D0092939

GLENN GOULD

Gould, 1962, CBC recording studio. Photograph by Herb Nott. Courtesy of the Canadian Broadcasting Corporation.

Gould, circa 1980, Eaton Auditorium. Photograph by Don Hunstein. Courtesy of Sony Classical.

Also by Peter Ostwald

Soundmaking—The Acoustic Communication of Emotion

The Semiotics of Human Sound

Schumann—The Inner Voices of a Musical Genius

Vaslay Nijinsky: A Leap into Madness

GLENN GOULD

The Ecstasy and Tragedy of Genius

Peter Ostwald

W. W. Norton & Company
New York London

Copyright © 1997 by the Estate of Peter Ostwald

All rights reserved

Printed in the United States of America
First Edition

For information about permission to reproduce selections from this book, write to Permissions,
W. W. Norton & Company, Inc., 500 Fifth Avenue, New York, NY 10110.

The text of this book is composed in Fairfield Light
with the display set in Fairfield Medium
Composition and manufacturing by the Maple-Vail Book Manufacturing Group
Book design by Chris Welch

Library of Congress Cataloging-in-Publication Data
Ostwald, Peter F.
Glenn Gould : the ecstasy and tragedy of genius /
by Peter Ostwald.
p. cm.
Includes bibliographical references and index.
ISBN 0-393-04077-1
1. Gould, Glenn. 2. Gould, Glenn—Psychology. 3. Pianists—Canada—Biography. 4. Genius. I. Title.
ML417.G68088 1997
786.2′092—dc20
[B] 96-43854
CIP

W. W. Norton & Company, Inc., 500 Fifth Avenue, New York, N.Y. 10110
http://www.wwnorton.com

W. W. Norton & Company Ltd., 10 Coptic Street, London WC1A 1PU

1 2 3 4 5 6 7 8 9 0

To my brother, Thomas H. Ostwald,
and my many Canadian relatives

CONTENTS

Foreword by Lise Deschamps Ostwald 11
Introduction 13

1 The Concert 17
2 A Little Night Music 25
3 Infancy 35
4 Child Prodigy 43
5 A Childhood Friend 57
6 New Teachers and Further Success 67
7 Gaining a Manager 81
8 "My Love Affair with the Microphone" 89
9 Self-Isolation 98
10 Triumph in the States 110
11 First Contact with Psychiatry 120
12 Conflicting Demands 130

13 Telephone Calls 142
14 Traveling Overseas 149
15 Strange Illnesses 159
16 In Search of a Home 171
17 Dr. Joseph Stephens 185
18 The Pitfalls of Composing and Performing 200
19 Retirement from the Stage 214
20 *The Solitude Trilogy* 230
21 Changing Views of Composers 244
22 Impersonator, Philosopher, and Technician 258
23 New Faces, New Challenges 271
24 Approaching Middle Age 286
25 The Last Years 304
26 A Fatal Stroke 320

Epilogue and Acknowledgments 332
Notes to Sources 337
Index 359

FOREWORD

Glenn Gould: *The Ecstasy and Tragedy of Genius* is the last book written by my husband, Peter. There is an underlying tragedy the reader may not be aware of, one that I report with great sadness. My husband will never read these lines, nor will he ever see this psychobiography in print. As the work he wrote with such ardor goes to press, Peter will have been absent from our lives since May 25, 1996. There are no words to describe the astounding courage my husband demonstrated while writing this book during the last year of his life.

Forty years have passed since the first meeting between Peter and Glenn took place. Why was this an unforgettable event, permanently engraved in both their minds? Was it the intuitive knowledge that this was the beginning of twenty-five years of friendship—and occasional collaboration—leading to the tragic tale of Glenn Gould's premature death at age fifty, which would be written by Peter Ostwald, a sixty-eight-year-old professor of medicine, a violinist, and a distinguished author, who fought an unrelenting battle with cancer for twelve years?

Peter's illness was demanding, marching forward at an unstoppable pace; but Peter was adamant—he would suffer, but his work would not. Only his physicians knew the extent of his illness, but they understood the immense creative energy that animated Peter and treated him accordingly.

I, alone, witnessed every day not only the suffering he endured, but also the amazing determination and admirable love he put into his work. He carried on with heroism and a valiant spirit that is not given to many, always striving to express quality and truth in his writings. He asked his children, Chantal, David, and Preet, to remember that he had fought the battle honorably.

As Peter had written an epilogue in which he thanks those who were helpful to him, I will not repeat those names; but I cannot conclude these remarks without acknowledging the tremendous assistance I have received over this book from the Deschamps family, especially my sisters Jeannine and Madeleine. I am grateful to my friends Mara Hill and Joan Murphy for their invaluable editorial help.

I hope this foreword sheds a little light on the remarkable man Peter was and the real pleasure he took in writing about Glenn Gould, a pianist he knew and admired greatly. To cite Peter's own accomplishments would require a chapter in itself, but it is with immeasurable pride that I introduce you to my husband's last work.

Both the subject of this book and the author will long be remembered for their outstanding legacy to the literary and musical world.

July 1996 Lise Deschamps Ostwald, M.D.

INTRODUCTION

In telling the lives of performing artists, one must separate their public personas, crafted to maintain a successful career, and the private selves they display to gratify fundamental psychological needs. Equally important is to recognize that these divergent aspects of personality—what is publicly concealed and privately revealed—can at times merge and at other times conflict. This problem of dual focus on the public and the private is especially critical when we try to understand Glenn Gould, who of all the century's great pianists was the first to seek out every opportunity afforded by the electronic media to illuminate and magnify one's artistic goals.

From the beginning of his career, and in ways never tried by classical musicians, everything Gould wanted the world to think of him was recorded, broadcast, filmed, videocast, and written about. Thus Gould managed to create a living legend of himself, incredibly versatile, highly eccentric, and so quickly a fascinating cult figure that his essential humaneness almost disappeared. "Unless I am much in error," wrote Geoffrey Payzant during Gould's lifetime, "his private life is in fact austere and unremarkable."[1] To get around this problem of public images eclipsing private realities, I have decided to approach Gould by combining personal knowledge with biographical data gathered since his death. The seed for this book was planted in May 1977, although I wasn't aware of it, during my last visit to Glenn, five years before his tragic death. We discussed biographical research—I was working on a book about Robert Schumann[2]—and he asked, in his typically provocative way, "Why such an inferior musician? You know very well that I cannot stand Schumann's music." Having learned a long time ago that Gould could not tolerate being contradicted, I let him go on. "Schumann wasn't even a competent pianist, and if it weren't for that clever little wife of his who managed to perform all those dreadfully mediocre compositions of his, we wouldn't know that he ever existed. What you should do, Peter, is write a book about a really important musician." Looking back, I wonder whether he might not have been thinking of himself.

As a medical person, I interceded several times when Gould needed professional advice, and I strongly supported a colleague's effort over seventeen years to preserve a psychotherapeutic attitude toward Gould. But he was never my patient. I never gave in to his repeated entreaties for drugs or requests to urge his manager to excuse him from concerts. Thus I feel I can speak more openly about Gould than the many doctors who undertook to treat him. Realizing now from archival research and interviews how crafty and mischievous Gould could be with physicians, I can—in retrospect—express relief for remaining simply a friend. At the same time, I regret that Glenn Gould never profited from the expertise he needed to deal with a complex of psychosomatic illnesses afflicting him. Many other musicians are luckier today, with the rising sophistication and coordinated practice of performing arts medicine.[3] Indeed, Gould's death in 1982, and the disclosures around that time by a number of other well-known performing artists of their serious physical and mental suffering, spurred me along with many co-workers to organize special programs of diagnosis, treatment, and research in this neglected field. From this evolved the birth of the Health Program for Performing Artists at the University of California.[4] In part, this book is meant to further interest in this new interdisciplinary specialty. Moreover, Glenn Gould gathers about him many timeless questions on that rare and astonishing phenomenon called genius. And finally, I wanted to remember a man who made a deep and lasting impression on my life.

Val des Champs, Howell Mountain Peter Ostwald, M.D.
March 3, 1996

GLENN GOULD

1

THE CONCERT

On February 28, 1957, two young men met on a California stage. One was an eccentric, fair-haired, world-famous pianist, barely over twenty-four, the other was a serious, already balding, twenty-nine-year old psychiatrist and violinist. Was this a chance encounter? Nothing in their background could suggest the possibility of such a meeting. The pianist was of Canadian descent, born and raised in Toronto, the only child of a prosperous furrier, and firmly entrenched in Canadian soil and Protestant values. The violinist was a Berliner child, star-marked by the Nazis, whose parents managed to flee to the United States in 1937, leaving behind relatives, friends, home, and property. The pianist, Glenn Gould, is now dead. His friend, Peter Ostwald, lives to write about him.

Looking back today on my initial contact with Glenn Gould, I wonder what made it so memorable. Surely the basic ingredients were this man's genius and my readiness for an overwhelming musical experience. Gould was then on his first transcontinental tour, following two spectacular recitals in Washington, D.C., and New York in 1955. Those recitals had led to his recording contract with Columbia and catapulted him to fame throughout the world with an astonishing LP of Bach's *Goldberg Varia-*

tions. The record cover shows young Gould in ecstatic poses, singing, playing, and conducting the music.

The night I met him was his debut in California. He was scheduled to perform the F Minor Concerto by Bach and Richard Strauss's *Burleske* with the San Francisco Symphony, conducted by Enrique Jordá. I had recently moved back to San Francisco from New York, after completing my psychiatric training, to take a faculty position in the School of Medicine at the University of California. Martin Canin, a friend and well-known pianist from New York with whom I had often played chamber music and who had introduced me to a number of leading musicians there, urged that I go to hear Gould. "You'll be amazed. He's one of the most interesting performers today, an astonishing technician, with a brilliant, keen mind. The real thing, and something of a nut. He'd be a good case for you! Be sure to go backstage and give him my regards." I couldn't resist.

The concert opened with a rarely heard symphony by the Spanish composer Juan Arriaga, who died tragically young, at age twenty, in 1826. It was beautifully conducted by the Spaniard Jordá, but received with only mild applause from a somewhat lethargic Wednesday-night audience. Next on the program was the Bach concerto, originally written for the harpsichord and a somewhat unusual choice for a pianist making his local debut—most performers will start with something more flashy. But it seemed fitting for Gould, since his reputation rested primarily on the astounding success of his first commercial recording of the Bach *Goldberg Variations,* which had instantly become a best-seller and identified him as an immensely original and effective interpreter of Bach.

His appearance on stage was unusual, to say the least. He strode out briskly but with a certain awkwardness, suggesting he was not at ease in a suit of tails that looked a size too big for him. His gaze at the audience seemed hesitant and unfocused. He didn't look like someone who enjoyed being in a crowd. His attention was more on the conductor and the musicians, whom he greeted warmly before ambling over to a Steinway Grand. It had been elevated on wooden blocks placed under the three legs. That, and the rickety folding chair on which Gould sat very close to the floor, brought his body into a strikingly unorthodox relationship to the keyboard. His arms were on a horizontal level, rather than angling from above, but he seemed quite relaxed in that unusual position. He smiled, rubbed his hands, and leaned forward, his face nearly resting on the piano keys.

The Bach F Minor Concerto opens with orchestra and soloist in unison. The keynote F is heard on the first beat and repeated, producing a syncopated effect reiterated in the next two measures with increasing ornamentation. Then there is a surprising ascent to the minor sixth, followed by a drop to the minor third and four notes of piano solo echoing the orchestra. Gould obviously enjoyed playing the music and had a profound sense of its structure. He swayed his body rhythmically, and the prominent jaw undulated, giving a rather simian cast to his pale, clean-shaven face. Indeed, he was articulating every note with his mouth; one could hear him vocalize at times. His playing was remarkable—sculptured, three-dimensional; each phrase seemed to have a life of its own. With the orchestra accompanying accurately and sensitively, Gould became ecstatic, his expression one of rapture, his eyes closed or turned inward, and his hands caressing the keyboard as if he were making love. This total involvement with the music also incorporated a curious tendency to elevate his left hand and make conductorlike gestures, giving direction to himself as well as the orchestra.

The combined visual and aural effect of Gould's performance quickly transmitted itself to the audience, who became raptly attentive, almost transfixed. His self-absorbed movements and embodiment in sound seemed to cast a spell. It was a kind of seduction. He was pulling his spectators into psychological orbits both close to him and far away, in some ethereal space. His interpretation of the slow movement of the Bach Concerto was truly a revelation. He projected the soulful melody like a silver thread by articulating each phrase with immense deliberation and creating smooth continuities between individual notes. The result was so songlike that it was difficult to believe one was listening to a piano. And the last movement, in strongly accentuated three-eight time, inspired such a rollicking sense of rhythm that the audience seemed to want to dance along with the joy and vitality of Gould's playing.

What a performer! I can recall very few pianists who had that magic, who triumphed in fusing bodily display with musical intelligence. We are told that Liszt did it in the nineteenth century. More recently there was Artur Schnabel, sitting in a comfortable chair and caressing the keyboard without appreciable effort, as though he were having a meal. I also remember Arthur Rubinstein's distinctive way of propelling himself upward in loud passages like a rocket, and then elevating his face as if he were praying to God. Sergei Rachmaninoff was another pianist who had to be seen to be fully appreciated. His granitic body, hunched solidly over the piano, hardly moved while nimble fingers extracted from it the most awesome and delicate sounds. These virtuoso musicians resemble dancers in their integrated appeal to both eye and ear. They play on one's responsiveness with the entire force of body and mind, communicating emotions that can range from religious devotion to sexual ecstasy.[1]

After intermission Gould launched into the *Burleske* by Richard Strauss, a mini-concerto that gave us the opportunity to marvel at his dazzling bravura. This piece is not one of Strauss's better known compositions, and Gould's selecting it for his West Coast debut again indicated a degree of nonconformity. But there could be no doubt that he was a technical wizard. Triplet chords and arpeggios literally flew off the keyboard, and the treacherous descending scales rippled like pearls. He was in absolute command of his instrument. Yet it all looked so easy. There were no exaggerated contortions, no deliberate attempts at showmanship. His hands remained close to the keys, and the wrists were horizontal except when his left hand was conducting.

As soon as the piece ended, Gould again became awkward. The applause seemed to startle him. When not making music, he became almost a different person, rather shy and embarrassed, like a young boy surprised to have evoked so much acclaim. After a quick, almost perfunctory bow to the audience, he waved to the orchestra but did not shake hands with the concertmaster as soloists usually do. He scurried backstage ahead of the conductor and came back briefly for a single curtain call. Jordá then returned to end the program with a vivid rendition of Igor Stravinsky's *Petrushka Suite*. I could barely listen. As soon as the *Petrushka* was over, I was planning to go backstage to thank Gould for an unforgettable experience.

In those days before San Francisco had a Symphony Hall, orchestral concerts were usually held at the War Memorial Opera House, where finding one's way to an artist's dressing room can be an exercise in frustration. The stage entrances from the lobby were controlled by zealous guards who screened and delayed any visitors, and the street entrances were equally inaccessible. But I had learned to get around these obstacles as a medical student, when I ushered at the opera house and occasionally turned pages for pianists who would accompany the famous violinists (Menuhin, Heifetz, Szigeti, Zimbalist, Elman) and other great soloists. In this way I learned how to enter the labyrinth of rooms and rehearsal areas backstage rapidly. The door to Maestro Jordá's dressing room was ajar, and I could see the conductor inside, combing his hair and preparing to welcome guests and autograph hunters. The soloist's room was locked. I knocked, but there was no response. After a second knock, the door opened and Glenn Gould politely invited me in. He had changed from his formal attire and was now dressed in gray pants, a white shirt without tie, heavy woolen sweater, and dark blue jacket. What shocked me was the temperature of the dressing room. It was stiflingly hot and muggy, like a sauna. All of the windows had been tightly closed, and the heat turned up full blast.

Gould was alone and seemed pleased to have a visitor, so I introduced myself as a violinist friend of Martin Canin. Then I told him that his playing had been enormously impressive, especially the concerto. Bach was my favorite composer and I had never heard this work played so well. The same was true for the Strauss piece. Gould's face grew radiant; he obviously enjoyed being complimented. But I noticed that he was ill-at-ease, his face tense, and there was some mild twitching of the muscles around his right eye which detracted from an otherwise youthful, handsome appearance. The way Gould began speaking also suggested substantial nervousness. The words poured out in a torrent.

"Thank you, that's very kind of you, especially coming from a friend of Martin, whose playing I admire very much. I hope we can get him to play in Canada some day. You know, we have a music festival there every year, at Stratford, and several musicians from the States have participated, the violinist Oscar Shumsky, and Leonard Rose, the cellist. Last year I became one of the directors."

"How does it feel being so far from home?"

"To be perfectly honest about it, I detest having to travel. Airplanes are a big problem for me because the cabins are never reliably heated and I'm extremely sensitive to temperature change. The air conditioning while waiting at an airport can be an ordeal; I have to be very careful to avoid drafts at all times. Large halls like this one make me very uncomfortable, as does the audience with its incessant coughing and sneezing. It is hard to protect myself from germs; I think I might actually be coming down with a fever, or a cold, as frequently happens. I'm not at all sure that I'll be able to play tomorrow night's concert."

"Well, you certainly played magnificently tonight," I ventured, hoping to direct the conversation away from the topic of health.

"It wasn't so bad, actually," he said quickly, with a look of false modesty. "The piano I was supplied with is really first-rate, one of the better Steinways I've played on in the States so far, only a little bit on the heavy side. I prefer something a bit lighter, a keyboard with a more pliable action." At home he had a Chickering, his all-time favorite. He agreed that the Bach concerto had gone well under Maestro Jordá, a splendid conductor. He had been easy to rehearse with, and the orchestra had responded to him quite well. "In the *Burleske* by Strauss—incidentally, he's one of my favorite composers and one of the most underrated figures of the twentieth century—the balance was never upset by the orchestral texture." Gould thought it difficult to maintain a proper relationship between the orchestral sound, which Strauss exploits in his inimitable manner, and the solo instrument, in this case the piano, an instrument Strauss didn't write all that much for. But he agreed that the orchestra "rose to the occasion splendidly."

Gould was beginning to relax, his voice stronger, more self-confident, pleasantly inflected. He obviously loved to talk and to hear himself talk—a brilliant monologue about orchestras he had played with, conductors he liked, his favorite composers, all delivered in densely constructed sentences with numerous embedded clauses. Words flowed out of him with unabashed vitality, making it difficult to interrupt. Not that one would want to stop a musician who possessed such a razor-sharp intellect and spun out words as delectably as he played music. Besides, much of what Gould had to say was very funny. He had a fantastic sense of humor, which he used provocatively rather than spitefully. One of his most devastating quips was about Wolfgang Amadeus Mozart, whom he described cattily as a composer who died too late. Had he not lived so long (to age thirty-five) and thus escaped the influence of Viennese opera, Mozart would have been a far greater composer. Such remarks were meant to shock, and my attempt to defend Mozart led to a vigorous rebuttal, with much laughter.

By now a few other well-wishers had arrived, including Enrique Jordá and several members of the orchestra who complimented Gould on his performance and wished him well for tomorrow night's concert. He asked me to wait while he spoke with each visitor briefly and courteously. After signing a few autographs, he turned to talk to me without interruption, until someone appeared to say that the dressing rooms would soon be closed and exits from the opera house bolted.

"Do you have a car?" Gould asked. "I'm staying at the St. Francis Hotel."

"It would give me great pleasure to drive you back to the hotel," I replied. "Perhaps you'd like to stop somewhere for a bite to eat or something to drink. You must be famished."

"Not especially, but I do get very thirsty." He pointed to a large bottle of water on his dressing table, and a box of soda biscuits alongside various lotions and vials of pills. "Poland Water is what my body tolerates best. I always carry my own supply." Suddenly Gould's brisk monologue reverted to aspects of his health; again he mentioned not feeling well. He feared he might be coming down with a cold. To alleviate his symptoms he was taking antibiotics and also using "pills to calm my nerves." In this context he mentioned a nagging pain in the middle of his back, and that he was experiencing some discomfort in his arms and shoulders.

"The bones of my back easily get out of alignment with my ribs, and I've found it of considerable benefit to visit chiropractors in Toronto who are very proficient in making adjustments to the spine." One of them also massaged the heavy muscles of his shoulders and advised him to have regular ultrasound treatments.

Chiropractors? Ultrasound treatments? During my last year in medical school I had several times visited the local chiropractic college in San Francisco with Peter Mark, a classmate who was as interested in unconventional medicine as I was, in order to find out about methods never included in our own curriculum. So Peter (who has become a successful dermatologist) and I knew about the techniques practiced by chiropractors. But I couldn't recall having heard much about ultrasound. "What does it do?" I asked now.

Gould, head and shoulder portrait, late 1950s. Courtesy of Glenn Gould Estate.

"It has a miraculous effect," Gould said, grasping his left shoulder with his right hand. "You see, the vibratory impulses break down tissue up here, in the bigger muscles, thinning them and thus reducing the bulky mass of muscles that are useless for a pianist. Muscles of the shoulder and upper arm are likely to get hypertrophied, like a boxer's, and that makes them far too powerful for the amount of work needed to play the piano. I am trying to minimize the strength of my shoulders—by sitting low in relation to the keyboard, with my arms level, I can accomplish that to a certain degree. But not sufficiently." His goal generally was to shift control from the upper arms to the hands and fingers. This was where ultrasound came in. He had his own machine at home and used it almost every day. But it was too heavy to transport on concert tours. "I'm already loaded down with thick blocks for the piano and my folding chair."

What Gould was saying about the use of ultrasound vibrations to destroy large masses of muscle tissue struck me as highly improbable, if not actually dangerous. At most, one might expect some warming of the tissues and other local effects. I decided it was time to tell Gould of my medical orientation.

"Well, don't worry, Mr. Gould. I happen to be a doctor—a psychiatrist." I hastened to add that I was not on duty this evening and he needn't fear that I was going to practice on him. "You've just performed two very demanding works, with spectacular results. My guess is that you must be somewhat exhausted and overwrought. Let's get out of this intolerably stuffy room and get some fresh air."

With that, Gould broke into a captivating smile and turned away from me to pack his belongings. He donned a heavy overcoat and cap, wrapped a woolen scarf around his neck, put on a pair of wool-lined gloves, picked up his folding chair, and we set off.

2

A LITTLE NIGHT MUSIC

In those days I drove an Austin-Healey sports car that offered minimal protection against the elements. But Gould didn't seem to mind. Despite his earlier complaints about sensitivity to cold air and drafts, he kept on talking, telling me excitedly that he was related to the Norwegian composer Edvard Grieg. "He was a cousin of my mother's great-grandfather. We all stemmed from a Scottish family to begin with, and in my mother's branch the original spelling, 'Greig,' was faithfully maintained. Those ancestors who settled in Norway inverted the two vowels so that the name would acquire a more authentically Nordic ring."

"You must visit that vast region to the north," he went on, adding that Canada had been rather neglected lately by Americans living in the neighboring States. He believed his country was blessed with some of the wildest natural beauty in the world and inhabited by amazingly cultivated people. Impishly he added "though I daresay the Eskimos haven't been attending too many of my concerts lately." The topic of Canada generally evoked Gould's most boyish enthusiasm. He spoke of his habit of regularly isolating himself for long stretches of time to study and practice in a cottage maintained by his parents at Lake Simcoe, near the little town of Orillia, sixty miles north of Toronto.

Gould annotating score at cottage, Lake Simcoe, 1956. Courtesy of Fed News and Glenn Gould Estate.

It was their summer and weekend retreat, and Glenn had many fond memories of childhood there. However, since late adolescence he had used it as his own private sanctuary, a place for withdrawing from the world and devoting himself to reading, listening to the radio, making music, and taking long walks with his dog.

"That sounds like a somewhat lonely existence," I said, breaking momentarily into the monologue.

He went on instantly to say that, although I might not approve, he was not at all the gregarious type. Indeed, he craved solitude, and up there in the north, in that freshness of nature close to the lake, his mind could dwell on essentials, "get to the heart of the matter, locate what's important and what isn't in the agenda of life."

Gould enjoying a peaceful walk with his dog, Lake Simcoe, late 1960s. Courtesy of Fed News and Glenn Gould Estate.

I interrupted to reassure him that I was able to share his passion for Canada. Having recently traveled to the provinces of Ontario and Quebec, I could appreciate the wild expanse of his native land and its engaging blend of European and American culture. But his quest for solitude struck me as contradictory. Here was a man preaching the virtues of isolation while traveling around the country giving concerts. That year alone, 1957, Gould performed thirty-eight times in five different countries.

And at that very moment he was demonstrating far more of a craving for companionship than for solitude. Speech flowed out ceaselessly and seamlessly, under great inner pressure. His vocal exuberance seemed like some kind of primal experience, a joyous discharge of emotion and intellect, mockery and fantasy, all designed to fascinate if not dominate the listener. At no time did he ask what my thoughts and reactions might be. I'd have to interrupt him to get a word in edgewise, which I was reluctant to do because he was such a charming raconteur, and one could feel a virtuosity in his speaking behavior that resembled his piano playing. It occurred to me that having been an only child forced to spend an inordinate amount of time at the keyboard, which is inherently a solitary pursuit, Gould might have been starved for social contact and developed a special way of communicating primarily with himself. Now, in the presence of someone who was so eager to listen, he could "let go" and show what it was really like to be Glenn Gould.

As we approached his hotel, I suggested stopping at a coffeeshop, where he ordered a bottle of mineral water and I ate a turkey sandwich. He continued to talk volubly about his current concert tour and the Stratford Music Festival, mentioning various musicians who had played with him there, including the Canadian cellist Zara Nelsova. It so happened that I too had played chamber music with Zara, who is a frequent visitor to San Francisco and a person I admire greatly.

Gould brought up his interest in listening to recordings of great artists, and I told him about my own collection. The first records I had ever bought were of Yehudi Menuhin playing Bach's G Minor Sonata for Solo Violin and Leopold Stokowski conducting his own transcription of the Bach Toccata and Fugue in D Minor for the organ. Gould's eyes lit up. Both Menuhin and Stokowski were among his favorite performers, and as the evening progressed it became increasingly clear that we shared a passion for the music of Johann Sebastian Bach. Later on I discovered other interests that put us on similar wavelengths. Gould spoke knowledgeably about the technology of radio and recording studios, while I was fascinated by medical research on designing a sound studio that could analyze the emotional inflections in speech.

I looked at my watch. It was past midnight, and I wanted to go home. He seemed unaware of my growing fatigue. "Aren't you getting tired?" I asked.

"Oh no, not at all. I have no trouble staying awake at night. In fact, I have difficulty falling asleep unless I take a sedative." He mentioned using Nembutal and some other barbiturate drugs that could be obtained fairly easily in Canada at the time, though in the United States they were more strictly controlled. As Gould spoke lyrically of sedatives that I knew to be potentially habit-forming and even dangerous when used in excess, I grew mildly alarmed. I had treated a number of severely addicted patients and had witnessed convulsions, comas, and suicides resulting from barbiturate overdose. But Gould would have none of it, claiming that barbiturates were "perfectly harmless." He considered himself an expert on the subject, one who needed no advice from a medical doctor. I didn't know it at the time, but just a month before we met, Gould had written to a pianist friend in Washington, D.C., touting the virtues of barbiturate drugs:

> Gould's Clinic for Psycho-Pseumatic [sic] Therapy
> 32 Southwood Drive
> Toronto, Ontario
> January 21, 1957
>
> Dear Thomas:
>
> I am delighted to hear that Dr. Gould's perscriptions [sic] as usual proved efficacious. Due to my long experience with internal medicine practice I am unusually alert to the problems of neurotic artists. Whenever you are planning a trip up to Canada my nurse will be glad to arrange an appointment.
>
> The yellow pills are called Nebutol [sic]. The white sedatives are called Luminal. I believe that both will have to be obtained through your doctor. Luminal is perfectly harmless and can be taken generally three times a day:—one after the noon meal and two at bed time. I strongly advise however that you do not make a habit of Nebutol [sic]. It should definitely be reserved for the nights before special occasions and to break chronic sleeplessness. . . .
>
> All good wishes.
> Sincerely
> Glenn Gould[1]

Having established that he was not about to go to bed, Gould now proposed that I join him in playing some piano-violin sonatas. He asked me to go home, pick up my violin, and then drive him back to the opera house, where he could play on the Steinway that he liked so much.

"But, Glenn," I remonstrated—by now we were on first-name basis—"the hall will be closed, and there won't be anybody to let us use the stage. If you're really serious about this, I think we should find another place to go." Since I didn't have a piano in my apartment, I suggested telephoning William Corbett Jones, a friend and classical pianist who at that time was working as the bar pianist at a popular North Beach nightclub called Vesuvio's. Bill probably would just have gotten home, and if not too tired might suggest a place for us. He did—Matilda Kogan's apartment on 35th Avenue. "But it's going to have to be an upright piano," I warned Glenn.

"That shouldn't be too much of a problem so long as it's in tune," he assured me. Glenn actually enjoyed the sound of an upright piano, saying, "The action can be rather comfortable. It reminds me of being at home with my parents in Toronto. I played on their upright almost exclusively when I was a child." So we drove to my apartment near the medical school to pick up my violin, and then headed for Matilda's place.

Bill had already arrived. He is a versatile musician with a superb memory who frequently performs in solo recitals and chamber music concerts in the United States and abroad. Now a professor of music at San Francisco State University, Jones played for many years in the highly acclaimed Alma Trio with the violinist Andor Toth and the cellist Gabor Rejto.

Jones greeted us at the bottom of the stairs leading up to the apartment, where we found two other musicians waiting: the pianist Sylvia Jenkins (later to become Jones's wife) and the violinist David Abel. Then just turned twenty, Abel had also been a child prodigy, studying with Naoum Blinder, who was Isaac Stern's principal teacher as well. "This is going to be an exciting evening," I said to myself.

After introductions were made, Glenn insisted that the heat in the apartment be turned up to eighty degrees Fahrenheit. He explained his sensitivity to cold and took off his heavy overcoat, scarf, and cap, which he wouldn't let anyone hang up for him, dumping everything unceremoniously on the floor. He set up his folding chair and suggested playing a Bach sonata with me. I chose the one in C Minor, which is one of my favorites and a work that I felt comfortable playing with such a distinguished performer. Piano and violin start the beautiful slow Siciliano together. Gould, as would be expected, played magnificently. The theme flowed with that structural clarity I'd noted earlier in the evening when he performed the Bach F Minor Concerto with the symphony. Every note was precisely nuanced; there wasn't a single mistake in sight-reading—perhaps Gould was playing from memory, which was one of his major talents, but he did look at the score. There wasn't much give-and-take in the ensemble playing. Glenn had his own expectations of how this music was to sound, and he assumed I would bend my playing to conform with his ideas about tempo and phrasing, which I was only too happy to do. Playing chamber music with Glenn was like conversing with him. He took the lead and obviously enjoyed being in control.

After we finished the four movements of Bach's sonata, Bill Jones and David Abel performed the great and difficult Duo for Violin and Piano by Franz Schubert. It was beautifully played, and Glenn turned pages for Bill listening with great interest. But afterwards he made it clear that Schubert was not a composer he especially liked. That led to a captious remark from Bill Jones, who began asking Glenn about his approach to the piano. Glenn vigorously defended the unusually low chair he used and his posture at the keyboard as being the correct one, at least for him, and he repeated almost verbatim some of the things he had told me earlier about the muscles in his shoulders. At one point he made everyone in the room feel his shoulder blades.

The atmosphere grew a bit tense, and I was surprised to see that in marked contrast to the zest for talking shown earlier, Glenn now became strangely inarticulate and seemed to want to avoid talking about himself. Only much later would I learn that he generally functioned far better in one-on-one conversations. When there were two people in a room with him, he would begin to feel edgy, and three or more caused his social anxiety to escalate sharply. The best solution then would be to seize control immediately, which he would do by going to the piano. Music allowed him to enter another universe, free of words and best fitted to his personal needs. Now he asked that I play with him the C Minor Sonata, opus 30, no. 2, for piano and violin by Beethoven. This is a very demanding composition, full of treacherous solo passages for both instruments and ensemble work that is difficult to bring off. I would have preferred that David Abel play the violin part, but Glenn insisted he wanted me as his partner, which made me feel very flattered.

In the opening Allegro I stumbled over several tricky runs, but Glenn negotiated the murderous double octaves in the piano part flawlessly. The Adagio he wanted to play at an unbearably slow tempo, a Gould trademark. He stretched the already-drawn-out opening theme for piano solo to an unmerciful length, which I found nearly impossible to replicate when it came my turn to play it. The Scherzo went hair-raisingly fast, and the Finale was done with passionate abandon. Afterward, Glenn seemed supremely happy. David Abel now wanted to play with him, and they gave a beautiful, almost concert-ready rendition of the Beethoven G Major Sonata, opus 96.

Then Matilda served ice cream, cookies, and coffee. Glenn seemed very relaxed and began to discourse about his love for animals. While there was gentleness in what he told us about his pets, especially his dog, he also spoke as an activist, arguing eloquently in favor of animal rights. His energy seemed inexhaustible, but the rest of us were getting tired, and I suggested taking him back to his hotel.

As we drove there, I noticed a peculiar quality of detachment and isolation. Despite his overt friendliness and jovial humor, Glenn radiated little warmth, almost as if the bodily coldness he often complained of had chilled him spiritually. He spoke of music but said absolutely nothing about the musicians we had just been with, neither their personalities nor their performance, nor did he have any comments whatsoever, positive or negative, about my violin playing. It suddenly occurred to me that during the five hours we'd spent together, Glenn had minimized all human relations; he'd said very little about his family and almost nothing about any friends, teachers, or other people who might have been close to him. The talk had focused primarily on himself, his musical activities, and his love of animals. He mentioned his interest in being a composer, talked about a string quartet he had just written, and expressed his desire to give up playing in public when he reached the age of thirty, so he could devote himself exclusively to composing and making recordings. One day, he said, he wanted to conduct a symphony orchestra.

When we arrived at the St. Francis Hotel, Glenn made it clear that he was wide awake and did not want to let me go, even though it was now 4:00 A.M. and I was obviously dead tired. He wouldn't get out of the car and just kept on talking. The thought crossed my mind that perhaps Gould was gay and wanted me to spend the night with him. But his behavior suggested just the opposite; there was nothing remotely seductive or erotic in his speech or gestures, nothing whatsoever to suggest he might be interested in physical intimacy. On the contrary, his way of persistently engaging in self-centered monologue tended to create distance, and it struck me that the envelope of heavy clothing he wore also was like a cocoon, sealing him from human contact.

I noticed that I was beginning to respond with ambivalence and lassitude to the demands on the one hand to "stay with me, listen, let me fill you with thoughts and ideas about myself," and on the other hand to "keep your distance, don't get too close, I want to be left alone and be fully in control." At this point I could take it no longer. Nudging Gould gently out of the car, I excused myself, saying it had been a wonderful evening but now I needed to go home and get some sleep. Before we parted, I gave him my address and telephone number and said I hoped we might have a chance to get together again before he had to leave town for his next series of concerts.

The next day, just before noon, I received a phone call. "Peter, I need to ask for your advice. I'm not feeling at all well. I couldn't sleep until eight this morning when I took a couple of Nembutals."

He had risen just a little while ago, "feeling quite feverish." After eating breakfast, he still felt unwell and not sure he could play in that afternoon's concert. "I think I'm coming down with some kind of infection, maybe a throat infection. Could it be streptococcal?" He described a kind of roughness at the back of his throat, which seemed to be getting worse. He was having trouble swallowing. "I'm wondering whether you could come down to the hotel and give me some penicillin? That should probably hold me over until the end of the concert."

"Have you mentioned this to the Symphony management?" I asked.

"No, but I did call my personal manager, Walter Homburger, in Toronto, and he recommended I see a doctor and then go ahead with the performance."

With a full schedule of patients and teaching that afternoon, it was impossible for me to rush downtown and visit Glenn in his hotel at such short notice. Nor did I think it wise to ask him to take a taxi to my office at the university. Like most psychiatrists in those days, I did not carry the necessary equipment for making housecalls and performing a physical examination, and did not have a supply of penicillin or other medications at hand. So I recommended that we get in touch with Dr. Herbert C. Moffitt, Jr., a colleague whose office was very close to Glenn's hotel. After calling Moffitt to explain the situation and make sure he would be available, I told Glenn to go there right away.

That worked. At 6:00 P.M., Glenn called me to say Dr. Moffitt had given him some "pink pills that gave immediate relief," and it had been possible to proceed with the concert. "What are the pills called?" I asked him. "Oh, that I can't tell you, because I took them out of the container and put the whole lot in my coat pocket, where I keep most of the things I need to take." Indeed, I discovered later that Glenn habitually kept handfuls of assorted pills in his coat pockets, which sometimes led to unfortunate results when he had to cross the border from Canada to the United States. Often he would be detained by suspicious customs officials.

He was feeling quite a bit better now, but described the matinée performance in somewhat disparaging terms, criticizing himself for having missed a run in the *Burleske* and complaining of the draftiness in the hall. I told him I would like very much to attend the following night's concert and hear him play again, but to my surprise he opposed this idea strongly. "Peter, I really would prefer that you not come to the opera house. Indeed, I must insist that you do not do so. It makes me very nervous when there is somebody in the audience whom I know, especially under conditions when I'm not at my best."

I was very sorry to hear that, and told him how much I regretted that we would not be able to meet again before his departure for Pasadena, his next stop in California before returning to Canada.

The friendship, formed then in 1957, lasted with various ups and downs for the next two decades, and ended just five years before Glenn's tragic death in 1982 at the age of fifty. But before telling the rest of the story, I would like to explore the forces that shaped this immensely gifted young artist. So, let us go back to the beginning of Glenn Gould's life and see what had taken place during the twenty-four years before our initial meeting in 1957. As disturbing as he could be, how did this fascinating, likable, and surely troubled musical genius get to be the person he was? Much of this information was so hidden during his lifetime that in many ways Glenn remained an enigma even to the people closest to him.

3

INFANCY

The family's name wasn't Gould when Glenn was born on September 25, 1932. It was Gold, and all of his early concert programs bear the name "Glenn Gold," a fact completely ignored in every book and article so far written about him. His birth certificate reads: "Gold, Glenn Herbert." His father filled out this document and signed his own name as Russell Herbert Gold. He described himself as "salesman" for the family business, called Gold Standard Furs, and noted his "racial origin," as well as that of his wife, Flora Emma Greig, to be "English and Scotch."[1]

Glenn, in keeping with family tradition, was not circumcised, but the ambiguity surrounding a possibly Jewish ancestry has never been satisfactorily settled. Stephen Posen recalls writing a letter stating that "despite Glenn's many virtues, he was not Jewish, though he would have chortled heartily at the mistake"; this was in response to an article written in the Canadian *Jewish News,* by Frank Rasky, about the great "Canadian Jewish pianist." When confronted with the Jewish question, Glenn, in typical prankster style, answered: "What? me? With the name Gould, and a father who's a furrier, and you're asking me if I'm Jewish?"[2] Surely it was a matter of discomfort within Glenn's family because in those days

Toronto, nicknamed "Hogtown," was not the cosmopolitan metropolis we know today, and there were strong elements of xenophobia and anti-Semitism. Glenn's uncle, Grant Gould, M.D., told me that Glenn's grandfather, Thomas Gold, "would get upset with all the Jewish people in the fur trade named Goldstein, Goldfinger, or Goldman. He decided he didn't want his kids to be taken for Jewish, and that may have been a reason for the name change later on."[3]

Thomas G. Gold, Glenn's paternal grandfather, was the son of a Methodist minister. He himself became an active worker in the early days of the Methodist Church where he was a Sunday School teacher and local preacher."[4] In 1902, Thomas Gold joined the staff of a well-known Toronto fur house. He established his own very prosperous fur business in 1913, which was later joined and taken over by Glenn's father, Russell "Bert" Gold.

Glenn's closest boyhood friend, Robert Fulford, remembers that Glenn's grandfather "was known as 'Papa Gold,' and he and his wife lived in Uxbridge. People would say, 'They're Jewish,' and yet they were members of the United Church of Canada. I never knew the answer. But one thing really sticks in my mind. We were in Glenn's father's office, and he gave us some pencils. They were commercial pencils with the stamp of a company on them, and as he handed them over—I remember this more than anything about this visit except for the skins of animals—he handed them over and then he took one of them back, saying, 'No, I'm not giving advertising from a Jewish firm.' And then he scraped the name off—I guess it must have said 'Shapiro and Sons' or something like that."[5]

Glenn's mother, Florence E. Greig, was nine years older than his father. Flora, as she was usually called, had been the second of three children and the only daughter. She was born on October 31, 1891, in Mount Forest, a small town in the province of Ontario. Her mother was Mary Catherine Greig (née Flett). Her father, John C. H. Greig, was a schoolteacher. The Greigs always were very proud of their Scottish-Presbyterian background, but they had difficulty tracing it, and the line to the composer Edvard Grieg was never as clear as Flora and her devoted son Glenn wanted it to be. Presumably a member of the Greig family (originally MacGregor) moved from Scotland to Norway, where the spelling was changed from Greig to Grieg. "I cannot offer you anything concrete as regards the Greig ancestry," writes H. A. Macdonald Greig of Aberdeenshire, Scotland. "I have always understood that we came over with William the Conqueror, but that is possibly wrong.

Gould's mother, Florence E. Greig Gould, circa 1920.
Courtesy of Glenn Gould Estate.

Another thing we claim [is] descent from Edvard Grieg, the Norwegian composer."[6]

Glenn's mother was musically gifted. She studied both piano and voice in Sault Ste.-Marie. Glenn Gould wrote an obituary for his mother in 1975, in which he noted that "already as a teenager she was attracted to music for the sacred service—being active in church and young people's groups. After she came to Toronto for further study in vocal and instrumental music, she devoted her talents primarily to church music. . . . She served as soloist in several large Toronto choirs, then as organist in a central Presbyterian Church. While serving as choir-leader at Uxbridge United Church, she taught both piano and vocal music in Uxbridge, Bradford, and Toronto. . . . Florence Gould was a woman of tremendous faith and, wherever she went, she strove to instill that faith in others . . ."[7] Given Glenn's amazing fluency in speech and writing, the style in which he describes his mother's achievements (a woman whose musical opinion he valued tremendously throughout his life) seems very dry and inhibited.

Bert Gold, as Glenn's father was usually called, met Flora through their musical associations. He was a devoted churchgoer and a gifted singer, who occasionally joined the chorus and played the violin until an accident caused him to retire his fiddle to a case underneath the piano. They married in 1925, on her thirty fourth birthday. Bert was already working in his father's prosperous business, which made it possible for him to purchase a house at 32 Southwood Drive, in an attractive, middle-class neighborhood called The Beach, with winding streets and hilly parks bordering Lake Ontario. Flora supplemented their income by working in a large Toronto church, and by giving music lessons in their comfortable home.

"Did she ever wish, herself, to be a performing artist?" I asked Glenn's father when I interviewed him in 1994. "Did she, as a child, teenager, or adult, have aspirations to play in public?"

"She was going to study operas. She studied with David Dick Slater, and a number of different singing teachers. Glenn's mother was a very accomplished musician."

"What kept her from pursuing a career on the stage? How come she didn't go on, in her own way, to become a famous artist?"

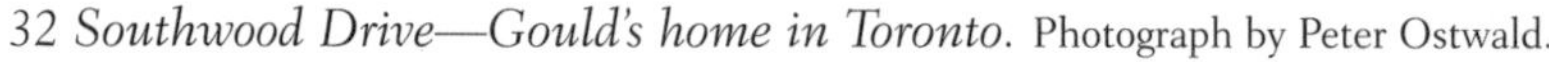

32 Southwood Drive—Gould's home in Toronto. Photograph by Peter Ostwald.

"I expect likely I came along at the wrong time and married her," he replied with a twinkle in his eye. "You see, in those days it would be unheard of for a married woman to pursue a career. Once you were married, why, you settled down to domesticity, and raised your children. Now it's very different."[8]

Flora became pregnant a number of times. But she repeatedly miscarried, and it was not until she was nearly forty-one years old (an advanced age for women having their first baby) that she succeeded in carrying a baby to term. Flora and Bert were understandably delighted by the prospects of finally becoming parents, and Flora, in particular, insisted that the child would have to be a successful musician, hopefully a great pianist. She believed that by exposing her unborn fetus all day long to her own piano playing, singing, and music from the radio and phonograph, its brain would gradually accommodate to this art from—a belief that has recently gained some support from scientists.[9] Glenn's father told me that "Flora would play all sorts of classical music while she was pregnant because she so much wanted the child to be musical and because she was so musical herself."[10]

Flora was known as a strict and demanding teacher, very conscientious with her students. One of them was Glenn's Uncle Grant, who recalls that "the impression she made on people was a little on the cold side. I think it was because all her drive was in music. And certainly when Glenn was born, she sort of instilled in him everything that she had ever known. She would play the piano, or sing to him, or have the radio on to classical music, convinced that in some mysterious way this would seep into his consciousness."[11]

Glenn's birth on September 25, 1932, was fraught with more than the usual amount of anxiety. "Of course we were all quite worried because of Florie's age and her previous miscarriages," his father told me. "But there was always somebody around to help her. There was Elsie, the 'housemaid' if you want to call her that, who lived with us permanently. And then we had a nurse who stayed there at least a week before he was born—you see, Glenn was delivered in our home, as was customary in those days—and the doctor came by every day."

"Was it an easy experience for your wife to have the baby, or were there complications?" I asked.

"It was a very smooth kind of labor. No difficulties."

"No difficulties at all?"

"None at all."

"Was Glenn breast-fed, or . . . ?"

"Well, I think he was breast-fed, possibly at the beginning, and I remember he used to have supplementary feedings with a bottle. It was heated at the bedside, in a tea kettle, something of that nature, electric. We'd stick the bottle in, and heat it in there."

A child's basic temperament is often exhibited right from the beginning. Some are sleepy and phlegmatic at birth, others vigorous and alert, depending on numerous factors, including the time that elapses before severing the umbilical cord.[12] We have no way of reconstructing Glenn's early development on the basis of objective observations. The family doctor is dead, and Glenn's pediatric records are no longer available. His Uncle Grant might have been of some help here, but he had not yet entered medical school and in any event did not have much contact with Glenn during his early childhood. His mother, who died in 1975, left no description of Glenn's early development. Thus we must rely on his father.

"What was Glenn like as an infant anyway?" I asked him. "Was he a lusty child, crying loudly, or more of a quiet baby?"

"He was reasonably lusty," Bert answered in his typically laconic, down-to-earth manner. "But something unusual about him struck us from the beginning. When you'd expect a child to cry, Glenn would always hum. I think it was something in his makeup that made him hum rather than cry."

That was a telling observation, I thought. Humming is a pleasure signal, soft and musical, whereas crying, which is louder and more noisy, indicates distress.[13] Was Glenn's father suggesting that his infant had an innate inclination toward music from the beginning? The origin of musical talent is a fascinating topic. There is some evidence for inborn, genetic factors—for example, the tendency to develop absolute pitch seems to be inherited, and certain parts of the brain appear to respond especially strongly to music if properly stimulated. The influence of prenatal exposure to music has already been mentioned. Future musicians often show their proclivities at a very early age, suggesting that their neurophysiological equipment may in some way have been "preprogrammed."[14]

"Do you mean that already at birth Glenn liked to sing?" I asked.

"Oh, sure. To his dying day Glenn liked to sing with the music; on the piano he'd always be singing along with it."

Clearly, his parents, so much in love with music themselves, perceived in their newborn a quality of musical talent, the tendency to respond selectively to musical sounds and rhythms, and to behave in a distinc-

Formal baby portrait of Gould, 1933. Courtesy of Glenn Gould Estate.

tively musical way. It was the fulfillment of his mother's fondest wishes. Much of what his father can remember conforms to her expectation that Glenn was destined to be a great musician. Bert enjoys telling the following story:

> When Glenn was three days old his fingers never stopped moving, just like this, as if he's playing a scale [the father demonstrates by wiggling his fingers]. His arms would be swinging back and forth, and his fingers going. It showed us that Glenn was musical. And the doctor said, "That boy is going to be either a physician or a pianist—one or the other."[15]

If this is an accurate recollection, it raises another question, the possibility that Glenn, the first child born to a woman already in her forties, might from infancy on have displayed some abnormal behavior. The absence of crying is distinctly abnormal,[16] and flapping movements of the hands associated with peculiarities in speech development are suggestive of a developmental disorder called infantile autism. Glenn obviously did not suffer from this disease. Had he been autistic, the remarkable success he had in a public career would have been impossible. But some of the behavior he manifested later in childhood and during his adolescence—a marked fear of certain physical objects, disturbances in empathy, social withdrawal, self-isolation, and obsessive attention to ritualized behavior—does resemble a condition called Asperger Disease, which is a variant of autism. Asperger Disease is occasionally associated with an unusual degree of giftedness in some particular field of expression such as music, mathematics, drama, athletics, or art. The composer Béla Bartók and the philosopher Ludwig Wittgenstein may both have been afflicted with this condition.[17] A number of similar cases have been reported more recently by the neurologist Oliver Sacks.[18]

The family doctor's prognosis when confronted with the baby's unusual dexterity as an infant was that the boy was "going to be either a physician or a pianist—one or the other." It so happens that Glenn fulfilled both predictions. His achievement at the keyboard turned out to be extraordinary. Less well known is that already at an early age Gould began trying to be a sort of medical expert—without benefit of formal education in the field. He read voraciously about clinical symptoms, diseases, and treatments. He repeatedly attempted to diagnose himself; he consulted numerous physicians; and he experimented with all kinds of remedies, thus managing to get through many immediate crises but probably damaging his health in the long run.

4

CHILD PRODIGY

As soon as Glenn was able to sit up, his mother would take him to the piano, prop him close to the keyboard, and play for him the music that she yearned to familiarize him with, including songs she had learned as a child, old Canadian folk tunes, some of the hymns and chorales she played at Sunday church services, and pieces by Bach, Chopin, and other composers that she was teaching to her piano students. She sang while playing, thus reinforcing the melodies coming from the instrument with her own pure, strong, and attractive voice. Glenn was an extension of her body, a physical connection between the warm, enveloping mother and the hard-edged piano keyboard facing them. Flora would encourage his tiny hands to reach out and grope those shiny black and white levers, pressing them down so that sounds emerged and mingled with her own copious singing and playing. Mother, child, and piano quickly became a unity. One could postulate that this may be the origin of Glenn's future posture when playing. His need to be very close to the piano would recall the warm feelings and earlier proximity of both mother and instrument.

Because Glenn's mother was always determined that he would be "a special child"[1] and make great future contributions to the world through music, efforts were made from the beginning to impose structure and order on his activity. He was encouraged to strike the "right" notes, and if he hit a "wrong" one, his mother grimaced, her body became tense, and words of disapproval crossed her lips. He picked up these cues instinctively and soon learned to avoid making mistakes. Innately possessed of musical talent, Glenn seemed to revel in learning to play correctly, and before he even knew how to speak, he was able to recognize that there was a logical system governing the universe of sounds. It was like a moral imperative controlling what one may and may not do with the piano keys. Conforming to these rules seemed to give Glenn pleasure, not only because it made his mother happy but also because of something deep in the core of his being, his basic or intuitive musicality. Both of his grandmothers loved music as well. They, like his mother, would take him to the piano and be astounded by his performance.

> As soon as Glenn was old enough to be held on his grandmother's knee at the piano [reports his father], he would never pound the keyboard as most children will with the whole hand, striking a number of keys at a time, instead he would always insist on pressing down a single key and holding it down until the resulting sound had completely died away.[2]

By the time Glenn was three years old and able to speak, his parents noticed that he was gifted with absolute pitch, one of the earliest signs of superior musical intelligence. What this means is that he now showed a foolproof ability to identify the pitch of a sound located in the musical scale. He knew, for example, when a tone was A rather than B, C-sharp rather than D, E rather than F; he could also sing tones at the correct pitch when asked to do so, for example, "Sing a G-flat." And he was able to recognize and name the different notes in a chord.

Absolute or "perfect" pitch is a neurological capacity that enables musicians instantly to identify tonalities (key signatures) and modulations (passing of one key into another), and also helps them in writing down music that they have heard or imagined. Many composers have absolute pitch. But this capacity can be a disadvantage for musicians when they have to play on instruments that are tuned higher or lower than standard pitch, or when they listen to recordings that are played faster or slower than normal, since the music they hear will sound distorted, "out of tune," or in the wrong key. Absolute pitch is a recognition skill that resides in the temporal lobes of the brain, where language abilities also are primarily organized. What makes this ability so special is that it is so rare. It seems to be based on a genetic predisposition that is activated by early exposure to music, tends to run in families, and can be enhanced through musical education in childhood. The psychologist Rosemary Shuter has convincingly demonstrated that children become increasingly less capable of absolute pitch recognition as they grow older.[3] And just as other spontaneous language skills—for example, learning to speak a foreign language without an accent—will diminish, absolute pitch rarely if ever develops after puberty.

It's not so surprising that Glenn's sense of pitch would turn out to be perfect. The hereditary element in his neurological makeup was being fortified by both his parents. Both loved to sing and were proficient on musical instruments, piano and violin. Bert often joined Flora in recitals at their local church. Both are reported to have had "beautiful voices."[4] Flora's incessant grooming of Glenn's taste and attitude by singing and playing for him must have enormously enhanced his precocious musical development. By the time he was three, she was regularly giving him piano lessons.

"He was never allowed to go to the piano and play a wrong note," reports his father. "If he did, she'd stop him immediately and make sure he'd correct it right then and there."[5] Playing correctly became firmly associated in Glenn's mind with pleasing his mother long before he could think consciously about what he was doing. He also assimilated very quickly her demand to sing every note that he played at the keyboard, a pedagogical device Flora strove to ingrain in all of her students. "She was very didactic and precise," recalls Glenn's Uncle Grant, who also studied with her, "no faking, and it was the ruler across your fingers if you made a mistake."[6] For Glenn, singing and playing the notes correctly seemed like child's play. It helped him to identify and remember the pieces he was playing, and he retained this habit all of his life.

Glenn was able to read music before he learned to read words, and it was soon discovered that he had a phenomenal musical memory, able to retain knowledge of every piece he had just heard or played, or whose notes he had merely looked at on the page. "His mother often compared him to Mozart," Glenn's uncle told me. "She thought that they had parallel courses in their upbringing and childhood, and she naturally thought Glenn had the makings of a genius at the age of three."[7]

And a cheerful genius at that. "I think that Glenn was, essentially, a very happy baby," is the way his father remembers him. "He had a very sunny disposition and a marvelous sense of humor." That impression is confirmed by many photographs showing an apparently calm and con-

Gould, in garden with stuffed animals, 1933. Courtesy of Glenn Gould Estate.

tented youngster, relaxed, never in pain or discomfort, playing and laughing. But snapshots rarely tell the whole story. Glenn's father makes the point that as a small child he already had a peculiar anxiety about his fingers, and seemed deathly afraid of hurting them. "From the time he was a tiny child, if you rolled a ball across the floor, he'd turn and get upset and wouldn't let it touch his hand at all. He always had that sensitivity to balls. He wouldn't have anything to do with them at all, wouldn't touch the ball. It was a natural way of protecting his hands, I think. It was just his instinct not to hurt his fingers."[8]

He also seems to have developed an oversensitivity to bright colors as a child. Years later Gould confided in Andrew Kazdin, his producer at Columbia Records who had become a trusted friend:

> When he was four or five years old, some woman gave him [Glenn] a present of a red toy fire engine. Despite the issue that no other color would have been appropriate for such a vehicle, the fact that it was red caused him to fly into a tantrum. He recalled that he became completely uncontrollable and had to be calmed down at some length. Exactly what it was about the color red was never made completely clear, but he stated that "I wouldn't have, as a child, any toy that was colored red at all." He went on: "I hate clear days; I hate the sunlight; I hate yellow. . . . To long for a gray day was, for me, the ultimate that one could achieve in the world."[9]

What better place to restrict one's visual colors to black and white, and to protect one's fingers while at the same time enjoying their deft motion and hearing them evoke beautiful sounds, than at the piano. The instrument became a safe haven for Glenn, his preferred place for spending as much time as possible—often to the exclusion of outdoor activity, mingling with other children, household chores, and other "normal" things that children are expected to do. The only way to discipline or punish the boy, his parents soon discovered, was "to close the piano down."

"You could tell Glenn, 'Stop practicing, go on out,' " his father said. "That didn't have a bit of effect at all. But if Glenn ever did anything wrong that he had to be punished for, his mother would just shut the piano down and lock it . . . that was far worse than any corporal punishment that could have been administered."[10]

On June 5, 1938, when Glenn was five years old, he was allowed to play the piano in public for the first time, as part of a Sunday afternoon church service held at the Business Men's Bible Class in Uxbridge, Ontario. This church held around two thousand people, according to Glenn's father. As the congregation gathered there was music played by an orchestra, then announcements, the singing of the Twenty-third Psalm, a prayer, and words of welcome. Then followed, according to the mimeographed program, a

VOCAL DUET—Mr. and Mrs. R. H. Gold
5 year old Master Glenn Gold at the Piano

Next came more hymns, speeches, vocal solos (one of them sung by Mr. R. H. Gold), orchestral offerings, and finally a benediction.[11] The name of the person who wrote the "Vocal Duet" that Glenn accompanied on the piano isn't given in the program, but presumably it hadn't been rehearsed, for his father commented that "he read the music right off."[12] Everyone in the audience was vastly impressed.

Six months later Glenn made his second public appearance, this time at a children's concert held in the Emmanuel Presbyterian Church on Friday evening, December 9. "Come and bring your friends and enjoy a pleasant evening at our concert," reads the printed announcement. Admission was charged—"Adults 25c, children, 15c"—to benefit the Chancel Fund. Glenn was third on a list of eleven numbers performed:

"Piano Composition . . . Glen [sic] Gold."

What that composition was is not recorded. But all the parents and children there were amazed by the superior quality of the little boy's performance, and he and his proud parents received so much acclaim that from this point on Glenn began telling people, "I'm going to be a concert pianist."[13]

This taking hold of his mother's long-standing ambition to produce a notable pianist had recently been stimulated by a concert Glenn was taken to, a recital by Josef Hofmann who was an exceptionally appealing stage personality. The Polish-born Hofmann was one of the most precocious musical prodigies in history, having toured Europe at the age of seven. His American debut in 1887 caused unprecedented excitement. One of the first professional musicians ever to make a phonograph recording, he was also a prodigious composer. Hofmann, a great Romantic pianist, was noted for his transparent tone and brilliant improvisations; he was a prime interpreter of works by Schumann, Chopin, and Liszt (Rachmaninoff had dedicated his Third Piano Concerto to Hofmann). He was also known to be gifted in mathematics, science, and business. In 1926, Hofmann became director of the Curtis Institute of Music in Philadelphia (founded by his heiress wife Mary Louise Curtis Bok), where two musicians who were to have a significant impact on Glenn's life, Leonard Bernstein and Lukas Foss, received their training.

Glenn was intoxicated by Hofmann's playing. A childhood dream suggests that he symbolically put himself in the older pianist's place and was able to identify with him:

> I was about six years old . . . the only thing I can remember is that I was being brought home in the car. I was falling asleep and I was in a wonderful state of half-awakeness in which you heard all sorts of incredible sounds going through your mind. And they were all orchestral sounds, but I was playing them all, and I suddenly was Hofmann. And this is something I'll never forget.[14]

The following year Glenn's mother, who until then had been the sole guide and arbiter of his musical development, wisely decided that it was time for his abilities to be judged by an outside authority. Questions had arisen about how to proceed with his general education, for it was already clear that Glenn was no ordinary child. After a year with a private tutor, he was enrolled at the Williamson Road Public School, just two blocks from his home, but he was clearly unhappy there and avoided social contact with the other children in favor of playing the piano. He detested group activities and seemed to be totally unfit for any sport. If someone threw him a ball in the schoolyard he turned away, petrified, and refused to pick it up or even touch it. Such behavior naturally led to taunts from the other boys, which made Glenn even more self-conscious and unhappy. According to John Roberts, later one of his closest friends, Glenn once was threatened by a bully at the school and found himself exploding with rage. "He told the boy never to come close to him again, and that if he ever did he would kill him."[15] This potential for naked aggression—we'll hear about another occasion shortly—frightened Glenn terribly. He habitually took pains to avoid situations where anger might arise, and to inhibit it, he would try to joke about it or wish it away.

Florence Gold had taken other exceptional pupils to the Toronto Conservatory of Music for testing and examination. Now it was Glenn's turn, and the results confirmed exactly what she had been hoping for. The test grades he received were the highest ever recorded in the province of Ontario, and he was awarded the Conservatory's Silver Medal. Clearly such great talent had to be nurtured. His parents, having no other children to take care of, gladly rose to the occasion.

Mr. Gold, always handy with tools and a practical man, built an annex to their house on Southwood Drive so that Glenn could have a special room of his own in which to study music and practice the piano. Mrs. Gold began restricting her clientele so she could devote herself more exclusively to training her exceptional child, though she continued helping other youngsters as well.

"Florie had quite a number of pupils go through the Conservatory courses and take Conservatory exams," Glenn's father told me. "Her students nearly always came highest in the class, or best in the province. After Glenn came along, she mostly took on charity students. However, when the mayor's son in Toronto was having difficulty with school reports, she put him through his music, and he got an extra credit for that, for his exams."[16]

Seeing other children competing for his mother's time and attention might have made Glenn somewhat anxious, if not jealous. But evidently he was sufficiently self-contained and able to work independently at an early age that these distractions did not seem to bother him, at least not consciously. We know, however, that competitiveness was a theme Glenn came thoroughly to detest. He later spoke and wrote disparagingly about every sort of competition—in sports, the arts, politics, and daily life. I would assume that his absolute dislike of rivalry and competition was a reaction against what he had to endure at home, where his mother's teaching of other children, young "competitors," deprived him of her total and undivided attention. Generally speaking, however, Glenn remained a pampered child.

"Was he ever expected to participate in any of the household chores?" I asked his father.

"No, Glenn was always for his music. He'd flee to the piano if there was anything to do."[17]

It was not something his father really approved of, but he admits that there was little that could be done in the face of Glenn's headstrong avoidance of more "normal" behavior, reinforced by Mrs. Gold's powerful ambitions for him. Mr. Gold did try to get his son involved in outdoor activities, but with little success, apparently. He tells the story, for example, of an ill-fated fishing expedition. Glenn's father had a boat at Lake Simcoe, the family's summer cottage near Orillia, about an hour's drive north of Toronto, and he thoroughly enjoyed going out on the lake with rod and reel to catch fish. He wanted so much to have Glenn come along and join him in pulling the big ones out of the water. One day he did succeed in prying his son away from the piano. But when the fish were hauled in, weighed, and displayed, Glenn expressed furious displeasure. He said it was the killing of the fish that disturbed him so terribly. After that he wanted nothing more to do with fishing, and the whole episode led to such intense argument that his father gave up the sport as well.

Gould boating at Lake Simcoe, accompanied by his dog and a playmate. Courtesy of Glenn Gould Estate.

However, Glenn continued to go boating with his dog, as well as with an occasional playmate.

But there's more to this story. The mysteries of life and death and the fusion between them are of common concern for children. In Glenn's case, such thoughts and fantasies were connected not only to his father's fishing expeditions, but to what took place in his father's fur business. (Glenn grew up in the days before television made gruesome scenes common for so many children.) His father worked in a shop prominently advertised as:

GOLD STANDARD FURS
Thos. G. Gould, Master Furrier
Designers and Creators
of Exclusive Fur Coats and Wraps
Repairs, Restyling, Cold Storage

The business, established by Bert's own father, was located on the upper floor of a downtown Toronto office building, at 33 Melinda Street. It consisted of selling fur coats to individual clients and bartering animal furs with other furriers. Freshly skinned pelts were always prominently displayed. Glenn's Uncle Grant remembers vividly how "Furriers would come in from their northern fur-trapping trails, and bring these horrible-

Gould with his favorite companion, Nick, 1942. Photograph by Charles du Bois.

smelling dead muskrats, and lay them out on the floor, and my dad [Glenn's grandfather] would say, 'This is good, this is good, this one isn't, take this one away, and I'll buy these.' "[18] When the little boy was taken there, he would gaze with horror and fascination at the dead beasts. Their heads, feet, and tails appeared amazingly lifelike. Slinky foxes were often draped around a woman's neck, their narrow snouts made into a clamp that held the whole thing in place. Glenn's mother would wear one occasionally, to his great distress.

Glenn's preoccupation with dead animals was enhanced by an unfortunate accident that took place at his home on 32 Southwood Drive. The story was related to me by his closest boyhood friend, Robert Fulford, who lived next door. "Glenn's father or someone was driving his car into the driveway and accidentally killed the family's pet dog—Glenn was

Gould called his pet bird "Mozart"—1944–46. Photograph by Gordon W. Powley.

inordinately fond of dogs. The one that was killed was a small dog, and that was the reason why the next dog they bought, who was called Nick, was so big, an English or Irish setter, a big, beautiful dog who was Glenn's favorite for many years. It was explained to me that the dog had to be very big so he couldn't be run down."[19]

For many years, Nick was Glenn's closest companion. They played and walked together, and Nick (officially Sir Nickolson of Garelocheed) would sit next to Glenn at the piano while he practiced. There were other pets in his life: a bird called Mozart; four goldfish named Bach, Beethoven, Haydn, and Chopin; and much to his father's amusement, a skunk that Glenn trapped and tried to tame. Themes of vivisection and protection of animals remained close to Glenn's heart. Often the child felt himself to be an animal, saying things like, "I am a collie-dog, woof,

woof."[20] After capturing a skunk, he wrote: "I am a skunk, a skunk am I. Skunking is all I know, I want no more. I am a skunk, a skunk I'll remain . . ."[21]

One of his childhood dreams was to create an idyllic home for old and stray animals on an island in the north of Canada, where he himself wanted to live out his old age. His father told me that "already as a child he wanted to have a farm for old cows and horses and everything. I even had to go up north with him on a trip to look at a farm on Manitoulin Island where he could put up all the old animals. It's a mystical place, full of Indian traditions, where the great god Manitou is said to have dwelt. Some of my wife's distant relatives had lived there."[22]

When we spoke of Glenn's love of animals and his great concern about

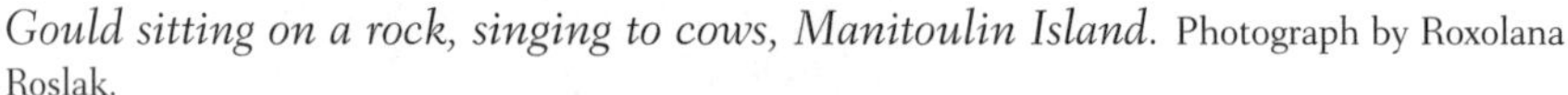

Gould sitting on a rock, singing to cows, Manitoulin Island. Photograph by Roxolana Roslak.

the harm done to them, Bert told me this may have stemmed in part from Grant Gould's biological studies. Uncle Grant was fourteen years older than Glenn. "During his vacations from medical school Grant would camp up at the lake. He had a tent up there, and he dissected frogs. Glenn was so upset. But Grant had to do it; you know, he was supposed to. Glenn and his uncle looked very much alike. I have pictures; you can't tell which is which. And Glenn, you see, would get so mad when Grant would come parading into a concert hall with an ice cream cone or something like that. That mortified Glenn."[23]

Grant A. Gould, M.D., now a distinguished surgeon practicing in Newport Beach, California, denies that he ever showed Glenn any of his dissections. But he acknowledges that already as a young child his piano-playing nephew was extremely squeamish about such things.

It was around the time when Grant was a medical student that the family changed its name from Gold to Gould. Court records of the change are reported as "gone missing," but the Toronto telephone book lists the name as Gould for the first time in July 1939, while the Toronto City Directory indicates the change in 1940. Glenn's last recital using his birth name was on October 26, 1941. He had just turned nine and performed "Piano Preludes" at the Islington United Church of Canada, followed by a "Song Service led by Glen Gold."[24]

How Glenn reacted to the change of his name is impossible to know. He never discussed this with anyone, and it has been ignored in all the literature and films devoted to his career. But I cannot believe that the boy had no feelings about being made to give up a name that has so many desirable associations—money, glitter, wealth, treasure—and that must have become part of his positive self-image in the course of his appearances under the name "Glen[n] Gold."

Surely there were discussions, if not arguments. The only evidence of serious friction or difficulty in Glenn's childhood is a confession he made many years later, again to his producer at Columbia Records, Andrew Kazdin:

> Apparently he had committed some infraction of the family rules and was engaged in an argument with his mother. He revealed to me that at the height of his rage, he felt he was capable of inflicting serious bodily harm on this woman—perhaps even committing murder. It was only a fleeting spark of emotion, but the realization that he had, even for a split second, entertained the notion frightened him profoundly. . . . The experience caused him to retreat into serious introspection, and when he emerged,

> he swore to himself that he would never let that inner rage reveal itself again. He was determined he would live his life practicing self-control.[25]

This memory, even if it was a fantasy, may to a small extent explain why Gould was so reluctant to come close to people, why he shielded himself behind music, and the personality quirks he developed in the course of becoming a professional musician. Gould was quite capable of feeling rage, but dreaded the possibility that it might lead to murder. And since one of the earliest objects of his homicidal impulse may have been his mother, the very person on whom he depended most for nurturance of his musical talent, the rage he felt and everything that went with it had to be suppressed.

Most likely that was also one of the reasons for his growing disenchantment with his father, whose values Glenn found increasingly difficult to accept. Bert would have preferred raising a son who could join him in fishing and other "normal" activities, perhaps even in the family business. But Glenn found all that revolting. The skins sold at Gold Standard Furs were a constant reminder of animal slaughter, the very thing Glenn had to turn against by becoming (later in life) a vegetarian and champion of animal rights. As he grew older, he often claimed to be fonder of animals than he was of people, and in his will he specified that a sizable part of his estate should go to the Toronto Humane Society.

5

A CHILDHOOD FRIEND

Lonely and alienated from his schoolmates, whose roughhousing frightened him and who could share none of his musical interests, Glenn as a child yearned to make contact with someone who might possibly understand and accept him. Fortunately such a person appeared when he was nine years old, a boy named Robert Fulford. Bob was only a few months older than Glenn and was another unusually gifted child, with strong literary and intellectual interests, as well as a keen appreciation for music. The two quickly became friends, and they significantly influenced each other's lives over a period of ten years.

Bob Fulford has an enviable talent for observing human behavior, for reporting accurately and vividly what he remembers, and for steady literary productivity. He is a marvelous raconteur, famous today as one of Canada's most popular journalists and authors. In one of his most successful books, *Best Seat in the House: Memoirs of a Lucky Man,* he describes his meeting with Gould:

> One day in my class at Williamson Road Public School the little boy in front of me turned around and said his name was Glenn Gould. We discovered that we were about to become neighbors: the house my family

> had just rented, 34 Southwood Drive, was next door to his. Soon we were visiting each other, and I immediately learned that Glenn was not an ordinary nine-year-old.[1]

Bob Fulford remembers Glenn as a nonconformist who was far more interested in his music than in school studies. "Glenn really didn't want to work very hard. He didn't want to do what the teachers wanted him to do a lot of the time. He was terrible in penmanship. All his essays and books and so on were always messy. But he was good in history, and of course in English and mathematics. He was an extremely likable person. Glenn was lovable in fact. He was very funny. . . . He took music very seriously, but he didn't take himself very seriously. He was very sweet-tempered and fun to be with."[2]

The decade of their friendship saw Glenn's career slowly progress from relative obscurity as a prodigy occasionally performing the piano or the organ, mostly during church events, to national prominence as a concert artist, making recordings and beginning to involve himself in radio broadcasting. The two boys saw each other nearly every day during those years as next-door neighbors, at school, and on many occasions when Bob was invited to join Glenn and his parents at their summer cottage at Lake Simcoe. Their backgrounds were different yet complementary. Glenn's family was more conservative and provincial, while Bob's was more liberal and cosmopolitan. His father was a newspaperman and an alcoholic, who had traveled widely and lived in New York; his mother was the daughter of an Ottawa bookseller. They had four children.

There was a marked economic gap between the two families. "The Goulds were extremely wealthy by the standards of our street," Bob Fulford told me. "At one point in the forties Mr. Gould told my father that he was spending three thousand dollars a year on Glenn's musical education, and that was my father's entire salary! So, if they could spend three thousand dollars on education on top of their house and their food and their clothing, that meant we were really poor people compared to them."[3]

If we had to rely on Glenn's own conversations, letters, and autobiographical reminiscences, nothing would be known about his friendship with Bob Fulford or its effect on his adolescent development. The same is true of other major relationships in his life. Glenn always sought to create an impression of fierce independence, of being someone for whom human interaction and intimacy were totally inessential. But in actuality he craved contact—always on his own terms, of course—and he often succeeded in drawing someone into his orbit, as he did later with me. His remarkable charm, playfulness, and intellect attracted people, and he reveled in the attention they were willing to give him so long as he remained in control and everything went the way he wanted it to go. In this way he could also make inordinate demands on his friends. Then, when the time came, as it inevitably did, that criticism or viewpoints were expressed that Glenn could not tolerate, he would quickly break off the relationship.

"I loved Glenn," Bob Fulford told me. "The last thing I would ever do was call him a sissy. I don't know if he ever got close enough to most kids to hear the cruelty that kids are capable of. He didn't have a lot of close friends. I was his closest boyhood friend by far. It never happened to Glenn that he would hang out after school around other kids just to be together, to tell jokes, even to sneer at someone. He really had none of that. I cannot see him in my mind standing with three or five people his age on a corner or another place, the sort of communion which I remember as some of the happiest I had in childhood."[4]

It was Bob Fulford who witnessed the development of many of Glenn's anxieties, which would plague him for the rest of his life, and he is convinced that Glenn's mother was largely responsible for giving shape to these fears. "If hypochondria could be inherited, we know who the villain was. His mother was constantly worried about his complexion. His complexion was too white, and his mother was worried about it, and it was, 'You must eat, you should eat more of this and you should do this and this, you should get out into the sun, why don't you and Robert go out and play.' "[5] John Roberts, a later friend of Glenn's, observed that "from childhood on, he had a fear of germs. If anyone was the faintest bit sick, they were not allowed to be near him. He was terrified of getting sick. His mother discouraged him from getting close to crowds. She urged him to keep away from the Canadian National Exhibition and other places where there are enormous crowds."[6]

Glenn seems to have accepted his mother's admonitions on health as gospel, without ever questioning them. In a film he made at the end of his life, he explained that avoiding crowds was necessary to protect oneself against the polio epidemics rampant in his childhood.[7]

Bob Fulford had some other important observations to make about Glenn's mother:

> Florence Gould was a woman of propriety; when she spoke it was from a tranquil world of rules and order, a world from which conflict and tension

had somehow been erased. She hated conflict, and she hated anything extreme or eccentric. Against impossible odds, she longed to see her son have a "normal" childhood, with the right amounts of fresh air and exercise and the right sort of friends. In retrospect it's occurred to me that my friendship with Glenn perhaps owed something to Mrs. Gould's view that I was appropriately normal.[8]

Fulford described the interaction between Glenn and his parents:

> Staying with them for a few days, I caught a glimpse of how intense family relationships could be. In my own home, affection and its opposite were diffused among seven people, but there were just three Goulds and the lines of love and tension were tightly drawn. Glenn was the classic only child, closely scrutinized and at the same time pampered and over-indulged. He explained to me that at the [Lake Simcoe] cottage he would sleep with his mother one night and his father would sleep with her the next, this arrangement having been worked out some years before.
>
> Theirs was a Christian home in which swearing of any kind was a grave effrontery. . . . Alone among all my male contemporaries, [Glenn] never told dirty jokes, never speculated about the sexuality of girls, and never said "fuck."[9]

That Glenn was allowed to sleep with his mother during those formative years when sexual urges become intense and conscious raises serious questions. Was he afraid to sleep alone? Was she attempting to soothe his anxiety? Why would his father give in to such an arrangement? Had the marriage failed, or was sexuality such a taboo issue in Glenn's family that sleeping arrangements simply did not matter?

According to Fulford, Glenn's marked avoidance of sexuality resulted from his having "internalized as a child is mother's distaste for anything having to do with the erotic. She was a strikingly unattractive woman, very angular—I think of her face as being sort of cubist, sharp, axlike—and anything bordering on the erotic had to be kept at a distance. My brother and I sometimes used dirty words, and that disturbed Glenn terribly. So he would start lecturing at us, tell us to stop, and even threaten us—'You'll have to stop coming over to my house'—if we disobeyed. He took this from his mother. His mother always said, 'You never use a word like that.' Well, he accepted that, and apparently believed it. Contrary to what you might expect from any teenage male on the planet, Glenn never said a word indicating physical interest in a girl."[10]

Fulford remembers Glenn and his mother remaining "terribly, terribly close" as he entered puberty, and his father offering little resistance to their intimacy, a point that is confirmed by Glenn's uncle, Grant Gould: "Glenn always felt very close to his mother. It was the complete dominance of the mother-child relationship, of this overpowering motherhood. I'm sure Bert never felt nearly as close to Glenn as he would have liked, and his fondness for Glenn was never really reciprocated."[11]

Bob Fulford told me that he remembers Glenn's father as being "gruff, not eloquent or impassioned. He wore a little mustache to go with the gruffness. And he could get angry—'don't do that; you shouldn't get into that'—the way fathers do with unruly kids. But as for sensuality, I can't remember anything like that. One got the impression that he was a bit overwhelmed by these two very powerful people with whom he was living. You know that he had to give up fishing because of Glenn's distaste for killing. I always thought it a little sad that he let Glenn push him around like that. At the same time he was immensely proud of the boy and did everything possible to foster his career."[12]

If Glenn had a rebellious streak, it took the form of playful jousting with his mother, mostly about differences in their musical taste. Her preference was for church hymns like "Still, still with thee, when purple morning breaketh" and "The day Thou gave us, Lord, is ended."[13] And she loved Italian opera. Among her favorite records were those by the tenor Enrico Caruso. But Glenn's taste as he approached adolescence was taking off in a different direction, and he was beginning to establish his own very determined and opinionated view of music.

Under the influence of Bob Fulford and Alberto Guerrero, the piano teacher Glenn worked with after age ten, he became interested in contemporary composers, especially the Viennese atonalists, Arnold Schoenberg, Alban Berg, and Anton Webern. Glenn also loved Wagner operas and used to say that listening to *Tristan und Isolde* made him weep. Soon he was articulating his opinions on music with the same vigor and faith with which his mother customarily espoused hers, and that led to clashes. As Fulford described it to me, "Glenn would say to his mother, 'Caruso is a clown, he's terrible, awful, horrible, a fraud, exactly what music shouldn't be.' And she would answer him in a hurt tone of voice, 'Oh, Glenn, you mustn't say things like that. Caruso was a great singer. You don't know anything about it. You've only listened to a few records he's made, and they're scratchy. How can you judge him on that?' But he would persist. 'I've heard enough. I've heard enough to know.' He knew that a certain kind of show business tenor was the enemy of whatever kind of music he was developing. And his views were amazingly fixed already at that early age."[14]

I was surprised to learn from Bob Fulford that a change had apparently occurred in Flora Gould's view of her son as a child prodigy. Whereas she had been delighted with his musical precocity as a baby and even compared him to Mozart, she now worried that his exceptional ability as a pianist might actually result in exploitation of his talent. "His mother's worst fear was that Glenn might end up not being normal," Fulford told me. "For example, the word 'Mozart' had become a swearword in the Gould household, because Mozart, as Glenn's parents and history perceived it, was ruined by being a child prodigy. He was exploited. And so 'Mozart' and 'prodigy' were two very bad words. Nobody in that house ever wanted Glenn to be spoken of as a prodigy, Glenn because he just thought it would be so silly, and Mr. and Mrs. Gould because they feared it. They feared the pressure of performances, so the number of his appearances in adolescence was severely limited—the rule was something like once a year on the radio and once a year on stage. They wanted him to be normal."[15]

Indeed, Glenn's public performances were few and far between. At age ten, a year after Bob Fulford first met him, he played the first movement of a Mozart sonata at the Wanstead United Church. The following year he played *Valse Oubliée* by Franz Liszt and a Waltz in A-flat by Levitsky, at the Cambridge Street United Church.

It was around this time, during pre-adolescence, that Glenn began to experience stage fright, so that public performance was no longer an unalloyed pleasure. "I always assumed that Glenn's later withdrawal from the concert stage was mixed with stage fright," Fulford told me. Gould revealed to a reporter who interviewed him many years later that his performance anxiety basically had to do with the discomfort of being looked at and the fear of humiliation. This surfaced when he saw another boy at school become physically ill. As the reporter put it:

> All eyes turned on the wretched child and from that instant on Gould was haunted by the specter of himself being ill in public. That afternoon he returned to school with two soda mints in his pocket, a small tousled boy on guard against the moment when he might lose face. The soda mints were soon supplemented by aspirins and then by more pills. In school, Gould literally counted each second until lunch hour (10,800 seconds at 9 A.M., a comforting four-figure 9,900 at 9:15), and prayed that nothing might happen to humiliate him.[16]

Gould playing a Heinzman Grand (age 9 or 10), 1941–42. Photograph by Charles du Bois.

The erosion of Glenn's faith in his ability to perform comfortably in public may also have been the product of an accident when he was ten years old that resulted in painful physical trauma and led to prolonged misgivings about his health. It happened at the summer cottage, where Glenn's father had installed railway tracks on an incline going to the lake. Bert Gould told me the tracks were designed to carry "a heavy stone-quarry car" down to the water. One day, as Glenn was scrambling to get into the car, he suddenly slipped and fell, landing on the tracks. "He was in great pain."

"Were there any signs of an injury, any bruises or bleeding?" I asked.

"No, but we did take him to the doctor. In fact, we took him to many doctors over the next few years, but he continued to complain. We tried everything—MDs, osteopaths. Nothing did any good. Only the chiropractor helped."

"Do you think there was a physical injury?"

"Yes, the chiropractor said his spine was out of alignment."[17]

The chiropractor was Dr. Arthur Bennett, whose office was only ten blocks from the Goulds' home. Glenn continued seeing him as a teenager, but we have no way of knowing what the diagnosis and treatment were because Dr. Bennett has been dead for over forty years and his records are no longer available.

Canada was then at war with Nazi Germany, having joined the Allies in 1939, when Glenn was seven. Bob Fulford describes the passion the two boys shared for radio, which was the medium that united the country and had such a strong influence on the young pianist that he later devoted large portions of his career to radio broadcasting. "We were vehemently a part of the first and last radio generation, the people for whom radio was the central means of communication," Fulford explained. "We were both born in 1932, just as the Americans and the Canadians were clicking into the idea of national radio. It grew during the thirties, and in the forties it really peaked because it became the center of our knowledge of the world. I can remember listening to the 1948 presidential conventions with Glenn. He knew every detail, which state was going for which candidate, and exactly how many votes each of them got."

"He had a fabulous memory."

"He understood all that. He had a feel for it. But that was a radio event for him, as was the music we listened to. A large part of music came to Glenn through the radio, a way which would not reach most young people today. Today it's the CD. For him it was radio and live performances, and records I think were a third place."

"He didn't buy many records?"

"I can't remember Glenn ever buying a record, although I remember him having them. What was especially important to us was the sense that radio really tied the country together. While listening to the Winnipeg Symphony one time on the CBC, I said to Glenn, 'You know, I find it somehow wild, I'm embarrassed to admit it, but I find it kind of thrilling to think of those guys in the middle of the prairie playing this music, and here it is coming down the wire.' And he said to me, 'Don't be embarrassed about that—it *is* thrilling.' In Canada it was very hard to get the country into your head. It's so damned big! There's so much of it, and there are so few people, and it goes so far. To Glenn this vastness of Canada was important, and radio was a way of encompassing that."[18]

Glenn's first experiment in electronic technology was conducted with Bob's assistance. They rigged up a couple of tin cans connected by long silk threads, and tried to communicate from their respective backyards. When that didn't work, they bought some microphones. "I guess we were at that time eleven or twelve," says Fulford. "I've forgotten how we set it up, but we could speak back and forth. I did a news broadcast from my side, and he played something from his side, and that was about all. We couldn't think of anything more to do, so we had to shut down our network."[19]

The power of electronic media in bringing music, news, and entertainment to Glenn's isolated existence seems to have kindled the ambition to exploit mass media for his own purposes, an ambition that far exceeded his mother's desire for his career.

"What exactly did his mother expect him to accomplish?" I asked Bob Fulford.

"She wanted him to be a pianist, or a composer. There was never any thought of him going into his father's business. What his mother wanted was that he be cultured, that he do something elevated and proper. She was very, very rigid and formal, and her attitude to music was almost the opposite of Glenn's. Hers was that music is good because it's educational, it's part of the respectable, proper, 'cultured' world. The whole side of music that involved the passions and the bohemian life—that would not be within her."[20]

Was there a battle of wits, with Glenn trying to differentiate his vision of the world from that of his mother? In Fulford's book, he remarks that "It could hardly have been otherwise, since they looked at the universe in entirely different ways. Put plainly, he was a born intellectual, and she was not. He saw no reason to accept conventional opinion, however well established, and she knew nothing but conventional opinion."[21]

According to Fulford, Glenn's way of talking—terrifically excited and knowledgeable while putting forth shocking ideas with great conviction—was already apparent by the age of thirteen. "The way he talked was free-ranging, almost wild, extremely irreverent, and full of surprises, a truly wonderful thing to hear, and nothing at all like the way teenagers normally speak. He already had a vision of the world in which all the pieces had to fit just right. And part of it was always aimed at his mother, with the idea of both arousing and mystifying her. I'll never forget the sound of her voice opposing him. She'd feel hurt and exasperated: 'Oh Glenn, don't be so extreme, don't be so opinionated.' "[22]

It seems that with the onset of adolescence Glenn was engaged in an enormous balancing act. Music, the connecting link to his mother, continued to be the supreme passion of his life. Other interests (such as radio and above all the polemical and expressive possibilities of speech) not only provided satisfaction but also a means of safely differentiating himself from his mother. How to manage his aggression and the fear of its consequences was obviously still a problem, and he was relying on his own ingenuity as well as family values for direction. Much later, he told the British filmmaker John McGreevy: "At age twelve I started writing the libretto for an opera, an aquatic *Tod und Verklärung* [*Death and Transfiguration*] about the self-destruction of the human race—the planet would be taken over by various animals."[23] Playing the piano in front of audiences was no longer as safe and pleasurable as it had been earlier, because of the fear, no doubt based partly on his mother's warnings about crowds, that something dreadful might happen to him. The injury to his back had further sapped Glenn's confidence in his body.

He relished the agility of his mind, with its remarkable memory and its capacity for verbal display, encouraged no doubt by his brilliant friend Bob Fulford. And then there was Glenn's pervasive sense of humor, which could suffuse the endless banter with his mother and transform aggression into harmlessly sarcastic attacks on Caruso and Mozart. With all this, sexuality seems to have been suppressed. Except for his father's observation that Glenn "had a beautiful voice, a beautiful boy soprano voice, but as he grew older it just deteriorated into a squawk,"[24] we hear nothing about the growth and maturation of his body, or of any erotic dreams and fantasies about the opposite sex. The staunch religiosity of Glenn's parents and their prohibition of any sex talk apparently had made this a taboo subject. Nor were there any signs of social interest in girls. Being friends with his next-door neighbor seems to have fulfilled Glenn's need for companionship. But above all he preferred the solitary splendor of playing music by himself on the piano or the organ.

6

NEW TEACHERS AND FURTHER SUCCESS

Let's step back in time for a moment. Already when Glenn was a child of seven he had passed tests and examinations at the Toronto Conservatory of Music with flying colors. At the age of ten, his mother enrolled him in classes there.

Surprisingly, if one is to judge from what he wrote in a test for his fourth-grade schoolteacher, Miss Winchester, his theoretical knowledge of music had remained rudimentary.[1] On his own drawing of a five-line staff, Glenn placed a simple tune that he had apparently composed when he was eight years old. It consists of sixteen bars in the key of G major. Below the staff he now wrote the letters "d," "m," "r," etc., to identify them as "do," "mi," "re." Miss Winchester gave him an A for this effort. Below that Glenn placed hand-drawn signs of the treble clef, bass clef, and alto clef, and the word "sempre," translated as "always." Then he added: "# sharp," "b flat," and "♮ natural." Miss Winchester wrote at the bottom of the page that "Glenn added the above signs of his own accord, June 1941."

Surely there is nothing here to suggest the abilities of Mozart, who at an equivalent age was already fully conversant with the musical language and had been writing numerous piano sonatas, pieces for violin and

Toronto's Conservatory of Music Silver medal winners, Gould, second from left, bottom line, 1942. Courtesy of the Royal Conservatory of Music.

piano, and symphonies. What made Glenn's musicality outstanding were the miraculous quality of his piano playing, his perfect pitch, his uncanny ability to read and memorize music at sight, and his enthusiastic singing.

But his expertise grew rapidly at the Conservatory. Professor Leo Smith gave him lessons in music theory, and before long the boy was filled with ideas about key changes, chord progressions, and sequences of vocal lines. He quickly mastered the basics of harmony and showed a particular aptitude for counterpoint, with its interweaving and overlapping musical themes. Professor Frederick C. Silvester instructed him in organ playing. Glenn had already played the organ in church, and he took a particular liking to this instrument, with its keyboards, pedals, and stops capable of projecting a huge array of multiple voices. Not only did the organ give him the chance to fill an entire hall with glorious sounds, it also offered him a safe haven where he was able to relax and collect his thoughts each Sunday after returning from the peacefulness of Lake Simcoe to face the noise and bustle of Toronto:

> Monday mornings, you see, meant going back to school and encountering all sorts of terrifying situations out there in the city. So those moments of evening sanctuary became very special to me. They meant one could find a certain tranquillity, even in the city, but only if one opted not to be part of it. . . . The organ was a great, great influence, not only on my later taste in repertoire, but I think also on the physical manner in which I tried to play the piano.[2]

Glenn's mother had introduced him to Johann Sebastian Bach's Preludes and Fugues on the piano. Now, playing Bach on the organ, he found that "one had to have an entirely different approach, something that was based really on the tips of the fingers doing the whole action for you, something that could almost have the wonderful whistling gasp of the tracker action of the old organs."[3]

Gould playing the organ at the Concert Hall, Toronto Conservatory of Music, 1945. Photograph by P. Toles. Courtesy of Glenn Gould Estate.

Gould and his music teacher, Alberto Guerrero. Courtesy of the University of Toronto Archives and the National Library of Canada.

The director of the Toronto Conservatory of Music was the eminent Sir Ernest MacMillan, also the conductor of Toronto's excellent Symphony Orchestra. He soon heard about the gifted boy enrolled at the Conservatory, became interested in his musical development, and met his parents. It was on the recommendation of Sir Ernest that Glenn changed piano teachers at the age of ten, from his all-embracing mother to the master pedagogue Alberto Guerrero.

Guerrero was considered the best piano teacher at the Conservatory and a formidable influence, although, typically, Glenn would later disown him as a teacher, claiming that everything he had ever learned about keyboard technique he had discovered on his own. Nothing could be further from the truth. Glenn's characteristic way of sitting on a low chair, of holding the fingers parallel to the keys, and of emphasizing digital dexterity at the expense of energy conveyed from the shoulders through the arms, all were acquired from his second, and last, piano teacher.

Alberto Guerrero was born and raised in Chile, where there was at that time a strongly Germanic musical tradition, exemplified by the famous Chilean pianist Claudio Arrau. A versatile pianist, Guerrero also had a wide knowledge of French music and had played works by Debussy and Ravel for the first time in Chile. He had worked as a music critic, and had founded and conducted a symphony orchestra in Santiago. After moving to Canada in the 1920s, Guerrero became one of the first musicians there to perform works by Stravinsky, Schoenberg, Milhaud, and other contemporary composers. According to the Canadian composer John Beckwith, who also studied with him, Guerrero's "performances of light rapid passages had not only fluency and great speed but also exceptional clarity and separation of individual notes."[4]

Glenn's parents evidently were very pleased to have Alberto Guerrero, then in his early fifties, accept their boy as a pupil. Bert Gould talks proudly of having helped Mr. and Mrs. Guerrero to find a piece of property close to their own cottage at Lake Simcoe. "He spent a lot of time at our home," Mr. Gould told me, remembering very clearly that Guerrero "sat very low at the piano himself. He would pull down the keys rather than hit them, claiming that's the best way to produce a good sound. That's where Glenn's ideas about the piano came from."[5]

Guerrero undoubtedly was a stern pedagogue, with very high standards. He could be "hard as nails,"[6] writes William Aide, a very fine pianist himself and currently a professor at the University of Toronto, who had studied with Guerrero. Mr. Aide has interviewed many of the pianists who were studying with Guerrero at the same time Glenn did and says that "Guerrero was very cultivated and artistically authoritative. He held very high artistic ideals and was a formative influence on major artists."[7] Central to Guerrero's method of teaching, as Aide explains it, was "the art of finger-tapping."

> Finger-tapping is a lowly, obsessive, and cultish exercise for acquiring absolute evenness and ease in tricky passage work. It eliminates excess motion in the hand and ensures intimate tactile connection with the pattern in question. I will explain the practice in its simplest application. Take the notes D, E, F sharp, G, and A, for which the right-hand fingering is thumb, 2, 3, 4, 5. The hand position is the natural one assumed when

> the arm and hand hang relaxed from the shoulder; the second knuckle is seen to be the highest point. Rest the finger pads on the key surfaces of the notes D, E, F sharp, G, and A. The left hand taps the fingers successively to the bottom of the keys. The right fingers are boneless; they reflex from the keybed and return to their original position on the surface of the keys. The left hand should tap near the tips of the right-hand fingers, either on the fingernails or at the first joint. The motion of the tapping should be as fast as possible. The second stage of this regimen is to play the notes with a quick staccato motion, one finger at a time, from the surface of the key, quick to the surface of the keybed, and back to the surface of the key. This is slow practice, each note being separated by about two seconds of silence.[8]

Guerrero claimed to have hit on the finger-tapping method independently, after attending a circus where he saw "a three-year-old Chinese boy do an astounding dance full of breath-taking intricacies. Guerrero went backstage to meet the child and asked his trainer for the secret. The teacher-trainer demonstrated how he placed his hands on the child and moved his limbs, while the child remained still and relaxed. Then the child was asked to repeat the movements by himself."[9]

How do we know whether Glenn actually engaged in the laborious practice of finger-tapping recommended by his teacher? According to William Aide, he was seen doing so by Ray Dudley, another piano student. "Ray heard the sixteen-year-old Gould practice every day, and claims that he tapped everything—passages, chords, whole pieces—that he studied with Guerrero. This would have included the Goldberg Variations. Ray Dudley testifies that Gould finger-tapped every Goldberg Variation before he recorded it . . . Gould boasted to Dudley that tapping the complete Goldberg Variations took him thirty-two hours."[10] Glenn's father confirms that Ray Dudley would have been in a position to observe Glenn's playing, if not his practicing. "Glenn and Ray used to play together; I've heard them," he told me. "At the cottage we had two pianos, which was useful when one of his friends would come up on the weekend. And sometimes we'd hear one playing the pipe organ, and the other playing the piano."[11] I would like to believe that Glenn's experience in finger-tapping while studying with Guerrero during his teenage years did contribute to his extraordinary fluency at the keyboard, one of the cornerstones of his piano technique.

Glenn's custom of sitting low in relation to the keyboard was also acquired during his tutelage with Guerrero. Posture had long been a bone of contention between Glenn and his mother. She insisted on having him sit up straight, while he preferred to slouch. Bob Fulford described to me "his mother saying over and over, 'Glenn, sit up.' How could you more violently defy your mother than by adopting in public the very posture that she predicted would be disastrous for him? She was just appalled by his posture."[12] Guerrero believed that to give the hands and fingers maximum freedom, a pianist's arms had to be on the same level as the keyboard. During their lessons, while Glenn was playing, Guerrero would firmly press his shoulders down, and Glenn had to reciprocate by pressing upward against his teacher's hands. This exercise was designed to help strengthen the pianist's back muscles.

Although his mother was unhappy with Glenn's posture, his father seems to have readily accepted Glenn's preference for sitting on a low chair and bending over the keyboard. He even went to the trouble of

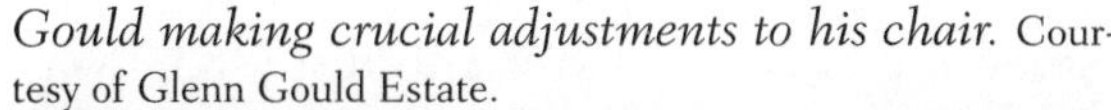

Gould making crucial adjustments to his chair. Courtesy of Glenn Gould Estate.

constructing a special chair for Glenn, just fourteen inches above the floor, which Glenn used for the rest of his life whenever he played the piano.

> I tried to find something fairly light in a folding chair, and then I had to saw about four inches off each leg, and I made a brass bracket to go around each leg and screw into it, and then welded the half of a turnbuckle to the brass bracket so that each leg could be adjusted individually.[13]

Under Alberto Guerrero's guidance, Glenn learned to play works by Chopin, Liszt, Levitsky, Scarlatti, Bach (already his favorite composer), Beethoven, Brahms, Mozart, Mendelssohn, and Haydn. A recording survives of Glenn and his teacher playing two of the Mozart Sonatas for Four Hands. As music teachers typically do, Guerrero arranged for occasional student recitals that were attended by parents and other guests, including prominent musicians living in Toronto. That was how the distinguished Viennese-born pianist and harpsichordist Greta Kraus, who later befriended Glenn, first met him. She told me, "When I heard Glenn play as a boy, he may have been with Alberto Guerrero for one or two years. It was in the evening, at his teacher's house, and he played, to my knowledge Chopin, certainly not Bach. I admired his natural, wonderful musicality, just so beautiful and lyrical and warm, all that which was not the essence of his playing later on."

"Did Guerrero have this natural musicality and warmth?"

"Yes, yes, he was one of the most relaxed players you can imagine. The most admirable part of his teaching was his ability to give technical facility and ease to his students, especially his students who had a problem. Now, Glenn never had a problem. He was born with a phenomenal technical talent. But I also think that his total, almost miraculous physical ability was greatly enhanced by that teacher, by Guerrero, because he had such an understanding of the hand and how to help people technically. And sometimes I wonder whether this was something Glenn didn't want to admit. He didn't want to acknowledge Guerrero's influence. I cannot understand that at all! But as far as I was able to make out, Guerrero was very much hurt, very much, by Glenn's refusing ever to give him any credit for his success."[14]

In addition to the private recitals organized by his teacher, Glenn also appeared in public performances, but sparingly, because his parents were still trying to protect him from too much exposure. On February 19,

1943, at age ten, as we have seen, he played the first movement of a Mozart sonata at the Wanstead United Church. On April 13, 1944, he took part in the annual spring concert of the Ontario Music Teachers Association, performing pieces by Liszt and Levitsky. On May 12 that year, he appeared on a program that also included "Entertainment by Mr. Ted Rust, Ventriloquist." Glenn's father sang a solo, "A Young Tom o'Devon" by Russell, and both of his parents sang a duet, "The Spider and the Fly" by Smith. Glenn himself performed the opening Allegro from Haydn's Sonata in A-flat Major and various short pieces by Liszt, Levitsky, Schubert, and "Patterewski" [sic]."[15]

In 1944, Glenn also entered his first competition. It was held in February as part of the Kiwanis Music Festival. His father, as an affluent businessman and devoted member of the Kiwanis Club of Toronto, was a moving force behind these annual festivals, which were organized to give young musicians a chance to be heard and to compete for prizes. The first time Glenn competed, he was awarded a $200 scholarship and immediately established his superiority over the older boys and girls who had performed on the piano. The Kiwanis Music Festivals were covered in the newspapers, which published the lists of first-, second-, and third-place winners for violinists, pianists, and other instrumentalists. One reporter described the eleven-year-old Glenn as having "that sort of commanding intelligence and responsibility which indicate an ability worth watching.[16]

The year 1945 was a banner one, with seven public appearances. On February 16, in an organ recital given by eighteen of Frederick Silvester's students at the Toronto Conservatory, Glenn played the Fantasia and Fugue in C Minor by J. S. Bach and a Concerto Movement by Dupuis. Glenn had recently gotten a job playing the organ for services at an Anglican church, but lost it because, so the story goes, he would make mistakes and "often lose his place whenever the congregation sang.[17] (I find this hard to believe.) Also in February he competed once again at the Kiwanis Music Festival, and this time won first place. He and some of the other festival winners were asked to perform for a convention of the Ontario Music Teachers Association on April 3. Glenn played the opening movement of Beethoven's Sonata in F Major, opus 10, no. 2. Another organ recital, at the Eglington United Church on May 6, featured him once more playing the C Minor Fugue by Bach. In a piano recital on June 22, he played Chopin's Impromptu in F-sharp Major and Brahms's Ballade in G Major. A major event was his performance of the Beethoven Concerto no. 4 in G Major in an Advanced Grades recital held at the

Toronto Conservatory on November 29. Alberto Guerrero accompanied him by playing the orchestra part on a second piano.

What Glenn and his family always considered to have been his official introduction to the public at large, his first truly important appearance, was a conspicuous concert held on December 12, 1945, when he was thirteen years old. This time he performed the organ in Toronto's large and attractive Eaton Auditorium, where many distinguished artists gave their recitals in those days. (Glenn would later use the auditorium as a recording studio.) The hall contained a magnificent organ built by Canada's famous Casavant Frères, and this particular concert was sponsored by the Casavant Society. It featured several performers, all chosen from the Malvern Collegiate Institute where Glenn had recently been enrolled as a student. With his friend Bob Fulford sitting next to him on the organ bench turning pages, Glenn played Mendelssohn's Sonata no. 6, the Concerto Movement by Dupuis he'd performed earlier that year in a student recital at the Conservatory, the Fugue in G Minor by Bach, and as an encore, a Bach prelude. This time the press gave him a real boost:

> Glenn Gould is just a child, really, a loose-jointed, gracious, smiling boy not thirteen yet [he'd turned thirteen on September 25]. But he played the organ last evening as many a full-grown concert organist couldn't if he tried. A genius he is, with the modesty that only true genius knows. . . . From start to finish and in every detail his playing had the fearless authority and finesse of a master.[18]

Glenn played the same recital a second time, on February 3, 1946, on the organ of the Metropolitan United Church. Later that month he entered his third competition at the Kiwanis Music Festival, held in Toronto's large Massey Hall, the city's major auditorium for classical music. (Glenn would later deny ever having played in any competitions.) And on April 10, he performed works by Bach and Chopin at an Alumni Association concert given by four advanced students of the Conservatory.

That year Glenn made a discovery which he felt was a "determining moment" in the way he would react to his own piano playing in the future. He was practicing a fugue by Mozart, K. 394, when the maid turned on a vacuum cleaner close to the piano. Suddenly his playing was shrouded in mechanical noise, a sensation he found not at all unpleasant. The way Glenn reported this experience later on was that "in the louder passages, this luminously diatonic music in which Mozart deliberately imitates the technique of Sebastian Bach became surrounded with a halo of vibrato, rather the effect that you might get if you sang in the bathtub with both ears full of water and shook your head from side to side all at once." The vacuum cleaner obviously interfered with his perception of the sound he was producing on the piano, but it heightened his perception of the movements he was making to produce that sound. "I could feel, of course—I could sense the tactile relation with the keyboard, which is replete with its own kind of acoustical associations, and I could imagine what I was doing, but I couldn't actually hear it."[19]

What had happened was that the masking noise of the vacuum cleaner had shifted Glenn's attention to the internal sensations of his body and away from the acoustical results of his playing. It was like a trip to the interior—and he enjoyed it. The interruption of auditory feedback led to a heightened awareness of how he moved his fingers while playing, a new tactile awareness of himself. Like forms of meditation, visualization, hypnosis, or other techniques for quickly changing one's level of consciousness, this experience with increased external noise seems to have led Glenn to a revelation about the nature of musical performance. It was like an epiphany, the sort of emotional "high" that teenagers, and other people of course, have at vulnerable moments when a new experience overwhelms them and changes their lives forever.

As a college student, the composer Robert Schumann experienced an epiphany while reading Jean Paul Richter's novel *Siebenkas,* in which a man pretends to be dead and goes through a mock burial; it nearly drove him mad.[20] For Gould, the result of his experience with impeded sound perception was that it made him more keenly appreciate the difference between music heard abstractly in the inner mind and music produced concretely by playing an instrument. The simple trick of vacuum cleaner noise had accomplished for him something akin to what deafness did to Beethoven. "I could imagine what I was doing," Glenn said, "but I couldn't actually hear it." And like many an introverted artist who may at times prefer the products of the imagination to the resulting creative effort, he enjoyed his inner hearing more than his outer performance. "The strange thing was that all of it suddenly sounded better than it had without the vacuum cleaner, and those parts which I couldn't actually hear sounded best of all."[21]

This alteration in the conscious experience of music when he was a young teenager had two long-term consequences. First, it influenced Gould's manner of practicing the piano. He wrote much later that "If I am in a great hurry to acquire the imprint of some new score on my mind, I simulate the effect of the vacuum cleaner by placing some totally contrary noises as close to the instrument as I can. It doesn't matter what noise, really—TV Westerns, Beatles records; anything loud will suffice because what I managed to learn through the accidental coming together of Mozart and the vacuum cleaner was that the inner ear of the imagination is very much more powerful a stimulant than is any amount of outward observation."[22]

The second consequence was that it became more difficult for him to feel satisfied with the actual sound of music, his own performances as well as those of other musicians. It forced him to become a perfectionist. From now on, whenever a work had to be prepared for a concert, he had to struggle mightily in trying to match his playing as closely as possible to the inner model of what it should ideally sound like. At piano lessons with Alberto Guerrero he tortured himself mercilessly (and his teacher as well) by trying to get pieces to sound absolutely perfect. "The lessons were of great duration because Glenn insisted on getting every sound just right," recalls Guerrero's wife. "He would linger over just one or two things until he had it. Alberto would say, 'Oh, it's all right, Glenn,' but Glenn would say, 'No, it's not.' "[23] In the course of time the lessons became "essentially exercises in argument," as Glenn put it later. "They were attempts to crystallize my point of view versus his on some particular issue, whatever it was and . . . I think that for me, anyway, it worked very well."[24]

In effect, Glenn's lessons with Guerrero had become the battleground on which he could fight for the validity of his personal inner vision and demonstrate that pieces of music had to be expressed on the piano keyboard in a certain way. That was the beginning of the highly appealing and unmistakable Gould sound, and his often original if not unorthodox musical interpretations. It was also the beginning of Gould's stubborn, obstinate way of defending, against opposition from other musicians, his personal views of how particular works must sound.

So long as he was playing a solo composition, he could indulge his own concept of the music. But when he had to play with an orchestra or in a chamber ensemble, conflicts with other musicians were likely to arise about matters of interpretation which Gould, so fearful of his own aggression, tried as quickly as possible to sweep aside. One of the first examples that he liked to joke about was "when I was a tad of thirteen [and] a misguided pedagogue at my alma mater, the then Toronto (now Royal) Conservatory of Music, suggested that I might prepare for my debut with orchestra . . . and play [the first movement of] Beethoven's Fourth Concerto." This was a work he already had performed twice in public, but only with Alberto Guerrero as his accompanist. The young Gould's inner concept of the Beethoven concerto had been evolving for at least two years, ever since he had acquired, "with funds painstakingly set aside from my allowance," a recording of this concerto by the great Austrian pianist Artur Schnabel. Gould listened to the recording "almost every day," thereby creating an ideal inner model for himself of how he felt this work must be played. "I faithfully traced every inflective nuance of the Schnabelian rhetoric, surged dramatically ahead when he thought it wise . . . and glided to a graceful cadential halt every four minutes and twenty-five seconds or so, while the automatic changer went to work."[25] (Those were the days of 78 rpm records).

The trouble started during rehearsals with the Conservatory Orchestra, conducted by Ettore Mazzoleni, for the concert on May 8, 1946. Suddenly the young Gould found it necessary to modify his preconceived interpretation and do away with the "graceful cadential halts" in order to avoid clashing with the orchestra. "There was a moment of stress, perhaps, at the D major entry, and the oboes and flutes didn't quite get the point at the E minor stretto, but I left in high spirits."[26] One critic commented on the discrepancies: "Not too much dynamic range here, phrasing a little choppy and sometimes puzzling to one familiar with Schnabel"[27] Another praised Gould generously: "[H]ow awesome are the ways of genius in a child. For Glenn Gould is a genius . . . his butterfly hands made the piano sing. . . . His phrasing was eloquent as poetry chanted by the poet himself."[28]

The observations of a teenage girl who attended this event give an even richer account:

> Glenn is fourteen [actually he was thirteen] but he looks much younger. I think he must have been scared, because at the beginning . . . while the orchestra was playing, he was sort of fidgety—kept pushing his hair back and mopping his brow with a large white handkerchief . . . his playing, however, more than made up for his idiosyncrasies. He was marvelous! The audience nearly brought the house down. Finally he played an encore—a Chopin Valse. His fingers moved like lightning.[29]

Another girl reacted quite differently. Her home was also on Southwood Drive, about fifteen blocks down the street from Glenn, and she was a few years his senior. At age nine, when she was awarded first place in a Kiwanis competition, Joyce Whitney had established a reputation for herself as the most outstanding child pianist in the neighborhood.

Glenn's winning the first place a few years later served to displace her from her favored position, and she took it badly. "It was like Christopher Marlowe having William Shakespeare moving into the same block," Bob Fulford told me. "Joyce was a wonderful pianist by the standards of her equals, but suddenly becoming the second-best pianist on Southwood Drive was devastating. Throughout her adolescence you could go to her if you wanted to know what was wrong with Glenn Gould. He was her obsession; she was terribly jealous of him."

"Did that bother Glenn?"

"Well, at school he'd say to me, 'That girl, don't look now, she's pretty jealous of me. She doesn't like me too much.' And I think, yes, it did bother him because nothing meant more to Glenn than to feel admired by people."[30]

He participated in two other public events that year, a "Symphony Week" program held on October 1, on the mezzanine of Simpson's Department Store, and the graduation exercises at the Toronto Conservatory on October 28, where he played the Sonata in C Major, opus 2, no. 3 by Beethoven, and Chopin's Impromptu in F-sharp, opus 36. Early the following year, on January 14 and 15, 1947, Glenn made his debut with the Toronto Symphony Orchestra, performing all three movements of the Fourth Beethoven Concerto, with Bernard Heinze conducting. By now, the fourteen-year-old pianist had become an established figure in the concert world of his hometown. Some of his odd behavior on stage had already become conspicuous. "Unfortunately the young artist showed some incipient mannerisms and limited his self-control to the periods when he himself was playing," wrote one news reporter. "As he approaches adult status, he will undoubtedly learn to suppress this disturbing fidgeting while his collaborators are at work."[31]

We know of course that he never did. Glenn's fidgeting was probably symptomatic of performance anxiety, but he sought to explain it away at the time by telling people that the problem stemmed from his having noticed "during a pause in the slow movement of the concerto" that his "best dark suit" was covered with long white hairs from his dog. "My father cautioned me to keep my distance from Nick, but that, of course, was easier said than done."[32] Now, in the middle of the Beethoven concerto, Glenn found himself thinking about how to brush the errant hairs from his trousers. It's a charming story, consistent with his sense of humor, which liked to make fun of serious things. But it did not brush away Glenn's underlying profound anxiety about having to perform in public.

7

GAINING A MANAGER

Walter Homburger, the distinguished Toronto concert manager whose portfolio included some of the world's most sought-after performing artists, as well as the Toronto Symphony for twenty-five years, was in great measure responsible for the escalation in Glenn's career during his late teens and early twenties. A modest, dignified man, Mr. Homburger, after living more than fifty years in Canada, still speaks with a heavy German accent.

"How did you first become acquainted with Glenn Gould?" I asked him.

"He was about fourteen years old, and I heard him play at one of the Kiwanis Festivals, where young musicians competed. I believe he played the Fourth Beethoven Concerto, with his accompanist being his teacher, and I thought it was phenomenal, you know. So I went to his parents, and met the parents, and said I'd like to manage his career."

"What was their reaction?"

"Fine. You know, he was just a kid of fourteen, and I visited their home, and they said 'fine' as I recall. It was just like any other family. And we made up a little agreement, which is a one-page thing which I don't think I even have any more, and that's how it started. I'd never managed an artist in my life."

One can assume there must have been more discussion with Glenn's parents than just "fine" and a quick contract, but Walter Homburger is circumspect when he discusses his clients, whose privacy he feels obliged to protect. I asked him what made him interested in assuming the responsibility of managing an artist like Glenn Gould when he had no experience in this field. Homburger told me that he was twenty-two years old at the time, only eight years older than Glenn. He had recently come to Canada as a refugee from Nazi Germany. Those were difficult times for refugees from enemy countries. They were kept segregated and under strict surveillance during the war; severely restricted in where they were allowed to travel and what they were permitted to do. But the idea of becoming a concert manager had appealed to Homburger long before he emigrated to Canada.

"I come from a banking family, but I was not interested in banking. My family lived in Karlsruhe, where I grew up, and they had a private bank there. Some of my childhood friends were very good musicians, for example, a young fellow by the name of Gerhard Kander, who was a child prodigy violinist and studied with Carl Flesch at the same time that Henryk Szeryng was there, and Ida Haendel, you know. That's how I got interested in music generally. But I'd never been in the business. People always told me, 'You can't manage an artist out of Canada; that's impossible.' But my attitude was that if Glenn is as good as I think he is, it makes no difference where he's managed from, because, looking at it the other way around, if I wanted to engage Horowitz in Toronto, I would find out where Horowitz's manager was living and contact him. In those days we didn't have faxes, naturally. And Glenn's parents went along with the idea that maybe I could be helpful, and that's how I started working with him."[1]

Here was a man able to recognize a promising musician and willing to take risks.

"What was it like working with Glenn?" I asked.

"Glenn in those days already knew what he wanted, and his parents left him alone to make his own decisions. And as far as I was concerned, my attitude was 'I'm not a musician.' You see, I can't even read music. I'm strictly a businessman. And so I had advantages and disadvantages. I mean, Glenn could never discuss anything with me musically. We might have a discussion about what I *liked* in a work and he'd ask for my opinion about such things as a trill before a cadenza, but I'd have to say, 'That doesn't interest me at all, it's the whole performance that I care about.' I'm like the public."

Homburger told me that when he first met Glenn, his parents were not "ambitious" for him to give many concerts, so there was relatively little for him to do as manager. Besides, Glenn's father continued to play a managerial role himself, writing letters on his behalf to arrange concerts, for example, a recital in Brantford, Ontario, in a hall that holds 560, at a fee, including Glenn's expenses, of one hundred and fifty dollars.[2]

Glenn was by now presenting full recital programs. His first one in Toronto was announced as "Glenn Gould from the Studio of Alberto Guerrero" on April 10, 1947. He played a Sonata in E-flat by Haydn, two Preludes and Fugues by Bach, Beethoven's Sonata in D Major, opus 10, no. 3, Chopin's Impromptu in F-sharp Major, and the Andante and Rondo Capriccioso by Mendelssohn. On June 8 he gave an organ recital at Grace Church-on-the-Hill, performing works by Dupuis, Mozart (the "Romance" from *Eine Kleine Nachtmusik*), Bach Choral Preludes, and a "Benedictus" by Rowley, assisted by choirboys of the church.

On October 20 of that year, when Glenn had turned fifteen, Homburger's managerial hand truly became evident. "I presented him in a recital at Eaton Auditorium as part of the 'International Artists' series."[3] This constituted Glenn's debut in a commercial sense. His photograph appeared prominently on glossy announcements and in the programs. He performed five sonatas by Scarlatti, the Sonata, opus 31, no. 2, by Beethoven; a Passacaille by Couperin transcribed for the piano by Alberto Guerrero; the Waltz in A-flat, opus 42, and Impromptu, opus 36, of Chopin; Liszt's *Au Bord d'une Source;* and the Andante and Rondo Capriccioso by Mendelssohn. Critics from three newspapers came to the well-advertised event. Wrote one: "Glenn Gould made every note a gem of loveliness. Scales at all sorts of speed were singing things of many-shaded beauty."[4] Another: "Here was a player who conceived movements, entire compositions as wholes, and whose every detail was calculated to reveal total structures."[5] And the third: ". . . he stupefied his audience, especially men. Spiderlike fingers, flexible rubberish wrists, pedals infallible, nose a foot above the keys, he was like an old man on a music spree . . . he outdid Rachmaninoff for intensely supple art."[6]

Glenn was delighted with the success of his first commercial recital. In mid-adolescence, when he was in front of an audience, he began to experience a "glorious sense of power"[7] that seemed to offset some of the uncomfortable anticipatory anxiety he always felt when performing in public. His repertoire was expanding. On November 4, he participated in a group recital for the Home Music Club, performing the Mozart C-

Minor Fantasy, Czerny's *Variations on a Theme by Rode,* and three pieces by Chopin. On November 16, he repeated his entire Eaton Auditorium program for a smaller audience at the Art Gallery of Toronto, and on December 3, he appeared in Hamilton, Ontario, playing Beethoven's First Piano Concerto in C Major with the Toronto Symphony, conducted by his mentor Sir Ernest MacMillan.

Glenn was still enrolled as a student at the Malvern Collegiate Institute, an excellent high school not far from the Goulds' home. His classes were limited to the mornings in order to give enough time for practicing at home and his musical studies at the Conservatory. At fifteen, Glenn wrote an essay entitled "My Plans for the School Year," which describes his view of academic studies with typical humor and literary bravado:

> I am at somewhat of a disadvantage in writing on this subject. . . .
>
> It must not be assumed, however, that I have a complete disregard for higher education. On the contrary, I find it stimulating, enlightening, refreshing, and capable of tremendous influence on otherwise stagnant minds. (For this well-defined phrase I am indebted to the preface of a Manitoba school textbook authorized and published in 1911, entitled "Crop, Cricket and Tariff Control.")
>
> My course of studies includes only three Upper School Subjects: French, English and History. I consider this a most happy choice, for, in French, one reads Rousseau and sides with the revolutionaries; in English one reads of *Wellington* and sides with the reactionaries while in History, one writes critical analysis of the Milan Decree and the Orders-in-Council, and shows how much better everything would have been if only some enlightened fifth-former had been present at the Congress of Vienna.
>
> My plan for this season is a number of solo recitals and appearance with the Hamilton and Toronto Symphony Orchestras. Although very little of this is relevant to the title [of this essay], I think it will be sufficient to show why I have not a moment to spend on extra-curricular activities at school. My plans for the school year, therefore, are non-existent. . . .[8]

"Clever" was his teacher's written comment. Glenn continued to be an outsider at the school, uninvolved in any social activities there. He was unhappy at Malvern, reports an older cousin, Jessie Greig, who was then living with the Gould family. "He was so vastly different and ahead of his age group that it was impossible for him to have much in common. I remember seeing Glenn at recess standing up against the fence all by himself, and that picture has always stayed with me, because he *was* lonely, even in those days. He didn't relate well. In fact, Bob Fulford was the only one I really ever remember him bringing to the house"[9]

Fulford disagrees, saying, "I don't think it was any more torture for him to be in school than it was for anyone else."

"Do you think that he was at all interested in forming relationships with his peers at Malvern?"

"If he yearned for the normal life of the normal teenager, I never noticed it, I never heard about it. It was his mother who wanted him to be normal. Glenn was committed beyond words, beyond any expression that he could make of it to us, to music. And what has always seemed so miraculous to me is that he knew, at the moment when almost no one in the music world knew he existed, that he was one of those people you see on album covers, and read about in the *New York Times,* and hear on the radio. It's true that the musical community of Toronto was aware of his extraordinary talent. But Glenn believed firmly that five or six years in the future the entire musical world would know about him."[10]

This quality of self-confidence evidently amazed Fulford and the other students at Malvern Collegiate Institute. While none of them understood exactly what a genius is, they all seemed to know intuitively that Glenn belonged in that category. Fulford writes in *Best Seat in the House:*

> When he walked home from school, waving his arms as he conducted an invisible symphony orchestra ("pa-puh, duh-*pa*"), the other students just assumed he was acting the way geniuses were supposed to act. . . . His fellow students came to accept it as a given that he would be a world-famous virtuoso, even though few of us understood what that meant or could even name one of the great pianists of the day.[11]

Although Glenn was only a part-time student, his intellectual brilliance became legendary at Malvern. "One thing I remember about school," says Fulford, "is how good he was at it when he felt like it. My favorite example is grade ten geometry. We got our books issued the week after Labor Day, and in October he was finished with that book, while the rest of us were still trying to get through chapter one. I remember another thing very well: his handwriting was terrible. We had a teacher who had that sadistic habit of rating the entire class in every subject, and when it came to handwriting, Glenn and I were always the last or next to last."[12]

Here is an example, from a not too illegible school essay, which shows how he was trying to hone his literary talent, using big words and dense sentences, as though he were a full-fledged musicologist as well as a learned historian:

> My pet antipathy is the reaction of the general public against contemporary thought in the arts in general and music in particular. The practitioners of this attitude are characterized by a firm resolution to resist conversion. Several trite arguments have become standard for the 20th century Cato. Music, for example, is reported to be without understandable melodic line, constructive purpose, and to have a nihilistic attitude in devoting itself to experimentation at the expense of the listening mass.
>
> The attention of by far the largest group of composers today is turned toward the establishment of a new classicism. The "Back to Bach" movement has claimed such diversified writers as Stravinsky, Schonberg [sic], and Hindemith. The aim of these men, and of hundreds of others who are less celebrated, is to recapture the pure subjectivity of the Renaissance, Baroque, and early classical eras. It is true that the reaction which I condemn is, in a sense, a reaction against reaction. However, the result of this return to bygone days has been more of a spiritual refreshner [sic] and aesthetic directive than a reproduction of the sounds or texture of these eras. . . .[13]

Glenn goes on to discuss three composers, Prokofiev, Poulenc, and Hindemith, who "have written occasional works in the style of the old systems." He concludes with the "opinion [that] the most significant refutation of all the arguments against the contemporary artistic idealism is to be found in the famous textbook by Johann Fux, Gradus ad Parnassum, which was written in the midst of another great period of transition—1725."

Glenn's schoolteacher graded his essay "B?" with the criticism, "Your line of argument is, to me, not quite clear." But what this essay makes abundantly clear is that the boy's musical loyalties were being pulled in two directions. Part of him yearned for the "bygone days" of Baroque and classical styles, while another part had gotten excited about contemporary, twentieth-century music. The intervening Romantic period he does not bother to mention. Except for Richard Wagner, it would never hold much interest for him, despite the fact that works by Chopin, Liszt, Mendelssohn, and other composers of the Romantic period were part of his repertory during adolescence. He would later drop these composers as quickly as he dropped many of his friends.

Glenn claimed that his passion for contemporary music was kindled when he first heard a work by the German composer Paul Hindemith:

> I was 15 at the time, a complete reactionary. I hated all music after Wagner, and a good deal of Wagner, and suddenly I heard *Matthias the Painter,* in a recording with Hindemith conducting, and flipped completely. This suddenly was the recreation of a certain kind of Baroque temperament that appealed to me tremendously, and I, as a 15-year old, came alive to contemporary music.[14]

The Czech-born composer Oskar Morawetz, who lives in Toronto, remembers meeting the young Gould at a student recital. "His playing was amazingly beautiful. He played a nocturne by Chopin, very soulful and legato. But I remember him being very opinionated already the first time I met him. At that time, studying with Guerrero, he was enthusiastic only about composers up to about Beethoven, which disappointed me, of course, since I'm a composer myself and I like people to be open to new music."

"How do you explain the later transformation in Glenn's taste?" I asked the genial, now elderly Morawetz.

"Oh, I know exactly how that happened. Glenn was a voracious reader in his adolescence. He used to borrow books from anyone willing to lend them, including myself, and seldom return them. One day he got hold of a book by René Leibowitz [the conductor, writer, and twelve-tone composer].[15] That book made a tremendous impression on Glenn, and after that it was only Schoenberg, Berg, and Webern. He talked about them constantly, listened to recordings of their music, and began playing it himself."[16]

Other influences steering Glenn toward these composers were his piano teacher Alberto Guerrero, who in his early years as a performer had championed contemporary music, and the opportunity of listening to modern composers on programs of the CBC, which Glenn tuned in to every day. Finally, there was his own interest in composing. This had started in childhood when his mother encouraged him to write songs. Later there were exercises in harmony and fugue writing assigned to him at the Toronto Conservatory. "I was good at fughettas," claimed the never-modest Glenn. "It was sort of like solving a jig-saw puzzle."[17]

He was sixteen years old when on February 18 and 19, 1949, an original work of his was heard in public for the first time. It was during a student performance of Shakespeare's *Twelfth Night* given by the Malvern Drama Club. Glenn played his own piano suite, in four sections, titled "Regal Atmosphere," "Elizabethan Gaiety," "Whimsical Nonsense," and "Nocturne." No complete score has survived, and it may be that parts of the suite were improvised. Glenn was very good at doing improvisations.

He also developed a passion for playwriting during his adolescence. His cousin Jessie remembers Glenn "writing plays that he wanted to produce, and he wanted each family member to be one of the actors or actresses in his plays . . . always he was the star. You were always a secondary character."[18] For a while Glenn seems to have seriously considered becoming a professional writer. "If I had not turned out to be a musician, I think the thing I would most liked to have done would be to be a writer," he said in his twenties. "I've always been strongly tempted to try writing fiction . . . one of these times I'll write my autobiography, which will certainly be fiction."[19]

But the pressures for a musical career proved irresistible. First, there were the internal pressures stemming from his extraordinary talent and agility as a pianist. Second came the external pressures and demands exerted by his mother, his teacher Guerrero, and now his manager Walter Homburger. The balance weighed in favor of a contrapuntal arrangement between music and words, with music framing the main subject.

Flora Gould bought Glenn his first Steinway in 1948. It was the model L Grand, 5 feet 11 inches in length, built of Honduras mahogany in New York in 1947. He practiced on this instrument for the next five years, until 1953, when his mother sold it to the mother of another Toronto child prodigy, Larry Miller, who played on it for the next forty years.

On October 9, 1949, Glenn, just turned seventeen, performed in recital the Seventh Sonata in B-flat Major, opus 83, by Sergei Prokofiev. This mighty, tumultuous work had been composed only recently, in 1942, at the height of the war in Russia. It expresses the bravura, heroism, endurance, and tragedy that inevitably occur during times of war. The sonata was associated with the famous piano virtuoso Vladimir Horowitz, who had given the work its first performance in America. Glenn mastered the demanding piece in just a few weeks, and, judging by his later recording of the sonata, it must have brought out all the energy and forcefulness the young pianist could muster. His performance also fortified the impression he wanted to make, that from now on his programs would feature original works and move away from the staple concert repertory of his earlier years. Haydn, Scarlatti, Liszt and Chopin were already the banished playmates of his childhood.

8

"MY LOVE AFFAIR WITH THE MICROPHONE"

Ever since Glenn and Bob Fulford had rigged up microphones as young boys to communicate between their backyards on Southwood Drive, Glenn had been experimenting with electronic devices. He was one of the first musicians in Toronto to use what he later called "primitive tape recorders—strapping the mikes to the sounding board of my piano, the better to emasculate Scarlatti sonatas, for example, and generally subjecting both instruments to whichever imaginative indignities came to mind."[1] Tape-recording one's practice sessions makes eminently good sense in that it allows a musician to review what he or she has been playing, to listen more objectively and critically than is possible during actual performance, to correct any mistakes, and to modify changes in tempo, articulation of consecutive notes, fluctuations in loudness and softness, and other nuances of interpretation. Using a tape recorder may be time-consuming but it is rewarding, enabling the artist to choose between endless subtleties of interpretive phrasing. Having taught himself how to use tape recorders at an early age, Gould would continue to rely on them for the rest of his life. "The greatest of all teachers is the tape recorder," he once told a friend. "I would be lost without it."[2]

Gould operating the tape recorder at the cottage, Lake Simcoe, circa 1956. Courtesy of Fed News and Glenn Gould Estate.

Equally important for Glenn's musical development was his involvement with radio, which became an overriding interest in his later career. The first professional radio broadcast he participated in took place on December 24, 1950, at 10:30 A.M. in the studios of the Canadian Broadcasting Corporation (CBC). This corporation, a unifying influence over a huge and multicultural nation, has had a great track record in championing young artists and composers, giving Canadians the opportunity to be heard live or in recordings, and thus to become better known throughout that vast country. For Glenn, at eighteen years old, his first performance over the radio was the beginning of "my love affair with the microphone":

> One Sunday morning in December 1950, I wandered into a living-room-sized radio studio, placed my services at the disposal of a single micro-

> phone belonging to the Canadian Broadcasting Corporation, and proceeded to broadcast "live" (tape was already a fact of life in the recording industry, but in those days radio broadcasting still observed the first-note-to-the-last-and-damn-the-consequences syndrome of the concert hall) two sonatas: one by Mozart [in B-flat Major, K. 281], one by Hindemith [in B-flat, opus 37].[3]

Other radio engagements soon followed, and they were to change Gould's development as a musician in a profound way. He recalled them as "memorable" for two reasons. In the first place "the immediate presence of a gallery of witnesses," which he had to suffer in the concert hall, had been magically eliminated, thus neutralizing one immediate cause of his stage fright. Second, he was assured of the proof of the pudding—"a soft-cut 'acetate,' a disc which dimly reproduced the felicities of the broadcast." For many years the disc would serve as a reminder of "that moment in my life when I first caught a vague impression of the direction it would take."[4]

His manager Walter Homburger was clearly aware of Glenn's fundamental problem with audiences. "He always said to me, 'I don't like playing in public so much because I always feel there are three thousand pairs of eyes watching what I do rather than listening.' And I think this was part of Glenn. Right from an early age, I mean fourteen, fifteen, he loved being in front of a microphone. He was exactly the reverse of most artists, who get petrified over a microphone and don't like television on top of it. Glenn loved it. We used to do Sunday morning recitals on the CBC Radio and he loved it. You know, he was a born ham."[5]

Indeed, Glenn was one of those rare musicians who positively disliked audiences. It seems as though the critical, fault-finding role of his mother was projected in an exaggerated way onto all the people who came to hear him play. He dreaded what he always felt was the intrusive gaze of live audiences, and compared himself to a Roman gladiator about to be torn to pieces. Glenn tried in a number of different ways to eliminate the terror of stage fright. One strategy was to pretend that there really wasn't any audience out there and that he was all alone. Another was to fortify himself with a feeling of "power" over those people. Finally, and most reliable, was his habit of taking sedatives before going on stage; and that, as we shall see, became his preferred way of maintaining self-control.

Some degree of performance anxiety seems to be universal among performing artists. It may be made worse by parental overprotectiveness and is undoubtedly related to physiological arousal, the outpouring of adrenaline and other stress hormones before going on stage. Usually the discomfort abates as the musician successfully communicates with listeners. Thrill or excitement may even take over as the concert progresses and the musician becomes stimulated and often exhilarated by the audience. Some performers overcome their stage fright by focusing on positive, receptive qualities felt to be out there; Arthur Rubinstein thought about beautiful women in the hall and directed his playing to them.[6]

For artists who find that audiences enhance their performance, the silent anonymity of a radio or recording studio may be acutely distressing and paralyze their interpretation. They feel keenly the solitude of the echo-proof place, the sterile environment, and the microphone becomes their enemy. It absolves no human error and makes every interpretation permanent. Gould's reaction was exactly the opposite. He much preferred playing in the privacy of a radio or recording studio. The sterile room was far more desirable to him than a large hall swarming with germs. The studio became a sort of refuge, a safe place where he could enjoy playing for himself and for what he felt to be an enormous invisible audience. It was almost like retreating to those peaceful, isolated organ lofts where he liked practicing as a child.

> I discovered that, in the privacy, the solitude and (if all Freudians will stand clear) the womb-like security of the studio, it was possible to make music in a direct, more personal manner than any concert hall would ever permit . . . I have not since then been able to think of the potential of music (or for that matter of my own potential as a musician) without some reference to the limitless possibilities of the broadcasting/recording medium.[7]

Glenn cherished solitude, and the public concerts he was required to give permitted little of that. Besides, Glenn's father or Walter Homburger was always setting limits. At this time, Glenn was not allowed to travel alone. When invited to give a concert in the province of New Brunswick, his father wrote to the organizer: "Sir Ernest MacMillan has intimated to me that he had given you my son's name as an artist available for a concert in Frederickton [at a fee of $600 for two appearances]. On account of Glenn's age [he was approaching sixteen] it is necessary that we send someone with him on such a journey."[8]

For years Glenn had been trying to increase the physical distance between himself and his parents while maintaining his psychological rapport with them. At Lake Simcoe he would alarm them by taking off by

Gould astride bicycle, with his dog, Nick, Lake Simcoe, 1945. Courtesy of Glenn Gould Estate.

himself on his bicycle. "Oh, it would be in his early teens," remembers his father. "He'd strike off on the bicycle, and his mother would get a little anxious wondering where he was . . . and I'd take the car and maybe find him five miles away on the side of the road. And one day I came along and he was singing to a bunch of cows. They were all lined up inside the fence." Or Glenn would escape in his motorboat. "If we missed Glenn, someone would have to get another boat and get out on the lake to hunt for him. He might be fourteen, fifteen miles away in his boat. We'd find him coming home singing, conducting."[9]

Glenn continued giving public concerts, of course, although by his early twenties he was already talking about retiring from the stage. The year of his radio debut, 1950, he gave four recitals in Toronto, as well as one in London, Ontario, and again played the Fourth Beethoven Concerto with the Conservatory Orchestra. His repertoire had expanded to include Beethoven's *Fifteen Variations and Fugue (Eroica),* opus 35, Bach's *Italian Concerto,* and the Third Sonata by Hindemith which he'd played on that first radio broadcast.

His enthusiasm for the works of twentieth-century composers persisted. He strove to get closer to the contemporary scene and to acquaint his listeners with fresh and daring works by composers who were almost unknown in Canada. He read whatever books he could find on the subject, and in 1950 he began to study the Third Piano Sonata by the Vienna-born composer Ernst Krenek. Glenn also wanted to learn about the music being composed in his native Toronto. He had met the composer Oskar Morawetz and liked him.

"When Glenn was nineteen," Morawetz told me, "I was at his cottage and brought him my Fantasy in D [written in 1948]. I came back two weeks later and he knew it already by memory and played the whole thing for me, and very, very accurate in everything. But I thought the tempo was anything but what I wanted, and, contrary to what I had written in the score, he used almost no pedal."

"What did it sound like?"

"Well, there was one passage where the melody was supposed to be very prominent, and everything else was meant to be a kind of underground color, muted by means of the pedal. He did just the opposite. The melody almost disappeared, not only because he didn't use the pedal, but because the melody, like in a *cantus firmus,* was much slower than the accompanying figures. And of course every pianist knows that if you have a slow melody and lots of accompanying figure, then you have to play the melody much louder than the rest, because the piano sounds die so fast."

"Did you object to what he was doing to your music?"

"Oh sure. But Glenn was always very argumentative. He told me he doesn't like Chopin because Chopin only wrote short pieces and didn't know how to develop his ideas, and that all his colors are dependent on the pedal. He said, 'I use pedal as little as possible, maybe just to emphasize a chord, but not to get the kind of overall crescendo, the type Franck and Liszt indicated.' "

"So what happened?"

"When he performed my piece he really played magnificently, but everything differently than I wanted, about twenty degrees faster than what I wrote, terribly fast. And when he was asked to record my piece for the CBC, he said to me, 'Oskar, I won't play it for you at all. I made up my mind how the piece should go, and that's it. When you tell me that one voice is more important than the other one, that's quite incorrect. All voices are equally important. And something else, it seems to me that the way you speak, you don't understand your own music.' "

"How could you put up with that?"

"Of course he played certain things wonderfully, but if you play something twice as fast, you completely change the character of the piece. When the record came out, I listened to it once and said, 'I can't listen to it again.' "

"Do you think Glenn was interested in being a composer himself?"

"Well, about that, I can't remember whether he told it to me directly or to Mr. Guerrero, who in turn told it to me. But basically it had to do with Glenn's wish to become immortal. He resented that composers, even when they are not the great ones, have a better chance to be remembered than performers. I really couldn't understand why he was so concerned about that, because he lived at a time when the recording industry had advanced so much that performers are almost better known than composers. And I'm sure that fifty years from now the great performers of today will be remembered just like composers."[10]

Yet Glenn wanted to be remembered as a composer, even though he produced a mere handful of compositions in his lifetime. During his later years, despite a phenomenal output of over one hundred recordings, he would downplay his identity as a pianist, calling himself "a Canadian writer, composer, and broadcaster who plays the piano in his spare time."[11] While still in his adolescence, Glenn had composed a number of pieces for the piano, and then a Sonata for Bassoon and Piano. They are well-crafted, original compositions, not too difficult to play and quite enjoyable to listen to. But they are difficult to obtain. I would recommend a recent recording of Glenn's solo piano compositions played by Emile Naoumoff: two short pieces for the piano and two movements of an unfinished piano sonata.[12]

The first piano piece is a slow and lyrical work, four minutes in duration, somewhat contrapuntal but not harshly dissonant, despite the wild tone clusters, wide-spaced intervals, and complex passages mirrored from the left to the right hand. The work sounds like an improvisation. The second piece, one minute nineteen seconds in duration, opens with an upward-moving theme of three notes, an ascending fourth followed by a descending third. This theme is repeated frequently, sometimes with the intervals inverted. A vigorous, marchlike tempo intervenes, after which the three-note theme returns, now with the pianist's fingers all over the keyboard.

The unfinished piano sonata is longer. The first movement, lasting about seven minutes, starts with a vigorous, dark introduction that breaks into a more relaxed, lyrical section before returning to the somber mood of the beginning. A captivating feature is the very prominent octave tremolos that are played very low in the bass and recur in the left hand. This is Gould at his most melodramatic. The second movement is the longest of all the piano pieces he ever wrote, lasting eight and a half minutes. It opens with a wash of soft, mysterious chords. The top notes gradually coalesce to form a theme, while the rest of the chord fades into the background. Then we hear a new section of dense polyphonic structure which recedes, to be followed by a short fughetta and a calm ending.

The Sonata for Bassoon and Piano, as played on the recording by Catherine Marchese and Emile Naoumoff, is an engaging work, not only because of the contrast provided by the low-pitched monophonic bassoon set against the piano's polyphonic full range of sound, but because of the originality of the musical ideas. There are three short movements. The first, lasting only two minutes, begins with the bassoon blowing a robust solo. This is quickly joined by the piano, playing a faster version of the same theme at gradually increasing speed. An intricate pattern of alternating duets and dialogues between the two instruments closes the movement. Rapid chords on the piano usher in the second movement, slightly over four minutes long. Soon the bassoon is also heard, but in a slower tempo than the piano. They continue playing together nonstop in a bouncy *perpetuum mobile.* The bassoon alone starts the third movement, slowly, until the piano enters in a faster tempo. Then they briefly agree on the same tempo and play a jumpy, fughettalike interlude that leads to a section where the two instruments scramble all over the map. A long improvisatory bassoon solo follows, interrupted by an imposing theme on the piano. After a sequence of duets and solos, the movement, only a little over three minutes long, ends undramatically on a few simple chords.

Glenn had enough confidence in himself as a composer to present his Piano Pieces and the Bassoon Sonata in a Recital of Contemporary Music at the Royal Conservatory, held on January 4, 1951. It was the first time he dared to present a program consisting entirely of contemporary works that included the Third Sonata by Paul Hindemith, the Fantasy in D Minor by Oskar Morawetz, and the very difficult Third Sonata by Ernst Krenek which he had been working on for the last year.

Further radio broadcasts, recitals, and solo appearances with different orchestras (Toronto Symphony, Hamilton Philharmonic, St. Catherine's

Civic Orchestra) occupied the rest of the year. In the fall of 1951, at the age of nineteen, Glenn toured Canada's western provinces accompanied by his mother. He performed the Fourth Beethoven Concerto with the Vancouver Symphony, conducted by William Steinberg, and gave a solo recital in Calgary. Steinberg happened to be a good friend of my parents, Kathe and Eugene Ostwald, and whenever he conducted in San Francisco he would have dinner with my family. Even before meeting Glenn, I had heard about his unusual interpretations directly from a conductor's point of view.

Thanks to these public appearances and his radio broadcasts—many of his Massey Hall concerts had been taped live—not to mention the efforts of his enterprising manager in promoting his career, Glenn was quickly rising to prominence throughout Canada.

9

SELF-ISOLATION

When he was nineteen, Glenn dropped out of the Malvern Collegiate Institute. It was simply too much to fulfill the demands of academic studies and a musical career at the same time. This marked the beginning of a self-imposed moratorium, a period of separation from parents and teachers and relative isolation from social involvements generally. During this period he lived alone in his parents' cottage at Lake Simcoe. He spent the time learning new music, practicing, reading, listening to the radio, playing the phonograph, and going for long walks. He did maintain contact with his old friend Bob Fulford, who had himself quit Malvern earlier, claiming that he was "a creative individual in rebellion against a repressive environment,"[1] which may have been another of Glenn's reasons. The two dropouts now decided to form a business together. Consulting with lawyers and bankers, they created a mini-corporation called New Music Associates, whose purpose was to organize and present concerts devoted to music by "new" composers who were then practically unknown in Toronto.

Fulford rented a concert hall seating three hundred people, at a cost of $31.50 a night. He printed the tickets, took care of publicity, invited two friends to serve as ushers, and wrote the checks—"all of them meager"[2]—while Glenn selected the composers and the performers, choosing himself, of course, as the main pianist.

The first event, a Schoenberg Memorial Concert, was held on October 4, 1952. Glenn, now twenty years old, played Schoenberg's Three Piano Pieces, opus 11; Suite for Piano, opus 25; and the piano part to *Ode to Napoleon,* opus 41. He also accompanied a singer in six Schoenberg Songs. As though that weren't enough to do, he wrote an explanatory lecture about the music heard that evening, in what Bob Fulford calls "the opaque style later familiar to readers of his liner notes; it was read to the audience by Frank Herbert, a CBC announcer who confessed to me afterward that he understood almost none of it."[3]

The second New Music Associates concert again featured music by Schoenberg and his two most distinguished pupils, Alban Berg and Anton Webern. This time, too, Glenn provided an explanatory lecture, which was printed—four typewritten pages, single-spaced—and distributed along with the program to members of the audience. This "lecture" not only demonstrates what Bob Fulford, himself an accomplished journalist, calls the "opaqueness" in Glenn's literary style, but reveals the young pianist's remarkable facility, at age twenty and without any special training in the field, to behave like a musicologist.

An example of his "opaqueness":

> There is common to most musicians who have come under the influence of the Schoenbergoan [sic] universe an approach toward music, classic as well as contemporary, which attempts through analysis, to reduce all sound forms to the lowest common denominator.

An example of his musical erudition:

> Webern began to use the twelve-tone technique consistently after 1925 and, subsequently the solidity and assurance which were absent in many of the works of his transitional period, are felt in the more forceful and extended treatment of his ideas. The Saxophone Quartet [included on the program] is one of the longer of his early twelve-tone works (it lasts almost eight minutes). The first movement is ternary in shape and canonic in texture. It opens with a five-bar introduction which lays bare the interval properties of his row in four three-tone groups which are echoed in inverted canon by a row transposed down two semi-tones. The canon is rhythmically altered to display subtle relationships between these two rows;

A		B	C		D
D♭ B♭ A	C	B E♭	E F	F♯	G♯ D G
B D E♭	C	C♯ A	G♯ G	F♯	E B♭ F
B		A	D		C

[4]

For this program, Glenn performed in four of the five difficult works presented. He played Webern's Variations for Piano, opus 27, and Berg's Sonata in One Movement, opus 1, a work he had recently recorded for Hallmark Records, his first commercial recording. With the mezzosoprano Roma Butler, Glenn performed Schoenberg's song cycle *Das Buch der hängenden Gärten (The Book of the Hanging Gardens),* opus 15, and he participated in the performance of Webern's Quartet for Tenor Saxophone, Clarinet, Violin, and Piano. The fifth work on the program, Webern's Five Movements for String Quartet, opus 5, required no pianist; but Glenn had scheduled himself to perform in yet another work, Schoenberg's Variations for Organ, which at the last moment had to be "regrettably canceled."[5]

A third concert organized by Glenn and Bob's shortlived corporation was devoted entirely to the music of Johann Sebastian Bach.

"But Glenn, if we are *New* Music Associates, why are we doing a Bach concert?" Bob asked him.

"Bach is ever new," is what Bob remembers as Glenn's explanation,[6] but that does not tell the whole story. There were strong personal reasons. Glenn had been working very hard on Bach's *Goldberg Variations,* written originally for the harpsichord and relatively unknown at the time. This remarkable work, about forty minutes in duration, consists of an opening and closing "Aria" plus thirty Variations all on the same ground bass. Glenn wanted to try it out in public, and the all-Bach program on October 16, 1954, would give him an opportunity to do so.

Only fifteen people showed up for this concert. The two contemporary music concerts had been well attended and well reviewed in the press, but the Bach concert was spoiled by Hurricane Hazel. A torrential rainstorm hit Toronto, producing catastrophic damage and much disarray. Also on this ill-fated program was an appearance by the gifted young Canadian contralto Maureen Forrester, making her debut in Toronto. "I paid her agent what seems to have been our highest fee—fifty dollars," writes Bob Fulford in his memoirs.

> I can still hear the applause echoing through the mostly empty building. One of those applauding was Sir Ernest MacMillan, the conductor of the

> Toronto Symphony, who was already familiar with Glenn's work but had not heard Forrester before. She was twenty-four that year, and still known mainly in Montreal . . . On that occasion we lost money . . . But while the Bach concert was no great financial blow, it was the end of New Music Associates.[7]

We don't know how closely Glenn's interpretation of the *Goldberg Variations* in 1954 resembled the phenomenal performance of this work he recorded a year later in New York. He had been searching for a suitable Bach style since his adolescent years when he listened to recordings by Wanda Landowska, Edwin Fischer, Pablo Casals, and other highly regarded Bach interpreters; he had liked none of them. However, there was one pianist, in New York—Rosalyn Tureck—whose recorded interpretations, especially of the *Goldberg Variations,* he had come to admire. As Glenn recalled many years later:

> Back in the forties, when I was a teenager, she was the one who played Bach in what seemed to me a sensible way. In those days . . . I was fighting a battle in which I was never going to get a surrender flag from my teacher on the way in which Bach should go, but her records were the first evidence that one did not fight alone. It was playing of such uprightness, to put it in the moral sphere. There was such a sense of repose that had nothing to do with languor, but rather with moral rectitude in the liturgical sense.[8]

Up at the cottage Glenn worked painstakingly on his Bach interpretations and other repertoire. It was a time of introspection and self-renewal. Here he could practice at all hours, play back his work on the tape recorder, read, study new scores, enlarge his repertoire, improvise, compose, listen to the radio and phonograph, all without outside interference or criticism. His solitude at Lake Simcoe was interrupted only by quick drives. Glenn was not one to obey traffic rules. He'd speed into Uptergrove and slam into a parking space in front of the coffeeshop. Here he chatted with the locals, who didn't think of him as a celebrated pianist. He also spent a good deal of time roaming in the woods with a new collie named Banquo, a recent replacement for faithful old Nick, who was ailing with a tumor of the back.

During those years of seclusion in his early twenties Gould put the finishing touches on his unique and inimitable piano style, a style that would differentiate his playing from that of every other pianist: marked contrasts between staccato and legato, unconventionally fast or slow tempi, exceptional rhythmic vitality, high clarity of articulation, respect for contrapuntal texture, and deliberate emphasis on inner or hidden voices. With this style went a number of bodily mannerisms that also made his performances unique. His mouth was incessantly in motion, articulating with lips and teeth the passages his fingers were executing nimbly on the keyboard. He always hummed or sang, as his mother had taught him to do, often loud enough to be heard by the public. Sitting on his low chair, he undulated the entire upper part of his body in a circular motion consistent with the tempo he was playing. And whenever one of his hands was not busy on the keyboard, he used it like a conductor's, making all sorts of expressive gestures and in effect conducting his own playing.

It was not uncommon for members of an audience or newspaper critics to remark on these physical mannerisms. Some found them amusing, others distracting or actively annoying. Many assumed that Gould did these things for purely exhibitionistic purposes, as a way of calling attention to himself. In fact, the movements were made primarily to satisfy some inner need. They were integral to his piano playing, not something artificially grafted onto it. One can observe them in films made when he was playing alone, and in segments of videotape ("out-takes") that were never intended to be shown in public.

Glenn always insisted that his "mannerisms" helped improve the quality of his musical performance. For instance, when playing on a piano whose sound he disliked, his singing and humming would get louder, like a masking tone (the vacuum cleaner) to enhance his internal perception of the music. And the undulations of his trunk as well as the conducting movements of his arms were geared to the experience of ecstasy while playing. Ecstasy is an intense state of emotion, a rapture, a swoon of delight, a trancelike feeling as if the mind has expanded beyond the limits of the body. Solitude and isolation can heighten an ecstatic moment, and it is quite likely that Glenn was using his moratorium of living alone in the country to experiment with such states.

Around this time the social traits that made Gould seem "eccentric" also blossomed: his odd way of overdressing, his excessive use of humor and joking, and his hypersensitivity to bodily sensations that he believed to be signs of disease. Already in those days he was running to physicians and chiropractors. (It was Colin A. McRae, M. D., in Toronto, who would prescribe tincture of opium for his complaints of diarrhea, and Chloromycetin, an antibiotic, for complaints of lung infection.[9] Gould's "neurotic" mannerisms, too, were integral to his artistic personality. They were part of a behavioral style that he seemed to need for expressing what he felt about himself as a highly nervous creative artist, striving constantly to excel and to become the world's foremost pianist. He was special but not secure. He wanted people to notice his vulnerability as well as his genius.

Bob Fulford, who probably understood Glenn better than anyone else at that time, has raised the question, "Were his eccentricities part of an intentionally self-created myth, or did they proceed inevitably from his neuroses?"

> [Glenn] could act oddly, laugh good-naturedly at the oddness of his behavior, and then act oddly again. When he was a teenager, and a young man, he had a curious habit of speaking with a German accent when he was discussing a German composer or a German book. The year he discovered Nietzsche's *Also Sprach Zarathustra,* the accent grew almost impenetrably thick. If you kidded him about it he would stop, and a few minutes later start again, all the while admitting that it was a funny way to talk. Was he satirizing himself or was he trying to work himself into a German mood?[10]

I think an additional determinant must be considered. Glenn's ego-boundaries evidently were so fluid that he could easily absorb into his own personality certain qualities observed in other people. He was a gifted imitator of their facial expressions, speech mannerisms, foreign accents, and body movements. As he grew older, he loved to engage in playacting and make-believe with friends. When he worked in radio and television, he found it possible, without any theatrical training, to impersonate a variety of fictional characters such as Karlheinz Klopweisser (modeled on the German composer Karlheinz Stockhausen) or Myron Chianti (a takeoff on Marlon Brando). But there was always something forced or excessive about these escapes into fantasy. "He's a real ham" was the judgment passed by a number of people who knew Glenn Gould well.[11]

His indulgence in German accents also suggests the growing influence of his very Germanic-sounding manager, Walter Homburger, who had now replaced Alberto Guerrero as an older role model and mentor. Glenn's withdrawal to the country to study and practice independently marked the final break in his ambivalent subordination to the teacher who had done so much to mold his posture and technique at the piano.

When Glenn entered his third decade, he closed the door on his student days, and all lessons with Guerrero ceased. Glenn felt they had become increasingly unproductive, mostly times for argument, while Guerrero thought Glenn was socially stunted.

William Aide, who knew both men, told me that "Guerrero strongly objected to Glenn's mannerisms and detested what he felt was a lack of authenticity in his performances. It was he who rejected Glenn, not the other way. Guerrero had a very cultivated and artistically authoritative influence on major Canadian artists. Rather than remain in constant disagreement with this particular student, he probably decided to set him free. Psychologically speaking, Guerrero had been Glenn's artistic father, a much stronger personality than Glenn's real father, who gave in to whatever his son demanded. Guerrero really left permanent marks on Glenn."

"What were they?"

"Well, in addition to his basic piano technique, the low chair and flat fingers and tapping method, Glenn further absorbed from Guerrero his basic seriousness, total intellectual concentration, and total necessity for supremacy. Guerrero had one ultimate concern—music. And he believed that one had to be a winner, whether playing the piano, or playing games like Monopoly or croquet, or arguing, which were what they did together regularly."

"Do you think that Guerrero might have reinforced Glenn's congenital sense of always having to be number one?"

"Definitely. It played right into Glenn's intense uneasiness about other pianists. For example, Glenn detested Claudio Arrau. Arrau really upset him because he was a friend of Guerrero, a rival, and a visitor to Toronto. Glenn would call him 'a child.' During the nine years Guerrero was Glenn's teacher, Guerrero aged a lot, and even before they parted company he stopped going to Glenn's concerts."[12]

For an interview published some years later in *The New Yorker,* Glenn had this to say about Alberto Guerrero:

> Our outlooks on music were diametrically opposed. He was a "heart" man and I wanted to be a "head" kid. Besides, nine years is a long time for anyone to be a student of the same teacher. I decided it was time for me to set out on my own snowshoes, and I developed an insufferable amount of self-confidence, which has never left me.[13]

Homburger was a very different kind of father figure. He was all business and didn't let himself get into arguments about musical matters, which basically didn't interest him. And rather than criticizing Glenn's

Gould playing croquet at Lake Simcoe with Alberto Guerrero, 1945. Courtesy of Glenn Gould Estate.

eccentricities the way Guerrero did, he defended them, realizing how necessary they were for his playing. "You know what my answer always was if Glenn was criticized for the way he behaved on stage? I'd say, 'I assume you go to concerts to hear music. So close your eyes, and listen. If you don't like to see him, eliminate it from in front of your face.' "[14]

Homburger also understood the publicity value of Glenn's reputation for odd behavior on the stage. At one point this included having glasses of Poland Water on the piano and placing little rugs under his feet to muffle the noise of his stomping. People who had never heard him play became curious and bought tickets so they could see him, thus rewarding

Glenn with the very thing he said he dreaded most—to be looked at. The money motive obviously was a factor in his agreeing to appear more frequently in public. Glenn liked making money and became good at it. Walter Homburger introduced him to an accountant, Patrick Sullivan, and an attorney, Morris Gross, for practical help with contracts and his money. Glenn also learned at an early age how to invest in stocks and bonds. When I first met him in 1957, he bragged about his assets in Canadian silver mines.

In the summer of 1953, Gould participated for the first time in the Stratford Music Festival. Stratford, seventy-five miles west of Toronto, already hosted an annual Shakespeare Festival. Musicians participated in the plays, and as their numbers grew it was decided to give concerts there as well, and to invite a roster of distinguished artists for a summer Music Festival. A full orchestra played in a hall open at the sides similar to the tent at the Tanglewood Festival in Massachusetts. The hall seated nearly a thousand people, with smaller spaces available for chamber music. The atmosphere encouraged informal mingling of musicians and actors, and led to performances of chamber operas. One of the most unforgettable was Stravinsky's *L'Histoire du Soldat,* featuring the French mime Marcel Marceau's North American debut, Alexander Schneider from New York playing the wandering violinist.

There are many stories about Glenn at Stratford. One of them concerns the rehearsals in 1954 for Beethoven's Trio, opus 70, no. 1 (the "Ghost"), which was to be recorded and televised. In 1950, the Canadian Broadcasting Corporation had inaugurated multimedia performances in Canada, and Glenn Gould had become one of their most popular stars. Now he would perform chamber music with two other outstanding musicians—Alexander Schneider, who for many years had been a member of the great Budapest String Quartet, and Zara Nelsova, the Canadian cellist, who had risen to spectacular prominence when only twelve years old and living in London. I'd gotten to know Zara when she performed in San Francisco, and we played string trios together with the violist Mary James. Zara clearly remembers her rehearsals with Glenn:

"There were many disagreements and arguments from the beginning. We'd start rehearsing in the morning, in blazing heat well up in the eighties. Glenn appeared wearing a heavy overcoat, muffler, gloves, and hat. Sasha [Alexander Schneider] immediately objected when Glenn kept his piano score closed and told Sasha he was used to playing everything from memory. Sasha and I were planning to play with our parts open in front of us."[15]

The practice of not using a score while performing music grew out of the era of virtuosity beginning at the end of the eighteenth century. Mozart seldom looked at the music when he played his own compositions; indeed, often he hadn't even put the solo part on paper. In the nineteenth century, playing "by heart" without the music became standard procedure, despite the fact that this terrorized those musicians whose memory was not totally reliable or who simply felt more comfortable with the score in front of them. Clara Schumann adhered bravely to the custom of playing from memory until advancing age forced her to abandon it. Franz Liszt was famous for his impromptu performances without looking at the music. Before the turn of the century the Meiningen Orchestra conducted by Hans von Bülow played entire symphonies from memory, and it has become almost routine for soloists, especially when performing with an orchestra, to do so. A number of string ensembles, including the famous Kolisch Quartet, which in the 1920's and 1930's introduced much modern chamber music, almost never played with the music in front of them.

There continues to be hearty debate about this practice. Some musicians say that visual dependence on the score reduces their spontaneity and expressive freedom. Others claim that the absence of the score increases their apprehensiveness about making mistakes, and interferes with the quality of their performance.

Glenn, who seemed to possess photographic memory and immediate recall, liked to say that he disdained anything smacking of nineteenth-century virtuosity, but when it came to performing, he acted like a virtuoso all the way and rarely used a score. Alexander Schneider, by contrast, felt that musicians "can relax . . . and make music" only when there is a score on the stand in front of them.[16]

But what bothered Schneider more than anything about Glenn was the pianist's arrogance, specifically over aspects of interpretation. Glenn as usual had made up his mind long before reheasals began about how the "Ghost" Trio must sound, and he now refused to budge from this perfect inner model of Beethoven's music.

"How many times have you actually performed this piece?" Sasha asked him.

"This will be the first time."

"Well, I've played the trio at least four hundred to five hundred times," Sasha said.

But Glenn got the last laugh: "My position has always been that quality is more important than quantity."[17]

Nelsova, a vastly experienced chamber music player, sided with Schneider. "I had made my London debut at the age of eight and since coming to Canada had formed with my two sisters a trio that concertized regularly. I sided with 'Sasha,' and that forced Glenn to play the trio in a more orthodox way. [A 33 rpm recording of this performance has survived.][18] As for his using the score, Glenn brought it with him into the concert hall and sat on it. Sasha later admitted that Glenn played 'very well' and had a promising future."[19]

Glenn made another personal contact with a member of the New York musical establishment before his phenomenal success there in 1955: Harvey Olnick, a newcomer to Toronto and the first music historian to occupy a chair in any Canadian university.

"How did you happen to meet Glenn?" I asked Mr. Olnick.

"He came to see me all of a sudden because his friend Ezra Schabas wanted me to do a review for Glenn in the States, something to publicize his inevitable debut there. Glenn asked me to go to his next concert in Toronto, and promised me the tickets if I'd give him a review. I'd heard, 'Yes, he's very good, you know,' but nothing like what I heard when I went to this concert. It was all Bach."

"What was your critical reaction?"

"Then I was just dazzled. It was the only kind of Bach playing I'd ever heard that was like this, particularly in this wonderful rhythmic pulse that he got, without accent and everything just going lickety-split. No one in Toronto that I knew of played that way at all. It was all very romantic playing, you know, with a very English calm. And so I was just bowled over."

"What did you do?"

"After the concert I went out to go to my office, and I found Glenn standing there. I said to him, 'Where did you come from? Who was your teacher?' I'd heard the *Goldbergs* done by Wanda Landowska, and now I heard Glenn playing them. Certainly this had the harpsichord technique of Landowska as well as the pianistic intensity of Rudolf Serkin."[20]

That was precisely the sentiment Olnick conveyed in the article he wrote, but did not sign, for the influential *Musical Courier,* published in the States: "If [Gould's] achievements in the music of Bach are matched by comparable insights into works by other masters, the public will soon be confronted with an artist in no way inferior to such artists as Landowska and Serkin."[21]

It was a dangerous challenge: to perform the works of other composers with the same degree of mastery he'd shown in playing Bach. Glenn was already experiencing some trouble with other composers, specifically Beethoven's Sonata no. 30 in E Major, opus 109. One variation in the last movement is famous for a sudden shift from sixths to thirds in the right hand. Glenn called it "a positive horror." After starting to practice the difficult passage, "one thing after another began to go wrong." Soon he developed "a total block about this thing—I couldn't get to that point [in the last movement] without literally shying and stopping." He later claimed to have solved the problem by practicing with two radios playing "as loud as possible," by concentrating his attention on "four unimportant accompanying notes in the left hand," and by playing the entire passage "as unmusically as possible."[22]

It apparently did not occur to Glenn to seek help from a more experienced pianist. The two years of isolation at Lake Simcoe had cut him off from the corrective influence of other musicians and taught him to be utterly self-reliant. He no longer wanted to be advised by older musical colleagues; at least that was what his behavior with people like Alexander Schneider, Harvey Olnick, and others like them suggests. He was listening more to business advisers—his manager, his stockbroker, and his accountant. Glenn's handling of money may have strengthened his masculine identification with his father, a prosperous businessman. But even these people couldn't always get through to him. Glenn always had to do things his own way.

Unfortunately, this willfulness was not matched by his sense of reality, which remained more childlike than adult. He believed that everything he wanted or fantasized or feared had to come true. A minor ache in his belly was treated as a medical emergency. Listeners at his concerts were out to destroy him. Glenn could imagine himself in a variety of roles—as piano virtuoso, music critic, composer, novelist, and medical expert—without being certain which really fit. Along with that went a chameleonlike quality of eccentric behavior, very appealing and entertaining, to be sure, but masking deep feelings of anxiety and fragility.

10

TRIUMPH IN THE STATES

Glenn's nervousness and indecisiveness about the future may be gleaned from a conversation with Zara Nelsova during the Stratford Festival just six months before his debut in the United States.

"We rehearsed in the morning, and his face had a yellow complexion, a really sickly color. Obviously he wasn't ready for the day yet, which for Glenn started in the afternoon. He told us he'd been up all night reading Tolstoy, that he had to read every classic he could get his hands on. That evening he took me aside and asked, 'How does one start a career?' which floored me coming from one of the most successful pianists in Canada. He seemed especially worried about how he might be received if he were to play in the States. There was little being done for Canadian artists abroad in those days, so I suggested a concert tour of Alaska. A good friend of mine, the pianist Maxim Schapiro, was active at that time in arranging such tours, and I recommended to Glenn that he get in touch with him."

"Did Glenn not tell you that he had a manager who was taking care of such things?" I asked Zara.

"Not a word. Glenn never mentioned a manager, which made me realize later, after hearing about his triumphal recitals in the United States, that he really had no need for my advice and was simply expressing insecurity, not to mention a bit of deceitfulness."[1]

Walter Homburger had booked two dates for Glenn's debut in the States: January 2, 1955, in Washington, D.C., and January 11 in New York City. Glenn fretted about what to perform. His repertoire was large enough by now to fill a dozen recital programs, but he was after something unique that would instantly identify him as a very special artist, display his Bach expertise, prove him loyal to classical as well as contemporary composers, and demonstrate his keyboard wizardry—a tall order. In addition, he was seeking a program that he would enjoy playing. After much agonizing and rearranging, he settled on a truly unusual selection: two organ pieces by outstanding composers of the seventeenth century transcribed for piano, a Pavane by Orlando Gibbons and a Fantasia by Jan Pieterszoon Sweelinck; five Three-Part Inventions (Sinfonias) and the Partita no. 5 by Bach; Webern's Variations, opus 27, Beethoven's Sonata no. 30, opus 109—the one with the dangerous variation—and the Piano Sonata opus 1, by Alban Berg.

His parents and Mr. Homburger came along on the trip to the United States, everyone trying to pretend that this was just an ordinary event, nothing very different from Glenn's many previous concerts in Canada. His Washington debut, a matinée, took place in the beautiful Phillips Gallery. A small audience appeared, but the critic Paul Hume wrote an extremely complimentary review in *The Washington Post,* mentioning among other things that "Few pianists play the instrument so beautifully, so lovingly, so musicianly in manner, and with such regard for its real nature and its enormous literature. . . . Glenn Gould is a pianist with rare gifts for the world. It must not long delay hearing and according him the honor and audience he deserves. We know of no other pianist like him of any age."[2]

The news spread like prairie fire through the network of musicians, especially pianists eager to know if it was true.

"I knew that Glenn's New York debut would be a sensational thing," says Harvey Olnick, whose recent article in *The Musical Courier* had helped pave the way to his success. Harvey had excellent connections in New York. "I called people up and told them they've got to go and hear this kooky guy from Canada. I called Mrs. Leventritt, who's an old friend [and a generous supporter of talented young musicians]. And I told her, 'This is a phenomenon, he's playing in Town Hall, go for God's sake and get the guys to go.' So she called Claude Frank, and Gary Graffman, and

I can't remember all the other guys. Who's the pianist who got killed in a plane crash?"

"William Kapell."

"Yea, Willy was there."[3]

Indeed, the elite of New York's younger pianists went to Town Hall to size up their latest competitor. The pianist Martin Canin has vivid memories of Glenn's recital. A brilliant Juilliard graduate, Canin had just returned to New York after two years of army duty in Europe. He'd met Gould earlier, through a mutual connection at Juilliard.

"Glenn had a recording with him. It was a small Canadian label called Hallmark. And we went into the library, and I put on this recording of the G-Major Partita. And it simply blew me away. It blew me away! First of all, the speed. I'd never thought of it that way."

"What do you remember about Glenn's Town Hall debut?"

"It was very poorly attended, maybe thirty-five people in the hall. Glenn was a total unknown at that time. I remember meeting somebody after that was over, and I asked, 'How did you like it?' and this person said, 'Oh, it was okay.' And I felt almost a tightness in my muscles as I expressed myself, 'You know, I think that's one of the greatest concerts I've ever heard. This is phenomenal.'

"He started with the piano lid down and the half-stick for the Gibbons—I still remember this because it ended so softly. The first half of the program he ended with opus 109, and the second part with the Berg sonata. Both pieces as you know end pianissimo. And he was so different, and the repertoire he played was so different. He was just great. I mean, he was *really* great. I don't think I was at the time familiar enough with the opus 109 Beethoven to say that it was authentic, and maybe his playing was less eccentric than it became later. He was then only twenty-two. But I was savvy enough to know immediately that this was a major league player. Triple A, no, not triple A, major leagues, quadruple A."[4]

Harvey Olnick told me about Rosie Leventritt's efforts on Glenn's behalf. "She had coordinated a party for him. She called David Oppenheim [the director of the Masterworks Division, Columbia Records] and I called him too, and Joe and Lillian Fuchs [the famous violinist and violist]. Of course you could have gotten tickets for nothing, but we knew the hall would be nearly empty unless we did some last-minute promotion. At any rate, Glenn played the concert and then went to the party. He didn't know there were going to be so many pianists there, all these rival pianists."

"He must have been petrified."

"He wasn't petrified! He was so unpetrified that he became sick and decided to leave within half an hour. He feigned illness, you know, but he wasn't really ill. He was just uncomfortable with so many people. Gary Graffman is very outgoing and may have asked him things. Well, when Rosie Leventritt called me the next day, she was furious because she'd made a good party, good food and stuff, and went to some trouble going to the concert. She said, 'What kind of a crazy kook have you sent me?' and she hated his guts ever since."[5]

The press was more generous. John Briggs of *The Musical Courier* wrote that "Gould's complete enthrallment with the abstract, abstruse,

Gould warming up his hands before Goldberg Variations *session.* Photograph by Dan Weiner. Courtesy of Sony Classical.

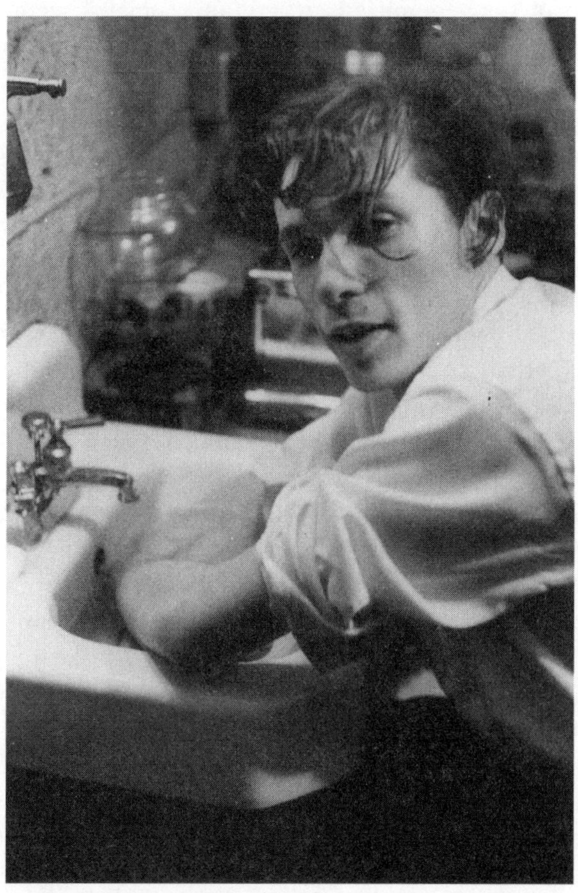

beauties of these contrastive works seems to result in a sense of almost other-worldly dedication. . . . I can only call him great, and warn those who have not heard him that he will plunge them into new and unfamiliar depths of feeling and perception."[6]

According to Glenn himself, the sudden illness, which Harvey Olnick described as "feigned," was an acute bout of chronic fibrositis that had come on just before the concert. The symptoms—pain, tension, and a clumsy feeling in his arms and hands—had been familiar to him for years and were to cause increasing stress and disability in the future. To have this happen just before a very important recital was extremely frightening. Glenn always sought to reduce the tension in his arms by bathing them in hot water thirty minutes before going on stage. And he relied on tranquilizers. We do not know what drugs he took for that Town Hall debut. (One of his biographers reports that Gould had been "rescued" that day by "a helpful druggist who applied the appropriate remedy.")[7] That, on top of his generalized anxiety and social insecurity, may well have contributed to the embarrassing episode in Mrs. Leventritt's drawing room.

Having run the gauntlet and finally played in New York was of course greatly satisfying to Gould, his family, and his manager. Besides, his debut there had been widely covered by the Toronto papers, and gave people at home something to celebrate. He'd proved that there actually might be some hope for Canadian artists being appreciated outside their provinces. Yet, in a practical sense, the debut itself did little to further his career. It had been an expensive investment—$450 to rent the hall, $1,000 for programs and promotion, plus the cost of coming to and staying in New York. Ticket sales were minimal, and only the few cognoscenti who attended were able to spread the word (not always favorably) about this extraordinary pianist. All of the eleven concerts he gave the rest of that year, 1955, took place in Canada.

It was not the Town Hall concert that catapulted Glenn Gould to international stardom. It was a lucky accident twenty-four hours later, which permanently changed Glenn's attitude toward himself as a performing artist. How this came about sounds almost like a fairy tale.

On January 10, just a day before the New York debut, Alexander Schneider, the violinist who had recently played chamber music with Glenn in Stratford, received a call from David Oppenheim, then director of the Masterworks Division of Columbia Records. Oppenheim had with him a recording by the Romanian pianist Dinu Lipatti, a sensation in Europe, whose career had been curtailed because of a severe chronic illness. In America, Lipatti was known primarily through a small number of exceptional recordings which had become collector's items after his premature death in 1950.

"Why can't we find another one like that?" Oppenheim asked Schneider, who told him that there was one, a person in Toronto named Glenn Gould, "who was, alas, a little crazy but had a remarkable, hypnotic effect at the piano."[8] Oppenheim went to the concert and liked what he heard. Glenn's playing "set such a religious atmosphere that it was just mesmerizing. . . . I was—thrilled."[9] Oppenheim looked around the small audience to see whether representatives from any other record company were there. Seeing none, he got in touch with Walter Homburger to work out a contract with Columbia Masterworks. At that time it was unheard of for a young musician to be offered a contract with a major recording company after only one hearing.

"I negotiated Glenn's recording contract, you know," Walter Homburger told me. "But I let him do all the arrangements with Columbia, what he wanted to record, and when he wanted to record. That was all his doing because I felt he knew more about what he wanted to do than I."[10] A wise decision, for Glenn Gould, as usual, had an agenda. He wanted to record Bach's *Goldberg Variations,* that masterful dusty relic of the eighteenth century which had remained obscure, reputed to be arid and unappealing for performers and audience alike.

It was a bold choice, and the Columbia executives at first tried talking him out of it. Ralph Kirkpatrick had brought out a scholarly edition of the *Goldberg Variations* in 1938 and made a recording, as had several other harpsichordists and pianists, including Wanda Landowska and Rosalyn Tureck, whose playing appealed primarily to Baroque music enthusiasts. Concert pianists generally preferred programming shorter works by Bach, say a selection of his Preludes and Fugues, or the *Italian Concerto.* For Glenn, however, the *Goldbergs* held enormous appeal.

As the most complexly organized and shrewdly integrated contrapuntal variations ever written, they challenged his ingenuity. The *Goldberg Variations* are not melodic variations on a theme as we think of them in the tradition of Mozart, Haydn, or Beethoven. In fact, the work is a majestic Passacaglia (or Chaconne, to use the French expression) that is built on a descending pattern, each variation restructuring the harmonic implications of the bass in a different way. Every third variation—there are thirty altogether—is a dazzling canon written at progressively higher intervals of the scale. The entire work is introduced and comes to an end with the playing of a lovely "Aria" that Bach had written some fifteen years earlier for the "Notebook" he gave his second wife, Anna Magdalena.

Glenn had fallen in love with the *Goldberg Variations* during his adolescence while studying with Guerrero, who also revered the work and had performed it. During the many hours spent mastering their intricacies, Glenn adorned the variations with unique vivacity, a youthful impetuousness, and occasional serenity, as well as scandalous tempi and ornamentation that broke traditional rules of Baroque interpretation. Exactly how Bach and other composers of the Baroque performed their music has been a subject for lengthy scholarly research and debate. But there's no evidence that Glenn approached the *Goldbergs* in a dryly scholarly way, although he did consult the wordy Kirkpatrick edition. Rather, he used his intuition and imagination to mold the music into a replica of his inner self, to make it express his innermost feelings and attitudes. This, perhaps, explains why of all the many works Glenn played and recorded in his lifetime, the *Goldberg Variations* have always been considered his finest musical achievement and the best example of his keyboard virtuosity.

The fact that Bach had composed them as a kind of music therapy for insomnia, one of Glenn's worst symptoms, may also be significant. Count von Kaiserling, the former Russian ambassador to Saxony, was victim to a neurological condition and sleepless nights. His court musician, Johann Gottlieb Goldberg, a student of Bach, tried to help Kaiserling by playing the harpsichord for him all night. One day, while visiting Leipzig, Kaiserling commissioned Bach to compose some clavier pieces "of such a smooth and lively character that he might be a little cheered up by them in his sleepless nights. . . . Thereafter the Count always called them *his* variations. He never tired of them, and for a long time sleepless nights meant: 'Dear Goldberg, do play me one of my variations.' "[11]

Finally, it would have been obvious and amusing for Glenn, whose family name had once been Gold, to identify with Goldberg. Occasionally, in jest, he spoke of playing the *"Gouldberg" Variations.* They became his signature work, heard repeatedly on documentary films and tapes honoring him.

The recording sessions for Columbia Masterworks took place during one week of June 1955, in an old church on East 30th Street in New York. The story has become legendary:

> Gould arrived in coat, beret, muffler, and gloves. "Equipment" consisted of the customary music portfolio, also a batch of towels, two large bottles

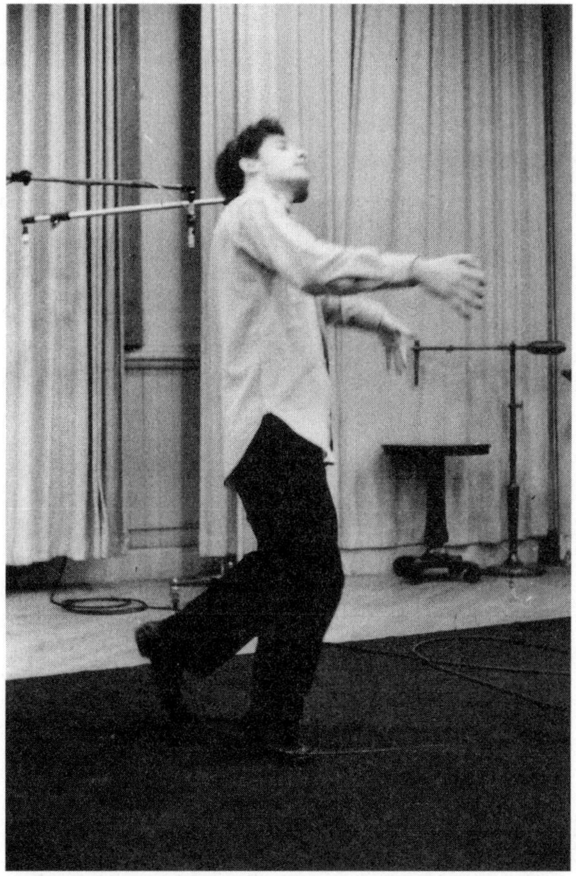

Gould conducting and dancing to the sounds of the Goldberg Variations, *CBS, 1955.* Photograph by Dan Weiner. Courtesy of Sony Classical.

> of spring water, five small bottles of pills (all different colors and prescriptions) and his own special piano chair. . . . Glenn was in perpetual motion, conducted rhapsodically, did a veritable ballet to the music. For sustenance he munched arrowroot biscuits, drank skimmed milk, frowned on the recording crews' Hero sandwiches.[12]

To Glenn's delight, press reporters were invited to observe him, and he rewarded them with capricious interviews that quickly turned him into a celebrity. (According to one biographer, he began to sound "like another new keyboard phenomenon named Liberace.")[13] Glenn obviously wanted and needed the attention. While recording the *Goldbergs,* he discovered a better and faster way of gaining it than by playing for live audiences. Here, in one of the technologically most advanced recording studios, he was able to repeat and correct his playing until the musical message was perfect. With engineers at his beck and call modulating the tapes electronically, the possibility for innumerable playbacks, and no audience coughing and staring to distract him, he created a recording of the *Goldberg Variations* that matched his inner ideal of Bach's artistic achievement:

Gould in a meditative mood, 1955. Photograph by Don McKague.

> It is, in short, music which observes neither end nor beginning, music with neither real climax nor real resolution, music which like Baudelaire's lovers "rests lightly on the wings of the unchecked wind." It has, then, unity through intuitive perception, unity born of craft and scrutiny, mellowed by mastery achieved, and revealed to us here, as so rarely in art, in the vision of subconscious design exulting upon a pinnacle of potency.[14]

When the recording was released in 1956 it quickly became a best-seller, and it has never been out of print, selling well even today. This huge commercial success gave the young pianist and his parents and manager vast amounts of pleasure and pride, not to mention sizable royalties. But, as Glenn confessed to one interviewer, "It also launched me into the most difficult year I have ever faced."[15] Suddenly in great demand around the world as a performer, he would find this role increasingly unbearable.

Thus it was a media event, the extraordinary and well-publicized recording of an obscure work by Bach, that catapulted a young Canadian to the sphere of select, great international artists. The spell this cast upon Glenn's life was to last until he re-recorded a final version of the *Goldberg Variations* shortly before his death, when this work, serving a dual purpose, also propelled him into the world of the immortal pianists.

11

FIRST CONTACT WITH PSYCHIATRY

Although in his writings and interviews Glenn occasionally made use of psychological terms, such as "ego," "catharsis," "traumatic associations," and, more often, spoke publicly about his psychosomatic problems and the sedatives he used for controlling them, he was always exceedingly coy about any personal experience with psychiatric or psychoanalytic treatment. In his own review of the first biographical study published about him,[1] Glenn commented:

> Payzant devotes three pages to a discussion of the various ways in which Gould has employed psychoanalytic terminology in his writing, presents evidence for and against Gould having been psychoanalyzed, and, in the end, leaves the question up for grabs. Given that Payzant and Gould are both residents of Toronto and that this sort of speculation could presumably have been settled with a simple "yes" or "no," such inconclusive testimony—verging indeed on idle musing—can produce a rather comical effect.[2]

Well, the fact is that after recording the *Goldberg Variations* in New York in 1955, Glenn did consult a psychoanalytically trained psychiatrist and even entered treatment briefly. Why this had to be kept secret from his closest friends and from his other doctors is a matter of conjecture. Most likely, the idea of having to seek help for emotional or mental problems was somehow offensive to his innate sense of independence, his desire to solve every problem by himself, and his general unwillingness to rely on other people for advice. Then there was undoubtedly the question of stigma, the fear that he might be looked down on or made fun of for turning to a doctor of the psyche. In those days, especially in staid, conservative Toronto, going to a psychiatrist still carried the implication of being crazy. While several of Glenn's musical colleagues were already calling him that, the reputation of madness was surely to be avoided by a young artist just beginning an international career.

Nevertheless, in 1955, Glenn went to see Dr. Albert E. Moll, one of the leading academic psychiatrists at McGill University in Montreal. We know about this from two sources, first, the recommendations Dr. Moll wrote on a prescription that Glenn filed among his private papers (now at the National Library of Canada in Ottawa),[3] and second, Glenn's gossipy conversations with the writer-photographer Jock Carroll, who in 1956 took him on a trip to the Bahamas for publicity purposes.[4]

Dr. Moll's prescription is undated, so the exact date of his meeting with Glenn is not known. Most likely it took place in August 1955, while the pianist was in Montreal to perform Beethoven's Fourth Piano Concerto, or perhaps in September when he played a solo recital there: the *Goldberg Variations,* Beethoven's Sonata no. 32, opus 111, and Hindemith's Third Sonata. How it happened that he was directed to this particular psychiatrist, again we do not know. However, it seems clear that both before and after his successful recording sessions in New York in June, Glenn had been experiencing more than the usual amount of anxiety, and that his customary ways of getting relief no longer sufficed to control the symptoms. The neighborhood chiropractor, Arthur Bennett, who had been treating him since childhood, had recently died, and his practice was taken over by his son, Denton B. Bennett. But according to another chiropractor who treated Glenn later on, the two "did not hit it off, Denton was kind of rough with Glenn."[5] On May 18, 1955, after two concerts in Ottawa and Toronto and just a month before leaving Canada to record the *Goldberg Variations* in New York, Gould's symptoms escalated to the point where he had to be seen on an emergency basis at the Toronto General Hospital.[6]

The hospital records are no longer available to document what the problem was. But during his two-week vacation in the Bahamas the following year, Glenn disclosed that he had been suffering from "a spastic stomach, diarrhea, and tightening of the throat. I've got three doctors treating me for it now."[7] He described to Jock Carroll what sounds like a psychogenic eating disorder, related in part to the panicky fear of soon having to give concerts in Russia:

> My hysteria about eating, it's getting worse all the time. Now, just the *prospect* of the Russia trip—I can see the Canadian Press writing from Moscow: GOULD THROWS UP! And I can see what it will be like in Moscow—embassy dinners impossible to avoid—and all the time this thing is getting worse. . . . Just the thought of eating and I get terrified. . . . What's really alarming is that the whole area of this thing seems to be spreading. Where it used to be just a fear of eating in public, now it's a fear of being trapped anywhere with people, even having any kind of dealings with people.[8]

That, incidentally, may have been one reason why Glenn had to run away from Mrs. Leventritt's party after his Town Hall debut in January 1955. He had been going to see Morris Herman, M. D., a highly respected family practitioner in Toronto for medical help, and Dr. Herman continued to be his primary physician for the next ten years. Dr. Herman told me that Glenn was always terribly afraid of having some kind of serious physical disease.

"He'd usually come in to the office very worried about symptoms for which no explanation could be found on the basis of a physical examination or by doing laboratory tests and X-ray studies. He had a tremendous amount of anxiety. Much of it was usually focused on the upper part of his body. Often there was a lot of generalized pain and tension in his arms and shoulders, and much of the time he was especially concerned about his mouth, throat, and chest. Any shortness of breath, a bit of coughing or gagging, or a random sensation in the chest would bring to his mind the absolutely terrifying idea that he was catching a cold and was about to develop a fatal pneumonia."

"Was that why he wore so much heavy clothing?"

"Even on the hottest days of midsummer he'd show up in the office dressed in an overcoat, sweater, muffler, woolen cap, and sometimes rubbers. As far as I could tell, this wasn't just a matter of artistic eccentricity. He really believed that he needed all that heavy clothing to protect him against the cold, and that without it he was sure to 'catch a chill,' as he always called it. It was purely a mental attitude, a conviction that something terrible was going to happen to him if he didn't dress that way. He joked about it at times, but the problem was really very serious."

"Hasn't it been conjectured," I interrupted, "that Glenn suffered from a circulatory disturbance that might have interfered with the control of skin temperature?"

"I found no evidence for anything like that. His fingers were never blue like someone with Raynaud's Disease. When you asked him to strip, his skin was always warm and moist underneath all those layers of clothing; in fact, he was often sweating copiously. Although Glenn did a lot of reading about medicine, he really had very little understanding of how the body works. But he was amazingly knowledgeable about drugs. He knew all the latest developments in antibiotics and many times asked me to prescribe something new he'd just read about. It was difficult to explain to him why this wasn't indicated. He'd just come back at you and to try to contradict you with many long-winded arguments."

"Did he talk to you about any of the drugs he was taking, or about treatment he was getting from other physicians as well as chiropractors?"

"No, he never did, except when I referred him to a specialist, which I had to do from time to time. Glenn was always very friendly and personally gracious. He gave me an autographed copy of one of his recordings, which I still have. But I must say that he was basically a very difficult and demanding patient. I felt honored to be his doctor, because he was a famous and very interesting man."

"Did you ever refer him to a psychiatrist?"

"It occurred to me to try to do that, but you know, in those days it wasn't so easy to find the right person. The older psychiatrists in Toronto were mostly neurologists, who had a very organic approach and administered shock treatment, which would have been wrong for Glenn. The younger psychiatrists were usually trained to be classical psychoanalysts. They wanted their patients to come to the office five times a week and lie on a couch to engage in free association. There were very few specialists practicing psychosomatic medicine, which I felt was the approach Glenn needed. I actually became interested in psychosomatics myself later on and have received training in the field. Many of the patients I see today respond well to a combination of psychological techniques, hypnosis or psychotherapy, along with medical care."[9]

Glenn's choice of Albert Moll in Montreal as a psychiatric consultant was an excellent one. Dr. Moll was one of the most highly respected specialists at McGill University, and a man noted for his tact and open-mindedness.[10] He was well versed in the older neuropsychiatric approaches and also experienced with the newer psychotherapeutic techniques. Indeed, Moll had been brought to McGill Medical School in order to organize a psychoanalytic training program there.

Unfortunately, Moll is now dead, and his professional papers are not available. But I can imagine a cordial meeting, with the always voluble pianist talking about himself and his many symptoms. As a psychoanalytically trained clinician, Albert Moll most likely would have guided the conversation as little as possible while listening carefully with the proverbial "third ear," picking up information about what might be going on inside this brilliant, charming, and troubled musician. At the end of the interview, Dr. Moll wrote on a prescription pad the names of four psychiatrists in Toronto he hoped might be able to treat Gould. It was clearly intended that the pianist would follow through and get into a therapeutic relationship with one of these doctors.

First on the list was Alan Parkin, a psychoanalyst in private practice. Dr. Parkin is also a medical historian who has written an informative book about the evolution and organization of psychoanalysis as a specialty in Canada.[11] He is the only one of the four psychiatrists recommended by Dr. Moll who is still alive, so I was able to interview him. In Dr. Parkin's opinion, the availability and quality of mental health care in Montreal at that time was more advanced than in Toronto.

"I didn't know Dr. Moll personally," Dr. Parkin told me, "but it was certainly a wise decision for Gould to consult him, and he would have been an excellent choice as Gould's therapist."

"Did you ever see Glenn Gould professionally?"

"No. He never called me. I knew nothing about the referral until you told me about it."[12]

Next on Dr. Moll's list of recommended specialists was Arthur M. Doyle, chief of psychiatry at St. Michael's Hospital. He is remembered by Parkin as "a general psychiatrist who treated his many patients with drugs and supportive psychotherapy,"[13] and by a younger colleague as "an old-style neuropsychiatrist, not the person I would have chosen for Glenn Gould."[14] There's no way to know whether Glenn ever made an appointment to see Doyle, nor is it possible to find out whether he consulted the third doctor on the list, B. M. Allan, then on the staff of the Toronto Western Hospital, or the fourth, Aldwyn Stokes, at that time chairman of the Department of Psychiatry at the University of Toronto. Dr. Stokes was described to me as "a real British gentleman who looked like the actor Charles Laughton and had a voice to match. He would have been friendly, affable, but not basically a psychotherapist. Glenn might have enjoyed meeting him."[15]

Thus it remains a mystery which one of these doctors Glenn finally decided to consult for treatment. That he did see a psychiatrist in Toronto is confirmed by what he told Jock Carroll during their Bahamas trip: "A Montreal doctor gave me a choice of three psychiatrists. One was into straight analysis. Second was a pill man. The third was a combination, so I went to him. His diagnosis was that nothing in the environment should be doing it [i.e., the eating disorder], nothing wrong with my sexual development, nothing physically wrong. So it was just a question of tranquilizers—bigger and better pills."[16]

That sounds like an overstatement. Most likely Gould wanted to deny to Carroll—and perhaps to himself—that there were any significant psychological roots to his illness. Of course we have no way of knowing how far the psychiatrist was able to get in analyzing Glenn's personality and psychodynamics. But I doubt that he ever established a psychotherapeutic relationship of sufficient duration to allow for deep exploration of his character structure. Barely twenty-three years old when he started treatment, he would have found many objections to the rules and discipline governing psychoanalytic treatment, for example, the need to make appointments in advance and keep them, and to see the therapist on a sufficiently frequent and regular basis. Glenn was on the crest of an international career that required many absences from Toronto. He had signed a contract with Columbia to make recordings in New York. He was becoming interested in producing broadcasts and films for the Canadian Broadcasting Corporation. And he was struggling to complete a string quartet that he had begun composing in 1953. Whenever he made an appointment to see a doctor, it was usually done impulsively, at a moment's notice, and at a time that suited Glenn's schedule. Since he generally did not get out of bed until early afternoon, he always insisted on medical appointments as late in the day as possible.

According to those of his doctors I've been able to interview, Glenn generally liked to be in charge, telling the doctor what to do rather than listening to his opinions. This would surely be an impediment to any collaborative setting. His fear of losing control would have been a further obstacle to the sort of psychotherapy which patiently uncovers sources of conflict that churn away below consciousness. Another defense would have been Glenn's willful demand for instant relief from his symptoms. His faith was in the sort of "quick fixes" that compliant physicians and pharmacists are able to provide by prescribing medication, and that chiropractors can give by physically manipulating the patient's body.

To work psychotherapeutically with someone as hugely talented and nonconformist as Glenn Gould would have called for an unusually toler-

Gould with the score of his string quartet. Courtesy of Glenn Gould Estate.

ant and resourceful therapist, someone free of dogma and open to the special demands that artists make on themselves and their milieu. It would have required a person with sufficient musical training and creative imagination to enter the labyrinth of his contrapuntal and musicological thinking. Glenn's mind could seize instantaneously the multiple levels of meaning inherent in language and music, twist them, and adorn them with rich and fantastic elaborations that surprised him as much as they did his listeners and readers. This became apparent, for example, while he was composing his string quartet. Glenn thought of himself as "a valiant defender of twelve-tone music and its leading exponents," only to discover that the quartet "would have been perfectly presentable at a turn-of-the-century academy, a work that did not advance the challenge to the laws of tonal gravity more boldly than did the works of Wagner, or Bruckner, or Richard Strauss."[17] We'll return to the psychological implications of this composition later.

Surely the contacts Glenn had with psychiatry and psychoanalysis in 1955 and 1956 helped him get through a major health crisis. The degree of his disturbance becomes apparent if one reads Jock Carroll's description of his behavior during the Bahamas trip. Before leaving, Glenn's mother had said to Mr. Carroll, "Please see that he sends out his laundry and get him to buy some decent clothes. If you can, try to get him out in the sun." On the plane, Glenn told Carroll about "a recurring nightmare in which he was being swept over Niagara Falls. At the very brink he always managed to catch hold of a protruding rock and hang on. 'At this point in the dream,' said Gould, 'some strangers appear and they begin banging away at my hands, trying to make me loosen my grip. This is where I wake up. My mother says as long as I can keep waking up at this point I'll be all right.' "[18]

The terror implicit in this nightmare fits well with the reality of Glenn's situation, up in a plane talking to a relative stranger and experiencing, as he usually did when flying, a tremendous fear of crashing down to earth, symbolized here by being swept over Niagara Falls. An aquatic death suggests something very primal, a return to the watery womb of which he speaks more positively at times, for example, when describing the womblike security of a recording studio. The protruding rock he hangs on to probably represents his yearning for support—from Jock Carroll sitting next to him, or a friend, or even a doctor. Rocks are solid and islands of safety, hard, fatherly. But a strange enemy appears, bangs on his hands, and tries to make him loosen his grip. This, I assume, is his unsettling neurosis coupled with the lifelong dread of damage to his hands. It's been there since infancy. His mother's reassuring statement that he'll be all right so long as he keeps waking up before he is swept over the brink of Niagara Falls in the dream suggests to me the beneficial influence of her pedagogy in directing his consciousness. Truly, it is a frightened lad who clings desperately to a lone rock for his survival, hanging by the sheer strength of his most precious asset, his long, supple, and strong fingers. The mother reassures him that, time and time again, he will overcome the danger and prove that indeed his hands are fit and whole. There are no dangerous enemies, no shadows lurking in the tempestuous mist; it is but a dream.

Arriving in Nassau, Glenn sealed himself into his room at the Fort Montague Beach Hotel for days on end, claiming, "I've gotten three bars of my opera written since we got here . . . a creative artist has to be a bit of an antisocial being in order to get his work done." He refused to go swimming because of a fear of what the saltwater might do to his hands. He joked about his eating disorder: "This tightening of the throat—I managed to avoid that when I was eating in my room . . . putting Oedipal relations aside, there's a womb-like feeling to your own room." One day he made such a commotion singing and conducting that the frightened chambermaid called the manager to report, "There's a crazy man in there."

Carroll was very worried about Glenn's aggressive way of steering their motorboat too close to larger vessels, and his whizzing their small red car much too fast through the narrow side roads.[19] "He seemed unable to connect the possibility of accidents with the way he was driving. Somewhat bitterly I was thinking to myself, 'Only a week ago Gould was talking about the emancipation of the blacks. Now he's roaring around their island with a total disregard for their safety.' "[20]

Although Glenn never again entered into formal treatment relationship with a psychiatrist, he seems to have maintained a positive interest in the field of mental exploration. I can imagine that the rapport he established with me when we met in 1957 was partly the result of helpful moments that had occurred with his Canadian psychiatrists. Similarly, the seventeen-year relationship that sprang up in 1960 between Glenn and the Baltimore psychiatrist Joseph Stephens came close to providing a psychotherapeutic experience for him, and can best be understood as part of a continuity of involvement with experts in mental health. Typically, the long association with Dr. Stephens was intermittent, crisis-oriented, and conducted largely over the telephone. Perhaps the multiple facets of his personality—pianist, composer, writer, would-be doctor—made Gould especially responsive to and fascinated by individuals who could pursue several interests at once, like Dr. Stephens and myself, who are both physicians and musicians.

Glenn made it a habit to satirize psychiatry. A clever man, he could exploit creatively those things he had not much use for. He took great pleasure in lampooning practitioners. In later years he invented a fictitious psychiatrist, "S. F. Lemming, M.D," who spouted such inanities as

> Paul D. Hicks, in his recent much-reviewed study "The Unconscious and Career Motivation," notes that most of us in middle life [Glenn was thirty-six when he wrote this] suppress occupational stimuli that, if indulged, would necessitate redirecting ambition-patterns. Among the upper-income stratum in American life, Hicks points out, this tendency is sometimes menopausally motivated, but more frequently, and especially among those active in the professions, it involves the reaffirmation of traumatic

associations deriving from childhood resentment pertaining to the intrusion of school discipline upon the parental security patter.[21]

This little satire may contain a core of revelations that apply to Glenn's own struggle with "ambition-patterns," "childhood resentment," and "school discipline." It demonstrates how a secretive individual used humor to allow himself both to disclose something personal but then to discount it through the flippancy of the preposterous Dr. Lemming. Gould's habit of spouting the jargon of psychiatry, making fun of this branch of medicine, and borrowing some of its concepts for his later essays and television programs, also betokened his deeper need for understanding the mysteries of the human mind—his own brilliant, elusive, and conflicted mind in particular. But entering into a formal clinical relationship with a psychiatric healer had evidently proved too threatening for Gould's powerful need to preserve his privacy and maintain his artistic identity. What he learned about psychiatry was acquired through his contact with Dr. Moll in Montreal and the specialist who treated him briefly in Toronto. Other sources of information were his extensive reading and the long conversations, often by telephone, with the two psychiatrists he had met on his travels.

Yet even with Dr. Stephens and myself, he maintained a certain distance. Only one person, his mother, was allowed to share his inner self. Until her death in 1975, Glenn spoke with her about his dreams and nightmares, his triumphs and defeats, his concerts and the reviews they received, the radio programs and television shows he planned and produced, everything he published, his every ambition and frustration. That is what his cousin Jessie Greig told me.[22] But whether he disclosed the intimate details of his private life to his mother, we will never know, for Florence Gould left no notes, diaries, or reminiscences about her son. Their relationship, despite its superficial teasing and nitpicking, was like a sacred trust. Even Glenn's father has little information about what was probably the most genuine, expressive, and supportive bond Glenn ever had with another human being. Their relationship was a touching testimonial to the intimacy that can exist between a mother and her child, in this case, an understanding that went beyond words to the realm of the unspoken, the world of music where feelings are shared without a single touch.

12

CONFLICTING DEMANDS

Until Glenn made his 1955 debut in the United States, he had been able to maintain a very light performance schedule averaging four to eight concerts a year. After that, the number of times he played in public grew exponentially: fourteen times in 1955, twenty-three times in 1956, thirty-six times in 1957. In 1959 he reached his maximum, fifty-one concerts, after which there was a gradual tapering off until 1964, when he stopped appearing in public.

Those eight or nine years when Glenn was heavily engaged in traveling and giving concerts proved stressful because of his fundamental revulsion against public performance, but also because of the conflicting demands stemming from his multiple ambitions to conduct, to record, to maintain his solitude, to compose, and to write. At the beginning he rarely complained openly about his biggest conflict: having to give concerts when he felt this was basically an unsuitable and unworthy way for him to be making music. But he shared this opinion with a few friends and, later, around the time of his retirement from the stage, publicized it in a series of provocative essays and interviews.

Basically, Glenn distrusted audiences. "There's a very curious and almost sadistic lust for blood that overcomes the concert listener," he told John McClure of Columbia Records. "There's a waiting for it to happen, a waiting for the horn to fluff, a waiting for the strings to become ragged, a waiting for the conductor to forget to subdivide . . . it's dreadful. There's a kind of gladiatorial instinct that comes upon the case-hardened concertgoer, which is why I suppose I don't like him as a breed and don't trust him, and I wouldn't want one as a friend."[1] Elsewhere Glenn described his perception of the audience as a hostile force whose "primal instinct was for gladiatorial combat."[2] Despite the acclaim and applause he regularly received, it seemed impossible for him to think of the people in the hall as individuals—some who might be indifferent to the music, others perhaps hostile, but still others who truly appreciated what he was doing, willing to overlook a mistake and wish him well. Glenn did not believe that audiences went to concerts for the sake of the music. Rather, they wanted to be lulled into a pleasant state of reverie that would evoke memories of the past. The concert hall was like a museum where relics are displayed rather than a place for exploring the future. Glenn believed it was on its way out as a place for listening to music; that could be better done at home with radio and recordings. And of course producing recordings interested him far more than giving concerts.

With such a strong bias against public performance, Glenn naturally felt more comfortable playing in a recording studio where a run or a scale or a series of chords or an interpretive nuance that he considered imperfect could be repeated as many times as he felt was necessary. Once he approved of it, the passage could then be spliced into the master tape and become permanent. Glenn coined the term "take two-ness" to describe this essential aspect of recorded music. There simply was no way of repeating or correcting something when playing in public: no audience would allow an artist to play a passage over again. This bothered him tremendously, and he made no secret of the fact that he planned soon to chuck "treading the boards" so he could devote himself exclusively to the electronic media.

Even during those conflicted years of playing in public, Glenn was actively engaged in broadcasts and telecasts for the Canadian Broadcasting Corporation in Toronto, and in recording for Columbia Masterworks in New York. Thus he gained expertise and developed friendships in the communications industry that would later become his primary arena for creative activity. For example, there was Franz Kraemer, the CBC producer who directed *Glenn Gould Off the Record; Glenn Gould on the Record,* the first film made about him by the National Film Board of Canada. This is a fascinating documentary showing Glenn at leisure in his Lake Simcoe retreat, practicing Bach on his beloved Chickering, playing parts of a Schubert symphony, discussing the art of composing with Kraemer, and going to New York to select a piano at Steinways and record Bach's *Italian Concerto* for Columbia.[3] Kraemer told me that his relationship to Glenn was like "father to son."

"I was the only guy who could criticize him. He was a genius and a monster—totally impossible in the studio, you could never trust that what he said or even what he felt was true—he was a man obsessed with controlling everything, the weather, temperature, his medicines, and other musicians. But he was the most unbelievably gifted, capable, and imaginative pianist I've known in my entire life."[4]

Another, deeper friendship sprang up between Glenn and John P. L. Roberts, who had recently come from Australia to assume the position of music producer for CBC Radio and assistant director for CBC Television in Winnipeg. They met when Glenn played the Beethoven First Piano Concerto with the Winnipeg Symphony on December 12, 1955.

"He got the reception of a pop star," Roberts told me. "The audience really went quite wild at the end of his performance. But as I got to know him better, I realized that crowds made Glenn very uncomfortable. It was quite intriguing, but he had an absolute thing about crowds. He could translate them into audiences, which aroused huge amounts of anxiety. To him they were hostile, intrusive, and dangerous. This got even worse as he became more famous. After I got to know his parents, I realized that his mother had instilled this attitude in him when he was a child by warning him over and over never to go to any special event where there were a lot of people, or to attend any public displays or exhibits—in order to avoid germs. Glenn rarely went to a concert, you know, except when he had to play, and it was always an agonizing experience for him."[5]

It made Glenn especially uncomfortable when someone he knew personally was in the concert hall. That always made it hazardous for him to play in Toronto, for example, and he preferred foreign cities because people coming to the concert were more likely to be strangers. Often he would beg his friends, even his manager, not to come to his concerts. John Roberts told me, "When my wife Christina and I would go with Glenn to the Stratford Music Festivals in the summer, he'd say, 'Please, don't come to hear me play. I can only play if the audience is completely anonymous. When there are people I know in the audience, if you were sitting in the audience, then I feel I can't ignore it.' " I assume that was the reason Glenn asked me not to come to his remaining concerts in San

Francisco when we met in 1957. Roberts described it as "a cat and mouse game Glenn played with the audience. He always cast a spell over them, and anyone sitting there whom he knew personally or was fond of broke the spell. It really upset him."

I asked Roberts what it was like when Glenn had to travel. He told me, "Glenn was still living at home as a mature artist, and very dependent on his parents. Whenever he had to leave for a concert tour, his father was very much at his beck and call, helping him with the chair, blocks, clothes, scores, and other paraphernalia that had to go along, driving him to the airport, and picking him up on his return. Of course, once he was on the road, he managed to cope, although very much in his own way, spending much time alone in his hotel room and eating by himself."[6]

Glenn's next United States appearance after the debut recitals of 1955 was for a performance of the Fourth Beethoven Concerto with the Detroit Symphony Orchestra on March 15, 1956. Paul Paray was conducting, and Glenn, still plagued by his eating disorder, must have been unusually nervous. The critics decided to spank him for his unruly ways on stage. The *Detroit Free Press* reported: "Gould's storm-tossed mane of hair, his invertebrate posture at the keyboard and his habit of collapse at the end of each solo line was sheer show business," and the Detroit Times noted that "it is his tragedy that his behavior at the piano produced laughter in his audience."

This was not the first time that Glenn had to confront press criticism of his so-called eccentric behavior. Even in hometown Toronto, the newspapers had occasionally objected to the pianist's deportment: "His left leg was carelessly draped over his right knee . . . why must he crouch like a panther over the keys? Why should he pounce upon the notes like a leopard leaps upon its prey for the kill?"[7] But it was after his painful Detroit appearance, and perhaps because of his recent consultations with a psychiatrist, that Glenn took the criticism to heart and allowed it to influence his level of self-consciousness. During an interview a few years later, he admitted that

> I had not regarded any of the things attendant upon my playing—my eccentricities, if you like—as being of any particular note at all. Then suddenly a number of well-meaning people in the arts said, "My dear young man, you must pull yourself together and stop this nonsense."
>
> I had never given any thought to their importance, at least to some people, of visual image. When I suddenly was made aware of it in about 1956, I became extremely self-conscious about everything I did. The

Gould in a typical slouch at the piano, 1955. Photograph by Dan Weiner. Courtesy of Sony Classical.

whole secret of what I had been doing was to concentrate exclusively on realizing a conception of the music, regardless of how it is physically achieved. This new self-consciousness was very difficult.[8]

In another article, he wrote:

> I hope people won't be blinded to my playing by what have been called my personal eccentricities. I don't think I am at all eccentric. It's true I wear one or two pairs of gloves most of the time and take a few sensible precautions about my health. And I sometimes play with my shoes off or get so carried away in a performance my shirttail comes out or, as some friends have complained, I look as though I were playing the piano with my nose. But these aren't personal eccentricities—they're simply the occupational hazards of a highly subjective business.[9]

Three days after the Detroit performance, Glenn repeated the Fourth Beethoven Concerto in neighboring Windsor, Ontario. This time he was on the verge of collapse. The increasing burden of nervous symptoms was taking its toll. "After extended discussion with symphony officials and insistence that he was too ill to play" reported the *Detroit News,* "Gould consented to 'try' and went to the piano." Finally he decided to go ahead with the concerto. According to the *News,* "The extraordinary contortions and twitchings were missing [but he gave a] performance that was almost colorless and marked by little of the brilliance for which Gould has been uproariously acclaimed."[10] Three days later he played in Hamilton, Ontario, the Bach Concerto in D Minor with Sir Ernest Macmillan conducting the Toronto Symphony Orchestra. Apparently this was a satisfactory performance.

There would be no other appearance for three weeks, when he was scheduled to play a solo recital in Toronto: three fugues from *The Art of the Fugue,* and the Partita, no. 5, by Bach; Beethoven's Sonata, no. 30, opus 109; and Hindemith's Third Sonata. It was a familiar program, but Glenn, still acutely distressed, felt the need for a quick remedy. On April 11, five days before the concert, he went to see J. C. Richardson, M.D., one of the leading neurologists at the Toronto General Hospital. Dr. Richardson wrote him a prescription for Largactil (25 mgm) and Serpasil (.25 mgm), each to be taken three times a day after meals and at bedtime.[11]

Bach D Minor Concerto with Gould and Sir Ernest MacMillan. Courtesy of Glenn Gould Estate.

Both of these drugs were widely used at that time for treating mental and emotional disorders. Largactil, also known as Thorazine, had recently been introduced as an effective remedy for insomnia, pathological excitement, and (in higher doses) schizophrenia. Serpasil, also called Reserpine, was also widely used as a powerful agent for treating agitation. Both drugs are known to have undesirable side effects if taken in doses larger than those prescribed by Dr. Richardson. Thorazine can produce motor spasms, tremors, a Parkinson-like syndrome, and, rarely, hepatitis. Reserpine tends to lower the blood pressure and can induce marked fatigue, lethargy, and suicidal behavior. Close supervision is necessary for patients treated with these drugs. Today they are rarely used because safer tools for treating psychiatric illnesses have been developed.

Glenn added the two drugs prescribed by Richardson to the large assortment of medications he was already taking with him on concert tours. Whether he obeyed the doctor's recommendations about dosage and frequency is impossible to tell, nor do we know whether he had ever taken Thorazine or Reserpine before. Glenn rarely kept records of his drug intake, and I haven't been able to locate any during this phase of his career. His tendency was to use pills before going on stage or into a recording studio; he also depended on them daily for sleep.

The recital in Toronto on April 16 evidently went well, as did another recital in New York later that month. June was devoted primarily to recording Beethoven sonatas at the Columbia studios in New York.

During the summer, he took part as usual in the Stratford Music Festival. He had been invited to be a co-director for new musical programs during the festival, along with the cellist Leonard Rose and the violinist Oscar Shumsky. The assignment gave Gould more responsibility and control over the repertoire, and greater authority in imposing his will on the interpretation of works that involved other musicians. From time to time he conducted the orchestra, usually from the keyboard, as in his filmed version of the *Fifth Brandenburg Concerto* by Bach.[12] At Stratford he could also plan unusual programs and play works that were not part of his traveling routine. In the years ahead, Glenn would enjoy organizing concerts that were devoted to a single composer, such as a Richard Strauss program in 1961 that included Shumsky and Glenn playing the Strauss Sonata in E-flat, opus 18, for Violin and Piano; Glenn's narration about Strauss's role in history; and Glenn's own transcriptions of *Elektra* and a scene from *Capriccio*.

The soprano Ellen Faull sang in these condensed performances of Strauss operas. She recalls Glenn's great warmth toward her: "He kissed me on both cheeks after the performance, a very unusual thing for him to do because he was so phobic about physical contact. We had a special friendship because my husband was a psychiatrist. Glenn was fascinated by what he had to say and always looked at *him* while we were together."[13] Ellen Faull later recorded a set of songs by Schoenberg with Glenn.

Another program, in 1962, featured the music of Felix Mendelssohn. Glenn with Oscar Shumsky and Leonard Rose played Mendelssohn's Trio no. 1 in D Minor, opus 49, and Glenn accompanied the baritone Leopold Simoneau in a song recital.[14] These annual musical festivals in Stratford gave him a chance to relax from the much more arduous work of touring around the continent and abroad.

Glenn yearned to get more involved in conducting. On July 9, 1956, at Stratford he led the rehearsals and performance of Schoenberg's *Ode to Napoleon*. The following year, he conducted the fourth movement of Gustav Mahler's immense Symphony no. 2, the "Resurrection," with Maureen Forrester singing the almost supernatural contralto solo "Urlicht." This performance was filmed by the CBC and is the only visual example we have of Glenn as a conductor away from the piano. He stands rigidly and appears to be quite tense in body. His face has an anguished expression appropriate to the mood of Mahler's music. Glenn's rather generous, flowing arm movements have a strange tendency to curve inward toward the conductor rather than outward to the orchestra. That would have made it difficult for some of the orchestra members to follow his beat, especially since Gould used no baton and directed time with his left rather than right hand as is customary. But to judge from the film and its not ideal sound track, his conducting led to a flawless and moving performance.

Less gratifying was the pain Glenn experienced each time he conducted, from keyboard or podium. He attributed the physical misery to an incompatibility between activity of the back and shoulder movements used for conducting and those required to play the piano. "I couldn't go near a piano for two weeks," he protested after the Mahler filming. "So I canceled all my other conducting engagements. Don't ask me why, I don't like to think about it."[15] But a letter written in 1958 to the conductor Vladimir Golschmann, whom Glenn greatly respected, shows that he did think about it:

> You have undoubtedly heard by now of my temporary retirement as a conductor which was due to a rather involved muscular reaction when I was

> doing some rehearsing up here [in Vancouver, B.C.]. I became quite alarmed about the danger of conducting at any time close to a piano performance. . . . This is one of my most fascinating symptoms and I would be happy to entertain you with it in great detail when I see you. For the present, however, my retirement after a successful career of one concert which was at once my debut and my farewell appearance [as a conductor] will, I am sure, be an irreparable loss in the music world. The one logical alternative is to retire from the piano and devote myself to conducting, which I'm seriously considering.[16]

Columbia Masterworks had released their second Glenn Gould recording in 1956. This time he chose not to play music by Bach but to shift to Beethoven, a composer for whom he had very mixed feelings. And he tackled the three last sonatas written by Beethoven, opus nos. 109, 110, and 111. It was a risky decision for so young a pianist. These works are far better known than the *Goldberg Variations* which had led to his instant world fame the year before. Revered by music lovers everywhere, Beethoven's late piano sonatas, like his final string quartets and the great "Choral" Symphony in D Minor, opus 125, epitomize the pinnacle of his musical development. They reveal the grandeur of his achievement toward the end of his life, when he broke away from the traditional rules governing his earlier works to create a wholly new style that reflected not only a remarkable degree of originality but his personal struggle with deafness and social isolation. Beethoven's late works are uniquely abstract, contrapuntal, and occasionally harsh in texture. They can also display heartbreaking degrees of lyricism and celestial serenity.

Glenn had been performing the Sonata no. 30 in E Major, opus 109, for several years, and included it in his debut recitals in Washington, D.C., and New York. But the other two late Beethoven sonatas, no. 31 in A-flat Major, opus 110, and no. 32 in C Minor, opus 111, were less familiar to him, and he had only recently begun playing them in public. To record these challenging works as a sequel to his explosively successful Bach *Goldberg* disc was surely a gamble, and the results were not entirely satisfactory.

Although the generally brilliant style of playing, the immense vigor, and the daring originality make these exciting recordings to listen to, one cannot help but be dismayed by Gould's defiance of Beethoven's careful instructions in regard to interpretation—specifically, his explicit indications for tempo changes in different movements. For example, in the E Major Sonata, opus 109, Gould totally ignores Beethoven's written demands for tempo differences between the variations in the last movement, which makes them sound uniform and lacking in emotional contrast. This is shocking. And in the grand C Minor Sonata, opus 111, he plays the *Allegro con brio ed appassionato* of the first movement so astonishingly fast that it sounds almost dehumanized, like a player-piano cranked up to its maximum speed. The performance resembles a caricature, and at that overly hasty *allegro* tempo the pianist can't get close to the *appassionata* Beethoven asked for. The meditative last movement, *Adagio molto simplice e cantabile,* is also played on the brisk side, with a kind of casualness that is out of character for this very profound music.

Not surprisingly, Glenn's recordings of the last three Beethoven sonatas stimulated much criticism. Reviewers used such terms as "childishness," "skimming the surface," "largely unacceptable," and "a botch."[17] But all such criticism of the recordings overlooks the fact that he was not aiming to produce an authentic performance, much less one that was meant to please the public. For him, the making of a record was a purely personal journey, a jubilant adventure into the unknown. He rarely had a preconceived notion of how a recording would actually turn out. He usually entered the studio and played a work or a movement through from beginning to end. That was "take one." He then stopped to listen to the take, noting any errors or other moments that did not please him and would therefore have to be re-recorded. Sometimes he recorded the entire piece for a second time, or as many times as he felt was necessary to achieve a satisfactory result. These were called "take two," "take three," and so forth.

After that, the business of editing could begin. Since multiple-track tape recorders were used, a certain amount of mixing had to be done, usually by the producer in charge of the project. Glenn himself designed a "splicing plan" to indicate where segments of tape that he disapproved of were to be cut out and replaced by an improved version. Thus the final product often turned out to be radically different from what Glenn's playing sounded like in a live concert. Furthermore, he expected the listener to modify the sound of a recording by turning dials on his hi-fi set, thus participating in what Glenn called "aesthetic narcissism"—"Through the ministrations of radio and the phonograph, we are rapidly and quite properly learning to appreciate the elements of aesthetic narcissism—and I use this word in its best sense—and are awakening to the challenge that each man contemplatively creates his own divinity."[18]

There is another form of narcissism, present in Glenn. Gould radiated his self-love onto the composer and music he performed. This is a form of artistic narcissism, different from the simple self-adulation of normal narcissism, or the selfish autistic love of the pathological narcissist.

Although Glenn never accepted a student, he felt he had a mission to educate, to impose his own insights and wisdom upon the world, thus fulfilling his mother's wish that he be "cultured, that he do something elevated and proper, that music is good because it is educational."[19] We've seen earlier signs of proselytizing in his efforts on behalf of Schoenberg and his followers, performing and recording their music, and writing learned articles about them. As for Beethoven, Glenn had very strong and iconoclastic ideas about this composer, which he wrote out, usually on reams of ruled pads of legal paper, in preparation for his published essays.

In the liner notes for his latest recording, the three last Beethoven sonatas, he objected to "the rather arbitrary chronological landmarks" by which the "creative estate" of a composer is often subdivided. In this respect, he maintains that Beethoven's late works have come in for "a greater preponderance of nonsense, not to mention contradiction, than any comparable literature."

> Typical is the comment of Joseph de Marliave, who in his work on the quartets recommends the exclusion from performance of both the "Grosse Fuge," Op. 133, and the fugue finale to the Hammerklavier Sonata, Op. 106. . . . Marliave's mention of "the intimate and contemplative appeal to the ear" illustrates an approach to these works based upon philosophical conjecture rather than musical analysis. Beethoven, according to this hypothesis[,] heaps one discordant effect upon another, and the general impression of tiresome waste of sound cannot be dispelled by the marvel of its technical construction. The giddy heights to which these absurdities can wing have been realized by several contemporary novelists, notable offenders being Thomas Mann and Aldous Huxley.[20]

In Glenn's opinion, the three last Beethoven sonatas are "a brief but an idyllic stopover in the itinerary of an intrepid *voyageur.* Perhaps they do not yield the apocalyptic disclosures that have been so graphically ascribed to them."[21] He saw himself in that role, obligated to provide the world with interpretations of Beethoven that had never been heard before.

Having already told a living composer, Oskar Morawetz, that he knew more about how his music ought to be performed than the composer himself, Glenn was now ready to cross swords with giants of the past.

But his audio recordings do not tell the full story of how he interpreted and misinterpreted Beethoven's music or that of other composers. His video recordings, now being released on tape cassettes and laser discs, give a much richer picture. For example, we can hear and see two totally different interpretations of Beethoven's Sonata no. 17 in D Minor, opus 31, no. 2, the so-called "Tempest." One version, filmed in 1960, is highly animated and dramatic, showing his body undulating and arms flying. It takes seventeen minutes, sixteen seconds. Another performance, filmed in 1966 after Glenn had stopped playing in public, is much slower and more sedate, and shows far fewer body movements. It takes twenty-one minutes, twelve seconds, nearly four minutes longer than the earlier performance. The second movement alone lasts nine minutes, eighteen seconds in 1966, compared to six minutes, forty-eight seconds in 1960, a difference of two and a half minutes. Only in the last movement does Glenn's tempo in the second version exceed that of the first.

There are other discrepancies between interpretations of the same work played at different times during his career. Thus it is a tragedy that he rarely re-recorded a work. What we hear of Glenn Gould on audio discs, especially some of the sonatas by Mozart and Beethoven, but even some of his Bach recordings, may sound artificial and insincere to those unfamiliar with Glenn's total conviction and commitment on how to interpret a certain work, or passage. The true grandeur of his performances is best appreciated on videotape or laser discs that show his ecstatic involvement with the music. Here there seems to be a magical fusion between pianist, composer, and keyboard, lending an ethereal, almost religious or mystical dimension to the music Gould plays.

13

TELEPHONE CALLS

In 1957, the year Glenn and I met in San Francisco, he fascinated me as one of the most exotic musical personalities I had ever met—very bright, witty, self-confident, and with a raging appetite for doing the unexpected. He in turn seemed attracted to me as an older man whose passion for music resembled his own and who was willing to pay more than casual attention to him. He talked almost incessantly and clearly needed someone who could reflect back the admiration he felt for himself. He appreciated my being a medical doctor because I could respond objectively and knowledgeably to the symptoms he brought to my attention. I in turn appreciated his enthusiasm about wanting to play chamber music with me and my friends.

But I had noticed from the beginning that his loquacity extended primarily to things musical; even his physical complaints seemed related in one way or another to his activities as a musician. Very rarely did he directly disclose anything of a more intimate nature, or talk about anybody who was close to him. His recent contact with psychiatrists who had tried to help him was never mentioned, and I must emphasize once again that I knew nothing of the stresses Glenn had to endure during childhood and adolescence. Thus almost anything he was willing to tell me about himself seemed new and tantalizing.

Sometime in April 1957, after our initial meeting, Glenn called long-distance from Toronto. I was happy and a bit astonished to hear from him. The conversation went something like this:

"Hello, Peter, this is Glenn."

"Well, what a surprise!"

"I'd like you to listen to a wonderful new tape I've just made in New York. Tell me what you think of it. It's the piano concerto by Beethoven that I played in my debut with the New York Philharmonic in January, the one in B-flat Major, an early work from that period in Beethoven's output when he hadn't yet gotten so detestably heroic and pompous."

"Oh yes, I remember your telling me about that New York performance when you were in San Francisco."

"Leonard Bernstein was the conductor, and now we're recording this concerto as well as the Bach D Minor with the Columbia Symphony Orchestra."

Before I could interject another word, Glenn went into a monologue. He obviously had an agenda. First he wanted to talk about "Lenny." He began by telling me about a party at the Bernsteins' where Lenny was entertaining his guests at the piano and had asked Glenn to join him with some four-handed playing.

"I really didn't want to do that. The room was very crowded, much too crowded for my taste, and I was already beginning to feel a bit sick. But Lenny can be very pushy and he insisted that I sit next to him at the piano. He'd put one of the Mozart sonatas for four hands on the stand and asked which part, the upper or the lower, I wanted to play. Well, it really didn't matter to me since I knew both parts. I'd played these pieces with my teacher when I was a child. So he took the upper part and we started playing. But, you know, I soon started to have this jelly-like feeling in my fingers. They just weren't up to their usual tactile accuracy."

Glenn wondered what was the matter and suddenly remembered that earlier in the evening he had consumed half of an alcoholic beverage. "Soon I was so sick that I had to stop playing. Lenny didn't seem to mind. There were plenty of other pianists there who could have finished the Mozart with him. So I went back to my hotel and swore never again to touch anything alcoholic before playing the piano."

I was amazed to hear this rather sad confession and couldn't help but observe that Glenn appeared to be more revealing over the telephone than he had been in our face-to-face conversations. Was it perhaps the veil of invisibility afforded by the telephone and the impossibility of any physical contact that allowed him to share this embarrassing episode?

He continued with his Bernstein monologue. There had been some sort of disagreement while rehearsing the Beethoven concerto. "Lenny didn't really understand the work too well. He actually wasn't prepared to make the recording." Nevertheless, they apparently agreed to proceed and, thanks to the miracle of "take two-ness" in the recording studio, some initial tapes were already available. Glenn told me he was going to play one of these tapes for me over the telephone. At this point it was past midnight in San Francisco (3:00 A.M. in Toronto), but I agreed and was dazzled by what I heard. The pianist did extraordinary things in blending the aggressive staccato style of the opening theme with the attractive lyrical passages that follow. The slow movement was truly moving and expressive. The Rondo Finale sparkled with wit. The entire recording displayed Glenn's masterful control of the keyboard and Bernstein's commanding way with the orchestra.

But before I had a chance to tell Glenn how much I liked it, he wanted me to listen to another version of the same concerto. "Peter, I believe that in take two we achieved an even better balance between the soloist and the orchestra, especially in the slow movement. What do you think?" There was no time to respond before he began playing the tape. I really wasn't able to detect much difference between the two recordings. Both sounded absolutely beautiful. But by now I was dead tired and found myself sporadically dozing off, something Glenn did not notice, but anyone else would have expected. I don't recall when this long telephone call finally ended, but it must have been at least another hour after the second tape before Glenn decided to hang up. I'm afraid I cannot recall a single word of it. Judging from the amount of time he spent talking, the telephone must have been his favorite instrument, after the piano.

His work with Leonard Bernstein interested me. The two musicians seemed to bring out the best in each other. Both were ex-child prodigies with enormous egos, narcissistic characters who shared a phenomenal commitment to music, as well as a need to make other people do their bidding. And both men were experiencing career conflicts. They were outstanding pianists who wanted to be composers as well as conductors. But Lenny was much more the extrovert than Glenn. He loved crowds and applause, had a knack for relating to other musicians with the greatest of ease, and lecturing about music without constraint.[1] Glenn was more the shy and sensitive introvert, who tolerated crowds poorly and had to struggle mightily to fulfill his ambition as an educator. Whereas Lenny spoke freely in front of a television camera, Glenn had to work laboriously to prepare scripts that he would memorize. Another notable difference was that Lenny was sexually liberated. He relished embracing and kissing his friends and fellow musicians in public, and he enjoyed sexual intimacy with men as well as women. To the emotionally restricted and puritanical Glenn Gould, such behavior was deeply offensive.

Nevertheless, Glenn wanted Lenny to be his friend. After their first performance together, Glenn wrote him a warm letter addressed to "Cher Maitre: Welcome home! I trust that the Caribbean sun did wonders for your slipped disc (or whatever)." He went on to recommend the use of a "high chair" for Lenny's conducting, mentioning that Otto Klemperer used one. "I personally can assure you that specially designed chairs have some fascination for the American public. We must do a concerto that way some time! . . . It was a real joy to work with you."[2]

Lenny in turn seems to have been quite fond of Gould. He raved about his rapturous playing: "He is the greatest thing that has happened to music in years."[3] One surmises there may have been an element of sexual attraction, and that Lenny probably found the slender, fair-haired young pianist erotically attractive despite his buttoned-up manners. Glenn in his youth was outstandingly handsome. At Bernstein's party for him following their concert performance of the Second Beethoven Concerto in January 1957 (I don't know if this was the same party Glenn told me about over the telephone), the conductor suddenly burst forth with "You played so beautifully in the cadenza that I almost came in my pants."[4]

It was not unusual for Glenn's fans, women mostly, but men as well, to find something "sexy" in Glenn's playing, especially in the swaying motion of his torso and the expressive gestures of his hands that accompanied it. Such an observation would make Glenn cringe; he didn't care to associate the erotic with the aesthetic. And yet after he recorded the Brahms Intermezzi in 1959 and 1960, he described them as "the sexiest interpretation of Brahms you have ever heard.[5] One time at the Bernsteins' apartment, Glenn did literally let his hair down by permitting Lenny's wife, Felicia, to wash and trim it. Bernstein remembered that "he came out looking like some kind of archangel, radiant, with this beautiful hair which one had never seen the color of, quite blond, and shining, haloed-ish. It was really a very beautiful thing to see, what she did, his acceptance, equally beautiful, and the result, which was thrillingly beautiful."[6]

About a week later, Glenn called again. This time he wanted me to listen to the liner notes he was planning to have published on the cover of his forthcoming Beethoven concerto recording. He had written a number of drafts and wanted to read all of them to help him decide which was the best. The notes were to contain several musical quotations which he sang over the telephone:

Musical example of Beethoven's Concerto no. 2.

The liner notes eventually used read as follows:

> Within this opening phrase the dual thematic character of the classical concerto allegro is summed up. The martial reveille of figure 1 (an inverted Mannheim skyrocket) makes an appropriate gesture of symphonic pomposity, is subtly modified by figure 1A and balanced by the lyric attitude of the consequent motive. At once is depicted that play of aggression and reluctance, of power and of pleading, which is the concerto idea.[7]

I complimented Glenn on his insight into the concerto's musical construction and the brilliance of his writing. But I had to admit there were some things in his piece I couldn't agree with. For example, Glenn started out by asserting: "The B-flat major Concerto is without doubt the most unjustly maligned of Beethoven's orchestral compositions. Until very recently it has been reserved for occasional appearance as a curiosity piece, and it is still greeted more often than not with critical reserve."[8]

"That's an overstatement and may not be true," I told him. "There are many other orchestral compositions by Beethoven that are rated lower and played less frequently than his B-flat piano concerto, for example, the Overture to *King Stephan* and his Fantasia for Piano, Chorus, and Orchestra."

Glenn responded with a rapid-fire defense: "Well, Peter, I was thinking mostly of his early period, which I'm especially fond of. The works you've mentioned both derive from Beethoven's later output, much of which I find questionable if not downright inferior. The Fantasia is just a lazy rehash of the 'Ode to Joy' from Beethoven's Choral Symphony, a work I've just never been sympathetic to, while the *King Stephan* is a useless excrescence from the end of his life, something simply not worth bothering with."

I suggested that Glenn's line of reasoning did not answer my objection, and that if anything it confirmed my feeling that he was attaching special status to this particular piano concerto.

"The point I'm making," he countered, "is that the concerto is *unjustly* maligned, whereas neglecting those pretentious works you've been mentioning is absolutely justified." Glenn's mind was made up; he really didn't need my opinions on the accuracy of his Beethoven essay.

But the phone calls continued. They invariably came at night, when Glenn was most alert and working. It was his habit to spend the sleepless hours calling people he liked and trusted. These were his captive audience, providing a sense of individual comfort that was exactly the opposite of the terror induced in him by crowds. He could be in absolute control, initiating and terminating the long-distance auditory contact at his own whim and without any concern for the other person's need for sleep or privacy. He never asked, "Are you busy?" or, "Is this a good time to call?" Nor did he allow people to telephone him directly. There was

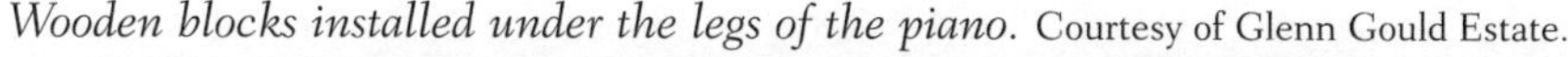

Wooden blocks installed under the legs of the piano. Courtesy of Glenn Gould Estate.

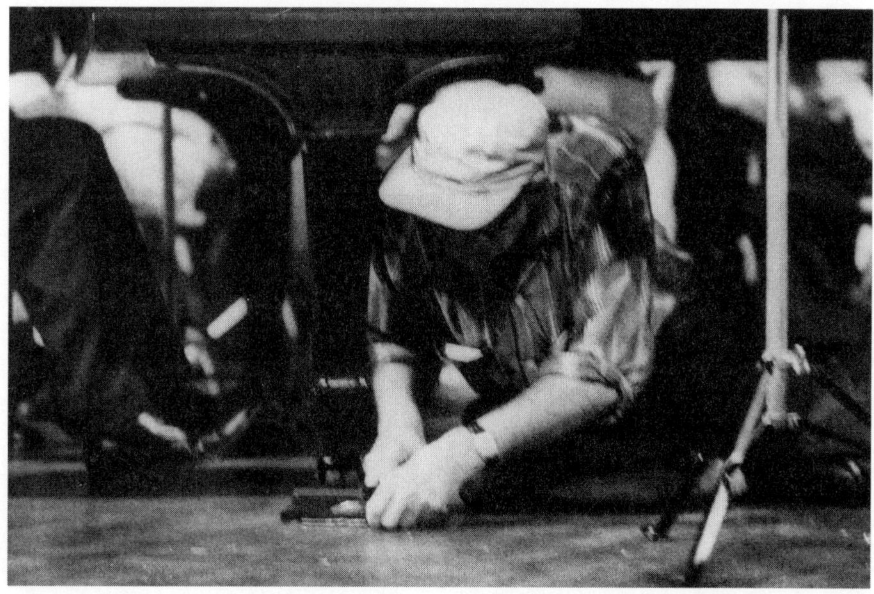

always an answering service or machine if one tried to reach him, and he would return the call only when he felt ready.

These nocturnal visits gave Glenn a sense of companionship that was absent in his daily life. He kept the calls focused on themes he was comfortable discussing, mostly aspects of his musical work that had become fairly routine and were emotionally neutral. He also liked to tell jokes, do imitations, and play guessing games over the phone. Disturbing or troublesome events were usually withheld. For example, in connection with the Second Beethoven Concerto, he said nothing about the embarrassing episode that had recently occurred while rehearsing this work with George Szell and the Cleveland Orchestra. I found out about it only many years later.

George Szell, in addition to the high level of musical excellence and discipline that he demanded from his players, was famous for his authoritarian manner and abrasive sarcasm. In preparing the Beethoven concerto with Gould, he apparently became annoyed at the time consumed by the soloist in adjusting his chair, and hiring a carpenter to build and position blocks under the piano. What exactly the irritable conductor said remains anybody's guess, but a *Time* reporter later wrote that it was: "Perhaps if I were to slice one sixteenth of an inch off your derrière, Mr. Gould, we could begin."[9]

14

TRAVELING OVERSEAS

During those two long phone calls in April 1957, Glenn mentioned nothing about a trip abroad that had been carefully planned for the month of May. He was scheduled to give concerts in Moscow, St. Petersburg (then Leningrad), Berlin, and Vienna. I suspect this was a subject he had compartmentalized in his well-organized mind and decided not to discuss with me. (Only the following year, when Glenn became ill in the middle of an European concert tour and canceled some of his concerts there, did he begin to share this kind of information more openly with me.)

There had been intense anxiety about this May trip for some time, and it escalated before his departure. A letter to a Mrs. Ford mentions his having "succumbed to the full fury of the intestinal flu . . . Friday night's concert had to be cancelled . . . it is comforting that you have written to Moscow re cereals et al—rest assured that I will remember you with each Shredded Wheat."[1] To Herbert Moffitt, Jr., the doctor I had referred him to when he had an anxiety attack earlier that year in San Francisco, he wrote on April 16: "I am enclosing an envelope, in which I hope that you will be so kind as to return a copy of the prescription which you gave me for some small yellow pills of some sedative property. . . . I am very happy to say that these pills were extremely effective and I would like to have a refill to take with me to Europe next week."[2]

The next day he wrote a woman in Quebec: "In two weeks I shall be off for Russia . . . if my stomach holds up with the Russian food I imagine that I shall have a really fascinating time."[3]

For the moment the whole complex of fears about eating, of vomiting in public, of being humiliated at the Canadian Embassy in Moscow had to be suppressed, along with other nervous problems: his fear of flying, his recurring panic that the plane might crash and he would be killed, and of course the old abhorrence of crowds. Performing in some of the great European capitals famous for their musical traditions was an opportunity he simply could not resist. Besides, Walter Homburger had worked very hard to arrange this tour, and was planning to come along. Prestige, fame, honor, and money were all at stake.

In 1957 the rulers of the Soviet Union, having lost their dictator, Joseph Stalin, only four years earlier, were eager to establish better relations with Canada. The new regime recognized that Canada was showing dissatisfaction with its status as a Dominion of the British Empire and planning to form stronger alliances with the United States. The time seemed ripe to open the Iron Curtain just a bit in order to promote trade and aid cultural exchange with the West. There was even some discussion about a music festival to be held in Moscow the following year, the Tchaikovsky Competition, where artists from around the world would in the future perform and receive prizes on a regular basis. Gould thus became a kind of cultural ambassador. He was the first classical musician from North America invited to perform in Moscow—being Canadian was clearly an asset. Many comparably exciting pianists in the United States would have been happy to play in the Soviet Union, but that was not yet possible.

Accompanied by Walter Homburger, Glenn flew to Moscow on a sleeper plane. "He had no problems flying with me," Homburger told me. "We flipped coins over who was going to sleep upstairs or downstairs." The two men were received cordially and given considerable freedom of movement. "In Russia I was with Glenn all over the place; never a problem," says Homburger. "They gave us a very nice translator, a woman. Glenn was like an ordinary citizen. We walked the streets. We went to the museums."[4] They were housed at the Canadian Embassy, where every courtesy was extended to the young pianist. Evidently he encountered no particular problems around meals. But something happened that Glenn later talked about with his friend, John Roberts, who shared it with me: "The wife of one of the diplomats tried to seduce Glenn, and this was probably the first time that he had ever run into that. I mean, he was horrified, and I don't think he could really cope with it at all. He coped with it by pretending that she wasn't there."[5]

Glenn's first concert was a solo recital on May 7, in the Grand Hall of the Moscow State Conservatory, where he played one of his typical, well-practiced programs: Bach fugues from *The Art of the Fugue* and the Partita no. 6 in E Minor; Beethoven's Sonata no. 30, opus 109; and the Berg Sonata. The audience was transfixed. They had never heard music by Bach and Beethoven performed with Glenn's verve and iconoclasm. As for the Berg Sonata, it was a totally new experience for the Russians because all compositions by twelve-tone composers had been officially declared decadent and were not allowed to be performed in the Soviet Union. According to Walter Homburger, who was writing glowing reports to be circulated in Canada by the *Toronto Star,* "by intermission, bravos could be heard all over the hall [and] as Gould took his second bow a huge basket of blue chrysanthemums was carried up the aisle toward the stage." Glenn had to play numerous encores: a Fantasia by Sweelinck and ten of the *Goldberg Variations.*

The following night, May 8, was even more auspicious: a concert at the famed Tchaikovsky Hall with the Moscow Philharmonic Orchestra. He played two of his favorite concertos, Beethoven's Fourth and the D Minor Bach. A telegram home that night reads: CONCERTS GREAT SUCCESS STAYING AT EMBASSY AM IN GOOD HEALTH LOVE GLENN.[6] Three nights later, again in the Tchaikovsky Hall, he presented the complete *Goldberg Variations* as well as two Intermezzi by Brahms and Hindemith's Third Sonata. By now his fame had spread, and subsequent concerts were packed. Fans in Moscow were calling their friends and relatives in Leningrad, Glenn's next stop, to tell them to be sure not to miss these extraordinary events.

Glenn spent May 12 playing and lecturing, with the help of his translator, for the students and teachers at the Moscow Conservatory of Music. In a long letter written the following year to the Ottawa-based photographer Yousuf Karsh, he described what he remembered about that appearance:

> I accepted with great delight but with the stipulation that I be allowed to play just whatever came into my head at the moment and that there would be no formal program. After some discussion with my manager and the

Gould lecturing in Russia, onstage with interpreter, May 1957. Courtesy of Glenn Gould Estate.

people at the Embassy, I decided to play for them a program composed entirely of contemporary music, most of it belonging to what is loosely referred to as the Viennese school—the Arnold Schoenberg, Anton Webern tradition. I began by re-playing the Alban Berg sonata which I had included on one of the regular programs. . . . It was written in 1908 and provided a wonderful point of departure from which to play for them and talk to them about the more serious facets of twelve-tone music. I talked to them, by the way, with the assistance of no less than four different interpreters [who] supplemented one another's vocabulary of technical terms and we made out amazingly well—at least the audience mostly laughed in the right places. . . . When I first announced . . . that I was going to play the sort of music that has not been officially recognized in the U.S.S.R. since the artistic crises in the mid thirties, there was a rather alarming and temporarily uncontrollable murmuring from the audience . . . many of the students were uncertain whether it was better for them to remain or walk out. As it turned out, I managed to keep things under control by frowning ferociously now and then and the only people who did walk out were a couple of elderly professors. . . . However, as I continued playing music of Schoenberg . . . Webern and Krenek, there were repeated

> suggestions from the student body, mostly in the form of discreet whispers from the committee on the stage but occasionally the odd fortissimo suggestion from the audience that they would prefer to spend their time with Bach and Beethoven.[7]

It might have been diplomatic for the young Canadian visitor to include music by a Russian composer in one of his programs. He was familiar with the Prokofiev Sonata no. 7 and had performed it occasionally in Canada and the United States. Earlier, he had made recordings in Toronto of pieces for violin and piano by Prokofiev and Shostakovich. But even these composers had aroused controversy and official condemnation under the Soviet regime. My guess is that Glenn wanted to play it safe by not presenting to Russian audiences music that might stir up even more contention. Besides, it was always his aim to differ from other pianists in his programming as well as his interpretations.

Leningrad gave him the most exuberant reception of his life. Extra seats had to be installed on the stage; special guards were assigned to control the huge crowds that gathered for each of his four concerts in this magnificent city; immense bunches of flowers were thrown onto the stage. The applause went on and on. Endless encores were demanded, and Glenn complied graciously. One day he received a handwritten note:

> Dear Sir, we implore you to play some Bach without the orchestra. Many of us had no opportunity of attending your concert on the 16th and had been waiting in the street for a long time and all in vain!
>
> Your Russian admirers[8]

Glenn again played for students at the Conservatory, and as he wrote later, "It was a sensation equivalent to that of perhaps being the first musician to land on Mars or Venus and to be in a position of revealing a vast unexplored territory to some greatly puzzled but willing auditors. It was a great day for me."[9] He also took an interest in the canine culture of the Russian cities, writing to "Banquo Gould" in Toronto: "I thought you would like to know about the dogs here. One sees very few indeed. Most of them were killed in the war. . . . The most prevalent variety [is] a sort of unclipped poodle—a few mongrels and no collies whatsoever. You would have the field all to yourself if you were here."[10]

Walter Homburger told me that Glenn enjoyed his Russia experience immensely and considered it the high point of his concert career—"there were never any problems." But later Glenn admitted that such wild displays of adulation had all been "overwhelming and just a bit frightening."[11] In fact, it was in Russia that he first noticed what he called "accruing bad habits" in his interpretation of Bach: "all sorts of dynamic hang-ups, crescendi and diminuendi that have no part in the structure, in the skeleton of that music, and defy one to portray the skeleton adequately. The reason . . . was that I had to play in very large halls which weren't set up with Bach in mind certainly, and try to project it to that man up there in the top balcony. . . . And I added this hairpin and that hairpin to a phrase that didn't demand it, didn't need it, and that ultimately destroyed the fabric of the music."[12]

Paradoxically, Gould would later feel guilty and ashamed about one of his greatest victories, the overcoming of performance anxiety in front of highly enthusiastic Russian audiences. In his article "Let's Ban Applause!", published in 1962, he expressed his true faith, that the best way to listen to music is in private, and with the "total elimination of audience response":

> I am disposed toward this view because I believe that the justification of art is the internal combustion it ignites in the hearts of men and not its shallow, externalized, public manifestations. The purpose of art is not the release of a momentary ejection of adrenaline but is, rather, the gradual, lifelong construction of a state of wonder and serenity.[13]

The best way to achieve this utopia was to do away with concert halls and rely exclusively on the electronic media. Not surprisingly, it was actually because of the media that Gould's reputation spread widely behind the Iron Curtain to places far from Moscow and Leningrad at a time when music lovers in the Soviet Union and its satellites had little access to what was happening in the West. Several of his concerts had been recorded live—for example, solo appearances in Moscow and both the Bach D Minor and the Beethoven Second Piano concertos played with the Leningrad Philharmonic. Though none of these recordings were officially released until after Glenn's death, they were broadcast much earlier, and pirated tapes soon began circulating among students and music lovers who found his interpretations revelatory.

"Here I was in Hungary in the 1960s," the pianist Andras Schiff told me. "Those were pretty dark years still, better than the fifties but we were completely isolated. We had to play Bach for our exams, and would play him in a terribly boring way, very dusty, with a lot of pedal, sort of moonlight-lit fugues. So along came these Gould recordings, and they were so alive, so rhythmically interesting. They were bouncing, there was something jazzy about it.

"And it really just liberated us somehow. Later, when I was already very much interested in Bach, it was wonderful to see that you could play his music in other ways. Certainly not to imitate Gould. I already knew, as a teenager, that he was a unique artist and it would be very dangerous to imitate him. But certainly he showed us that when you play Bach on the piano it was possible to play not in a nineteenth century manner, and not by using all that pedal as if you were playing Chopin or Liszt. The clarity of his playing, and the part-playing, the polyphony, was extraordinary.

"And it was all from Russia. In a way, I think those were the most beautiful Gould recordings, like those *Inventions,* they are infinitely more beautiful than his studio recordings, wonderful."[14]

Following Russia, Glenn's next triumph was in Berlin, then still divided into East and West. On May 24, 25, and 26, 1957, he played the Beethoven Concerto no. 3 in C Minor with the Berlin Philharmonic led by Herbert von Karajan. Glenn was much taken by this stern, self-possessed, fabulously successful musician, who exerted what the pianist described as "a magnetic attraction" on him. "I don't mind confessing it," Glenn wrote in one of his imaginary dialogues. "As you know, Karajan tends—in late romantic repertoire particularly—to conduct with eyes closed and to endow his stick wielding with enormously persuasive choreographic contours, and the effect, quite frankly, contributed to one of the truly indelible musical-dramatic experiences of my life."[15]

Glenn hadn't played the Third Beethoven Concerto for about six months before he was scheduled to perform it with Karajan. He often asserted that he practiced rarely, if at all, for his concerts, but that was obviously untrue. According to the pianist Gary Graffman, who saw Glenn in Berlin, "he was practicing a lot"[16] at the Steinway Building to prepare for the three appearances with the Philharmonic, the last to be broadcast. Clearly, Glenn wanted to be at his best in Berlin. A recording of the broadcast proves that the additional practice had paid off. Glenn always spoke very highly of his success in the still war-damaged German metropolis. Indeed, he often expressed a special fondness for Germany and the Germans. He took pleasure in mimicking the German language although he never learned to speak it.

The concerts with Karajan led to an exceptionally flattering review, written by one of Europe's leading music critics, the composer H. H. Stuckenschmidt, who had studied with Arnold Schoenberg and later wrote a biography of the composer. Stuckenschmidt was impressed: "A young man in a strange sort of trance. . . . His technical ability borders on the fabulous; such a combination of fluency in both hands, of dynamic versatility, and of range in coloring represents a degree of mastery which in my experience has not appeared since the time of Busoni."[17]

The name of Busoni evokes a gigantic image of intellectual and pianistic excellence. Born in Italy in 1866, Ferruccio Busoni was a child prodigy pianist who at an early age became interested in composing. After extensive travels throughout Europe and to Russia as well as the United States, he decided at age twenty-eight to settle in Berlin, where he became one of Germany's most highly regarded performers, musicologists, and composers, writing numerous works for the piano, including transcriptions of other composers' music that are still played today. He also composed many orchestral works, concertos, and five operas. To be compared to this giant was extraordinarily flattering, and it pleased Glenn enormously. He often quoted the Berlin review to colleagues and friends as proof of his own worthiness. Stuckenschmidt's equating him with Busoni seems to have resonated with Glenn's view of himself as a man who could make important contributions not only as a performer but also as a creative artist and philosopher.

The famous pianist Egon Petri had worked closely with Busoni and became his assistant. He spoke of Busoni as a man of great culture whose knowledge encompassed art, literature, philosophy, as well as music. He was widely known as an influential teacher, whose ideas were valid in the context of changing musical style from late romanticism to early modernism. But while the musical cognoscenti respected him, he never achieved the sort of mass acclaim or cult status that characterized Glenn Gould's public career.

Vienna was the next and final place for Glenn to perform, and because of recurring "colds" and "sinus pains," he decided to go there by train. Some of the dramatic events of this trip were described in a delightfully long letter he wrote home, to "Mouse, Possum, Bank" (nicknames for his mother, father, and dog Banquo).

> I was getting on the train at Frankfurt when I noticed a distinguished looking white-haired man on the platform taking the air (the train was the Amsterdam-Wien-Express). I looked twice to make sure, then said—"Excuse me, but isn't it Mr. Stokowski." He winced as though he thought I were a reporter or autograph-hunter and without turning to look at me mumbled "It is." I ploughed ahead and said "Permit me to introduce

> myself, sir. I am GG." Suddenly he smiled "Are you Glenn Gould!" Whereupon like a benevolent long-lost grandfather he came into my compartment and chatted for half an hour.[18]

The letter also describes his train trip through southern Germany: "The most wonderful pastorale imaginable. I stayed up till 11:30 specially to sing *Die Meistersinger* as we went through Nurnberg." A scary accident occurred while crossing the border to Austria: "this morning at 6:30 the porter came around to give me back my passport . . . and as I was opening the door to my compartment he suddenly pushed it shut again on my left thumb and said thumbnail is now turning slightly blue and making it a bit difficult to write—Hope it will be allright by Friday."[19]

Glenn's recital in Vienna on June 7, was yet another triumph. He played fifteen Sinfonias by Bach, Beethoven's Sonata no. 30, opus 109, and Webern's *Variations,* plus "encores upon encores [with] cheers upon cheers, houselights on, stage lights out, more applause, and a final bow in overcoat, hat and gloves."[20]

He wasn't quite sure what to do with himself after Vienna. To his parents he wrote about possibly renting a car if he could get an international driving permit, and then driving either south to visit Trieste and Venice and maybe Milan, or west for sightseeing in Salzburg, Munich, Stuttgart, and Frankfurt, before flying to London and then home. Walter Homburger had returned earlier, and Glenn surely deserved a vacation. He wouldn't have to be back until July for recording sessions at Columbia Masterworks in New York.

> If I do get the car [he wrote home] please rest assured I shall not speed and shall generally exercise utmost caution. If I don't get it you will likely see me home a lot sooner than expected. I am not a good tourist—I'm afraid—I never have had the energy to traipse around from village to village. . . . This does not minimize the fact that I have had a wonderful time in Europe. In fact I am seriously thinking of taking up residence here for six months of 58–59. . . . I shall be establishing my European residence (sounds imposing, what?) probably in Germany in the early fall of '58 (concerts permitting) and you could come over and visit me. . . . Dr. von Karajan has offered to introduce me to any city where he happens to be conducting if our schedules fit. So things are in good shape for Germany in the future.[21]

But it seems that he had difficulty in obtaining a driver's license, and he didn't want to stay in Vienna because "It is absolutely impossible to get much practise in here—So many concerts going in all the halls. I should have stayed in Berlin. . . . I find Vienna much less attractive than I had imagined it. Too much rococo architecture for my rather severe tastes."

Besides, Glenn's psychosomatic fears were once again inhibiting him. The eating disorder seems to have come under control. He wrote his parents about a dinner he had "in my room as usual in Frankfurt where the food was 1st class. Steak, vegetables, fruit juice, ice cream with all kinds of trimmings, coffee." The offending problem was that "my cold is still with me and gives signs of the annual hayfever."[22] Finally he decided to curtail further traveling and fly back home to Toronto.

15

STRANGE ILLNESSES

Upon returning to Toronto in mid-June 1957, Glenn plunged immediately into his usual routine. During July and early August, he visited New York and the Columbia studios in order to make a recording of Bach's second book from *The Well-Tempered Clavier.* His interpretation of these glorious Preludes and Fugues was highly personal, with startling dynamic shifts, unexpected ornaments, and extreme fluctuations in tempo. Many passages that are traditionally played legato, Glenn plays staccato, and vice versa, and where several notes are to be struck simultaneously as in a chord, he often plays them successively in a quick arpeggio. The recording made a hit because of its freshness and unorthodoxy.

No one had ever heard the Preludes and Fugues performed like this, but connoisseurs found some of them offensive and objectionable. Glenn rationalized this with his general dictum, applied also to other questionable recordings he made, that to sound new and original and to distinguish his recordings from those of other pianists, he had to do what he did, and of course one does recognize a Gould recording instantly. He also used a historical explanation to defend what he had done with the Preludes and Fugues:

Gould playing piano onstage to an empty hall. Courtesy of Glenn Gould Estate.

> The *Well-Tempered Clavier,* or excerpts therefrom, has been performed on the harpsichord and on the piano, by wind and string ensembles, by jazz combos, and by at least one scat-scanning vocal group as well as upon the instrument whose name it bears. And this magnificent indifference to specific sonority is not least among those attractions which emphasize the universality of Bach. . . . One cannot, therefore, entirely sidestep considerations pertaining to the manner in which [the piano] should be employed in its behalf.[1]

His first concert after returning from Europe was in Montreal, and it included a performance on August 20, 1957, of the Brahms Quintet for Piano and Strings in F Minor, opus 34. His fellow musicians were the renowned Montreal String Quartet. The hall was packed; spare tickets were being hawked for thirty dollars, an unheard-of figure at that time, and CBC made a recording of the quintet.[2] It shows, again, Gould's distinctive approach and his determination to produce an "original" recording by playing games with the tempi. The opening movement, marked *Allegro non troppo,* is driven forward so aggressively that it loses its stately character and permits no lingering over Brahms's luscious harmonies. The second movement, marked *Andante, un poco Adagio,* ignores the composer's direction "un poco Adagio" and takes so fast a tempo that much of its marvelous lyricism is obliterated. The third movement tries to do the opposite by reining in the tempo and thus reducing the bombast of this powerfully syncopated *Scherzo—Allegro.* The Finale, *Poco sostenuto—Allegro non troppo,* sounds lackluster and mechanical, as though little imagination was used in rehearsing and performing it.

Gould's German biographer, Michael Stegemann, suggests that friction between the pianist and members of the quartet was responsible for the production of this mediocre recording. "Anyone whose ideal of chamber music is based on the principle of absolute homogeneity of sound and interpretation is bound to view this ensemble as a mismatch."[3] In addition, one might postulate the exhausting effects of the pianist's recent whirlwind tour abroad, plus his unhappiness at having again to plunge himself into concerts.

However, Eric McLean, the music critic of the *Montreal Star,* a Gould fan, was enchanted with what he heard, and pointed to the composition itself as a source of potential disunity among the players. Brahms had originally intended this work to be a quintet for strings. "The performance of the Brahms was electrifying. . . . There was, for me, a sense of rightness about the tempo throughout. . . . There was an admirable unity of thought and feeling in the playing of these five musicians, without a trace of push or pull from any one member."[4]

By the end of August, Glenn was flying across the country for a concert in Hollywood and then back to Toronto, Washington, D.C., Syracuse, Rochester, Toronto again, Pittsburgh, Cincinnati, New York City, and Miami. But the integrity of the folding chair he always sat on while playing the piano—was being questioned by his manager.

"Glenn's old chair was rickety already in those days," Walter Homburger told me, "and I worried one of these days it would collapse, and I wanted to have some security behind him."[5] A year before the Russian tour, Homburger had written to ask the director of an aluminum company in Canada whether a new chair could be made for Glenn, since "his excess baggage bill on airplanes is considerable."[6] Glenn wouldn't cooperate with this plan at all. Three weeks later, Homburger made a similar request to another manufacturing company, adding that "Mr. Gould's greatest fear is that a chair made out of aluminum might be so light that when he would play and possibly sit at the edge it might slide away from under him."[7] Finally, Homburger had a new chair built for Glenn in Berlin. "But then he never used it. Nobody knows what ever happened to it. The chair was made out of metal. It was more solid."[8]

For the rest of his life, Glenn always used the wooden chair made for him by his father. As far as I know, there were never any mishaps. However, the leather-cover on the seat deteriorated down to the last scraps of padding, which tumbled down the sides of his chair; in time, the seat disintegrated completely. Later recordings (when he no longer gave concerts) were made with Glenn sitting on the bare wooden cross-beams. This must have been extremely uncomfortable, but he never complained or sought to have the seat repaired.

In 1958, he embarked on his second overseas tour, a longer one this time. He was scheduled to appear at the Salzburg Music Festival in Austria on August 10, then to perform in Belgium, Sweden, and Germany, and finally to go south again for concerts in Italy and Israel ending in mid-December. The USSR was not on his agenda in 1958. That year a new American star, Van Cliburn, won the Tchaikovsky Competition and the hearts of the Russians. Glenn would have nothing to do with competitions.

Unhappily, before leaving for Europe, he had exhausted himself with a steady stream of twenty-two performances in Canada and the United States, and his playing was beginning to show the strain. Several music critics had mentioned it:

> *New York:* "His tone was harsh, at times downright brutal."
> *Buffalo:* "He has nothing like the technique of a young Horowitz."
> *Montreal:* "The finger-work of the fast movement [in the *Goldberg Variations*] was not as clean as usual."[9]

At a performance of the Beethoven Third Concerto attended by the pianist James Tocco, "Gould didn't come out on the stage for a long time. Finally, a stage hand appeared with this enormous score. It was wider than the music rack of the piano, and had a black cover. He placed it on the music rack, opened it up, went back into the wings, and again no Glenn Gould. About a minute after that, the man came out again, this time with a glass of water which he placed to the right of the music. That kind of got everybody stirring. And then finally Glenn Gould came out, to rather warm applause. He bowed once to the audience and sat down. And at the same time that he sat down, he turned his back to the audience, swiveled in his seat, crossed his legs, propped his left arm up on his knee, and rested his chin in his hand. That's the way he stayed during the entire opening tutti."[10]

In Boston, Glenn had behaved quite inappropriately by telling the audience that because he hadn't practiced enough he would substitute a Mozart sonata for a late Beethoven sonata. He later admitted having felt "terribly depressed" about the tour. "I was going to be in Europe for three months [actually for five months], terribly out of touch with all the life that I knew, and everything seemed ridiculous. . . . Well, who the hell said it was supposed to be fun anyway?"[11] Evidently he had abandoned the idea of residing in Europe, the plan proposed to his parents the year before.

Walter Homburger did not accompany him on his second overseas tour, so this time Gould had to make many more decisions for himself. In Salzburg, musical colleagues were struck by his discomfort and indifference. "He sealed himself in his hotel, and I distinctly remember things he didn't do," the pianist Anton Kuerti, who was also in Salzburg, told me. "I mean, Glenn was never one for doing much walking; he was definitely an indoor type, and I'm much more an outdoor type. And you know there would be some things in Salzburg that one could sightsee, but I'm quite sure he never did anything like that."

"Did he overdress there in the typical Gouldian fashion?" I wondered.

"Yes, even though it was midsummer."

"Did that seem to create any sort of special interest over there? It was blown way out of proportion, as you know, on this side of the Atlantic. But how was it in Europe, where I guess people are a little more used to various lifestyles and behaviors?"

"I don't recall his way of overdressing as causing any interest. At that time maybe he wasn't that well known, and nobody would have said, 'Ah, there's the famous Glenn Gould.' "

Kuerti, who had met Gould earlier when they were introduced by John Roberts, tried to cheer Glenn up:

"We had this session where we both attempted to write a little fugue on the subject of Strauss's *Burleske*. After a page or so we looked at each other's fugues, and he was sort of surprised that I hadn't introduced any sixteenths into mine—the theme of the *Burleske* is all in quarter notes, and a dotted quarter note and an eighth note, several eighth notes—and I sort of expressed surprise that Glenn's had lots of sixteenths in it, and I said something like, 'Well, was this supposed to be an exercise in species counterpoint?' . . . He looked quite thin and was obviously neglecting his diet. So, much against his normal habits and principles, I convinced him to go and eat in a restaurant, and we went. It was in his hotel, and we looked over the menu. There were various things on it, and for whatever reason I decided I would order brains, which was quite a popular Austrian delicacy. It's called *Hirn mit Ei*. They mix calf's brains with scrambled eggs. It really doesn't look very different from an omelet. But when it was brought to the table, Glenn said, 'I can't, I can't. I'm sorry. Please forgive me. I'm going to have to go to my room.' And he left."[12]

Glenn's first appearance in Salzburg on August 10, 1958, went well. With Dimitri Mitropoulos conducting Amsterdam's Concertgebouw Orchestra he played the Bach D Minor Concerto, a work in which the piano is relatively unexposed, playing in unison with the orchestra much of the time. Glenn had been performing it quite frequently over the past three years, most recently five months earlier in New York, again with Mitropoulos conducting. However, after this performance he began complaining that he was seriously ill. He said he had contracted a bad cold due to the air conditioning in the Salzburg *Festspielhaus*. Now it had settled into his windpipe, producing tracheitis, which is an inflammation that causes painful breathing and may interfere with voice production.

Expecting trouble, Glenn had a list of doctors in Europe that Dr. Michael Lenczner of Toronto had given him. But it contained no recommendation for a physician in Salzburg. The closest would have been a Dr. Brunner in Vienna.[13] The man Glenn consulted in Salzburg was Gerwald Maybegg, M.D., who came to the Hotel Bristol four times on August 13, 14, and 15 to administer intramuscular injections of a broad-spectrum antibiotic and a thyroid-gland stimulant. We do not know how Glenn reacted to the medications, but because of his illness he canceled a solo recital planned in Salzburg.

Cancelations are not supposed to happen very often in the concert world. Most performers adhere to the slogan "The show must go on," and prefer to appear on stage even under circumstances that are less than ideal. Unless they can be explained on the basis of problems that genuinely threaten the integrity of the performance, cancelations reflect badly on an artist's reputation and are costly for the manager, who may have to supply a substitute at short notice. For example, an upper respiratory infection like tracheitis would be a legitimate excuse for a singer or flutist to cancel a concert, but not for a pianist unless he is running a very high fever (and even then, many have been known to perform).

Similarly, the paralysis of a hand would disqualify an instrumentalist, but not a singer.

Gould's situation was exceptional for several reasons. In the first place, his singing was integral to his piano playing, so that an upper respiratory infection or the loss of his voice might be considered a legitimate handicap. Second, he was so tuned in to disturbing sensations anywhere in his body that these quickly led to a general feeling of malaise, distracting him from playing as well as he wanted. Third, he basically detested the concert scene so much that a cancelation meant immediate relief from stress. In this case, he withdrew for a few days to a resort in the Alps to recover from the tracheitis. Finally, Glenn did not have to rely on concerts as a source of financial security, so that canceling a performance here and there imposed no great economic burden on him. Recordings provided regular income, and he was a clever businessman who knew how to benefit from stock- market transactions. As early as our first meeting in 1957, he told me how successful he had been with his investments in Canadian silver mines. On his overseas tours Glenn always kept in touch with his Toronto stockbroker's office, Bache & Co.

By August 25, Glenn had recovered sufficiently to give a concert at the Brussels World Fair. He again performed the Bach D Minor Concerto, this time with Boyd Neil conducting. The following month he played the same work in Berlin, with Von Karajan conducting, on September 21 and 22. This time, however, there was a mishap at the start of the first performance, attributable to a momentary lack of attention on Glenn's part and possibly associated with his growing fatigue. He fouled up by coming in prematurely at the beginning of the opening movement where piano and orchestra play in unison. Glenn later called it "one of the most embarrassing beginnings this concerto ever had."

> I looked up at K, saw, or thought I saw, his preparatory upbeat, and three-quarters of a second later, as his arms emphatically described the bottom of their trajectory, I made my entrance—alone—For K., up is down and vice versa—in the matter of prep. beats. The orchestra entered as I answered at the second beat—Happily canonic voice-leading met all academic requirements—I took 3/4 of a second off to compensate and rejoined them in the middle of the bar.[14]

By this time Glenn was becoming aware that something was seriously wrong with him. He was having new symptoms that worried him ceaselessly, and the trip north was beginning to resemble a nightmare: "Premonitions of disaster . . . the sweat in the night . . . the continuing unwellness. . . . The chiropractor . . . 'the flu.' . . . Nordic hedonism."

These brief observations, made with the intention of one day writing a kind of autobiographical survey of his travels, to be called "A Season on the Road," remind me of similar notes kept by the German composer Robert Schumann while traveling in Switzerland and Italy. They are like fleeting memories intended to be elaborated and explained in greater detail later on. But unlike Schumann, who incorporated ideas from his travel diaries into letters and essays, Glenn never made literary use of his reminiscences about this trip. He traveled as far north as Stockholm, and played Mozart's Concerto in C Minor, k. 491, now available on disc. He returned to Germany, visited Cologne, and, on October 9 performed the Third Beethoven Concerto in Wiesbaden, with Wolfgang Sawallisch conducting.

Glenn's travel notes report: "Wiesbaden, Sawallisch; cut finger; the drive down the Rhine; Koln, the paternoster; cancellation No. 1; the endless bath . . . the flight to Hamburg—fever and pain; the chiropractor (Palmer method); 102 in the eve.; to Vier Jahreszeiten [hotel in Hamburg]—the Inner Harbor. Dr Storgaharm: Remember Chopin."[15] Again, without further explanation, it's difficult to understand what was actually going on. "The chiropractor" might refer to Martin Müller, a practitioner in Berlin whose card, retained in Glenn's files, mentions "the Palmer School of Chiropractic."[16] We also know that Glenn did take up residence at the Hotel Vier Jahreszeiten in Hamburg. "Remember-Chopin" suggests that he may have been thinking about the great Polish pianist who frequently became ill, collapsed during concert tours, and died at the early age of thirty-nine.

I had heard from our mutual friend Martin Canin that Glenn was in Germany, but knew nothing about his misery during the Europe tour. Unaware as yet of some of his deeper problems, I sent him the following letter on October 1:

> Dear Glenn,
>
> I was very happy to see that you will be in San Francisco again [for three concerts in February 1959] to play with the Symphony. It would give me great pleasure indeed to be your host while you are here, and I'd like to invite you to stay here [in my apartment] where you might be more comfortable than in a hotel. Perhaps I could also do something in the way of arranging a party for you—after one of the concerts, if you like, or later if you can stay in town for a few days.

The year has been a good one for me, except for the fact that medicine has kept me away from music more than I would have liked. I visited New York recently and saw Marty Canin. He told me about your Carnegie Hall recital which, I hope, you'll repeat in San Francisco one day.

Please let me know in what ways I may be of service to you. Looking forward to seeing you again,

Sincerely,
Peter[17]

Gould answered my letter on October 29 (this reply will be cited shortly). Meanwhile, on October 2, whil still traveling, he had written Walter Homburger to explain his health worries: "I have fallen victim to another flu à la Salzburg (current temperature 101 degrees). Sunday's concert had to be canceled."[18] On October 18, he wrote another letter to Homburger, from Hamburg: "I have chronic bronchitis in the right lung. This we found out by X-rays recently. Since I don't know too much about this I am not sure that the practitioner who is seeing me is the best person for the job."

Glenn described this doctor as "very much a Nature Boy type—milk and honey, cold cloths on the right side—all that sort of thing—I am sure this kind of doctoring would suit you perfectly but it doesn't seem to be getting me any improvement." He also told Homburger, "I have a high fever every evening (last night up to 100.8)."[19] This rise in temperature cannot be considered a "high fever." The normal body temperature, taken by mouth, is 98.6 degrees Fahrenheit in the morning, and can rise one degree, to about 99.6, in the evening. Thus 100.8 degrees would be considered a mild to moderate elevation unless the patient was elderly or seriously debilitated, in which case such a reading might be more serious cause for alarm.

It is difficult to evaluate Homburger's reactions to Glenn's reports of himself as sick. When I asked him about this, he told me, "If Glenn said, 'I'm sick, I can't play,' then I said, 'So we cancel.' "[20] But matters could not have been quite that simple. Canceling a performance usually means loss of income for both artist and manager, and often involves a considerable amount of work for the manager, who has to make explanations and negotiate alternate arrangements. Glenn seems to have shown little sensitivity to Homburger's dilemma. From Hamburg, he wrote, "If I see no hope of speedy recovery, I am going to cancel the works [i.e., all of his remaining overseas concerts] and head for Die [sic] Zauberberg."[21] A week later, he reported to Homburger even more portentously:

> The doctor concluded his diagnosis yesterday and I have been put to bed for ten days on a no-protein diet. The idea seems to be to give the kidneys a rest as much as possible. X-rays showed there was nothing wrong with them whatever organically but that they had some way been affected by this virus. Quite frankly, I don't think I can stand ten days with nothing substantial to eat.[22]

This was alarming and puzzling news. How had the doctor reached the conclusion that Glenn was afflicted with kidney disease? I wish I could answer this question, but so far I've been unable to identify who the "Nature Boy type" was. On a piece of stationery from the Hotel Vier Jahreszeiten, Glenn scribbled the names "Dr. Harders" and "Dr. Kaufman"; they can no longer be located. Nor do we have objective information about X-rays or other tests. According to Glenn's notes, the diagnosis of "focal nephritis" was made on the basis of a urine test that showed "bacteria [and] blood cells clumped together."[23] To Walter Homburger he also once mentioned "blood in the urine," which the manager took to be "a false alarm."[24] I would like to know how a bladder infection was ruled out. And if there were bacteria, why wasn't Glenn given antibiotics in Hamburg?

Even before receiving the bad news of "kidney disease," Homburger had written to Gould about the problem of his cancelations. The two men also communicated by phone. "Dear Glenchick," Homburger wrote on October 22, "I don't know what would give you the idea that I would wish you to play when you are *really* ill, as this is obviously the case at the present time. After all, your health comes first and if the Drs. should tell you that you should rest for one, two, or three months, that is all there is to do." Yet Homburger expressed skepticism about how ill Glenn really was. "After they have diagnosed your ailment, it will be interesting to try and find out what the causes were. Naturally, I shall have my own ideas about it but we won't go into that now. When [Vladimir] Ashkenazy arrived in town, he was already carrying two of your recordings under his arm and I shall present him with two additional ones tonight. Now, if you only get on your feet, then everything will be in clover."[25]

Homburger's misgivings about the true nature and severity of Glenn's illness was justified in that there had been numerous psychological and self-induced factors such as poor diet, insufficient sleep, lack of exercise, and overuse of medications. Glenn had a long history of unreliability when it came to reporting on his health. My impression is that he was probably suffering from a recurring viral infection, complicated by massive anxiety about his body. It is difficult to know what to make of the diagnosis of "nephritis." Much later in life Glenn developed high blood pressure, a condition that may result from kidney disease. But there was no evidence then of structural changes in his kidneys, nor was any kidney damage reported in the autopsy done after he died. There's no doubt that Glenn used medical diagnoses, some real and some imaginary, to stir up sympathy and concern among his friends, relatives, and manager. He once wrote Leonard Bernstein, "I have several titles for diseases which I am expecting to use in later life and have not yet had occasion to make use of. I always find that a good disease title will impress your average concert manager no end."[26]

Hearing about Glenn's "nephritis," his Grandma Gould wrote from Canada advising him to "try my remedy, a *thin* coating of mustardine or musterole spread on a cloth and worn over the aching spot. It eases all my aches."[27] The Berlin harpsichordist Sylvia Kind recommended a massage by her half-Indian masseur. She was convinced that "when the circulation is intensive, the poison goes out from the body."[28]

Glenn's letter to me of October 29, 1958, suggests that after several weeks in the ultra-luxurious Hotel Vier Jahreszeiten, he was comfortable, happy, and probably symptom-free:

Hamburg, Oct. 29,

Dear Peter,

Many thanks for your note which was forwarded to me here. It was good to hear of you again.

I am indeed very grateful for your invitation to be your guest in San Francisco. However, in the year and a half since I saw you, I have become inured to hotel existence and in fact find that on the whole I study better and work easier in a climate of indifference such as hotels provide. I shall, however, try to search out a less claustrophobic cubbyhole than what they gave me at the St. Francis [Hotel]. But anyway, much thanks for your kind suggestion. If I am not mistaken it was (or is) this week that Marty [Canin] plays at Carnegie Hall. . . . Last August, he played the Elliott Carter *Sonata* for me and I was greatly impressed though perhaps more with his playing than the work itself. But I think his plan to include it on the program a striking idea.

I have been over here since the middle of Sept. [actually August] and will be on tour until middle of December. However, the tour has been seriously interrupted by some complications after a relatively minor flu. It was diagnosed as nephritis and I have had to stay here 3 weeks (2 of them on a no-protein diet) and I consequently had to cancel 9 concerts. However I am now almost fully recovered—I never really did feel very ill which is the nice part of having something interesting but relatively bearable and I shall be able to get on with the tour and eat something beside rice porridge and fruit salad in another week.

Glad to know that all is going so well with you in medicine. I look forward to seeing you again in January.

All the best,
Glenn Gould[29]

Looking back on his convalescence in Hamburg, Glenn later used such terms as "the best month of my life . . . the greatest blessing in the world . . . really marvelous . . . a sense of exaltation . . . it's the only word that applies to that particular aloneness."[30] (These words remind one of the ecstasy expressed by Beethoven when he composed the poignant and magnificent slow movement for his String Quartet no. 15 in A Minor, opus. 132. On top of the manuscript he wrote: "Heiliger Dankgesang nach einer Erkrankung"—A Holy Song of Thanks after an Illness.")

Glenn used some of his free time to take care of pressing business affairs, in particular, the costs resulting from his many cancelations. Wolfgang Kollitsch, an impresario who had been involved in planning concerts for him in Germany, was especially insistent on getting his money back, and Glenn offered a bountiful settlement, to which Homburger, in a letter dated October 28, objected vigorously:

I am sure he knows as well as all managers, that there is no recourse in an "act of God" case, such as yours, and I am frankly astounded by his demands. Your suggestion to let him have the money which he still owes to you is most generous—but definitely uncalled for. If you were to analyze the figures you'll find that in the end he'll even make a profit on the deal. . . . So if you were to pay him a total of around DM 1250.00 I think it would be very fair. Believe me, I have never heard of an artist paying expenses and profit on a canceled recital because of sickness!![31]

By November 1958, Glenn was ready to resume his tour.

16

IN SEARCH OF A HOME

On the agenda for November and December 1958 was a tour of Israel. Glenn wanted to cancel it and give concerts elsewhere. But Homburger talked him out of that and flew to Europe to help Glenn fulfill his obligations, writing to him in October that

> your suggestion of getting out of the Israeli tour, but continuing in Europe, is based on dreams rather than reality. It just can't be done. They would know about your playing [elsewhere] and it would antagonize them in such a degree that it might even have reverberations over here. They know the chances they are taking with your health. . . . I personally believe that in your own mind you have now blown up any difficulties and problems in Israel to such a degree that you have become frightened. From where I sit I firmly believe that once you get there you'll enjoy playing in their environments. And I also know that while you might presently be afraid and worrisome about the pianos there, you will, as always, come through with flying colors.[1]

Glenn played eleven concerts in eighteen days, some of them under very difficult conditions. The hall in Jerusalem was so impossibly cold

Gould extends a hand to concertmaster of Israel Philharmonic Orchestra, 1958.
Photograph by Isaac Berez. Courtesy of Glenn Gould Estate.

that even with eight electric heaters placed on the stage, he was reluctant to play there. The piano in one of the communes where he performed was "absolutely rotten." It helped Glenn to use his powers of imagination to overcome these handicaps. At one point he decided simply to project himself into the coziness of his Lake Simcoe environment and think of himself playing on his own Chickering. That seemed to make the deficient instrument feel better to him. On the whole he had happy memories of the Israel tour. To one friend he wrote, "Although I was about done in at the end of it, it was nevertheless one of the most exciting experiences of my life. . . . Even I, you will be amused to know, with all the bourgeois thinking of my Western background, was in a very happy mental condition while I was there and felt myself very much attuned to stone huts, donkey carts, shepherds and flocks of goats."[2]

With typical grandiose humor he wrote Malka Rabinowitz of the *Jerusalem Post* a letter thanking her for galley proofs of plans for an improved auditorium heating system: "I am very happy to know that it has finally been achieved and I think the least they could do, since I made such a spectacle of myself over the issue, is to put a plaque bearing my name over one register so that in future all comfortable artists in the hall will be able to celebrate the martyrdom of St. Glenn!"[3]

Despite his eccentricities and carryings on, Glenn's playing made a tremendous impression in Israel. The love and admiration he evoked there is symbolized by one of the letters he received after the tour:

> Dear Mr. Gould!
>
> I am just an ordinary Israeli housewife. I know you don't care about the public, almost hating us. Nevertheless I will say thank you from all my heart, for letting me hear you playing. I went home changed for days to come. God bless you.[4]

Back home in Toronto, however, another housewife might have felt neglected had it not been for the intervention of an astute manager. Walter Homburger wrote Glenn on October 31: ". . . Your dad called me today—it seems you forgot your mother's birthday today—unless you called her or sent her a wire. Anyhow, I sent her flowers with a message 'Happy Birthday—Love—Glenn.' Hope I did all right."[5]

In January 1959, Glenn came to San Francisco for his second series of concerts, and we were able to get much better acquainted. He visited my apartment and played on my piano, a Blüthner made in Leipzig in 1896 and rebuilt during World War II in the Bösendorfer factory of Vienna. To Glenn's delight, I had dubbed it the "Blüthendorfer." It has a light action which he liked immediately, and he wanted to buy the instrument, which I couldn't agree to because I needed it for my own chamber music evenings.

Glenn's relationships with pianos have become legendary. He treasured the memory of those he played on as a child. In an emergency, when a piano he was using was truly inadequate or unresponsive, he would get through a concert, as he did in Israel, by conjuring up memories of playing his beloved old Chickering and vicariously enjoying the pleasant tactile sensations in his hands. Because Glenn's nimble fluency and keyboard style called for an action that was especially light and supple, adjustments constantly had to be made to his pianos, to the dismay of technicians who sometimes thought he was going too far or expecting the impossible. Here is all of one letter he wrote in 1956 to Winston Fitzgerald of the Concert and Artist department, Steinway & Sons in New York:

"An explicit summary of my complaint [about Steinway CD 90] can scarcely fail to do justice to the incredible negligence on the part of your firm, of which I have been victim since our first dealings 18 months ago. . . . I am now totally unable and unwilling to play for even the briefest period on this instrument."[6]

Despite such stinging criticism, Glenn preferred Steinway pianos, and his favorite instrument by far was the Steinway Grand CD 318. It had been his preferred instrument in his early career in Toronto, and he continued to favor it for most of the recordings he made in New York until 1971, when CD 318 was severely damaged while being transported to Toronto. Glenn was constantly on the lookout for new pianos, and at the end of his life switched to the Yamaha. Part of his performance anxiety was the fear of having to grapple with a bad instrument. The Steinways he played in San Francisco generally pleased him, one reason that he enjoyed visiting there.

This time he had come to perform Beethoven's Third Piano Concerto in C Minor with the San Francisco Symphony, Enrique Jordá conducting, on February 14, 15, and 16, 1959. Glenn was in a good mood and did not ask me this time to stay out of the hall. His playing was immaculate—refined, vigorous, and without any objectionable distortions of the music. The audience response was terrific.

Before his final performance, on the sixteenth, Glenn called me from the opera house around ten o'clock in the morning to say he was all alone on the stage and wanted to practice. But there was nobody around to help him put the wooden blocks under the piano which he needed to raise the instrument to its proper height. The piano tuner had left; the stage hands refused to do the job because it was not in their contract and they feared they could be sued if something happened to the piano. Glenn asked whether I could come down to the opera house and help out. I accepted the challenge, but only on condition that I would bring my violin along so we could play some sonatas together. He agreed. The blocks were about three inches high and placing them under the legs of the piano was not as difficult a task as it seems, although it left me with a sore back. Glenn, always fearful of physical injury, didn't lift a finger to assist me. But our spirited performance—to an empty house—of sonatas by Bach, Mozart, and Beethoven made up for everything. To be on the stage making music with Glenn Gould was an experience to remember.

Our relationship was very cordial for most of that year. Glenn allowed me to give a party for him, a small group of musicians. Iris Fath, wife of the Symphony's first clarinetist Philip Fath, commented afterwards, "He seems awfully shy." Glenn was seldom comfortable in a group, always preferring one-on-one communication where he could be in control and do most of the talking. However, he had a certain disarming modesty. For instance, he never mentioned being awarded the Bach Medal for Pianists by the Committee of the Harriet Cohen International Music Awards in London.

One evening in January, I invited him to join me for a chamber music session with my string quartet, which met once a week, and he accepted. This meant having to drive across the Bay Bridge to the home of Fred and Helen Stross, in the town of Orinda. Despite the cold fog and the draftiness of my small convertible Austin-Healey, Glenn didn't complain at all and seemed to enjoy the forty-five-minute ride. Helen was then the cellist in our group; the others were Mary James playing viola and Austin Reller playing violin. As we entered the house we were greeted by the Strosses' big Belgian shepherd. Glenn liked the dog immediately and stopped to pet it, saying, "People have to be nice with a dog like that."

We usually began with a quartet by Haydn, then went on to one of the Beethoven quartets, followed by a Romantic work, Brahms or Dvorák, or occasionally a more modern quartet by Bartók or Kodály. We would close with a short early quartet by Mozart or Schubert. We asked Glenn what he preferred to listen to, and whether he might join us in a piano quintet. He declined the invitation to play because there was "no applebox" for

Gould singing and conducting. Courtesy of Glenn Gould Estate.

him to sit on, but he suggested that he conduct our group while playing Beethoven's *Grosse Fugue,* the outrageously complex and dissonant fugal movement that forms the conclusion to the String Quartet no. 13, opus 130. We agreed, and after starting with the customary Haydn quartet, launched into the Beethoven. It was a wild performance, with Glenn singing and waving his arms and the four of us playing this most difficult work with more enthusiasm than accuracy.

After that we played the String Quartet by Claude Debussy, which was not exactly to Glenn's taste, but he listened quietly without commenting, unusual for him. Glenn wore his woolen gloves throughout the evening, even when we stopped for coffee and cake. (If I remember correctly, he ate nothing and drank only coffee.)

As we drove back to San Francisco, Glenn told me that several years earlier he had written a string quartet. It was in one movement reminiscent of the style of Bruckner and "very contrapuntal." He wanted our group to play the work and told me he would send me the music. He never did. Later he wrote me, "Let me thank you for the dinner Saturday night, which I neglected to do as I was creeking [sic] out of the Austin-Healey. I really enjoyed the evening at the Stross' very much and it did my spirit good to know that there are still homes in which chamber music is done live."[7]

Glenn's departure from San Francisco for St. Louis, where he was to play Beethoven's Fifth ("Emperor") Concerto, was stressful and uncomfortable. He mentioned his dissatisfaction with having to do so much touring and talked of all sorts of horror stories and mishaps. Not one but two overseas trips were on his agenda for 1959, the first from May 16 to June 1 for a recital in Berlin and the first four Beethoven concertos, to be played in London with the London Symphony Orchestra conducted by Josef Krips; the second from August 25 to 30 for two concerts in Salzburg and a performance of the Concerto in D Minor by Bach at the Lucerne Festival in Switzerland, with the Philharmonia Orchestra conducted by Herbert von Karajan.

In a letter soon after Glenn's visit to San Francisco, I expressed my anxiety in a way that mirrored his own habit of worrying about himself:

> How are you? I was slightly (or more than slightly) concerned about you when you left, what with bad weather, your oversleeping, the piano story, and other excitements. Please let me hear from you so that I don't have to elaborate various fantasies about your demise at the hands of careless

> pilots, sadistic piano tuners, incompetent doctors, or lethargic taxi drivers.[8]

We were having quite a lively exchange of letters and phone calls because Glenn had recommended me to the management of the Stratford Festival as a violinist they might want to engage to play in the orchestra that summer. Soon I received a letter from Louis Applebaum, the music director at Stratford, explaining what would be involved. Five weeks of concerts, opera, and chamber music were being planned for the summer of 1959, and Mr. Applebaum would be pleased to consider me as a potential member of the orchestra. That made me very proud, but since I was not a professional musician with union membership (absolutely required at Stratford) and had other pressing obligations, I regretfully declined.

While Glenn was in San Francisco we had talked about books we liked. Both of us were very fond of *The Last Puritan* by George Santayana. There were times, over the telephone, too, when Glenn talked about this book incessantly. It reflected much of the spirit of his own aestheticism and Glenn almost seemed to be thinking of himself as "the last puritan."

"Have you ever read the correspondence between Henry James Sr. and his sons (William and Henry) and Emerson?" I wrote at one point. "I think these would appeal to your Santayanism."[9] In another letter I wrote, "If you should have a few hours to spare, tear yourself away from Mr. Santayana and read Lewinsohn's *A History of Sexual Customs* (Harpers) a recent translation from the German, and a masterpiece."[10] Obviously I felt there was room for Glenn to move away from his professed puritanism. In the same letter I praised a recording he had recently made of the Beethoven C Major and Bach F Minor concertos with Vladimir Golschmann conducting the Columbia Symphony Orchestra.

> [I] wish to compliment you not only on the performance, which is superb, but also on the scholarship and literary skill that went into the article printed on the cover. Your insight into the psychology of the soloist amazes me; I was stimulated by the notion that, after all, composers are responsible for more than the music. They must somehow synthesize the social prejudices of an era, the mental attitudes of individual performers, and the physical limitations of the instruments in every composition.[11]

On February 23, I mentioned a book by J. Ma Corredor called *Conversations with Casals* which I had recently read. Glenn liked it and later (January 15, 1974) made a documentary for the CBC, *Pablo Casals: A Portrait for Radio,* honoring the great Spanish cellist. I also recommended that he read *And the Bridge Is Love,* by Alma Mahler Werfel, for "the light it sheds on the death throes of European romanticism, and especially the small personal vignettes of Schoenberg, Berg, Pfitzner and other composers who interest you." And I enclosed a clipping of Van Cliburn's concert "to show you that your playing has created some sort of standard against which other pianists are being compared. Aren't you ashamed to make life so difficult for other pianists???"[12]

Glenn had told me he might return to San Francisco following his New York recital and two concerts in Utah in mid-February. He was talking about spending more time on the West Coast. He'd found an exceptionally good Steinway and was thinking of renting a house in San Francisco. But on March 13, 1959, he wrote,

> Cher Pierre:
>
> Many thanks for your letter of the 23rd. I didn't inform you that I wasn't coming back because, knowing your telepathic insight, I realized that you would be aware of it even before I was. In point of fact, I have encountered a couple of other reasonably good pianos in the last month and hence, while I have by no means forgotten my affection for old 123, it does occupy a somewhat more remote niche in my consciousness.
>
> I have not altogether given up the idea of spending some time in the summer out there but I have found I think quite a nice piano in Boston which I may take to New York. This would certainly simplify matters considerably. The New York concert [February 13] was, I think, the best I have done there, despite what you might have read in the Times. . . .
>
> All the best for now and I shall let you know when I will be dropping in again. . . .
>
> Sincerely,
> Glenn[13]

The reference to telepathy deserves comment. Glenn had been phoning me so often I could almost anticipate the next call. One time he did call just as I was thinking about him. I mentioned this to him, and he said, "Aha, you are telepathic." Actually, this was an example of syncronicity (two meaningful events coinciding, i.e., my thoughts and his call), rather than telepathy, which is the ability to communicate mentally without benefit of speech, writing, telephone, or other media. Nevertheless, we would banter about our "telepathic rapport," which I suppose symbolized the closeness we enjoyed that year. After his January visit to San Francisco I had written, "I hope that next time you'll be able to stay here a little longer and that we can have a more leisurely and predictable exchange of ideas . . . drop me a line from St. Louis about your concerts, and in any case I'll be in a state of readiness for any telepathic messages during your performance."[14] Glenn loved playing around with such parapsychological concepts.

The year 1959 proved to be an exceptionally stressful one for him. In addition to a very busy concert schedule and the two trips to Europe, he made numerous recordings and participated in several radio and television programs. It was also a year of transition in the sense that Glenn finally decided to move out of his parents' home and establish his own residence. His friend John Roberts and others at the CBC had been urging him to do so for some time. John felt especially strongly about the constant commotion at 32 Southwood Drive, with Glenn coming home at all hours of the night and playing his tapes and records at top volume way past midnight, which clearly disturbed his parents. Besides, he was now twenty-seven years old, spending much time away from Toronto giving concerts, and needed a place to return to that offered privacy and security. Having become fond of the solitude of hotel living, his first choice was a room at the Windsor Arms Hotel, a wonderful old hotel, rather run-down, where many musicians, including the Beatles, liked to stay. Glenn had his piano there and later graduated to a suite. His old teacher Alberto Guerrero had died that year, but we do not know whether this affected Glenn emotionally. The accidental death of his beloved Banquo, a few years later certainly did. The dog had run in front of a car while on a walk with Glenn's father and was killed instantly. That news upset Glenn terribly.

In October, he was back in California to give recitals in Berkeley and San Francisco. But he looked unusually thin and pale, and seemed exhausted from the constant touring. His Berkeley concert, held in the University of California's Men's Gymnasium on October 25, was limited entirely to twentieth-century music, by Berg, Schoenberg, Hindemith, Krenek, and Morawetz. Despite the difficulties of such a program for listeners as well as performer, the gymnasium was packed and the audience wildly enthusiastic.

The recital in San Francisco, a matinée at the Curran Theater on

November 1, was a more traditional affair, featuring Sweelinck's Fantasia for Organ, Schoenberg's Suite, opus 25, the Mozart Sonata in E Major, K. 330, and after intermission Bach's *Goldberg Variations.* A few days before the concert, Glenn told me he wasn't feeling well, feared becoming ill, and wanted to cancel it. That made me very unhappy not only for him but because I had never heard the *Goldbergs* played live. So I recommended that he go to see Malcolm Watts, a professor of medicine at the University of California and one of my former teachers. Dr. Watts gave Glenn a clean bill of health and he reluctantly went ahead with the performance. But in the middle of the Bach he suddenly stopped playing and complained to the audience about a draft coming from an open door way up in the balcony. The door had to be closed for the concert to continue. This struck me as exceedingly odd behavior for a seasoned concert artist.

In December, Glenn had the time to do some serious house hunting, and with the help of a real estate agent he found the home of his dreams. It was a very large country estate fifteen miles outside Toronto called "Donchery." The mansion had twenty-six rooms, seven bathrooms, a tennis court,—even a swimming pool. Glenn signed a long-term lease on December 13 and asked John Roberts to help him furnish the empty building. They made lists of items needed for the different rooms, including the kitchen, but because of Glenn's fear of crowds and the fact that he was easily recognized wherever he went and often asked for autographs, he asked John to do the actual buying. Stove, refrigerator, and "lots and lots of other things" were purchased and installed in the house.[15] Glenn told people that he was planning to occupy one wing, while the other wing was to be reserved for his "manager." But it wasn't exactly clear who that was meant to be. Problems had been brewing between Glenn and Walter Homburger, whom he regarded as being deficient in the area of publicity. So at one point he asked Winston Fitzgerald of the Steinway Company to be his manager. According to Glenn's biographer, Otto Friedrich, Fitzgerald "almost went through the floor." Friedrich cites Fitzgerald as saying,

> I ultimately did not go to manage him, for many reasons, not the least of which was that he had a habit of calling me at two or three o'clock in the morning, and this happened several times a week for years. I did not tell him I was afraid of being a prisoner of his whims. I said I had a life-long obligation to Steinways, and he accepted that.[16]

Very quickly Glenn got cold feet and at considerable expense pulled out of the lease agreement for Donchery. He then moved into a suite in an apartment building on Avenue Road. It was at the rear of the building where he thought it would be quiet, and it was furnished. But he didn't feel comfortable there either and stayed only briefly.

Late in December 1959 I received a phone call from Glenn that worried me because it indicated something was seriously wrong. Although his speech sounded calm, he told me that people were spying on him from the roof of an adjacent building, shining lights into his windows, making strange noises, and sending him coded messages. He said he could hear them talking about him and wondered if this was part of a plot involving an illegal business deal. The whole thing, he said, was rather "disconcerting." That's as close as Glenn came to admitting any fear. In his usual deliberate way he asked me: "Should I deal with these people directly, invite them in, go to their place, or write to them? Or is that a dangerous thing to do? Would it be better to call the police? Can you help me straighten this thing out?"

I wondered what in the world was going on. Was he trying to pull my leg? Was it a prank, or some kind of experiment in telepathy? Or had Glenn taken too much medication and developed a drug delirium? Might he be clinically paranoid and showing signs of delusions? As I found out much later, John Roberts also noticed some bizarre behavior around this time.

"I asked Glenn one day where a piece of furniture, a cabinet which had been in the corner, had gone, and he said, 'I've had it moved into the spare room.' And he said to me quite seriously, 'I didn't like it, it was looking at me, it was staring at me.' Glenn also would ask me whether I could hear the voices that he heard talking to him. I told him that I heard nothing, but that he shouldn't worry. There was nothing wrong with hearing voices."[17]

As a psychiatrist, I couldn't be that sanguine about it. Glenn was probably suffering from a brief paranoid delusional episode. Such disorders can be focal and transitory, and do not necessarily impair judgment or other aspects of reality orientation. One sees them among isolated people, most commonly among the elderly. My advice to Glenn was, "Don't call the police, but try to get hold of your doctor right away." At that time I didn't know that he had actually seen a psychiatrist in Toronto. I tried to explain that he was experiencing symptoms that could easily be remedied by treatment from a competent physician, but that it was not realistic for me to try to intervene over the telephone and at such a distance. "Of course not," he replied, seemingly relieved by what I told him, "but there's more to this than meets the eye, and I will send you a letter to explain what it's all about."

The letter arrived several days later. It consisted of a copy of the contract forms Walter Homburger used for engaging artists, plus a handwritten note that read:

Dear Pierre,

Herewith the contract! As I said on the phone clause 9 is the only possibility of escape—

Do think it over and let me know if you feel moved to become a conspirator. Rest assured, no further attempt will be made to persuade you if you decide against it—

Best,
Glenn[18]

In the margin of the contract next to clause 9, Glenn had scribbled a smiling cartoon face and the word "regardez." This clause states that artists are "under no obligation for failure to appear or perform in the event that such failure is caused or due to physical disability of the Artist." (Not a word about mental disability.) Now it became clear what it was that Glenn expected me to do. He wanted me to be "a conspirator" against his manager, certifying that he was too sick to honor the obligations of his contract to give concerts.

This request put me in a terrible bind. I wanted to help him in any way possible, but giving him an official medical excuse would have been unethical, since I was not Gould's physician or psychiatrist. I'd never examined or treated him. So I decided to do the next best thing: send a formal letter on my office stationery, giving an opinion that might perhaps carry some weight with his manager.

Dec. 31, 1959

Dear Glenn:

I cannot tell you how dismayed I was to hear about the trouble you are having. When you were here in the fall and almost canceled your concert I began for the first time to suspect that there is more to this than some kind of artistic eccentricity. You did tell me earlier about your illness in Hamburg, but I'm afraid that I took your statements much too lightly.

When it became necessary for you to call Dr. Watts to see you just before the concert I realized how serious your disturbance really is.

Since you have asked for my advice, I feel it necessary to state that I think you should under no circumstances make any definitive decisions about your trip to Europe until you have consulted a physician qualified to understand and deal with your problem. Something is clearly amiss, and I think you owe it to yourself and to your career as an artist to seek whatever consultations and treatment may be medically indicated. I hope that you will feel free to call me again as soon as possible so that we may discuss this matter further.

I have put these remarks in the form of a letter at your request, and

Gould's penthouse apartment, 110 St. Clair Avenue West, Toronto. Photograph by Peter Ostwald.

give you permission to use this letter in any way that you think may be of help to you. I do hope that the statements I have made may carry some weight and may assist you in ironing things out. My comments, as you know, stem as much from a sincere feeling of friendship and concern for your happiness as they do from medical knowledge.

Yours,
Peter[19]

What Glenn did with this letter I do not know. There's no sign of it in his otherwise scrupulously maintained correspondence in the National Library of Canada at Ottawa. I assume he either lost or destroyed it. Walter Homburger, when I interviewed him recently, said he had no memory of this entire episode and knew nothing about my letter. Nor did Glenn respond by calling, writing, or giving me any further information about what was going on. This left me greatly concerned since I assumed that Glenn had probably been mentally ill.

Fortunately, the episode was short-lived. During the early months of 1960 he was able to continue his search for a suitable place to live. While looking at different places with John Roberts, he liked to call himself "Mr. Roberts" and to call Roberts "Mr. Gould," a switch of identities that led to rather comical situations when John would receive "strange calls from potential landlords and landladies" asking what he wanted to rent.[20]

Finally, a six-room penthouse apartment was discovered at 110 St. Clair Avenue West in Toronto, which Glenn liked. It was in a quiet neighborhood and the rooms were spacious. Glenn managed to purchase the furniture from the previous owners and asked his lawyers to buy him out of his earlier lease on Avenue Road, again at considerable expense. In the course of time, he adjusted well to the new place, which would remain his official home for the rest of his life. But restlessness drove him to move back into hotels or to stay in auxiliary residences from time to time. And later he spent many of his nights—Glenn generally slept in the daytime—in a studio-apartment at the Inn on the Park, a modern hotel in a beautiful, wooded part of Toronto, where he installed his electronic equipment and did much of his tape editing. This was to be the scene of much of his later creative work, as well as an ideal retreat from the world at large.

17

DR. JOSEPH STEPHENS

Back in 1952, I had met Joseph Stephens when both of us were working at the New York Hospital. Joe's great knowledge and love of music was a key ingredient of our friendship. He plays both the piano and the harpsichord extremely well and over the years we have had many enjoyable chamber music sessions together. Joe's home is in Baltimore, where he joined the Psychiatry Department of Johns Hopkins Medical School, developed a private practice, and became well known in both medical and musical circles. His many years of research into the course and outcome of schizophrenia have brought him international attention. He is also a highly respected consultant and therapist.

After the difficult episode in December 1959, when Glenn told me about his acute mental illness and then asked me to intervene with his manager, I decided to ask Dr. Stephens for advice. He was familiar with the pianist's recording of the *Goldberg Variations* and admired it, but he had never heard or met Gould personally. So I urged him to go to a concert on March 2, 1960, when Glenn was to perform Beethoven's Piano Concerto no. 4 in G major, opus 58, with the Baltimore Symphony Orchestra. I explained my concern about his health and urged Stephens to go backstage and try to find out how he was getting along. He agreed,

Drs. Peter Ostwald and Joseph Stephens, both psychiatrists at Payne-Whitney Clinic, 1952. Courtesy of Dr. Joseph Stephens's personal collection.

and told me afterwards that he had introduced himself to Glenn by saying, "I'm a friend of Peter Ostwald," which seemed to have an instantaneous effect.

After the formalities were over, Glenn proposed leaving the hall with him right away. The snow was falling heavily, so Joe wisely headed for his home nearby. But Glenn, accustomed to driving in storms and blizzards in his native Toronto, immediately rebuked him. "You understand nothing about driving in the snow. Let me show you how we Canadians do it." Within moments Glenn had driven through an intersection nearly ramming into a car, put his foot on the brake, and caused the car to skid on the icy road. "I was scared to death," relates Joe, who was hoping to initiate a significant conversation about Glenn's playing. Instead, he found himself wondering how this man had managed to survive all those Canadian winters.

Fortunately, Stephens's house was close to the concert hall and they arrived safely. Glenn noticed the harpsichord there and told Stephens he didn't want to touch it because he had the idea that everything in his playing had to do with "tactile sensation," and that the secret of his playing was the feeling at "the very tip of his fingers." Stephens asked him what he meant by this, and he said the tactile feeling would be disturbed if he touched the harpsichord, because he remembered from the past the last instrument that he played. "He couldn't switch from the piano to the organ or the harpsichord without disrupting this tactile sensation which was so important to his playing."[1]

"I liked him very much," says Joe Stephens. "Glenn seemed very warm, very natural, very unaffected, and for some reason he seemed to like me, because before the evening was over I was already invited to come to Canada to visit him." It was apparent that Glenn was the one who would do far more of the talking. Joe recognized that Glenn "was always a monologist." Two-way conversations were hardly possible because he was always pontificating to anybody who wanted to listen. He soon discovered that Joe was a perfect listener. Only a week after they first met, Glenn began calling Joe, always late at night, after eleven. "There was never, 'Am I disturbing you? Do you have company? Are you alone?' or anything like that.' The calls usually started with 'Ah, Joseph' or 'Ah, Herr Doktor,' or one of his awful imitations of someone. And soon followed the 'Twenty Questions' business where he would want to play guessing games with me."[2]

Thus began one of Glenn Gould's most important friendships, conducted largely by telephone two to three times a week and consolidated by occasional meetings. Glenn invited Stephens to visit him in Toronto, and several times they stayed together in the country retreat at Lake Simcoe; also, they saw each other in different East Coast cities where Glenn gave concerts. The relationship lasted for seventeen years, and I think it was as close as Glenn ever got to being involved in a kind of psychotherapy. Although there was never an exchange of fees, Stephens tried consistently to maintain clinical objectivity with Glenn. He kept his personal views in the background and never criticized, teased, or belittled him in any way, whereas I did occasionally raise questions about Glenn's behavior and criticize certain recordings. (For example, after his oddly manneristic version of the Preludes and Fugues from Bach's Well-Tempered Clavier was released, I asked him whether it was really necessary to break chords as often as he did. He became ruffled and replied, "Ah, don't you see, that's my trademark.")

With Stephens, Glenn found it possible to converse at length about aspects of keyboard technique. As Stephens recalls it, "I once told him that the whole secret of his piano playing is the internal precision. For example, if there is a passage with sixteenth notes and eighth notes, the secret is that it's the sixteenth notes which are so beautifully precise. And I said, 'That's why your playing is so marvelous.' " Of course this appealed to him because he knew it was true. It was at a time when people were playing very sloppy Bach, and he was playing extremely rhythmically precise Bach, very much like Landowska. He told Stephens he hadn't been influenced by Landowska at all, that the person he admired was Rosalyn Tureck. Stephens didn't especially care for Tureck's playing and felt that Glenn's approach to the piano bore absolutely no resemblance to hers. And so was established an interplay of likes and dislikes between two very intellectual musicians. One time Stephens asked Glenn to improvise for him. He was amazingly good at that. "Brahms, Schubert, Rachmaninoff—you name the composer—he improvised them all beautifully in their styles."[3]

Another reason why the relationship with Dr. Stephens worked so well and lasted so long is that, unlike many of Glenn's other friends (including myself), Stephens wasn't immediately taken in by the pianist's charisma. Because he had befriended many celebrities, Joe Stephens was not in awe of famous people. He explained, "To me, Glenn was a secondary pianist in terms of genius compared to Gina Bachauer, whom I had met when I was about twenty-seven and had really been a follower of, and had kept a very close contact with and gone out of my way to go to her concerts. Stephens was thirty-three when he met Gould, and by then he had learned how to deal with celebrities. Maybe that's why the two men got along. Joe sensed from the beginning that Gould couldn't stand criticism, so that even when he heard records that he despised, he never said anything. However, he did defend Gould's tempi in the Bach Partitas, which had been widely criticized for being too fast. "I actually compared them with many other recordings of the Partitas and found there really wasn't much difference,"[4] Stephens admitted to Glenn, who was delighted with this research and urged Stephens to publish it (which he did, under the name of Timothy Swanson).

Their relationship had another side as well. "One of Glenn's attractions to me was the fact that I was a doctor, and that he was a superhypochondriac," says Stephens. Indeed, during their initial meeting in Baltimore, Glenn had opened up about a serious problem with his left shoulder. It had been bothering him for some months, but he had said nothing to me about it during that stormy period in December when I was supposed to be his "conspirator." To Dr. Stephens, he now explained that during a visit to New York in December he had requested that the

Steinway technicians make certain adjustments to his favorite piano, CD 318. Glenn wanted the action to be much lighter, which led to arguments with William Hupfer, the chief technician assigned to work on two demanding pianists' instruments, Gould's and Horowitz's.

Hupfer was worried that the modifications Glenn was asking for would interfere with the true Steinway sound. During one of Glenn's visits to the Steinway workshop, Hupfer, trying in a coarse way to be friendly, apparently slapped him on the back. The move was a shock and a surprise to this vulnerable individual, who abhorred physical contact. (The jolt may also have activated forgotten memories of Glenn's childhood back injury.) Glenn immediately started to complain about severe pain, and he claimed that he had been badly injured. In describing the incident to other people, he often insisted that "Hupfer had actually grabbed him by both shoulders and shaken him so violently as to cause physical damage."[5]

After this frightening incident, Glenn had rushed to see his general practitioner, Morris Herman, who examined him carefully and told him there was "no evidence of an injury"[6] But to be on the safe side Dr. Herman recommended a consultation with one of Toronto's leading orthopedic surgeons, Morris D. Charendoff.

Dr. Charendoff examined Glenn on February 4, 1960. His report to Dr. Herman contains the following information:

> Glenn presented with complaints referable to his left upper extremity. He also informed me that about six weeks earlier, when he was in a sitting position, someone had pressed down firmly in the region of his left shoulder and scapula as a "demonstration of their affection." Since that incident he has been experiencing several rather vague complaints with reference to his left arm, consisting chiefly of a sense of fatigue, aching, and a sense of incoordination in the left arm and especially the left hand. He had noticed the latter symptoms particularly in his attempts to play the piano. He had also been aware of attacks of numbness and tingling affecting the 4th and 5th digits so that he was unable to properly co-ordinate these fingers in difficult technical pieces on the piano and that the above problems had represented a disability to him.
>
> Examination of Glenn at the time revealed no unusual findings relating to his cervical spine. There was a full range of motion in his shoulders and all joints of the upper extremities. There were no signs of any major motor nerve dysfunction or other lesions affecting the nerves of his left arm. The

> movement of the fingers and hand were entirely within normal limits, although he himself did not feel able to co-ordinate these movements as easily as usual.[7]

The symptoms Dr. Charendoff had described so far—fatigue, pain, incoordination, tingling and numbness in the fourth and fifth digits, all coupled with the absence of physical findings—constitute a syndrome that has often been observed among pianists and other musicians who seek help from physicians specializing in the care of performing artists. It is a condition that not infrequently develops among those who drive themselves mercilessly, practice and play their instrument excessively, and work under conditions of undue tension and stress. A recent change of instrument or playing technique occasionally contributes to the problem, and some studies have shown predisposing anatomical factors such as disproportionately large or small hands.

The labels usually attached to this syndrome include "overuse disorder" and "repetitive strain injury." It occurs also among other professionals who do high-speed work with their hands over long periods of time—such as computer operators. To what extent an overuse disorder is associated with some structural or physiological damage in the arm or hand is moot; but rest, physical therapy, and improvement in work habits are usually recommended to avoid permanent disability.[8] If not promptly treated, the disorder may lead to more serious complications like tendinitis or focal dystonia (abnormal muscle movements).

What Dr. Charendoff concluded in 1960 was that Gould "could have suffered a minor traction injury to the various nerves entering his upper extremity and particularly the roots of the ulnar nerve. Such injuries are referred to as neuropraxia. They can usually last anywhere from six to eight weeks, but do not lead to permanent disability."[9] Glenn's condition had quite a different course, however. First of all, he developed some rather bizarre theories of his own as to what was causing his symptoms: He became convinced that his left shoulder had been pushed lower than his right shoulder. X-rays taken at the time do show the shoulder blade on the left side to be slightly lower, but this cannot be considered a significant finding since many people who have no symptoms whatsoever demonstrate the same inequality. But Glenn treated the whole thing as a major catastrophe. He canceled concerts, fretted that he would never be able to play the piano again and that his career had been ruined. Furthermore, he instructed his lawyer to take legal action against the

Steinway Piano Company for $300,000 in personal damages. The case was later settled out of court for a lesser amount.

Glenn also sought several different kinds of treatment for his shoulder. Between January 8 and October 22, 1960, he received a total of 117 (almost daily) home visits from a masseur, Cornelius Dees.[10] A number of these massage sessions were witnessed by Joe Stephens, who says that "the massage consisted of Mr. Dees continually rubbing and kneading Glenn's chest, shoulder, arms, and back while Glenn talked and laughed non-stop. He obviously enjoyed being massaged, and I sometimes wondered, considering the sexually inhibited person he was, whether maybe this gave him some erotic pleasure. Ordinarily, Glenn had an aversion to physical contact. He let me shake hands with him only once, the first time we met."[11]

Glenn also received chiropractic treatment from Dr. Herbert Vear, who told me: "Regarding the Steinway matter, I found a lot of tension around and above the scapula [shoulder blade] on the left side. He also complained of numbness in the left hand. I treated him with ultrasound, and he felt that what I did gave him relief. But I often felt he had imaginary problems. He was a very difficult patient, coming for treatment only sporadically, and always telling me what was wrong with him and how I should treat him."[12]

On the recommendation of the conductor Eugene Ormandy in Philadelphia, Glenn began consulting an orthopedic surgeon in that city, Irwin Stein, as well, who would treat him intermittently for the rest of his life. At this point Dr. Stein placed Glenn's upper body into a firm plaster cast, elevating his left arm over his head, so that the left shoulder presumably would rise to a higher position. This had the effect of totally immobilizing him and making piano playing completely impossible. Joe Stephens once accompanied Glenn to Philadelphia to observe this procedure and found it appalling. Dr. Stein also recommended: "It would be nice to have vitamin B_1 (100 mgm), B_{12} (1000 micrograms) around three times a week—cut down frequency in 2–3 weeks."[13] Whether Glenn had this treatment I do not know, but he did take cortisone, a synthetic adrenocortical steroid, for some time, apparently with little relief.

Dr. Stephens wanted him to have a neurological examination to rule out any nerve damage. Numbness and tingling in the fingers can be caused by compression of a peripheral nerve, and Dr. Charendoff had earlier postulated an injury to the ulnar nerve supplying Gould's hand. So Stephens took him to the office of a neurology professor at Johns

Hopkins, Dr. Lutrell (since deceased), who examined the upper part of Glenn's body very thoroughly and also tested all of his cranial nerves and tendon reflexes. Lutrell pointed out to Stephens that although Glenn had "a slight tic, a little involuntary twitch on the right side of his face, there's not a thing in the world wrong with him neurologically. It's purely hysterical—a conversion reaction."[14] (The "slight tic" can readily be seen while Glenn is talking with Yehudi Menuhin in a film made for television in 1965.)[15]

I have asked Stephens, "Would there have been any way of explaining to this highly intelligent individual that emotional conflict, fear, anxiety can have an effect on the body, on the way we feel about the body, the way the body feels to us, and how well it functions?"

He answered, "I think that I had already sized Glenn up as one who didn't want to hear anything like that."

"Did you ever think of saying to him, 'Look, maybe you're seeing the wrong kind of doctor; maybe you should consult a psychologist or a psychiatrist?' "

"Never, I wouldn't have dreamed of it."

"That never crossed your mind?"

"Of course it did, but I would never in a million years have suggested such a thing. It would have been the end of our friendship."

To this day Joe Stephens feels that "the whole business with his shoulder was too absurd. Never for a minute did I think he had been hurt by anybody at the Steinway Company."

"What about the lawsuit?"

"Much ado about nothing. But I thought, 'Well, they're litigious people.' "

"So how did you, as a psychiatrist, interpret what was going on?"

"Well, Glenn already had the reputation of being a great hypochondriac, so I thought this was part of it."

"And what does 'being a hypochondriac' mean to you?"

"Well, that he gave undue importance to physical symptoms that really were not on an organic basis, and that he exaggerated their significance. Actually, the concern about his shoulder was out of proportion to anything that made physiological sense. It bordered on the delusional."

My own view is that Glenn probably had been physiologically damaged in some way, most likely because of the wear and tear resulting from his incessant piano playing under conditions of poor posture and emotional strain. I doubt that William Hupfer's "slap on the back" had more to do with it than to provide a focus for Glenn's complaining. There had been earlier nasty run-ins with the people at the Steinway Company, and we know that their artist liaison, Winston Fitzgerald, had recently turned down Glenn's invitation to move into his intended home, Donchery, and become his manager.

I agree with Dr. Charendoff that Glenn may have been suffering from a minor traction injury to one of the nerves entering his upper extremity. Such conditions are extremely difficult to diagnose and may require specialized electrophysiological tests of nerve conduction that were not done on Glenn. His misery was made much worse by his hypochondriacal tendency to exaggerate and dramatize physical symptoms. And the conflicting opinions and multiple treatments he received from different doctors probably confused him further. Being encased in a body cast may even have worsened his illness by forcing him to experience the terror of immobilization, something we will return to shortly.

Final proof of the ephemeral nature of Glenn's disability in 1960 is that he continued giving concerts that year. In the summer, he participated in the Vancouver Music Festival both as pianist and conductor. There he met the London writer and radio director Humphrey Burton, who was interested in the newly upcoming field of television for music. They developed a friendly rapport and agreed to collaborate in the future on a series of films about major composers.

It was unusual for Glenn to find any merit in the nineteenth-century piano literature, but around this time he began to feel an affinity for Johannes Brahms, whose Quintet for Piano and Strings in F Minor, opus 34, he had recently performed and recorded. Much of Brahms's music is suffused with a characteristic bittersweetness, a blend of melancholy and elation. In his personality, Brahms also shared some of Gould's qualities. Both men were outstanding pianists who wanted to compose and to conduct. Brahms, like Gould, was keenly involved in contrapuntal study and musicological analysis. Both led an isolative, almost secretive lifestyle, and both remained unmarried.[16] It is reported that Gould, as well as Brahms, experienced an intimate relationship with a woman who was married to another well-known pianist-composer. As with all great men, gossip will endure, whether or not it is based on fact.

Glenn had taken a special interest in Brahms's very demanding Piano Concerto no. 1 in D Minor, which he performed for the first time in Winnipeg, Manitoba, on October 8, 1959, then in South Bend, Indiana, on April 24, 1960, and in Vancouver, B.C., on August 17, 1961, with the young Zubin Mehta conducting. He also spent much time in 1959 and 1960 recording all ten of Brahms's Intermezzi for Columbia Masterworks. These are stunningly original performances, some with unexpectedly slow tempi and exposure of inner voices. Glenn himself called them "sexy," which was a very unusual statement coming from him, but he never explained whether it meant that the music stimulated him sexually or whether he thought it might turn on other listeners. In 1960 he also recorded three important works of Beethoven, the Sonata no. 17 in D Minor ("Tempest"), the "Eroica" Variations, opus 35, and the Variations in F Major, opus 34.

In 1961 Glenn was still complaining about problems with his left arm and shoulder. He again canceled several concerts, including performances with the San Francisco Symphony, which I regretted especially because I had hoped to introduce him to my wife, Lise Deschamps. Lise and I had met two years earlier after a concert of the Santa Rosa Symphony conducted by Corrick Brown, in which her teacher, Egon Petri, performed the Beethoven "Emperor" Concerto. I was playing in the violin section and met Lise at a reception after the concert. Lise did not suspect that I was a psychiatrist, nor did she know that I was a violinist. Seeing me in a tuxedo serving champagne, her initial impression was that I must be the butler of this beautiful home with two Bösendorfer grands. One source of attraction between us was our mutual fascination with Glenn Gould, whom we spoke about that first evening. Lise, too, is a professional pianist. She had been so enthralled by Gould's rendition of the *Goldberg Variations* that she performed them at age sixteen shortly after his recording was released. When we met, Lise was preparing to enter the Chopin Competition in Warsaw. A French-Canadian from Montreal, Lise shared with Glenn similar cultural attributes.

After the "conspiracy" episode late in 1959, Glenn had stopped communicating with me; no more phone calls or letters, but I continued to hear about him from Dr. Stephens. Glenn knew nothing about my marriage to Lise Deschamps, on December 22, 1960, and when he received our bilingual wedding announcement he must have been quite surprised. He had been traveling, and the news did not catch up with him for several weeks. It clearly disturbed him, as we see in the letter he sent me on February 17, 1961:

> Dear Peter—you dog:
>
> What the h . . . do you mean by announcing your marriage two months after the fact. The nerve! And may I say that you have incensed not only the musical but the psychiatric community as well. Our mutual friend, Joe Stephens, fully shares my wrath at receiving such tardy notice. [Glenn

Peter and Lise. Photograph by Audrey Larsen. Courtesy of Peter Ostwald's private collection.

was being hyperbolic; Joe had been informed much earlier] I realize, old man, that you do all things casually, but, after all, there is a limit. And while I am in the mood to tell you off, may I say that you must never again come to Montreal [I'd gone there to meet Lise's family] without looking me up when you are that close. . . .

Now that I have let off steam, let me say seriously how delighted I am to hear of your marriage and compliment you on having the good taste to marry a Canadian. I certainly look forward to meeting her in April.

All the best for now,

Glenn[17]

As a wedding present he sent us several months later a magnificent book about Yugoslavia, with illustrations of superb frescoes from the old churches and monasteries, most of them probably destroyed by now in the recent civil war. Thus our line of communication reopened, and Lise and I both thanked him for his thoughtful gift.

Some cancelations were easier for Glenn than others. A particular problem arose in 1961 when he was scheduled to perform Beethoven's "Emperor" in Philadelphia with Eugene Ormandy conducting. Glenn was fond of Ormandy, who like a good father figure had earlier recommended the orthopedist, Dr. Stein, in Philadelphia, who had put him into a plaster cast. That, as we shall see, was one reason for Glenn's terror in contemplating a concert there. He agonized over how to explain this to Ormandy and prepared several drafts for the letter he finally sent. Here is one of the drafts:

> Dear Eugene
>
> I daresay you have received some strange requests from time to time, but I daresay that few of them will have been as stealthy(?) as the one I'm going to make to you now. (I have been trying to summon courage to call you for the last several days, but I felt that what I have to ask of you is so extraordinary that only by writing can I give it some better form.)
>
> I have developed (if that's the word) over the past months what can only be described to you as a great apprehension in regard to giving concerts in Philadelphia. Never before in my life have I experienced anything at all similar to it, for I have come to feel something approaching terror at the thought of playing there. I'm afraid that Philadelphia in my imagination has become inextricably confused with my weeks there and with the fact that during those weeks I was immobilized at least pianistically. . . .
>
> [The draft breaks off, but in another one he adds] I can only say how dreadful and quite idiotic I feel about this whole business and can only hope that you will not judge me too harshly.[18]

There were further drafts, including one for a letter to Ormandy's wife Emma. They are riddled with apologies, with concerns about letting the orchestra down, with misgivings about his fee. Gould views himself as a bad person, not a sick person. There is clearly an emotional illness involved here, a phobic reaction to the idea of making a public appearance in Philadelphia, which is associated in his mind with becoming "immobilized" again. "It is so much easier to develop a phobia of this kind than to shake (dislodge) it," he writes. He cannot chase the horrible fantasy away; it is obviously connected with the saga of the bad shoulder. He even reports a dream about self-injury: "I had a dream, for instance quite a few nights ago—in which I seemed to be waiting first offstage in the [Philadelphia] Academy and as I moved toward the stage fell over a rope of some kind and the dream ended as I apparently broke an arm. . . ."[19]

Tragically, Glenn couldn't simply admit himself to be emotionally ill and seek help from an appropriate professional. Not once did he mention the Philadelphia phobia to Dr. Stephens. Instead, he had to make a big deal out of it to Ormandy, dramatize and mystify it, and blame himself as though it was "idiotic" and "an aberration." He had to maintain control by dealing with it entirely on his own.

Ormandy took the situation in stride. Van Cliburn, recent first-prize winner in the Moscow Tchaikowsky Competition, replaced Glenn as soloist. Trying to shield Glenn from embarrassment, Ormandy wrote him: "Perhaps it will give you a chuckle when I tell you that every time I talked to Van, for some psychological reason, I called him Glenn. The third time it happened, he said he didn't mind at all because he loved Glenn and he considered it an honor and a pleasure to be called by that name."[20]

That sort of flattery always went a long way with Glenn. "He was such a maniac in search of praise and attention," says Joe Stephens. "Yet he couldn't see that the very things that he did were giving him that. The best example possible [from the perspective of his music making] is that he would play things at a speed which was absolutely remarkable, but [to him] this was not to gain attention in any way. This was the way he perceived the music. Whereas to me it was, 'I can play faster than anybody else, and with great accuracy, and so I'm going to be a show-off.' He was the consummate show-off, and he couldn't see it at all. He was always talking about the purity of the music, and how he hated virtuosity for the sake of virtuosity. He didn't have the insight to know that he was the supernarcissist who wallowed in attention."[21]

Although Stephens expresses skepticism that "somebody who is so out of touch with his own motivations" could benefit from psychotherapy, he did at one point attempt, subtly and diplomatically, to introduce him to a colleague in Toronto who might have been able to treat him. This is how it happened. In the summer of 1962 Glenn asked Stephens for the name of an internist in Toronto, and Stephens wrote to Stanley E. Greben, a recent Canadian graduate of the Johns Hopkins psychiatric training program:

> Dear Stan,
>
> I suggested that Glenn Gould call you about being referred to an internist. What he needs, I would assume, is someone who will take him seri-

ously but reassure him that there is nothing wrong with him if this is the case. Knowing Glenn, this could take patience and some psychological sophistication. . . . You might like knowing Glenn who is a fascinating person even when he's being hypochondriacal. Maybe he might come over to visit you some evening since you are practically neighbors.[22]

Glenn did call Dr. Greben, who is now a professor of psychiatry and psychoanalysis at the University of Toronto and a leader in the treatment of performing artists. But the request was for an ear-nose-throat specialist because of "a persistent cough," and Greben gave him the name of Dr. W. Goodman. About six weeks later Glenn called Dr. Greben to invite him and his wife for drinks at his apartment on St. Clair Avenue and dinner at Benvenuto, a restaurant in the apartment-hotel on Avenue Road where he had once considered living. "He was cordial," Dr. Greben told me. "He was clearly a very sensitive and shy person, but not standoffish. He didn't behave in a way which said, 'I'm a celebrity and you're lucky to be with me.' On the contrary, he was gracious and as comfortable as a shy person can be, and he obviously felt indebted for what little I did, which was five minutes over the telephone. But he was repaying my debt."

"What kind of impression did he make on you as a psychiatrist?"

"He wasn't finicky about his food, and he wasn't difficult about it, and he didn't give anybody a hard time. He wasn't difficult with the waiter, or demanding in any way. I'm very cautious to make any psychological interpretations of any kind, but the impression I got was of a person who was worried and frightened, and I would have to say phobic."

"What would make you say phobic?"

"Well, the way he dressed, for one. He seemed to me a person who was afraid of being chilled, of being infected, of being ill. It just seemed that way, and he seemed a little bit asthenic [weakened, debilitated], a little bit worried about himself, but not in a way that he put into words. He didn't seem hardy in his attitudes about his health. He seemed excessively self-protective, and I would think that was based on fear for his health."

"Did you feel you might want to be his therapist?"

"The inclination was there. He was a man I would very much liked to have befriended. But his shyness felt like a barrier to doing that. I felt I didn't want to intrude on him. I did have the feeling that Joe [Stephens] was hoping something might click. I would have been very positively interested, and somewhere in me I always regretted that Glenn didn't choose to ask me if we could work together. As you know, I've worked with many artists, and I have a great respect for highly creative, artistic people, and so I admired his way of handling himself, and I would have loved to see if he could be helped with what I took to be a phobic condition and avoidance. I've worked with a lot of people like that, so it would have been interesting."

"You opened the door as widely as you possibly could."

"Yes, but Glenn never got in touch with me again."[23]

Glenn certainly would have benefited from treatment sessions with a man as sensitive and knowledgeable as Stanley Greben. Since this did not materialize, it is my belief that Glenn, laden with terrible fears, was fortunate to have enjoyed the therapeutic friendship, professional objectivity, musical rapport, and subtle guidance which Joe Stephens provided so generously for many years.

18

THE PITFALLS OF COMPOSING AND PERFORMING

As he approached the end of his twenties, Glenn felt a sudden urge to compose again. This time he wanted to write an opera. He hadn't composed anything since 1955, when, at twenty-three, after two years of intermittent work, he completed a string quartet, his "opus 1." As we learned earlier from his composer friend Oskar Morawetz, Glenn's ambition to be a composer was linked to his wish for "immortality"—a desire that something tangible, stamped by the uniqueness of his personality, would remain after his death.

According to an interview given in 1962, Glenn thought of himself as "a sort of musical Renaissance Man capable of doing many things. I obviously wanted to be a composer. I still do."[1] And some people were convinced that it was true. Franz Kraemer, who had directed Glenn's early film and recording projects at the CBC, used to have long discussions with him about composing. (Kraemer himself had wanted to be a composer before emigrating from Austria to Canada; he had been a student of Alban Berg.) "Basically Glenn was a composer," Kraemer told me. "He worked everything out in his head, and his approach to music was absolutely contrapuntal and logical. His sense for counterpoint was absolutely extraordinary. While playing he always sang an extra voice.

Glenn was so highly creative, and if he'd lived another twenty-five years he would have composed more."[2]

The successful completion of his string quartet had made Glenn feel both proud and embarrassed—proud because he felt it to be a genuine expression of his musical creativity ("a subjective synthesis of all that has most deeply affected [my] adolescence"),[3] and embarrassed because he knew that the quartet betrayed his unfamiliarity with the capabilities of string instruments. While working on it he had asked for technical advice from several experienced musicians, including Harvey Olnick.

> He used to call me sometimes at one o'clock in the morning because he had written three more bars to the quartet and he wanted to play the whole thing [Olnick recalled]. He wanted admiration the whole time, and indeed I thought what he was doing was miraculous. But as a piano piece, not as a quartet. Because he didn't really learn that you have to move registers around in order to make things interesting. And the composition was an act of will, of deciding beforehand that he wanted to do this.[4]

Glenn seems to have learned quickly, for in its final form his quartet makes quite effective use of the string medium and is surprisingly free of pianistic clichés. What immediately strikes the listener is the seriousness of this work. Rarely does the music show any of that lightheartedness or facetiousness which Glenn radiated in his social behavior. Instead, we have thirty-five minutes of deeply somber, occasionally agitated, and at times almost unbearably intense polyphonic music. The underlying tonality, F minor, sets the basically melancholy mood. The quartet is composed in a style that has become thoroughly outmoded, sounding at times like something Anton Bruckner or Richard Strauss might have written. There is no trace of the atonality of those twentieth-century composers, Schoenberg, Berg, and Webern, whose work Glenn was so familiar with and had been championing in his concerts.

Glenn wrote a long essay about his string quartet, commenting that it does not reflect "my great admiration for the music of Schoenberg" and that it happily declared an equally strong affection for "the Viennese romantics of a generation before Schoenberg."[5] Indeed, he was coming to develop a strong partiality for the music of Richard Strauss, a contemporary of Schoenberg who adhered stubbornly to the late Romantic style while totally ignoring the new twelve-tone method of composing. Glenn devoured Strauss's tone-poems and operas. He knew many of them by heart, and he loved playing his own piano transcriptions of these works while singing or mouthing the vocal lines. Among his favorites were the string sextet that opens the opera *Capriccio,* and the *Metamorphosen* for string orchestra written when Strauss was eighty-one years old. Both compositions may have served as models for Glenn's string quartet. "I was writing a work within a harmonic language utilized by composers whom I adored," he observed, "yet I was working in this language with a kind of contrapuntal independence which I had learned from more recent and, indeed, from much older masters."[6]

The quartet begins mysteriously, with a four-note motive played by the second violin hovering over a fog of notes held by the lower strings:

Musical example of Gould's quartet.

This nuclear motive generates everything that happens throughout the entire work. It permeates the lengthy introduction, empowers the gorgeous, songlike second theme, controls the very complicated development section, and is even transformed into a fugue. At one point, in three hundred measures of what Glenn was hesitant to call a "Coda," the instruments replay many of the contrapuntal evolutions induced earlier by the four-note motive. A long recapitulation section mingles the various themes in a dense counterpoint and again exposes everything that has happened before.

Glenn's quartet tends to exploit the mid- to low ranges of the four string instruments almost exclusively, seldom venturing into high-register sonorities, which produces a sense of uniformity. But the resulting monotony is dispelled by occasional dramatic "subclimaxes," achieved by a sudden brightening of the texture through harmonic resolution. Finally, he puts this great slithering contrapuntal beast of a string quartet to rest amidst layers of calm tremolos played by the different instruments.

One is left with the impression that the composer has done a first-rate job resurrecting the juicy Romantic style that was in fashion during the latter half of the nineteenth century and that Richard Strauss so successfully carried forward into the twentieth. Gould shows great skill in mimicking this style while displaying an adroit use of counterpoint. Although the work seems overly long in places, listening to it can be a moving experience. But considering that this music stems from an iconoclast who prided himself on being highly innovative, its downright conservatism is exasperating. Perhaps Gould as composer hadn't yet found his own voice, the ability to "speak in a tongue that has not previously been heard," as the musicologist Maynard Solomon puts it.[7] Or, more likely, this was his own true voice, and he was using it to express what was most certainly a conservative side of himself. In many ways Glenn did indeed have the qualities of an old Canadian backwoodsman, settled in his own beliefs, loyal to his national origins, self-sufficient, and disinterested in progress. He wore the same kind of clothes all his life. He seldom varied his diet; for a while it was steaks, then fish, later nothing but scrambled eggs. He had a passion for solitude, and he pursued his projects with single-minded energy. Besides, Richard Strauss was a musician Glenn worshipped, so why not borrow the mantle of this older man while exploring how far he himself could go as a composer.

Perhaps that is the most important message of Gould's string quartet. He regarded it as a highly personal expression of his formative years. One of the things he had enjoyed most in his youth was listening to Wagner's *Tristan und Isolde,* which he said made him weep.[8] (Weeping was something Glenn was never observed doing.) He recognized that there had been unconscious factors motivating him to compose the way he did, remarking, "I was not shaping the quartet—it was shaping me."[9] And he knew that he could do better. "The system must be cleansed of Opus Ones," he wrote; "the therapy of this spiritual catharsis will not remedy a native lack of invention. It's Opus 2 that counts!"[10]

But there would never be an opus 2 during his lifetime, nor did Glenn ever again try to write a strictly instrumental work. (However, other compositions were published after his death.) His desire to articulate his ideas in speech and writing rather than pure music, and to dramatize them through performance and filmmaking, was to consume much of his creative energy, so that "being a composer" remained largely a matter of fantasy, part of his imagined self-image but very rarely a reality. Only sporadically did he try to make the fantasy come true, as can be seen when one looks through his personal papers and here and there finds a reference to something he wanted to compose or a fragment of music he had actually written. For example, in a letter to the composer David Diamond in 1959: "I am struggling with the sonata for clarinet and piano, which I am desperately trying to prevent from becoming a quintet. My piano writing always has a habit of getting over-rich and assuming a short [sic] of organ pedal for the left hand which always ends up being unplayable except for the cello."[11] No trace of such a composition has survived.

As soon as he finished writing the string quartet, Glenn was pushing to have it performed. He browbeat the violist Otto Joachim, a founding member of the Montreal String Quartet, into taking a look at the score.

> Reach for your most reliable sedative [he wrote Joachim]. You are about to receive a blast! As you will no doubt recollect—the quartet has been in your possession for well nigh on 2 months [. . . .] I have waited with exemplary patience, not usually identified with my temperament. And in the past couple of months, I have given you guys a helluva lot of free publicity. Your performance? of [the quartet] has been mentioned in numerous interviews on my trips—Naturally, all this stems from motives of the greatest altruism.[12]

The Montreal String Quartet made a broadcast transcription of Glenn's quartet for the CBC in 1956, and in 1960 it was recorded for commercial release by the Symphonia Quartet of Cleveland (Columbia MS 6178). An excellent recent recording is the one by Bruno Monsaingeon, Gilles Apap, Gérard Caussé, and Alain Meunier (Sony SK 47 184). These recordings probably exist only because Glenn was such a famous musician. No major string ensemble has made his quartet part of their repertory. At one point he buttonholed Mark Gottlieb, first violinist of the Claremont Quartet, about playing it, but was turned down. "This juvenile work was just impossible for us," Mark told me. "It reeked of a bygone age; no audience today would want to sit through such a piece."[13]

Glenn spoke repeatedly about wanting to compose an opera, and at twenty-nine his infatuation with the music of Richard Strauss actually inspired him to jot down some ideas for an opera to be called *Children II* or *Richard Strauss Writes an Opera.* The intended cast was:

1. The composer
2. The composer's daughter
3. her husband
4. 12-tone composer
5. Diatonicist
6. Electronicist

An autobiographical element is very obvious in the few surviving fragments of dialogue (I assume it is the composer's daughter who is singing here):

> Father, what is success if you cannot enjoy it . . . you need the proof that you have succeeded—look at Wagner, how the world was at his feet—did it prevent him from writing more? No, it inspired him. . . . Think of it father, your opera given by Karajan, your sonata played by Cliburn—your symphony given by Bernstein.

Here's another fragment, presumably the "12-tone composer" is talking to "the composer":

> Surely, doctor, you must know that this infinitely heaving romantic style of yours is ludicrous. This is the day of atonality, not tonality . . . this is the only way to express your age, doctor, an age in which the man creates and orders all, commands all, doesn't kneel, doesn't beg, doesn't cry—because there's no one to lift him up, to grant him favors, or to wipe his tears.[14]

If Gould composed any music for this or any other operas, he must have destroyed it, for nothing resembling notation for an opera can be found among his papers. But one shouldn't belittle his creativity. He just didn't have it in him to be a composer of operas or other large-scale works. His String Quartet, opus 1, is sufficient proof of his talent as a composer. But the time and energy needed for doing this kind of work he directed elsewhere.

The period 1961–62 saw recordings of three piano concertos—Mozart no. 24 in C Minor, K. 491, with Walter Susskind conducting the CBC Symphony; the Schoenberg Piano Concerto, opus 42, with Robert Craft conducting the CBC Symphony; and the Beethoven Concerto no. 4 in G Major, opus 58, with Leonard Bernstein conducting the New York Philharmonic. In addition, Glenn recorded Richard Strauss's setting of Alfred Lord Tennyson's epic poem, *Enoch Arden,* with Claude Rains as the narrator; Beethoven's Sonata no. 3 in A Major for Cello and Piano, opus 69, with Leonard Rose; Beethoven's Trio in D Major, opus 70, no. 1, ("Ghost"), with Leonard Rose and Oscar Shumsky; Bach's *Art of the Fugue* Nos. 1–9, played on the organ of All Saint's Church in Kingsway, Ontario; and the Preludes and Fugues Nos. 1–8 from Bach's *Well-Tempered Clavier.*

During those twenty-four months Glenn also made five television programs and participated in five radio broadcasts. Most of the television programs featured his discussion and presentation of various musical works, many with the collaboration of other musicians and singers, and

Gould at the organ, 1962. Photograph by Dale Barnes. Courtesy of CBC.

often on a very ambitious scale. For example, a Richard Strauss Festival televised on October 15, 1962, included, in addition to Gould's discussion of his affinity for this composer, three sets of songs by Strauss with the soprano Lois Marshall; the Suite, opus 60, "Le Bourgeois Gentilhomme," with an orchestra conducted by Oscar Shumsky; and the first movement of Strauss's Sonata for Violin and Piano in E-flat Major, opus 18, played by Shumsky and Gould.

Notable among the radio broadcasts was Glenn's first venture into a documentary style focused on an important musician. This one was called *Arnold Schoenberg: The Man Who Changed Music.* Over the years it would be followed by other radio documentaries on Leopold Stokowski, Pablo Casals, Richard Strauss, and a series called *Master Musician* presenting Yehudi Menuhin. When Glenn was in San Francisco for concerts in February 1962, he mentioned the Schoenberg documentary and I told him that I had met the composer in 1948 when he was teaching at the Music Academy of the West in Santa Barbara. I was enrolled there as a summer student and privileged to attend Schoenberg's lectures on musical analysis. He would explain in a breathtakingly precise way the detailed structure of a major composition, and I'll never forget his brilliant analysis of the Brahms Second Symphony. Schoenberg also invited selected students and faculty members to his home. Since I was studying with Sidney Griller of the Griller Quartet from London, which was planning to perform one of the master's string quartets, I was able to attend an evening totally devoted to Schoenberg's chamber music at his own house. He played recordings of the four string quartets and commented liberally on their construction. There was little small talk, and when Sidney Griller asked me at the end of the evening to make a thank-you speech, I became completely tongue-tied.

Glenn wanted to interview me for his two-hour Schoenberg documentary. His plan was to include interviews with people who felt strongly about the composer and would have contrasting opinions of him and his work. The final selection was Aaron Copland, Winthrop Sargeant, Goddard Lieberson, István Anhalt, Schoenberg's wife Gertrude, and myself. Glenn then edited the tapes in such a way that we seemed to be talking to each other, at times contradicting each other. When the project was nearing completion, he wrote to me:

> Dear Peter:
>
> Just thought I would let you know that our interview has become a most valued contribution to the Schonberg [sic] documentary. We have tried to surround it with rather good company including Aaron Copland, Goddard Leiberson [sic] and Winthrop Sargent all of them reminiscing to various degrees about experience with Schonberg or giving their views of his music. But I must say that, in some ways your interview has proven the most valuable of all, since it throws an especially human light on Schonberg. I am grateful to have it.
>
> There is one moment in Copland's interview in which he says something to the effect that "Schonberg was really not my kind of person—not the sort of person I would want to spend an evening with." He says this by way of indicating that he found Schonberg rather reluctant to absorb the views of others in conversation, but I am going to truncate his comment, I think, with that in which you begin "I spent an evening with Schonberg"—or words to that effect. In any case, between you and Mr. Copland, at this point there will be, I hope, a rather delicious dialogue which should provide, if not a clear picture of Schonberg in toto, at least an illuminating contrast of view.
>
> Do give my best to Lise and, of course, best to you.
>
> Sincerely,
>
> Glenn Gould[15]

The Schoenberg documentary was broadcast by the CBC on August 8, 1962. A month later Glenn wrote me that "the show was apparently a great success and [the CBC] now wants to re-run it (gad, Sir, you should have been on a commission)."[16]

Although he continued to give concerts—thirty-two in 1961 and twenty-two in 1962—they were getting to be increasingly joyless affairs. Dr. Stephens was with him on January 2, 1962, when he played Bach's Fifth *Brandenburg Concerto* and Strauss's *Burleske* in Baltimore.

"I remember he had to take his pills to calm himself down," Stephens says. "The pill he took was called 'Soma' [carisoprodol, manufactured by Wallace Laboratories; usually prescribed as an adjunct to rest, physical therapy, and other measures to relieve discomfort in the muscles and joints, it also has sedating effects]. While playing the *Brandenburg Concerto,* he got lost in the first movement and made mistakes. Afterwards he absolutely insisted that the tape of this performance never be used in any of the orchestra's broadcasts."[17]

In Oakland, California, on February 6, with Gerhard Samuel conducting the Oakland Symphony, Glenn played the Fourth Piano Concerto by Beethoven, a work he knew backwards and forwards, but he had the miniature score open in front of him and even while playing the cadenza consulted notes in the back of the book. "The first movement was slow and ponderous," wrote Alfred Frankenstein in the *San Francisco Chronicle,* "but the whole was nevertheless suffused with the irresistible poetry of Gould and with his incomparable singing tone."[18]

Five days later, during an all-Beethoven recital at Hertz Hall in Berkeley, he didn't rely on the printed music but played quite a few unexpected notes in the Sonata opus 31, no. 2, (the "Tempest"). My wife had recently performed that sonata in a concert at the San Francisco Conservatory. We couldn't tell whether Glenn was improvising to cover a memory lapse or had mislearned the sonata. (None of his recordings of this work contain the notes in question.) After the concert, Lise congratulated him on his beautiful performance and added, earnestly: "We must be using different editions for the 'Tempest' because I heard you play some very unexpected note sequences in the recitative." Glenn brushed the comment aside with "Oh, it's quite possible; I don't recall."

For a solo recital on February 15 in the San Francisco Opera House, he again relied on the score, pasted on very large pieces of cardboard, for the Beethoven Sonata opus 109, no. 30. This was another work he had played many, many times and recorded. Evidently he had lost confidence in his memory. But the playing was outstanding. "Gould's supremacy is partly a matter of rhythm," wrote Alfred Frankenstein, "a living, breathing, free rhythm held in check by perfect taste and partly a matter of tone. Nobody draws so richly colored and singing a sound from the piano."[19]

After the concert, Glenn came over to our house. By now we had a six-month-old baby, so I drove home in our car to relieve the baby-sitter, while Glenn drove with Lise in his own rented car. First they stopped at the Huntington Hotel to deposit his folding chair and pick up a few items of clothing. "The disorder in his room was unbelievable," Lise remembers. "Clothes, music, and boxes of books were strewn around helter-skelter, and I had to help him find what he needed, because he couldn't leave the room without an extra scarf, a warmer pair of gloves, and a heavier sweater." She found Glenn's driving "as unpredictable as his musical style." Red lights were sometimes ignored and he veered erratically between lanes (1962 was one of the years Glenn nearly had to forfeit his Canadian driver's license). Just before getting to our house, you make a sharp right-hand turn off the boulevard into a street that goes uphill. "Glenn turned so abruptly that he landed on the sidewalk, and he continued to drive on for a moment, nearly hitting a tree while trying to avoid the cars parked along the curb," says Lise. "I was surprised to be in one piece when we got home. But I must add that he apologized in a most charming manner."

Once there, he was a delightful guest, relaxed, charming, full of humor. We sat down in the dining room for a midnight supper. Lise had prepared one of her elaborate meals, thinking he would be famished, but he spent more time singing than eating. "Oh, it's very good," he said about the food, "but let me sing you my latest composition, *So You Want to Write a Fugue*." After that he made a bee-line for the Blüthner which he'd always liked. "But Lise, how can you possibly play on this chair," he scolded after spotting the Chippendale with a conventional high seat she was then using. "We searched for a box he could sit on to approximate his own chair. We found none, so he had to settle for the Chippendale." And then it was Strauss, Strauss, Strauss nonstop for the next two hours. Glenn played huge selections from *Elektra, Der Rosenkavalier, Die Frau ohne Schatten,* and *Capriccio,* mimicking all the vocal parts and producing a lush orchestral sound from the piano. He was having great fun, and it was an exhilarating experience for us. But we were getting tired, and when Lise suggested preparing an early breakfast for the three of us before our daughter's six o'clock feeding, he took the hint and drove back to his hotel.

Only three months later an unhappy event took place that proved embarrassing to Leonard Bernstein and hurtful to Glenn Gould. They were scheduled to perform Brahms's First Piano Concerto in D Minor, opus 15, with the New York Philharmonic on April 6 and 8. Glenn had already performed it three times and had been doing a lot of thinking about this concerto, which is one of the more problematic works in the piano literature. Conceived originally as a chamber music piece, it generated a very negative response when Brahms himself first performed it as a concerto. To understand Gould's interpretation of this work, one must recognize that he held an exceedingly biased view of the conventional concerto. Gould thought of it as a vehicle for "competition" between soloist and orchestra:

> . . . the monumental figures like Beethoven and Brahms almost always come off second best as concerto writers, perhaps because their native sensibilities balk at pampering the absurd conventions of the concerto structure: the orchestral pre-exposition setup, to titillate the listener's expectation of a grand dramatic entrance for the soloist; the tiresomely repetitive thematic structure, arranged to let the soloist prove that he really can turn that phrase to a more rakish tilt than the fellow on first clarinet who just announced it, and above all the outdated aristocracy of cadenza writing—the posturing trills and arpeggios, all twitteringly superfluous to the fundamental thematic proposition. All these have helped to build a concerto tradition which has provided some of the most embarrassing examples of the primeval human need for showing off.[20]

Of course we know Glenn to have been a notorious show-off himself. Nevertheless, he claimed that his interpretation of the Brahms D Minor Concerto (he never performed the other one, in B-flat Major) was concerned with "an attempt to subordinate the soloist's role, not to aggrandize it—to integrate rather than to isolate. . . . I have chosen to minimize [the concerto's] contrasts. I have deliberately ignored the masculine-feminine contrasts of theme which have become the cornerstone of sentiment in the classical concerto tradition. . . . In the process, certain traditional accents have been avoided; certain dynamic proclamations have been understated; certain opportunities for the soloist to take the reins firmly in hand have been bypassed."[21]

What immediately bothered Leonard Bernstein was Glenn's approach to the tempo. The first movement is in 6/8 time, marked *Maestoso,* and Brahms had written into his own score the metronome mark 56 for the half-measure. Conductors therefore usually give two beats to each measure. But Glenn wanted Lenny to conduct six beats to the measure, which drastically slows down the tempo. Bernstein remembered their discussion: "You're not going to really do it this way. You're just showing me what you've found, with these mathematical relationships between one movement and another. And he said, 'No, this is the way we'll play it.' And I said, 'All right.' "[22]

Even after rehearsing the New York Philharmonic using Glenn's slow tempi, the conductor remained unconvinced. For Bernstein and the orchestra, this basic pulse was embarrassingly slow. But Bernstein had too much respect for Gould's musicianship to withdraw.[23] He decided that some words of explanation were needed to prepare the audience for what they were about to hear. Bernstein began by telling them, "Don't be frightened—Mr. Gould is here," which precipitated gales of laughter. Then he went on:

> You are about to hear a rather, shall we say unorthodox performance . . . I cannot say I am in total agreement with Mr. Gould's conception, and this raises the interesting question "What am I doing conducting it?" [laughter] I am conducting it because Mr. Gould is so valid and serious an artist that I must take seriously anything he conceives in good faith. . . . But the age-old question still remains, "in a concerto, who is the boss, the soloist or the conductor" [laughter]. . . . Almost always the two manage to get together, by persuasion or charm or even threats [more laughter] to achieve a unified performance. I have only once before in my life had to submit to a soloist's totally new and incompatible concept, and that was the last time I accompanied Mr. Gould [loud laughter]. But this time the discrepancies between our views are so great that I feel I must make this small disclaimer. So why, to repeat the question, am I conducting it? . . . Because I'm fascinated, glad to have the chance for a new look at this much played work; because, what's more, there are moments in Mr. Gould's performance that emerge with astonishing freshness and conviction; thirdly, because we can all learn something from this extraordinary artist who is a thinking performer; and finally because there is in music what Dimitri Mitropoulos used to call "the sportive element," that factor of curiosity, adventure, experiment. And I can assure you that it has been an adventure this week collaborating with Mr. Gould on this Brahms Concerto.[24]

It was a risky thing to do, and totally out of line for a renowned conductor whose protocol requires him either to perform without complaining to the audience, or, if he feels so much at odds with the soloist, to ask an assistant conductor to take over. Lenny always claimed that he had given Glenn advance notice of what he was going to say. "I'll just tell them that there is a disagreement about the tempo between us, but that because of the sportsmanship element in music I would like go along with your tempo and try it," and he insisted that Glenn even thought this was "a great idea."[25]

The performance was very slow indeed, but at that tempo Glenn was able to bring out aspects of the concerto that one rarely hears. The performance was recorded and one can hear the audience applauding enthusiastically. Except for a few moments that really test one's endurance, I too rather like this leisurely interpretation of the Brahms concerto. But there were people in the hall who disapproved. Anton Kuerti told me, "It was not a performance I remember very favorably. The tempi were not just slow, they were ludicrously slow, heavy. I guess it was boring as well."[26] The professional critics were unusually cruel. "Mr. Gould is indeed a fine artist, unfortunately at present suffering from music hallucinations that make him unfit for public appearances," wrote Paul Henry Lang in the *New York Herald Tribune*. And Harold Schonberg, writing in the *New York Times*, made totally outlandish statements under the guise of an imaginary letter to Ossip Gabrilowitsch (Gabrilovich, according to the *New Grove*), a famous Russian pianist who died in 1936, and a frequent performer of the Brahms concerto:

> Such goings-on at the New York Philharmonic concert yesterday afternoon! . . . I tell you, Ossip, like you never saw. But maybe different from when we studied the Brahms D Minor Concerto at the Hohenzellern [sic] Academy. . . . So then the Gould boy comes on, and you know what, Ossip? . . . The Gould boy played the Brahms D Minor Concerto slower than the way we used to practice it. (And between you, me, and the corner lamppost, Ossip, maybe the reason he plays it so slow is maybe his technique is not so good.)[27]

It is perfectly obvious from the many television films Gould made around this time and later, which could not have been tampered with by splicing the tapes, his technique was in fact miraculous, impeccable. He could have played the Brahms concerto flawlessly at any tempo he chose. Schonberg's diatribe was completely uncalled for, and Glenn felt very hurt by it. As for Lenny's undiplomatic behavior, Glenn showed no open animosity, although their friendship definitely cooled after this incident.

Among Glenn's private papers the following comment is scribbled in pencil:

> . . . the only misinterpretation of Mr. B's remarks which troubles me is that the oddities of his performance were perhaps calculated. . . . It was Mr. L. Bernstein who drew undue attention to certain departures in the norm in my interpretation of this work. . . . He suggested that it was the slowest most intractable performance he had ever heard.[28]

One result of this grotesque episode was that it reinforced Gould's already jaded view of the "competitiveness" and "destructiveness" inherent in concert life, and strengthened his resolve to get out of the business of public performances as soon as he possibly could.

19

RETIREMENT FROM THE STAGE

It was not so much an abrupt withdrawal from the concert stage in 1964 as a gradual petering out of an activity he had never really liked, and one that had led to increasing amounts of strife and discomfort over the preceding years. There had long been talk about retiring from his performing career. I heard about it when we first met in 1957, and over the years he had mentioned it to numerous people, including news reporters who didn't keep it a secret. Lately he had been canceling performances left and right. A note Glenn wrote at the Beverly Hills Hotel discloses that he had developed a painful, severe, and unexplained rheumatic condition in neck area, "which makes it extremely difficult to perform. Regret terribly that have no alternative but to cancel all Seattle engagements."[1] In 1962, he wrote to his friend at the BBC in London, Humphrey Burton: "I decided that when the next season is over, I shall give no more public concerts. Mind you, this is a plan I have been announcing ever since I was 18, and there is a part of my public here that does not take these pronouncements too seriously, but this time I think I really mean it."[2]

Lise and I, together with Joe, visited Glenn one month later in Toronto during the 1962 conference of the American Psychiatric Association

Gould at Lake Simcoe. Courtesy of Dr. Joseph Stephens's personal collection.

there. He seemed elated at the prospect of his concert career coming to an end but didn't want to discuss it. Glenn was very fond of different guessing games. He initiated Lise into his favorite and most mystifying one. After that we chatted about a variety of things. Glenn admired the blue dress Lise was wearing, and when it became time for us to leave—we were due at a banquet of the Psychiatric Association—he seemed to have difficulty letting us go. "The only reason you're leaving," he said to me peevishly, "is because you want to show Lise off to your friends." To smooth his ruffled feathers we agreed to visit him again the next day, while Joe stayed behind. The following evening Glenn invited us to have dinner at his "club"—his rather grandiloquent way of referring to the restaurant where we ate—and talked endlessly.

In 1963, Glenn gave only nine concerts, three of them in San Francisco in February, playing the Bach D Minor and the Schoenberg concertos. He had stopped flying because of his fear of being killed in an airplane crash, a very real fear since several important musicians had been killed in crashes—the pianist William Kapell, the conductor Guido Cantelli, and the violinists Jacques Thibaud and Ginette Neveu. So

Glenn was now relying on train transportation, which proved to be time-consuming and uncomfortable. He complained especially of cold, drafty compartments and thoughtless porters. When he visited us that year, he asked Lise all sorts of personal questions such as, "How old are you? . . . Oh! you're just a baby," and then quipped, "You know, I'm in love with Jacqueline Kennedy." He also treated us to anecdotes about recent train trips, and I suggested he ought to look into the possibility of purchasing a private railway car. A book of lavishly photographed railway antiques, with luxuriously appointed private cars, had just been published,[3] and I gave a copy to Glenn. His letter of thanks included the sentence, "I must say looking at them makes me realize that even if some of that collection did survive till the present, they probably would need such extensive re-springing et al that one would take quite a chance on trying to buy one, so I guess I'm talked out of that successfully."[4]

Paradoxically for someone who feared crowds and hated to appear in public, just before retiring Glenn began a brief stint as a lecturer. He read a long, erudite paper at Hunter College in New York about harmonic relationships and musical structure in Beethoven's Sonata, opus 109, that seems to have been way over the head of his large audience. They apparently had assumed that Glenn would perform the sonata for them, but he played only a few snippets to illustrate points. The same lecture was repeated at the Gardner Museum in Boston. Next, he spoke at the University of Cincinnati about the music of Arnold Schoenberg, and this time was so well appreciated that the university published his lecture.[5]

And of course there was the constant involvement in radio, recording, and television work, which interested Glenn much more than the giving of concerts. In 1963, he recorded many works by Bach: the Partita no. 4 in D Major, the Toccata in E Minor, *Well-Tempered Clavier* Book 1, Nos. 9–16, and the Two- and Three Part Inventions. That same year he masterminded a remarkable television program for the CBC called *Festival: The Anatomy of Fugue,* in which he analyzed the historical development of fugal structure in music, and with help from other musicians and singers gave examples of contrapuntal writing from the fourteenth century (Landini), the Renaissance (Orlando di Lassus, Luca Marenzio), the Baroque era (Bach), the Viennese or Classical period (Mozart), Romanticism (Beethoven), and modern times (Hindemith). Then came what for Glenn was the high point of the program, a performance of his own recent experiment with counterpoint, the piece for four singers and string quartet called *So You Want to Write a Fugue.* (Lise and I had been liberally treated to early versions of it when Glenn was in San Francisco.)

He called it "a five-minute, fourteen-second singing commercial. . . . What it plugs is one of the most durable creative devices in the history of formal thought and one of the most venerable practices of musical man."[6]

So You Want to Write a Fugue is both a delightfully effervescent spoof and an earnest advocacy of fugue writing. The bass sings encouragingly, "You've got the nerve to write a fugue, so go ahead." The tenor is concerned about practicalities: "So go ahead and write a fugue that we can sing." The contralto wants to discard the rules: "Pay no mind to what we've told you . . . just forget all that we've told you and the theory you've read," to which the soprano lends support: "Pay no mind, give no heed." Finally they all agree, "For the only way to write one is to plunge right in and write one, just ignore the rules and write one, have a try." When the string quartet starts playing, they briefly quote four of Bach's most popular themes, as well as Wagner's Overture to *Die Meistersinger.* "But never be clever for the sake of being clever," cautions the contralto, "For a canon in inversion is a serious diversion and a bit of augmentation is a serious temptation."

Glenn would have been the first to admit that *So You Want to Write a Fugue* is no profound or entirely original composition. "It is an ingenious, ironical and playful work showing Gould at the helm of fugal sailing, uttering whiffs of themes attributed to illustrious composers."[7] His basic wish was to make it sound like Bach, but in a lengthy analysis of the piece he confessed that the harmony is "Mendelssohnian."[8] Yet this is probably the most appealing piece he ever composed. His ardor for fugal structure is infectious. As he explained in his long essay about the work, "The idea to which fugue is most conspicuously the servant is a concept of unceasing motion. It is this nonstatic concept which makes fugal structure the perfect vehicle for the adventurous and subjective traffic of baroque art. And since this concept is carried forward into other eras, it offers us a partial explanation of the extraordinary historical unification of fugal practice."[9]

Glenn gave only two concerts in 1964, one in Chicago in March and his last one, in Los Angeles, on April 10. Appearances with the San Francisco Symphony were scheduled for that same month while he was still in California, but he canceled them and was replaced by the pianist Moura Lympany. On returning to Canada, he went to the Lake Simcoe retreat for rest, rejuvenation, practicing, and work on intended new projects. One of them was an important essay to be called "The Prospects of Recording," in which he articulated his philosophy about the demise of the concert hall and the superiority of recorded over live performances. He called it a "radical pronouncement," predicting that "the public concert as we know it today would no longer exist a century hence, [and] its functions would have been taken over by electronic media."[10]

Glenn wrote that public concerts have predominated in musical culture for only "a brief span," primarily because of the "substantial managerial investment" currently committed to them. These were not accurate statements, however, and they betray the fact that Gould's approach to musicology was artistic and intuitive, not scholarly. Though it is true that certain kinds of musical performance have been called "concerts" only since the seventeenth century (in contrast with operas, church music, music for dancing, etc.), the playing of music in public goes back to the very beginning of civilization. And many other factors besides economic ones have contributed to the way in which music is composed, played, and listened to, including changes in the notation systems, the kind of musical instruments used, room architecture, acoustics, and social as well as religious attitudes.[11]

Gould's long essay touts recent changes and improvements in the recording industry that have resulted in "conventions which do not always conform to those traditions that derive from the acoustical limitations of the concert hall." He praises the recording industry for the "astonishing revival in recent years of music from preclassical times . . . the neobaroque enthusiasm of our day."[12]

> But most important, this archival responsibility enables the performer to establish a sense of contact with a work which is very much like that of the composer's own relation to it. It permits him to encounter a piece of music and to analyze and dissect it in a most thorough way, to make it a vital part of his life for a relatively brief period, and then to pass on to some other challenge. . . . His analysis of the composition will not become distorted by overexposure, and his performance top-heavy with interpretative "niceties" intended to woo the upper balcony, as is almost inevitably the case with the overplayed piece of concert repertoire.[13]

Glenn envisioned a time when listening to music would be entirely a matter of manipulating a radio, record, and tape-playback system to produce whatever the listener wanted to experience. "Dial twiddling is in its limited way an interpretive act."[14] Listeners would "compose" acoustical events for themselves by picking the composition, the interpreter, even shuffling between different interpreters of a work, and of course controlling the parameters of loudness, direction, and balance. This vision has to some extent been fulfilled. It is possible today to create musical experiences entirely in one's home by using electronic equipment. But Glenn never seemed able to admit, or to accept, that the electronic approach is really quite compatible with the tradition of concert giving. Indeed, the practice of recording "live" concerts has brought the two media very close together. It was his own exquisite discomfort with public appearances that led him to disparage the concert hall, plus his conviction that only in the recording studio could he get results that matched his expectations of musical perfection.

Glenn was only thirty-one years old when he stopped playing in public, and at first it wasn't exactly clear whether this was to be a temporary situation or whether his "retirement" was permanent. Walter Homburger kept making future bookings and Glenn himself hinted that he might return to the stage from time to time. Homburger told me he had warned Glenn that "there's one thing you have to realize. Generally when an artist comes to town and plays, record sales go up, because there's renewed interest in him. . . . If you retire, what can happen is that your record sales income is going to drop. So every six months he would call me and say, 'I got my statement. Guess what?' So I would guess, and of course I guessed high and was still low . . . and he would tell me how much, and then he got suspicious of whether it was reported right, from Finland or wherever it may have been, and I said, 'It's not worthwhile checking.' "[15]

In fact, Glenn never again played in public. He became ever more convinced that it would be "a terribly retrogressive step to retreat back into the embrace of a concert."[16] In his box of mementos called "Keepers," he placed a note from Marshall McLuhan: "Bless Glenn Gould for throwing the concert audience into the junkyard."[17] With the hated crowds out of his way, he was free at last to indulge his fascination with radio and television. The problem, as everyone who worked with him soon came to realize, was that Glenn didn't have the same natural flair for these electronic media that he had for playing the piano. As John Roberts explains it: "Music was the talent with which he was born, and he had been perfecting his piano playing since he was a tiny child. His education in other areas was really quite limited. He didn't finish school and never attended a university, so that when he finally quit giving concerts there was this great vacuum that needed to be filled. He had to begin amplifying talents that had been more or less latent until now, and that were not as reliable as his immense musical talent. This required a tremendous effort of will."[18]

As music program organizer, and later head of Radio Music at CBC,

John helped Glenn enormously by facilitating his use of the studio, giving him access to the technicians there, occasionally suggesting projects, and at the same time letting him have the freedom to do anything he wanted. John made an office for Gould by installing a desk in a corner of the Music Department, adding dividers, and giving him his own telephone. He also commissioned a number of Glenn's radio recitals, some documentaries, and both sessions of *The Art of Glenn Gould* series.

For Glenn all this was certainly a step upwards in the communications industry, but it was by no means a total transformation in his life. He had long been doing radio and television programs at the CBC, sometimes with assistance from Vincent Tovell, one of the most gifted directors there, whom Glenn had handpicked a decade earlier and felt he could trust. Tovell, ten years his senior, was vastly experienced in techniques of broadcasting after years of radio work in New York and Toronto.

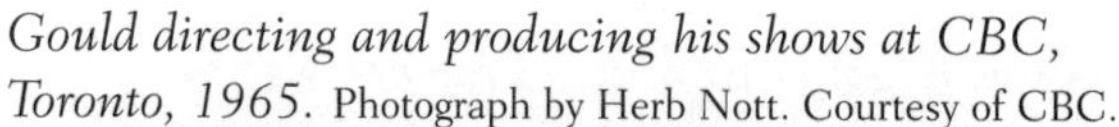

Gould directing and producing his shows at CBC, Toronto, 1965. Photograph by Herb Nott. Courtesy of CBC.

He worked closely with Glenn and became deeply impressed with what the young pianist was able to contribute to radio.

"Over the years Glenn had become his own producer in radio," Tovell told me, "and he had mastered the business of taking a microphone and recording what he wanted to record, when and where he wanted to do that. He was extraordinarily good at extracting material from people in conversational situations, then removing his own voice, and in fact making his own program compositions."[19]

Unfortunately, that was not the case with television. "You couldn't do television the way Glenn did radio, not then," Tovell explained. "It still was a matter of four cameras and a studio for a performance program. And the complications organizationally, that you could only have the studio for certain hours, and that there would be unions and all those problems of the costs."[20] Glenn would write the scripts and be one of the performers, but in contrast to his radio work, he did not operate the equipment, did not handle the tapes, and never directed his own programs. Tovell observed him closely:

"One of the curious things about seeing him in the studio is that he was at home. He was friendly with the crews, not gregarious, but certainly comfortable in that milieu. And he enjoyed the process of putting the elements together. He would have loved, I suspect, the possibilities now of videotape and all the ways in which one or two people can manage the material and make of it what they want. It was very clear that he always wanted to be his own director. But with television you couldn't do that. It was not easy to perform between 10:00 and 10:20 and then have to take a break. That was like the whole concert business which was so unsatisfying to him, because he didn't really have the kind of control of circumstances that his temperament required. . . . He wanted to think of himself as visual, but he really was very dependent on other people for all of that. His mastery was of the sound, and of the words."[21]

There wasn't much for Glenn to do in the studios that first year of retirement. Only one television program was produced in 1964–65, called *Concert for Four Wednesdays.* It shows Glenn performing (without an audience) one of his typical concert programs: Variation no. 30 and the nine canonic variations from the *Goldberg Variations;* Beethoven's Sonata, opus 109; Sweelinck's Fantasia in D Minor; and the Webern Variations, opus 27, all impeccably and beautifully played. And he did appear in public twice that year, but as a speaker, not a pianist. In June 1964, he was awarded an honorary Doctor of Laws degree by the University of Toronto and gave the graduation address. In November, he gave a talk, "Advice to a Graduation," at the Royal Conservatory of Music. He began his somewhat pompous speech by advising the graduates to reject advice and not live "too much by the advice of others." Then he presented them with a partially incomprehensible thesis:

> All aspects of the learning you have acquired, and will acquire, are possible because of their relationship with negation—with that which is not, or which appears not to be. The most impressive thing about man, perhaps the one thing that excuses him of all his idiocy and brutality, is the fact that he has invented the concept of that which does not exist. . . . The implication of the negative in our lives reduces by comparison every other concept that man has toyed with in the history of thought.[22]

I wouldn't call that a particularly upbeat message for music students about to enter the professional world as teachers, performers, and composers. But in view of the difficulties ahead, perhaps Glenn was realistic to inject a bit of negativism, for work opportunities in the field of music were discouragingly limited in the sixties, as they continue to be today. Only a tiny percentage of these well-trained graduates of the Conservatory and the university would find employment in orchestras, choruses, and academic institutions. Some might go into the not very lucrative, often demeaning business of giving private lessons; the majority would probably have to find other careers and be retrained in a non-musical field. So it was not inappropriate for Dr. Gould to warn them of "the dangers of positive thinking."[23] Besides, he himself was in the throes of a career change.

In 1965, the Russian-born Vladimir Horowitz returned to the concert stage after a prolonged absence due to emotional illness. Horowitz's success alarmed Glenn, who, while saying how much he despised competition between artists, had long harbored a distinct feeling of envy toward the older pianist. He discussed this at great length with Joe Stephens.

"That Horowitz business was so ridiculous," Stephens recalls. "Glenn felt that he had to outdo Horowitz. He told me, in no uncertain terms, 'I can outplay Horowitz. What is the mystery of Horowitz?' My answer to that was, 'I have no doubt you could outplay him.' Glenn had to prove that to himself by learning and recording two of the big pieces most closely associated with Horowitz [the Prokofiev Sonata no. 7 in B-flat Major, opus 83, and the Scriabin Sonata no. 3 in F-sharp Minor, opus 23]."[24] But that did not diminish Glenn's childlike sense of rivalry. He told many people that Horowitz "faked" the octave passages he was so famous for, and even made the outlandish claim that he once showed the RCA Victor technicians in New York how to repair a Horowitz tape by inserting a measure played by Gould.[25]

Glenn went to New York many times that first year (1964–65) after his retirement to make recordings for Columbia Masterworks. He put on tape an amazing amount of music by Arnold Schoenberg: all of his solo piano works (Six Little Pieces, opus 19; Five Pieces, opus 23; the Suite, opus 25; and Pieces, opus 33a and 33b); the *Ode to Napoleon,* opus 41 (with the Juilliard String Quartet and speaker John Horton); the Fantasy for Violin and Piano, opus 47 (with Israel Baker); and numerous songs—all the early songs, opus 1 (with Donald Gramm), opus 2 (with Ellen Faull), opus 3 (with Donald Gramm and Helen Vanni), and *Das Buch der hängenden Gärten,* opus 15 (with Helen Vanni). He also recorded three sonatas by Beethoven, no. 5 in C Minor, no. 6 in F Major, and no. 7 in D Major, and three sonatas by Mozart, nos. 11, 12, and 13 (K. 331, 332, and 333).

In January 1965, Glenn aired his *Dialogue on the Prospects of Recording,* a formidable radio program that comprised interviews with seven people, including Professor Marshall McLuhan, the pianist Leon Fleisher, and Diana Gould Menuhin, who had been a ballet dancer before marrying the great violinist. Glenn introduced the program:

> Electronic media have in the last half century drastically altered the effect that music has had upon our society. Music surrounds us as it has never done before. Music comes out of speakers in our homes and in our cars. Music provides background for the images on our television screens, helping those images convince us to purchase things we don't need; music is piped into restaurants to relieve us of the nuisance of conversation, into public places to make us less riot-prone, into elevators to make us less claustrophobic. . . .[26]

He then demonstrated the different qualities of sound that can be obtained when music is recorded in a large concert hall, in a studio, and with microphones placed close to or at a distance from the instruments. Next, he elicited comments from his guests. Their discussion, most carefully sculpted by Gould, was about the function of music in modern society and the influence of critics, editors, technicians, and others who are part of today's communications industry. Paul Myers, a producer at Columbia Masterworks who had been working with Glenn, said:

> I think one of the glories of music is that every performance is a little different, and that no two conductors, no two pianists, will ever play the

same piece exactly the same way. In the case of many artists they will play the same piece slightly differently on each different occasion. This is what makes music so interesting, and this is why so many people listen to it, and I would see no harm in having a performance of the Beethoven Symphony with a Klemperer first movement, a Karajan second movement, a Toscanini third movement, and a George Szell finale. . . .[27]

Another record producer, John Hammond, took a less optimistic view of current acoustic trends:

I feel that what has happened to recorded sound . . . can be summed up in the word inflation. I think the reasons for this are perhaps the egos of the artists . . . the soloist rather prides himself in being able to be heard in over one hundred pieces. . . . In a string quartet very often nowadays, I am sorry to say, four microphones are used as with stereo. . . . In emphasizing the parts you so often destroy the unity of the whole, and my feeling is that people who are not musicians, in recording, very often take over the role of the musician [and] most recordings by the major companies of symphony orchestras are so cluttered with microphones and engineers who give equal importance to all the voices that the composer's wishes are almost invariably flouted.[28]

Robert Offergeld, the music editor of *Hi Fi Stereo Review,* commented on the "unprecedented" revival of interest in Baroque music attributable to the recording industry.

The pianist Leon Fleisher was more negative about the value of recorded music:

I don't think that art should be governed by the media that are available to it. . . . The record retains vitality only as long as there is something unfamiliar in it. The moment we get to the point in our relation with a record where we know exactly how each phrase is going to be shaped, how long the fermata is going to be held, the record has served its purpose, it should be thrown away, because it no longer contains the essence of what music is and that is—a renewing of life at each performance.[29]

Diana Menuhin also had critical things to say about both recorded and live musical performance:

I am afraid of pinning things down too much. I am afraid of the modern scientific way of analyzing too much, the modern way of trying to catch

> what should be elusive. I always think of the studio interpretation of the record as something that crystallizes too much. [But, regarding live concerts] I've often thought . . . about people beating their hands together . . . this is absolutely absurd, it is something so prescribed, so idiotic . . . you cannot meet Beethoven on these grounds.[30]

Schuyler Chapin, director of Columbia Masterworks, was enthusiastic that "for the first time through records, through electronics, a new media has been given to the composer. . . . We are talking about something that has never been in existence before."[31]

Marshall McLuhan of the University of Toronto addressed the electronic revolution in visionary terms:

> With the recorder, the electronic drum as it were, the music of the world becomes available at any moment, just like an encyclopedia. We begin to develop a vast tribal encyclopedia of musics. Music becomes plural—you cannot speak of it any more in the singular—and as an international language. . . .
>
> I think there is a strong tendency in the electronic age on many levels for the general audience to become more creatively engaged. We are moving into an age, for example, when children will be taught how to program computers, when the entire production making process at the highest levels of industry can be entirely run from homes by housewives under a type of computer technology.[32]

All of these comments were interlarded by Glenn's brilliant monologues, as well as musical illustrations from the work of such contemporary composers as Lukas Foss, Henk Badings, Henri Pousseur, and Igor Stravinsky.

At the beginning of his radio career, Glenn had been criticized for his highly intellectualized and often arcane way of speaking. "There are times," reported the producer of one of his radio programs, "when even I couldn't understand what he was talking about."[33] And when it came to participating in impromptu interviews, Glenn was reticent since he'd once had the painful experience of being called "you nut" by someone who disagreed with him.[34] That convinced him to write out in advance not only the questions he planned to ask but also the responses he expected from anyone he was to interview or be interviewed by. He also learned to simplify his language and make his scripts sound more colloquial. TelePrompTer machines were used in his television shows to

Yehudi Menuhin joins Gould in the CBC recording studios. Courtesy of CBC.

remind the participants what they had to say and to avoid digressions and errors.

An outstanding piece of television work was made in October 1965 when Yehudi Menuhin joined Glenn in the CBC studios. "It was very easy playing with him," recalls the violinist, "because when we had different points of view we resolved them by just playing. It's no good talking. Music isn't resolved like that, any more than any emotions are rational. You just play, and you adjust, and if you're of goodwill and respect the other person, you adjust and you find your true meeting place. And that's what happened, because he was so genuine, so great."[35]

The program began with a flawless rendition of Bach's Sonata no. 4 for Violin and Piano in C Minor. Then the artists briefly discussed the piece they were to play next, Beethoven's Sonata no. 10 in G Major, opus 96. Glenn, as usual, had scripted the text in advance:

> *Gould:* When I approached this piece . . . I had in mind the pipe and peasant aspects of Beethoven, the quasi-militaristic quality of the early period.

Menuhin: I was wondering—because at first you took certain liberties dynamically and in phrasing of the line; you were very strict rhythmically and then later on you seemed to become less strict rhythmically—whether that was my bad influence. I hope not, because it was rather romantic!

Gould: I did find one compromise a little difficult to achieve . . . I found the Fughetta in the last movement a bit odd in that way, because I had thought of it as something terribly angular and tense and involved and looking toward the sort of Bachian counterpoint of the last Beethoven period, something in this fashion, *Sturm und Drang* [he demonstrates at the keyboard]. And I know that you—well you tell me what you feel about it, it's quite different.

Menuhin: Well, I wish Beethoven were here to hear you, because the way you do it is absolutely convincing. I don't have quite the courage to go against the indication in the score, which is simply *pianissimo* [both laugh].[36]

Following their well-integrated and not at all dissentient rendition of the Beethoven sonata, Glenn had programmed the Fantasy for Violin and Piano, opus 47, by Arnold Schoenberg, a work that Yehudi had never played before and didn't much care for.

Gould: The Fantasy is full of all sorts—I suppose, I don't know, correct me if I'm wrong—genuinely violinistic things. [It] exploits harmonics on the instrument and—

Yehudi (beginning to break away from the lines Glenn had written for him): Yes, and yet it's curiously clumsy in another way. . . .

Gould (also speaking more freely now and with a slightly mischievous smile): Putting all your cards on the table, Yehudi, you really don't like the Schoenberg, do you?

Menuhin: Well, Glenn, I was very anxious to take you up on the invitation to play it because I admire you and know that you know more about Schoenberg and have a genuine understanding of Schoenberg perhaps than anyone else. And I'm always interested in learning about something through the eyes of someone who understands it and loves it . . .

Gould: But if you could put it into one or two basic complaints other than the registrational ones and the fact that it doesn't quite fit the instrument, what is your *real* anxiety about this piece. I mean, what basically disturbs you the most about it?

Menuhin: Well, the fact that there is the curious discrepancy between the gesture and the words. It's as if you had taken the words apart of say a

> play, *Hamlet* of Shakespeare, and merely strung together an arbitrary sequence of syllables which had no meaning as such, but the rhythm and the gesture of the play were copied absolutely so that the person who knew the play would recognize where the love scene takes place and where the ghost turns up.
>
> *Gould:* That's a marvelous analogy.[37]

A closer look at Glenn's face during this disputation reveals his acute discomfort with Yehudi's deviation from the carefully prepared script. The right side of his face twitches conspicuously. But Yehudi was not one to kowtow to Glenn's way of putting words into people's mouths. He told me recently that he had warned Glenn, "I really would prefer to have a genuine conversation," to which Glenn responded rather arrogantly, "But I know exactly how you think." Indeed, Glenn never did understand why Yehudi wanted to digress from what had been so conscientiously written out for him in advance. "The man just doesn't know how to read," Glenn explained to the CBC technicians.[38]

"You see, Glenn's mind was so well organized that he didn't trust himself ever to be taken by surprise," says Yehudi. "He didn't like a situation where he wasn't in total control, of the music, of the people, of the voices."[39]

These two musicians had much in common, both having been extraordinarily successful child prodigies, but that was a topic they never discussed. They had met in New York a few years earlier, "quite by chance," says Yehudi, and Glenn immediately was "much taken by [my wife] Diana, he loved Diana and she loved him."[40] This might have cast an Oedipal tinge on the relationship, had there not been such mutual admiration and genuine friendship. Diana would send long, affectionate letters to Glenn, full of sarcastic and not altogether complimentary reports on "the old fiddler's" busy life, to which Glenn responded gallantly, in a rather sardonic mode:

> My dear, I am at one with you in your embarrassment [over Yehudi's attaining honors throughout the world]. . . . But what a comfort it must be for you to know that men of goodwill will rally round in this your hour of adversity. . . . One thing more, dear Lady Diana: I have chosen not to comment directly upon Sir Yehudi's elevation to the Knighthood because frankly, my nose is out of joint.[41]

Yehudi had enormous admiration for Glenn and invited him to participate in one segment of his eight-part television series, *The Music of Man,* originated with CBC in the 1970s. They debated the relative merits of live versus recorded musical performance. Glenn did not wish to expose himself as an artist, nor disclose his true self, to a live audience. He preferred the insulation of the recording studio. The following excerpt gives a wonderful insight into their differences both as artists and as human beings.

> *Gould:* It seems to me, Yehudi, that what technology is all about is the elimination of risk and danger.
>
> *Menuhin:* Has technology really reduced risk and danger, apart from music. Isn't there a risk of losing the sense of life, the sense of risk itself?
>
> *Gould:* Obviously, technology has its own dangers, but I think the purpose of technology is to give the *appearance* of life.
>
> *Menuhin:* Are you satisfied with the *appearance* of life only?
>
> *Gould:* Well, a recorded performance is not exactly real life.
>
> *Menuhin:* So we have to live on two different levels. . . .[42]

Indeed, Yehudi's idealistic perception of Gould even today seems to be on two different levels: "1. He was not an ordinary man, eccentric in his own ways. 2. People who were attached to the country, who hunted or fished or worked or belonged to the land—these were his kind of people. Ones that had to do with his own musical life, agents and others, those interested him less."[43] In reality, Glenn's contact with "people of the land" was very peripheral and limited to his outings to rural communities northwest of Toronto. He no longer spent much time at Lake Simcoe, and he was heavily involved with directors, writers, engineers, and technicians at the CBC.

Glenn's reciprocal admiration of Yehudi was made manifest in a radio program, *Master Musician/Yehudi Menuhin,* aired on May 7, 1967, in which he played a recording Yehudi had made at the age of fourteen of the Violin Concerto by Sir Edward Elgar. He also published a laudatory article about the violinist in *Musical America,* concluding that "For many of us, Yehudi Menuhin, artist extraordinaire, human being nonpareil, seems to be one of those rare individuals who could in time succeed to that unique place in the affections of mankind left vacant by the death of Albert Schweitzer."[44]

20

THE SOLITUDE TRILOGY

In 1967, when Glenn was thirty-five, he successfully accomplished two of his most burning ambitions. One of them was to create a new art form—something related to but not quite the same as musical composition, in fact, a way of fusing musical structure with literary expression. His other long-term ambition, not unconnected to the first, was to acquaint himself with the experience of solitude by visiting that vast, icy, and sparsely populated region of Canada called the Northern Territories, or simply the Canadian North.

Solitude was for Glenn a cherished state of existence. He preferred being alone. "People are about as important to me as food," he said in 1964, the year of his retirement from the stage. "As I grow older I find more and more that I can do without them; I separate myself from conflicting and contrasting notions. Monastic seclusion works for me."[1] Solitude reduced the tensions he felt in the presence of other people and allowed him to focus exclusively on himself—his thoughts, feelings, music, and artistic aspirations. He often said that only under conditions of solitude was he able to experience ecstasy. The negative side of this, unfortunately, was that conditions of solitude also brought into Glenn's

Sitting in doorway of boxcar, Gould embarks on a long northern journey. Courtesy of CBC.

consciousness those bodily sensations that he all too easily misinterpreted as symptoms of disease.

Yet he claimed that "isolation is the indispensable component of human happiness . . . for every hour you spend in the company of other human beings, you need x number of hours alone."[2] He believed, along with many prominent artists, writers, scientists, and scholars, that solitude is beneficial if not essential for the creative process. And he shared with many Canadians a sense of awe and respect for the inhabitants who sought or were forced to endure solitude through much of their lives, in those mysterious northern Canadian lands stretching all the way up to the Arctic Circle:

> The north has fascinated me since childhood. In my school days I used to pore over whichever maps of that region I could get my hands on . . .

> but my notion of what it looked like was pretty much restricted to the romanticized, art-nouveau-tinged, Group-of-Seven paintings which in my day adorned virtually every second schoolroom. . . . When I went to the north . . . I began to draw all sorts of metaphorical allusions based on what was really a very limited knowledge of the country and a very casual exposure to it.[3]

Indeed, Glenn never actually penetrated the Northern Territories. To do so would have required traveling by boat or plane, neither of which were acceptable to him. But in June 1965 he took a train as far north as trains could go, to the little town of Churchill on the western shore of Hudson Bay, in the province of Manitoba. Here he found the solitude he needed to start working on what he later called "technically a documentary [but] at the very least a documentary which thinks of itself as a drama."

The idea had been proposed to him by directors at the CBC who were looking for special projects to celebrate Canada's centennial year, 1967. Glenn wasn't quite sure what this was going to lead to, but his strategy was to invite four "guests"—a nurse, a geographer-anthropologist, and two writers who "had a remarkable experience of the north"—and ask them to talk about the North into his portable tape recorder. Then he added a fifth speaker, "a pragmatic idealist, a disillusioned enthusiast," to be the narrator.[4] These people did not know each other, nor did they ever meet. They were interviewed separately. In this way Glenn collected an enormous amount of tape-recorded material that he brought back to Toronto for the complex job of editing and splicing into a one-hour radio program to be called *The Idea of North.*

With assistance from technicians at the CBC, he fashioned the material into a "prologue" and six scenes focused on different topics such as "the Eskimo" and "Isolation and Its Effects." But that led to a program which would have run to nearly ninety minutes. A possible solution was to eliminate a scene or two, but Glenn was unwilling to make the sacrifice. And that is how he came to the crucial decision of using overlapping voices, "contrapuntal radio," as he called it, a way of constructing programs by having the speakers talk simultaneously rather than sequentially.

Although simultaneous dialogue had been experimented with in Hollywood in the 1930s, Glenn claimed it as his own invention. He had long been expressing dissatisfaction with the "linear" way radio programs were structured according to the tradition of having speakers follow one another in conversation. Influenced by Marshall McLuhan's writings on non-linearity, and under the sway of his own contrapuntal way of thinking (not to mention his pathological experience a few years earlier of hearing hallucinatory voices along with normal conversation), Glenn felt that his discovery of "contrapuntal radio" might represent a new art form. His confidence in this method of recording simultaneous dialogue was braced by the belief that human beings tend to underuse their ears. He believed that we can take in far more information by ear than we are willing to admit, and he enjoyed demonstrating his own capacity for multichannel listening by tuning in on multiple conversations in diners and other public places.

Glenn's technical approach to *The Idea of North* and the docudramas that were to follow was based on his deep understanding of counterpoint. He wove the voices in and out as a composer might write lines of music in a fugue. The prologue of *The Idea of North* he referred to as "a sort of trio sonata," alluding to the way three speakers interact. The first voice is that of the nurse:

> I was fascinated by the country as such. I flew north from Churchill to Coral Harbor on Southampton Island at the end of September. Snow had begun to fall, and the country was partially covered by it. . . . I could see ice floes over Hudson's Bay, and I was always looking for polar bear or some seals that I could spot, but unfortunately there were none.

After a while the second voice enters, that of one of the writers. Exactly what he says is a bit difficult to make out because he and the nurse continue talking at the same time, but here are his opening lines:

> I don't go—let me say this again—for this northmanship at all. I don't knock those people who do claim that they want to go farther and farther north, but I see it as a game, this northmanship bit. People say, "Well, were you ever up at the North Pole?" and, "Hell, I did the dogsled trip of twenty-two days," and the other fellow says, "Well, I did one of thirty days"—you know, it's pretty childish.

Then we hear a third voice, the second writer. He talks along with the two previous speakers, making it even more difficult to follow what each of them is saying:

> And then, for another eleven years, I served the north in various capacities. Sure, the north has changed my life; I can't conceive of anyone being

> in close touch with the north, whether they lived there all the time or simply traveled it month after month or year after year—I can't conceive of such a person as being really untouched by the north.

In addition to the voices of these three speakers—simultaneous and barely comprehensible—there is a background noise: the steady beat of a train rolling along on its tracks. Glenn likened it to a "basso continuo." At the end of the program he lets us hear a few bars from the last movement of Sibelius's Fifth Symphony. One might equate this symbolically to a six-voice fugue (five voices plus a continuous bass), being conducted by Glenn in a manner that was difficult for the ear to comprehend but not far removed from the tonal effect of contrapuntal writing.

As Charles Rosen states in his impressive book *The Romantic Generation,* speaking of the unparalleled contrapuntal art of Johann Sebastian Bach's *Musical Offering*: "The independence of the voices in a fugue of this kind is absolute, but it can only be partially heard. . . . A constant aural perception of six individual parts is neither a reasonable nor a desirable goal."[5] Perhaps this was what Gould was trying to emulate, imbued as he was with the masterful language of Bach. If Gould could not write musical fugues such as Bach's, he could and would produce sound images related to a style that had so permeated his soul.

He deeply enjoyed working on *The Idea of North*. The way Glenn applied his knowledge of musical structure to the verbal material he had collected during the trip north made him feel that he was actually engaged in a form of musical composition, a satisfying experience considering his relative lack of success as a more orthodox composer. He was in fact creating what he called "totally new sound perspectives" for radio. But he wasn't using the sounds of musical instruments; he was manipulating the sounds of speech. Glenn knew the difference only too well: "Sometimes one must try to invent a form which expresses the limitations of form, which takes as its point of departure the terror of formlessness."[6] Had he been more familiar with the visual arts, he might have compared his work with sound painting—a way of presenting voices in a veiled, shadowy manner that resembled the Impressionist painters, who had created a new way of viewing nature, of coloring, and of interpreting structure and shape. Instead, he stubbornly and incorrectly compared it to opera:

> It's perfectly true that . . . not every word is going to be audible, but then by no means every syllable in the final fugue of Verdi's *Falstaff* is either,

> when it comes to that. Yet few opera composers have been deterred from utilizing trios, quartets, and quintets by the knowledge that only a portion of the words they have set to music will be accessible to the listener . . .[7]

This shows the degree to which he was willing to delude himself, for what Glenn was doing was totally unlike opera. His protagonists never sing, nor do they act, and there is no plot or libretto. All they do is talk, often at the same time. Nor did the production of contrapuntal radio have much to do with working in solitude, the condition Glenn so often touted as a creative necessity. Gathering the voices by doing interviews was a social activity, and the laborious job of editing, splicing, and repeated re-editing and resplicing, until Glenn's demanding aesthetic sensibility was satisfied, was a collaborative enterprise. It required daily and nightly contact with technical experts at the CBC who helped Glenn to achieve his extraordinary effects. One of these technicians was Lorne Tulk, a man ten years younger than Glenn, who became his dedicated co-worker and a close friend.

"Glenn was a wonderful person to work with," Tulk told me. "What was very noticeable in him was his tremendous intensity. I mean, when

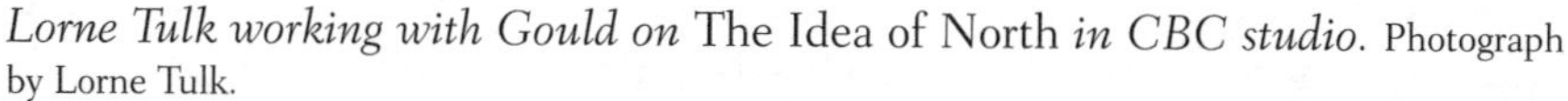

Lorne Tulk working with Gould on The Idea of North *in CBC studio.* Photograph by Lorne Tulk.

Glenn took hold of a subject or he decided to do something, his intensity was focused and so he just zeroed and focused in to where he was going. There was no room for anything else. If he worked on a project for a month or two months or three months, he was completely focused in that area."

The first project they worked on together was called *The Search for Petula Clark,* a radio program based on Glenn's frequent exposure to the voice of this popular singer from his car radio while driving along the northern shore of Lake Superior on Queen's Highway 17, a road that "defines for much of its passage across Ontario the northernmost limit of agrarian settlement. It is endowed with . . . fishing villages, mining camps, and timber towns that straddle the highway every fifty miles or so."[8] Experimenting with solitude less than five hundred miles from home, Glenn would stay for a week or two in motels at villages like Marathon or Wawa on Lake Superior. There he wrote and edited many of his preliminary radio scripts.

Petula Clark's voice had the double appeal of stimulating Glenn's thoughts about pop music and giving him the illusion of an imaginary companion. The program he wrote about her in the Marathon Motel is a manic melange of ideas about "the Max Reger–Vincent d'Indy chromatic bent which infiltrated big-band arranging in the late thirties and forties . . . more formidable precepts of Princetonian Babbitry such as 'pitch class' . . . the Beatles hav[ing] as little regard for the niceties of voice leading as Erik Satie for the anguished cross-relation of the German postromantics," and other heady themes. While listening to Petula Clark's voice, Glenn would speculate about her emotional state as expressed through song: "After the prevailing euphoria of [her first three] songs, [her most recent one] 'Who Am I' reads like a document of despair. It catalogues those symptoms of disenchantment and ennui which inevitably scuttle a trajectory of emotional escalation. . . . Clearly it's a question of identity crisis, vertiginous and claustrophobic, induced through the traumatic experience of a metropolitan environment and, quite possibly, aggravated by sore feet."[9]

Lorne Tulk remembers that *The Search for Petula Clark* was first presented "for a children's program, a young people's program. It was primarily a disc jockey show. He had a bunch of records and he simply talked between the records, and played the records while he continued talking. It's a brilliant piece of work, and it's really in many ways a compliment to Petula Clark and the way she was able to publicize herself, to market herself. I think he was fascinated by that element."

"Did he like to work at night?"

"Yeah, it was always nighttime. That was actually my wish. I'd spent most of my career working evenings and nights, which obviously was the time when he was coming off performing, in the days when he still gave concerts. And so I think the fact that I liked to work nights, and I suspect he did too, sort of coincided."

"Are conditions in the studio better at night?"

"It's quieter in the sense that there are fewer people around, so you could get into a studio and work for many hours without somebody opening the door and saying, 'Gee, Lorne, have you seen so-and-so?' That just immediately breaks your concentration, and as I said, Glenn was a very intense person. And so I think working evenings he enjoyed for the same reasons I did, because somebody didn't intrude on you. But I got the impression that Glenn had never really stayed up the entire night. It was a new experience for him."

"Really?"

"Because when we finished it was like five or six in the morning, and when we walked out the sunlight was coming, the dawn. It was getting quite bright, and Glenn was like a little boy. It was like he was having some new experience. The bogeyman hadn't gotten him. [Laughs] It was like he'd been a bad boy and nothing bad had happened to him. In many respects Glenn was a little boy, you know, there was this very boyish quality about him."[10]

Lorne Tulk's technical collaboration in splicing Glenn's tapes was an essential ingredient in completing *The Idea of North* in time for the broadcast on December 28, 1967, Canada's first centennial year. The critical response was gratifyingly favorable: "A poetic and beautiful montage of the North emerged . . . more real than the entire ten-foot shelf of standard clichés about Canada's northlands . . . likely to stand as the forerunner of a new radio art, a wonderfully imaginative striving for a new way to use the only half-explored possibilities of an established form."[11]

The following year, the CBC celebrated the introduction of its national stereo network and invited Glenn to do a follow-up to *The Idea of North.* This time the subject was to be the people of Newfoundland—Canada's most recent acquisition, in 1949. Hence the title of the new radio program, *The Latecomers.* In the summer of 1968, Glenn drove east and took a boat up the St. Lawrence Gulf for his first visit to this fiercely independent community, at that time battling the provincial government's decision to move people from their isolated outports into larger urban centers. Again Glenn's purpose was to depict aspects of solitude and to defend nonconformity. "Newfoundland itself is a fantasy [he wrote]—a disadvantaged piece of real estate set adrift between two cultures, unable to forget its spiritual tie to one, unable wholly to accept its economic dependence on the other. . . . The reality is in its separateness."[12]

With help from Howard Moore, a local CBC technician, Glenn interviewed and tape-recorded thirteen individuals. He then instructed Moore to make extensive recordings of the ocean, rumbling waves, crashing surf, gentle backflow on beaches to be used as a "basso continuo" background, similar to the railway noise heard in *The Idea of North*. Glenn's return trip was also by boat. "Gale warnings were hoisted . . . the coastline disappeared. The gulf was turbulent that night; the coast of Cape Breton was a welcome sight next morning. But Newfoundland itself remained behind, secure."[13]

Now began again the arduous labor of splicing and editing. Glenn told Arthur Rubinstein, when they met a few years later, that he "spent almost four hundred hours in a studio."[14] He worked mostly at night, with the loyal Lorne Tulk always in close proximity. "Lorne and Glenn loved each other, and so between them there was utter peace," is the way Janet Somerville, one of the CBC directors, later described it to Glenn's biographer Otto Friedrich. "It was like a knight and a page, you know, on a great adventure. Lorne should have lived in the Middle Ages. I mean he has that kind of loyal devotion, which was *the* human virtue of that relationship. And Lorne is just so rich in it. And Glenn . . . felt that *of course* people would feel that way about him."[15]

Lorne Tulk sees it more as a kind of sibling relationship. "Glenn's father has mentioned this, and so has his cousin, that I was probably the brother he never had. I remember he asked me one time whether I minded him thinking of me as a brother, and I said, 'In all deference to my own brothers, if they don't mind I don't mind.' And he was so touched by that, you know, that I had mentioned my own brothers first."

Lorne was concerned about Glenn's drug taking. "He would carry Valium in his pocket, and if he met somebody and it looked like there might be a confrontation, the first thing he would do was go down to the washroom and pop a couple of Valiums, and then come back. He disliked confrontations immensely and would avoid them at all cost."

"How do you explain that he would be so fearful about confrontation?" I asked.

"He was an extremely sensitive person, and confrontation intruded on that sensitivity and tended to dull it. He preferred to remain sensitive and sharp, and I think he tried desperately to avoid confrontation or conflict."

"Do you think that the feeling of anger might have interfered with his ability to concentrate?"

"Oh sure, no question. His feeling toward anger was that anger kills not just the person, but it kills the incentive, and it kills the artistic ability."

"An impressive piece of insight. But whose was it," I wondered. "Did Glenn put that into words as well as you just did?"

"Well, this is what he told me—I'm only describing what Glenn told me," was Lorne's reply.[16]

Working together in the studio, and with other technicians at times, there had to be moments of tension, disagreement, confrontation, even anger. To prevent them from "killing" him, Glenn usually relied (in addition to his drugs) on three psychological mechanisms of defense. First, he would adopt the pose of a conductor, the superior musician who directs his lowly minions in their grinding drudgery. (Tulk : "I was just a technician, given the job of working with him on this program. I'm just a button-pusher. I had nothing really to do with the concept. I'm not a creative or artistic individual.")[17] A film called *Radio as Music* shows Glenn at work on one of his contrapuntal docudramas. He is seen hovering over the control panels in a CBC studio, waving his arms to the technicians as though he were leading an orchestra. And he refers to the work of editing almost entirely in musical terms: "Let's give this voice a little crescendo . . . more diminuendo here," etc. In keeping with the idea that he is creating a musical composition, at one point he holds up a piece of paper that resembles the sort of score conductors use, claiming it is his master plan for the work.[18]

Glenn's second way of protecting himself and his studio colleagues against undue tension was suddenly to lapse into sophomoric humor. He would do hilarious imitations of some of the characters he had met on his trips, or begin talking in a mock German accent: "Now zis iss ze place vhere ve haff to be zuper careful not to drown out poor Mr. Scott." This would provoke laughter and induce a moment of relaxation. Then the work continued.

Finally, there was the process of symbolic transformation, the opportunities inherent in the work Glenn was doing of deflecting aggression from himself and targeting it on various characters in his drama. For example, one of the women he had interviewed had given him a hard time. "[She] turned on me with a fine fury, stopped short of insult, but indicated that my line of questioning was foolish." When Glenn edited her tape-recorded voice, he removed himself completely from the dialogue and fused her annoying comments with those made by one of the men he had interviewed. That made it sound, thought Glenn, like "a man and his wife, certainly a lady and a gentleman who are engaged in rather intimate conversation."[19] Using a razor blade to cut the tapes, which is the first step in engineering a tape splice, can also be seen as a sublimation of aggression. To create something original, an artist must know how to destroy. In a debate three years later with Arthur Rubinstein about the merits of tape splicing, Glenn gave the example of "a delightful man" he had tape-recorded in Newfoundland:

> [He] was very articulate and very perceptive, but he had a habit of saying "um" and "uh" and "sort of" and "kind of" constantly—so constantly, in fact, that you got absolutely sick of the repetitions. I mean every third word was separated by an "um" and an "uh." . . . Well, we spent—this is no exaggeration—we spent three long weekends—Saturday, Sunday, and Monday, eight hours per day—doing nothing but removing "um"s and "uh"s and "sort of"s and "kind of"s and righting the odd syntactical fluff in his material . . . there were sixteen hundred edits in that man's speech alone in order to make him sound lucid and fluid, which he does now.[20]

Glenn employed the principles of contrapuntal radio, now enhanced with stereophonic sound, in several other documentaries, including the one about Leopold Stokowski, which was aired in 1971. Here the juxtaposition involves only one speaker, the octogenarian maestro himself, whose mellifluous voice is heard against samples of the recordings he had made over half a century. His philosophy of music and culture mingles beautifully with the rich orchestral sound that was Stokowski's trademark. *Pablo Casals: A Portrait for Radio* (1974) also makes use of the contrapuntal radio technique. It consists of interviews with several of Casals's students and his biographer Albert Kahn, as well as segments of the cellist talking about Bach.

Glenn began working on the third installment of what was finally called his *Solitude Trilogy*[21] in 1972. He had again driven north along Lake Superior, then west into the province of Manitoba with the hope of interviewing nine members of a Mennonite community in Winnipeg for a radio program to be called *The Quiet in the Land*. He also tape-recorded two services in a Mennonite church in Waterloo to be used as background sound, along with church bells, choral singing, cars on the road, children at play, and other local noises. But a strike by the CBC engineers delayed the project. Hoping to obtain additional material, Glenn wrote to a community member, requesting an interview:

> I should point out that this program will not, unlike many others which have been done about various Mennonite communities, be unduly concerned with the purely historical aspects of the evolution of those communities. Inevitably, the history of the communities—the sense of transience, of the threat of materialism, of one's relation to the state, etc. makes itself felt, but what I hope to achieve, primarily, is a "mood-piece"—a radio-essay dealing with the degree to which, as one of my interviewees put it, the Mennonites are able to remain "in the world but not of the world." It is, in short, a reflective and, I believe, rather poetic program and, if it succeeds, will, I hope, capture the essence of the Mennonite communities and the life style of the peoples involved more faithfully than any recitation of historical facts possibly can.[22]

Glenn did not complete this third installment of his *Solitude Trilogy* until 1973. It is by far the most appealing of the three docudramas on Canadian themes. His editorial skills had by now advanced tangibly as a result of accumulated experience with the new medium and what he had learned from master technicians at the CBC. In *The Quiet in the Land,* he gave speakers more time to be heard individually before other voices were superimposed, thus improving their intelligibility. He added a rich tapestry of background sounds: fragments from a Bach Suite for unaccompanied cello, snippets of Janice Joplin crooning "Mercedes Benz," some informal piano playing, and reverberations from a children's chorus being trained to improve their singing. Several scenes include the sonorous voices of preachers telling their congregation about the ethics of a Mennonite life, followed by men and women commenting on the background of the Mennonite faith and the tension between more conservative believers who wish to remain isolated and those who seek greater contact with surrounding communities.

However, *The Solitude Trilogy,* did not always go over well with those who had contributed to it. There were some dissenting voices. One speaker in *The Idea of North* expressed his irritation at "the absence of a coherent series of statements," while a Mennonite professor of economics Glenn had interviewed for *The Quiet in the Land* objected that he had been "led to believe that my ideas would be used not as the expression of an individual but as a foil for the ideas of others. You can't abstract an individual much more than that, even in a totalitarian society. . . . Each person becomes a note in a larger symphony. . . . The dictator is a social composer."[23]

Such remarks expose the ambiguity of Gould's position as a creative artist. He was a musician who had abandoned his personal contact with live audiences and now moved exclusively into the bigger, more modern and more popular area of electronic communication. In clear defiance of an ethos that required musicians to be heard and seen in public, he was now ensconced in studios and getting to be known as one of Canada's more original and provocative radio and television personalities. Janet Somerville called him "an authentic National Treasure."[24]

The rest of the world, which didn't hear and see Glenn Gould's programs, thought of him more as a recluse or a hermit. Yet he continued to have a major impact on the music world. Outside Canada it was only the steady stream of recordings he produced, and the hope that he would one day return to the stage, which kept the image of him as a great pianist alive. Glenn had given up his Canadian manager Walter Homburger in 1967 and, hoping to get more worldwide publicity, signed on with a New York manager, Ronald Wilford, who helped many celebrated conductors with their careers. But Glenn no longer did any traveling, except to New York for his recording sessions at Columbia, and even that, as we shall see, diminished after it was agreed he could do the taping in Toronto. Sporadically he went to Philadelphia for consultations with the orthopedist Dr. Stein. After the completion of *The Quiet in the Land,* he was invited to do a radio documentary on China but turned this down because of his unwillingness to travel such a long distance.

Glenn claimed that his health had improved since he stopped giving concerts in 1964. "Most of my earlier illnesses were psychosomatic—a sheer protest against my regimen," he told one interviewer.[25] Perhaps he was referring to his health crises while abroad, for he continued consulting doctors in Toronto regularly. The radiologist A. A. Epstein told me that "Glenn worried constantly about his chest and having pneumonia all the time, and he complained of gas and flatulence. He was worried that he might have cancer. His family physician, Dr. Morris Herman, followed him very carefully and would send him to me once or twice a year for X-rays, usually a chest film but sometimes some GI series and esophageal studies. The findings were invariably negative."[26]

In a letter to Leon Fleisher, the pianist, who himself was having an agonizing hand problem, Glenn writes: "As you know, no one is in a better position to realize what you have been going through . . . than I, even though my own experience with this sort of malaise is by comparison limited both as to duration and, I expect, severity . . . you are one of the few original performers and, as such, far too valuable a person to absent the scene for long." Glenn also mentions having seen their mutual orthopedic counsel, Dr. Stein (who had once put Glenn in a body cast), in Philadelphia, "because I threw my left leg out of whack."[27] Dr. Stephens, for his part, noticed absolutely no difference in Glenn's "hypochondriacal complaining" after leaving the stage. He maintains that "It was a terrible tragedy that this musical genius felt so compelled to fritter away his energies by making radio documentaries for which he was far less gifted than he was as a pianist. Just think what he might have accomplished with the music of Debussy, Schubert, Schumann, other composers whose works he tended to ignore or dismiss."[28]

But Glenn had sworn never to return to the stage. "I think that [the life of the concert artist] has no relevance to the contemporary music scene . . . I couldn't conceive going back to that life," he said in a lengthy interview in 1968. "It was an experience that I wanted to be rid of and to shuck off as quickly as I could, and when that moment came I did it . . ."[29]

In my opinion, Glenn's retirement had the great benefit of allowing him to go in new directions and explore aspects of his creativity that had lain dormant for years. It also brought him closer to an understanding of solitude. But at the same time it cut him off from important human interaction throughout the world—contact with other musicians, conductors, critics, and above all audiences whose reactions to his playing, even when he complained about them, might have been helpful to his self-esteem and breadth of artistic vision. Working now primarily in studios with technicians and engineers, he no longer had to contend so much with either the flattery or the fault-finding directed at his earlier musical performances. (That happened only when a new recording was released.) The result was a kind of diffusion of Glenn's identity, a certain loss of the primary image of himself as a pianist, an image that had been built up in childhood under his mother's guidance.

Did this indicate personal maturation, a step in the direction of greater autonomy and strength of character? Or did it betoken weakness, a capitulation to his performance anxiety and social withdrawal in the face of fear-provoking crowds? Perhaps both factors were at work simultaneously, so that Glenn lured himself into believing he was on the right track, and at the same time remained riddled with doubts as to where his career was going.

21

CHANGING VIEWS OF COMPOSERS

Glenn felt that his break from giving concerts provided greater freedom than ever before to explore the range and variety of musical compositions. "It's about four years now," he told John McClure, music director of Columbia Masterworks, in 1968,

> and they've been four of the very best years of my life, four years in which I've come to terms with music and with myself qua music in a way that I didn't realize was possible before . . . it's been a remarkable experience to start thinking about music not via an instrument, not by having to decide what Beethoven was really like, or Bach was really like, in terms of an instrument by which I might translate that decision to an audience. It also . . . means first of all that you cover an immense terrain of music. You can look down from a fairly considerable height upon a vast literature that's spread out before you . . . really encountering music as a totally enjoyable and personal experience. That encounter does curious things to you. It makes you aware not just of a tremendous range of repertoire which is good for you by itself, it makes you aware of the mental process of assimilating repertoire very quickly, which is also very good for you. But it also makes you aware of the—it sounds a little corny—of the magnitude of music.[1]

It was this newly felt freedom to explore music—not necessarily to perform it—that had generated, in 1966, four forty-minute television programs for BBC2 called *Conversations with Glenn Gould,* "which were produced here in Toronto, with the immense help of Humphrey Burton, who came out from London for a ten-day period last March . . . more fun to make and, all in all, more satisfying than any television I've ever done."[2]

In an informal studio setting, with cables on the floor and electronic gear standing about, Glenn sat at the piano talking with Humphrey Burton, the British producer with whom he had collaborated on several features for CBC during the 1960 Vancouver Music Festival. The first program was primarily about Bach, the second about Beethoven, the third about Richard Strauss, and the fourth about Arnold Schoenberg. Glenn would play examples of their music, talking in a typically effervescent and controversial way about diverse challenges their music presented for performers and listeners. Burton recalls the astonishing amount of preparation that went into each of these programs: "He liked the public debate. He loved to shock. Despite the apparent high-spirited, almost jokey informality of the conversations, they were in fact carefully structured, the result of many hours of talking (round the subject) at Glenn's incredibly disorganized Toronto apartment. The spontaneity was rehearsed—a paradox Glenn enjoyed."[3]

That same year, Glenn proposed a totally different kind of enterprise to John McClure, hoping Columbia Records might be interested. It was to be a "spoof" of the recorded public piano recital.

> I would be presented in recital at White Horse, Yukon Territories; Yellowknife, Northwest Territories; or some other such romantic spot . . . we [could] fake the whole event studio-wise [and] concoct an irreproachably chronological recital format consisting exclusively of pieces that I would be unlikely to record as part of any more sober project. . . . It would, of course, be recorded to the best of our ability with perhaps just a few conspicuous clinkers left in to give it credence. . . . Then we would overdub the splutters, sneezes, and sighs of the noisiest damn audience since Neville Chamberlain was shouted down in the House.

Did Glenn really mean it? His sense of humor could lead to exorbitant fantasies, and in his letter to McClure he admitted, "This all sounds quite mad." Yet he tried to justify the recording because "it is from such madness that the [Gerard] Hoffnung concerts and the Baroque Beatles

Book grew."[4] Columbia Records was unwilling at first to indulge Glenn in this whimsy, but fourteen years later did allow him to go ahead with a similar parody. Still spurred by jealous memories of Horowitz's successful return to the stage after a lengthy absence, Glenn mimics a public concert held on an oil rig in the Canadian Arctic. The recording was released in 1980, under the title *A Glenn Gould Fantasy,* as part of an album celebrating his silver anniversary with Columbia Records.[5] It is a prime example of Glenn's use of humor to deal with a painful subject—every unflattering reference to Horowitz was painstakingly deleted.

A very satisfying recording event was Glenn's work with Leopold Stokowski, a musician he truly venerated. He'd interviewed the maestro in 1965, and Stokowski himself raised the question: "Why have we never been invited to make records together?" An agreement was reached with Columbia to record Beethoven's Fifth Piano Concerto in E-flat Major (the "Emperor") with Stokowski's own orchestra, the American Symphony. Conferring beforehand about their interpretation, Glenn told the elderly conductor that "whatever the tempo, we can make this piece into a symphony with piano obbligato; I really don't think it ought to be a

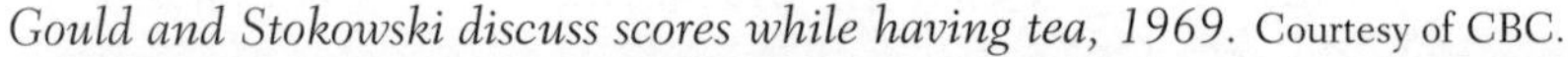

Gould and Stokowski discuss scores while having tea, 1969. Courtesy of CBC.

virtuoso vehicle," and Stokowski couldn't help but agree.[6] This concerto was not one that Glenn had much respect for. He remarked that "Like most of Beethoven's middle-period blockbusters, the 'Emperor' Concerto is a rather simple-minded work harmonically. It concentrates on primary chord materials, modulatory subtleties are at a premium, and nowhere this side of Grand Old Opry can one encounter more unadorned II–V–I progressions."[7]

The recording was made in March 1966. Glenn phrased his opening cadenzas in a truly original way, and he acceded to Stokowski's tactful admonitions about modulating the tempi: "But do you not think there are a few moments which should perhaps go a little faster and a few which might go a little slower?" Miracles of acoustic balance and coherence were achieved by the Columbia producer, Andrew Kazdin, who was beginning to play a major role in Glenn's recording career, working closely with him to achieve the many discs that were now forthcoming. Another version of the "Emperor" Concerto was made for CBC Television four years later, when Glenn was a last-minute substitute for the Italian pianist, Arturo Benedetti Michelangeli, another musician famous for his last-minute cancelations. When conductor Karel Ancerl heard about Glenn's willingness to step in, he is supposed to have said: "Michelangeli? Gould? Where do you people get such kooks?"[8]

During the intervening years, Glenn went to New York about once a month, and his record output in 1966 and 1967 was stupendous, including

Beethoven Sonatas:
No. 8 in C Minor ("Pathétique"), opus 13
No. 9 in E major, opus 14, no. 1
No. 10 in G major, opus 14, no. 2
No. 14 in C-sharp Minor ("Moonlight"), opus 27, no. 2
No. 18 in E-flat Major, opus 31, no. 3
No. 23 in F Minor ("Appassionata"), opus 57
Beethoven, 32 *Variations* in C Minor
Numerous *Lieder* by Richard Strauss, recorded with his favorite singer, the German soprano Elisabeth Schwarzkopf ("no vocalist has brought me greater pleasure or more insight into the interpreter's art").[9] Of these, only the *Ophelia Songs,* opus 67, were released because Mme Schwarzkopf objected to Glenn's improvisatory way with the accompaniments
Bach, *Well-Tempered Clavier,* Book II, Nos. 1–8

Bach, Piano Concertos no. 3 in D Major and no. 7 in G Minor, with Vladimir Golschmann conducting the Columbia Symphony Orchestra
Hindemith, Sonata no. 1 in A Major, and no. 3 in B-flat Major
Prokofiev, Sonata no. 7 in B-flat Major, opus 83
Various pieces by William Byrd
Canadian music in the twentieth century: Oskar Morawetz, István Anhalt, Barbara Pentland, and Jacques Hétu
Six Sonatas by Mozart:
No. 1 in C Major, K. 279
No. 2 in F Major, K. 280
No. 3 in B-flat Major, K. 281
No. 4 in E-flat Major, K. 282
No. 5 in G Major, K. 283
No. 15 in C Major, K. 545.

Glenn's policy in recording was always to make the music sound different from what might be expected. It made no sense to him to record anything that resembled what had been produced by other pianists. Thus he took enormous liberties, especially with tempi and dynamics, if necessary "recomposing" parts of a work to give it that special Gould touch. This could lead to interpretations that were at best startling and at worst outlandish. For example, the opening of the "Appassionata" Sonata is played so slowly that one wonders if something is wrong with the playback equipment. At that lethargic tempo, the music loses all forward momentum and caves inward like a cold soufflé. Given Glenn's outstanding control of the keyboard and how awesome his interpretations could be, one can only be dismayed at his choosing to play in this manner. Of course, this is a subjective reaction; no pianist on earth can elicit constant approval. As for the Mozart sonatas—Gould ultimately recorded all of them—these have stirred up more contention than almost anything he ever put on tape.

He had a most peculiar attitude toward Mozart in the first place, and it had started "as far back as I can remember," suggesting that his myopic view and the love-hate relationship he had with Mozart's music was determined by childhood conflict. The conflict, as far as I can figure it out, was between loyalty to what he had learned from his mother and fidelity to his own personal beliefs. Mrs. Gould, as we saw earlier, feared that her son's musical talents might be exploited prematurely, and she fiercely resisted any attempt to compare his early accomplishments with those of the Salzburg child prodigy. The very mention of Mozart's name was forbidden at home. This may have kept Glenn as a boy from forming a more positive view of one of the greatest musicians of all time; a pity, because children thrive on the inner images of desirable role models.

It would not have been surprising if the young Glenn Gould, with his immense musical gifts, had aspired to be like Mozart. But that's exactly what his mother did not want to see happen. "You're no Mozart, and don't let anybody think that you are," was the attitude she conveyed to her son. Yet the negative implications were contradicted every time he picked up pieces by Mozart. "The actual playing of them [i.e., the piano sonatas] was always very enjoyable," he recalled. "I had a lot of fun running my fingers up and down the keys, exploiting all those scales and arpeggios."[10]

Playing Mozart's music evidently was a positive, enjoyable experience, but at odds with his negative way of thinking about Mozart as a person. On the one hand he was ready to denigrate Mozart, saying that he had died too late rather than too early, and that his musicianship had been spoiled by involvement in opera, which made his music too theatrical. Glenn even tried to write an essay on "Why Mozart is a Bad Composer."[11] And in keeping with his preference for the Baroque period and his antipathy toward romanticism, he said he "hated" late works by Mozart such as the Symphony in G Minor, K. 550.[12] (Had Glenn never listened to the late viola quintets? How could anyone "hate" such sublime music?)

On the other hand, his favorite childhood pet was the little bird named Mozart, and the only surviving recordings of his pre-adolescent piano playing (four hands with his teacher Albert Guerrero) are of works by Mozart. One of Glenn's most sublime interpretations in his twenties was Mozart's Concerto no. 24 in C Minor, K. 491.[13] And a major project in his thirties was to record all of Mozart's Piano Sonatas and Fantasias. He confessed that "I had more fun with these things than anything I've ever done, practically, mainly because I really don't like Mozart as a composer."[14]

These recordings were made over a period of nine years—between March 1965, when he was thirty-two, and September 1974, when he was barely forty-two. Considering Gould's simultaneous involvement in many other projects, as well as his change in recording techniques and studios (from the New York Columbia studio to Toronto's Massey Hall and Eaton Auditorium) during that stretch of time, the unevenness of the product should not come as a surprise. Glenn was the first to admit its deficiencies, for example, to the critic and writer Tim Page, who told him, "Your performances of some of the [Mozart] Sonatas strike me as possibly your least successful records."

> Yes, a couple of the later Mozart Sonatas [he told Tim Page]. The early works I love, the middle ones I love, the later sonatas I do *not* like; I find them intolerable, loaded with quasitheatrical conceit, and I can certainly say that I went about recording a piece like the Sonata in B-flat major, K. 570, with no conviction whatsoever. The honest thing to do would have been to skip those works entirely, but the cycle had to be completed.[15]

Listening to these recordings, one is immediately struck by the vigor of Gould's interpretations. This is not the porcelain-doll Mozart in powdered wig and silk brocade. The playing is full-blooded and powerful. It defies many conventions: the texture is jangly and percussive; there is very little legato phrasing but a great deal of staccato; especially in the accompanying passages which, in keeping with Glenn's contrapuntal bias that all voices should be equal, often overwhelm the theme. Dynamic changes are minimized or ignored entirely; tempo markings are rarely acknowledged; accents are choppy and ordinary chords are often arpeggiated in bizarre ways. Above all, what's missing is the charm and repose that make Mozart's music so universally appealing. And yet there are some model performances. The Sonatas no. 6 in D major, K. 284 (Glenn's favorite), and no. 7 in C Major, K. 309, are especially well played. I disagreed with him that the Sonata no. 17 in B-flat Major, K. 570, should have been eliminated, because as a violinist I think of Mozart's other version of this work for violin and piano, and actually enjoy listening to Glenn's performance. But the beginning of the second movement of the Sonata no. 16 in C Major, K. 545 ("Sonata facile"), is in my opinion a disaster, an ugly caricature, and an insult to both the composer and those who love his music. It's Glenn's demonstration of how *not* to play Mozart. This movement is marked *Andante,* yet Glenn plays it at the speed of an Allegro, much too fast, hiding the fluidity of the theme under bluntly detached configurations of the left hand. Further on, Glenn softens this and actually plays quite lyrically. Thus, in the same movement, one can appreciate Glenn's ambivalence toward Mozart.

He was far less ambivalent toward Richard Strauss, who, according to the laudatory essay Glenn wrote about this composer, "always fancied himself as a kind of twentieth-century Mozart, and this is not an altogether insupportable conceit."[16] Glenn was seventeen years old when, listening to *Ein Heldenleben,* he grew naturally into a sympathy "with the flamboyant extroversion of the young Richard Strauss . . . [and] I have never grown out of it."[17] Considering how passionately he defended the radicalism of Schoenberg, his simultaneous advocacy of the ultraconservative Richard Strauss exemplifies Glenn's striking capability for embracing opposites. Thus he could think of Schoenberg as "one of the greatest composers who ever lived,"[18] and also believe that "Strauss was the greatest musical figure who has lived in this century."[19] Such "high prejudice," as Glenn called it, led him to produce innumerable radio and television programs about Strauss (including the two-part radio documentary in 1979 called *The Bourgeois Hero*), to record many of the composer's songs as well as his very limited output for solo piano (the Sonata in B Minor, opus 5, was Glenn's final recording, made shortly before his death in 1982), and to write the persuasive essay "An Argument for Richard Strauss."

In that essay, Glenn expressed his opposition to "those cunning currents of fancy which . . . make haste to consign old Strauss to the graveyard for romantics, pronouncing him a great nineteenth-century character who had the audacity to live fifty years into the twentieth." Instead, he regarded Strauss as "a central figure in today's most crucial dilemma of aesthetic morality—the hopeless confusion that arises when we attempt to contain the inscrutable pressures of self-guiding artistic destiny within the neat, historical summation of collective chronology." It intrigued Glenn that Strauss "had the good fortune to be writing masterpieces in the days of Brahms and Bruckner and the luck to live beyond Webern into the age of Boulez and Stockhausen." And he admired enormously Strauss's concern "with utilizing the fullest riches of late romantic tonality *within* the firmest possible formal disciplines . . . his interest was primarily the preservation of the *total* function of tonality. . . . Strauss is able to produce by the simplest and almost deceptively familiar means an overpowering emotional effect."[20]

Glenn's endowment for contrapuntal thinking and his strong attraction to polyphonic music made him search for these qualities in his hero's compositions. He had to admit that Strauss "was by no means a composer who practiced counterpoint per se. In his music the absolute contrapuntal forms—the fugue, the canon, etc.—appear primarily in the operas (and even there infrequently) and are almost without exception the occasion for a self-conscious underlining of the libretto . . . but one always has the feeling that Strauss is saying 'Look, I can do it too!' and that he regards such diversions simply as a means to enliven an otherwise static situation on the stage." But Glenn couldn't leave it at that. He had to project onto Strauss an expertise that he either didn't possess or seldom chose to exercise. "[I]t cannot be overemphasized," wrote Glenn in a spasm of hyperbole, "that Strauss, on his own terms, was the most contrapuntal-minded of composers. The fundamental strength of Strauss's counterpoint . . . lies in his ability to create a sense of poetic relation between the soaring, dexterous soprano melodies, the firm, reflective, always cadential-minded basses, and, most important of all, the superbly filigreed texture of his inner voices."[21]

Finally, Glenn had to pay Strauss the highest compliment of all, by comparing him to Beethoven. "Indeed, short of the last quartets of Beethoven, I can think of no music which more perfectly conveys that transfiguring light of ultimate philosophic repose than does *Metamorphosen* or *Capriccio*—both written when [Strauss] was past seventy-five." Yet Glenn's amazing musical erudition, gained, as I have said before, not so much through scholarship as by attentive listening and conscientious review of scores, made him take note of one fundamental difference between the two composers. "Beethoven, after all, in the last quartets did . . . afford a link with the taut motivic complexities of the Schoenbergian generation," whereas Strauss "has promised nothing whatever for the future."[22]

In his panoramic view of Western musical history, Glenn seems to have had blind spots for most of the accomplishments of nineteenth-century composers. He tended to dismiss their work, or worse yet, to denigrate and ridicule it, especially the piano compositions of that so-called Romantic period.

> I have always felt [he told Tim Page] that the whole center core of the piano recital literature repertoire is a *colossal* waste of time. The whole first half of the nineteenth century—excluding Beethoven to some degree—is pretty much of a washout as far as solo instrumental music is concerned. This generalization includes Chopin, Liszt, Schumann—I'm tempted not to say Mendelssohn, because I have a tremendous affection for his choral and chamber works, but most of his piano writing is pretty bad. You see, I don't think any of the early romantic composers knew how to write for the piano. Oh, they knew how to use the pedal, and how to make dramatic effects, splashing notes in every direction, but there's very little real *composing* going on. The music of that era is full of empty theatrical gestures,

> full of exhibitionism, and it has a worldly, hedonistic quality that simply turns me off.[23]

He did play Chopin's Sonata no. 3 in B Minor, opus 58, for a CBC Radio program in 1977 about the revival of interest in Romantic composers. It is a bombastic, insensitive rendition of this magnificent work, with peculiar voicing of the opening chords and delicate right-hand themes buried under brutal left-hand accompaniments. One is reminded of a frigid woman being forced to kiss a man she despises. It is regrettable that Glenn took this attitude toward the Romantic composers, because I am told he performed Chopin beautifully when he was quite young. In his later years he rarely played music by Chopin and one clearly senses that his affections were directed elsewhere. Also on the program were five *Songs Without Words* by Mendelssohn, played far less objectionably.[24] Another foray into unwanted territory was Glenn's recording, in 1968, of the Schumann Piano Quartet in E-flat Major, opus 47, with members of the Juilliard String Quartet. I discussed this with Robert Mann, first violinist of the quartet.

Ostwald: What do you think led Gould, despite his strong reservations regarding Schumann and the Romantics, to agree to record the piano quartet?

Mann: In his own kind of inverted and ego-centered thought about the way he saw music, he thought it would be a challenge to see what he could make of it.

Ostwald: So it was actually on his initiative?

Mann: No, it wasn't on his initiative. We'd recorded all the three string Schumann quartets, and we'd recorded the piano quintet with Lenny [Bernstein], and we wanted to do the piano quartet with somebody else. Since we had done any number of other things with Glenn, Columbia Records at that time wanted us to do this with him.

Ostwald: Had you ever performed with Glenn in public?

Mann: Well, to tell you the truth, no. The only time I'd ever experienced any music making with Glenn had always been in non-public situations. We did the Schoenberg, you know, *Ode to Napoleon,* and also he wrote kind of a funny little Christmas Cantata that was not really a serious piece, but he wrote it and we recorded it.

Ostwald: Was that *So You Want to Write a Fugue?*

Mann: Yes, and also he wanted very much for us to record his string quartet, and we had some experience with that. So when Columbia said,

> wouldn't you consider doing the Schumann with Glenn Gould, we said, well, find out if he wants to do it.[25]

There was trouble during rehearsals because of Glenn's fixed opinion that the piano quartet should be played in a "symphonic" style.

> The difference between a string quartet and a symphony of the classical period, or even the romantic era, is purely textural, in no way formal [Glenn expostulated on a radio program about the Schumann quartet], so I just don't buy that whole elaborate mystique of the chamber music cult. I don't believe that it takes some "holier-than-thou" dedication, some selfless renunciation of the virtuoso ambition, in order to play chamber music effectively. . . .
>
> I would have to depict my own contribution as oversymphonicized, relentlessly up-tempo driven. . . . We weren't speaking to each other by the time the sessions came to an end, which was pretty childish, but that's the way it was.[26]

Another deviation from the obstinate neglect of the nineteenth-century piano literature was his interest in Franz Liszt's keyboard transcriptions of the Beethoven symphonies. This interest stemmed more from Glenn's curiosity about their technical construction—he himself later made piano transcriptions of Richard Wagner's operatic music—than from any true admiration for the Hungarian pianist, whom he often referred to as "a second-rate composer."[27] Although Glenn disapproved of some of the devices Liszt habitually used for converting orchestral sound to the piano, for instance, having octave tremolos on the keyboard imitate drum rolls, he gave very serious thought to recording all nine of Liszt's Beethoven Symphony transcriptions.

As it turned out, only the Fifth Symphony and the first movement of the Sixth ("Pastorale") were ever recorded. Glenn thought the latter was "by far the best of the Liszt realizations—quite a miracle really"[28] But both recordings are excellent examples of Glenn's ability to toe the line musically, to play with authentic respect for the composer without perversely distorting the tempi or dynamic shifts, and to use a full palette of tone colors from songlike purity to percussive bombast.

The Fifth Symphony's last movement contains passages of such difficulty that Gould applied the technique of "overdubbing," i.e., recording separate two-hand versions and combining them into an essentially "four-hands" performance. His playing of the "Pastorale" Symphony's opening movement was broadcast on one of CBC's Tuesday night Glenn Gould recitals (June 11, 1968), and also filmed for a television program that shows the pianist first playing the transcription in an empty auditorium, later strolling along the shore of Lake Superior in the little town of Wawa. This was one of his favorite hideouts, a "therapeutic" environment for his creativity.

> [Wawa] is an extraordinary place [says Glenn] . . . something very strange happened to me the first time I was up here. I was away for about two weeks, away from Toronto and away from cities and away from city living and city thinking, and I did I think some of the best writing of my entire life at that time, and I decided it was the sort of therapy I needed, and I've been coming back for more of the same ever since.[29]

Three unlikely candidates for Glenn's enthusiasm, Edvard Grieg, Fartein Valen, and Georges Bizet, caught his attention when he was searching for new works to record in the early 1970s. Grieg's popular Piano Concerto in A Minor was an odd choice for someone who claimed to despise the virtuoso tradition of the nineteenth century. Yet Glenn was hoping to record this concerto with Herbert von Karajan while the maestro was engaged to conduct operas at the Metropolitan in New York. There were rumors that Karajan might wish to make use of the CBC facilities in Toronto, but nothing came of that. In a letter to his new manager, Ronald Wilford, Glenn mentioned plans for recording the Grieg concerto with the Cleveland Orchestra, conducted by Karel Ancerl, and by way of promoting himself, he suggested that "Uncle Edvard's opus 16 deserves inclusion in whichever token library of 'serious music' is initially made available via cassette."[30] (Although there is no objective evidence for it, Glenn always wanted people to believe that he and "Uncle," sometimes "Cousin," Edvard were blood relatives.) John Roberts was present when Glenn, claiming never to have played the Grieg concerto before, tried it out for the first time.

"I had never heard the concerto played at such a fast tempo," Roberts told me. "The treacherously difficult arpeggio passages and octave runs were incredible. He played with such intensity that it was frightening. The difficult cadenza came off perfectly. I couldn't believe that he had never played the work before, but he insisted that this was the first time he had ever taken a look at it, and he was using the music. He played all the orchestral parts he could, and sang the others. 'Glenn,' I told him, 'this is sensational, you'll have a tremendous success with the Grieg.' 'No, John,' he answered, 'this piece is not for me.' "[31]

Nevertheless, plans were made in 1971 for Glenn to record the Grieg concerto, as well as Beethoven's Second Piano Concerto, in Cleveland. His Steinway CD 318 had already been transported from New York to Severance Hall, and the Columbia recording team was poised for action with portable equipment to be shipped to Cleveland. But at the last moment Glenn canceled, with the excuse that "he had contracted the flu or some other illness."[32] Instead, he recorded Grieg's Sonata in E Minor, opus 17, which is a more subdued piece. In the liner notes he wrote about having been "at almost perverse pains to underline those dour, curiously dispassionate qualities of Ibsenesque gloom that I feel to be on predominant display in even the earliest works of cousin Edvard."[33]

Glenn was contemplating a radio program devoted to a "Scandinavian theme . . . Grieg Sonata, Nielsen suite, and possibly a sample of the current Baltic avant garde,"[34] but dropped Carl Nielsen in favor of Fartein Valen, an obscure Norwegian twelve-tone composer whose Sonata no. 2, opus 38, he presented along with the Grieg sonata in a CBC Tuesday night radio recital on July 18, 1972. Glenn had first heard about Fartein Valen from the American composer Alan Stout, who was introduced to him by Joseph Stephens. "Valen's music," wrote Glenn enthusiastically in a letter to Jane Friedman of CBS Records, "provides the most 'refined'—if that's the appropriate word—utilization of conventional 12-tone techniques this side of Alban Berg [without having] any of the frenetic hyper-romantic qualities of Berg. . . . I really do feel, for the first time in many years, that I've encountered a major figure in 20th century music."[35]

Coupled with his not very ingratiating Columbia recording of the Grieg sonata is a vivacious rendition of Bizet's *Variations Chromatiques,* opus 3, a fascinating composition that Glenn lifted out of relative obscurity by calling it "one of the very few masterpieces for solo piano to emerge from the third quarter of the nineteenth century" and giving it an unusually erudite performance. Also on that side of the record was the *Premier Nocturne* in D Major by Bizet, "[c]hiefly concerned with frustrating the cadential inclinations of a melody of Methodist primness. . . ."[36]

Finally, in summing up Glenn's "new look" at composers and their music, one must mention his resurgent interest in two English Tudor composers, Orlando Gibbons and William Byrd, a selection of whose works (Rounds, Grounds, Pavanes, and Fantasies) he recorded with great vitality and exuberance in 1968 and 1971. Gibbons had long been Glenn's "favorite composer," he told Jonathan Cott. "There is . . . a spiritual attachment that I began to feel for his music when I was fourteen or fifteen and first heard some of the *Anthems;* I fell in love with them, and consequently I've wanted to make a Gibbons album all my life."[37] It thrilled Glenn to discover that this late Renaissance music "sits surprisingly well on the modern piano," and he enjoyed comparing Gibbons to the "more introverted Gustav Mahler" and Byrd to the "decidedly extroverted Richard Strauss."[38]

22

IMPERSONATOR, PHILOSOPHER, AND TECHNICIAN

Glenn's high level of anxiety did not change as a result of the transformation in his career; it was merely displaced from one kind of activity, the public concert, onto another, the recording session. When the writer Jonathan Cott asked him to talk about his anxiety dreams, Glenn disclosed, "I only have one dream of that kind, which one would think would have abated the moment I stopped giving concerts, but it didn't. It simply transferred itself to other media, and I now have it in relation to recording sessions." He went on to describe "the most elaborate variation" on this dream, in which he was supposed to sing the baritone role in a Bellini opera with Maria Callas. He protested—"This is absurd, I'm no singer"—but was forced to go ahead anyway, and started to sing. "But all of a sudden a diminished chord, which I thought was heading back to E major, decided to veer off and go to G—as diminished chords have a tendency to do. And I was left hanging there."[1]

This dream, to the extent that we can take it at face value, suggests that Glenn's unconscious mental processes were intrinsically connected to musical symbols, probably as a result of his having been shown by his mother how to manipulate tones, scales, keys, and other musical concepts before he learned how to read and write words. The dream also points to his high striving—singing an opera with Maria Callas—and the sense of being forced to perform even when he wasn't ready for it.

Fortunately, along with the transition from concert artist to radio and television star, Glenn perfected a way of coping with anxiety that had its roots in earlier patterns of pretense and make-believe. He became an expert in impersonating fictional characters of his own invention. By feigning someone other than himself, Glenn would feel more relaxed and less burdened by self-imposed artistic responsibilities.

> . . . my most joyous moments in radio, as opposed to my most creative ones, perhaps, are those when I turn to impersonation [he told Jonathan Cott]. I was incapable of writing in a sustained humorous style until I developed an ability to portray myself pseudonymously. I started this in the mid-sixties. I wrote a few articles for *High Fidelity* in which I turned up a critic called Herbert von Hochmeister who lived in the Northwest Territories. The reason for that metaphor was that Herbert could thereby survey the culture of North America from his exalted remove, and pontificate accordingly. The character was also vaguely based on Karajan: Von Hochmeister was a retired conductor and was always spouting off about Germanic culture and things of that nature. Once having gotten into it, I had to make him sufficiently aware of other and more recent innovations so that he could speak of them with some authority. But in any event, once I did that, I found it no problem at all to say what I wanted to say in a humorous style. Until then, there was a degree of inhibition that prevented me from doing so. But then the floodgates were open, and subsequently I developed a character for every season.[2]

Except for an occasional impersonation over the telephone or with his studio colleagues, Glenn at first confined this activity to his writing. In the liner notes for his Beethoven/Liszt recording issued in 1968, for example, he expressed himself in the guise of no less than four invented characters.

Sir Humphrey Price-Davies comments that "in the releases for the current month, that colossus of American industry, CBS, includes an offering it rather immodestly describes as a 'keyboard first'—Franz Liszt's transcription of the Beethoven Fifth Symphony as rendered by that extravagantly eccentric Canadian pianist Glenn Gould."

Professor Dr. Karlheinz Heinkel draws attention to "bars 197 and 201 of the first movement of this work, in both of which a middle C is missing. . . . If these notes are dismissed by this Hungarian transcriber [i.e., Liszt] we must ask why has this been done? Is it that this transcriber thought to be helping Beethoven? Does he dare to instruct us with our own musik? Does he presume to a private knowledge of Beethoven's notes?"

S. F. Lemming, M.D., having attended "several recording sessions in New York City," contributes some psychoanalytic insights:

> As recording ensued . . . it became evident that career disorientation was a major factor. The work selected by the artist was, in fact, intended for symphony orchestra and the artist's choice clearly reflected a desire to assume the authoritarian role of conductor. The ego gratification of this role being denied by a lack of orchestral personnel, the artist delegated the record's producer and engineers as surrogates and, in the course of the session, attempted to demonstrate approval or disapproval of various musical niceties by gesticulating vigorously and in a conductorlike manner. He developed increasingly laconic speech patterns as the session progressed. . . .

And Zoltán Mostányi cites an article from the *Journal of the All-Union Musical Workers of Budapest*. "What would you think, beloved Franz [Liszt] . . . if you could know that this, your work, your enterprise, distorted, serves only to enrich, impoverish the many. You played for them, good Franz. . . . No glory did you seek, nor profit either. But eighty men denied the right to work, dear Franz. Eighty men whose children will be colder still tonight. And all because one timid, spineless pianist [Gould] sold his soul to the enslaving dollar, and in his lustful quest exploited yours."[3]

Glenn's impersonations also began appearing in some of his CBC radio programs. Sir Humphrey Price-Davies spoke up during an imaginary musicologists' conference on one of the 1969 series of weekly broadcasts called *The Art of Glenn Gould*. Another program in that series featured a character named Theodore Slutz. A 1972 program called *The Scene* debated the merits of competitive sports, with Glenn taking on several roles, including the boxer Dominico Patrono. Only three times in his life did he actually disguise himself to resemble one of his surrogates. This was for a series of television commercials in the mid-seventies promoting a radio program called *CBC Tuesday Night*. First Glenn would show up undisguised, asking the audience to listen to the programs, and then he appeared dressed up as one of a number of characters.

Sir Nigel Twitt-Thornwaite was a "superannuated" British conductor, with shoulder-length hair, spectacles, and a long baton, who stood on the podium fussily instructing an imaginary orchestra. As Gould explained in his staging instructions, Adrian Boult was his model. "Sir Nigel is utterly dotty . . . the epitome of Edwardian mod—he should, I think, have a sort of Pearson-like bow-tie [Lester B. Pearson, prime minister of Canada from 1963 to 1968, usually wore a bow tie], and, if possible, the camera should cut from a rather low angle to emphasize the enormous honor which his presence confers upon our studios."[4]

This impersonation obviously allowed Glenn to express disdain for some of the more conservative British conductors who did not conform to his image of Stokowski. (Stokowski actually was born and raised in England.)

Myron Chianti was Glenn's takeoff on Marlon Brando in the film *On the Waterfront.* He wears jeans, a leather jacket, and cap, slouches about

Gould as "Sir Nigel Twitt-Thornwaite." Photograph by Robert Ragsdale. Courtesy of CBC.

the studio mouthing inanities, stumbles into the piano, and holds a stick like a microphone. Here we see Glenn portraying a tough, uncouth character, barely literate and strikingly bad-mannered, the very opposite of himself and yet the image of someone he admired. Myron Chianti also afforded a way for Glenn to enter, vicariously, the contemporary world of filmmaking that fascinated him.

Karlheinz Klopweisser combined two characters, the German composer Karlheinz Stockhausen and his ex-wife, the painter Mary Bauermeister. For this impersonation, Gould was dressed in a blond wig and golden tunic. He strode about the stage barefoot carrying a huge Geiger counter that emitted whistling noises when he brought it close to different empty frames hanging about. "Stockhausen is much given these days to pronouncements on the state of the cosmos," Gould wrote in his staging instructions, and he followed suit by having Klopweisser mouth absurdities in a high-pitched mock German accent. "I am convinced that my world is concerned with the resonance of silence—verstehen Sie?—but although with German silence which is organic, as opposed to French silence which is ornamental. My work can only be properly understood seen in the proper perspective in the radio."[5]

Role-playing had by now become a fundamental ingredient of Glenn's personality. It helped him, as he said, to inject fluency and humor into his writing, but also provided opportunities for externalizing aspects of his contrapuntal mind. Glenn's make-believe characters allowed him to step outside of himself and give voice to inner doubts and conflicts. They provided a harmless, even ludicrous vehicle for bringing internal preoccupations out into the open, in much less threatening ways than the hallucinatory phenomena he endured in his late twenties, trying to break away from his parents' home. Disguised as "Hochmeister," "Thornwaite," "Chianti," or "Klopweisser," Glenn in his late thirties and early forties could bring himself to articulate the most absurd, fantastic, even crazy ideas, which no longer had to remain dormant or unexpressed.

The practice he gained in doing impersonations also led Gould to create imaginary dialogues in which he talked to himself. Two of these have been published. The first explored Glenn's ideas about Beethoven. Here is a fragment.

> *g.g.*: . . . like most professional musicians, you have a pronounced penchant for the late [string] quartets and piano sonatas.
>
> *G.G.*: I listen to them a lot, yes.

g.g.: That's not really what I was asking you, Mr. Gould.
G.G.: Well, those are very problematic works, you see, and I—
g.g.: Please, Mr. Gould, with all due respect, we don't need you to tell us that. If I'm not mistaken, even one of Huxley's characters—what was his name?—
G.G.: Spandrell or something, wasn't it?
g.g.: Yes, thank you—even he committed suicide more or less to the accompaniment of Op. 132, didn't he?
G.G.: That's right. Well, I apologize for the clichés, but those works really are very elusive, you know—very enigmatic, very—
g.g.: How about "ambivalent"?
G.G.: Don't be hostile.[6]

A much longer imaginary dialogue, in which Glenn interviewed himself about himself, makes the cantankerous nature of his inner voices even clearer:

G.G.: May I speak now?
g.g.: Of course, I didn't mean to get carried away, but I do feel strongly about the—
G.G.:—about the artist as superman?
g.g.: That's not quite fair, Mr. Gould.
G.G.: Or as the interlocutor as controller of conversations, perhaps?
g.g.: There's certainly no need to be rude. I didn't really expect a conciliatory response from you—I realize that you've staked out certain philosophical claims in regard to these issues—but I did at least hope that just once you'd confess to a personal experience of the one-to-one, artist-to-listener relationship, I had hoped that you might confess to having personally been witness to the magnetic attraction of a great artist visible at work before his public.
G.G.: Oh, I have had that experience,
g.g.: Really?[7]

It is difficult to think of Glenn's philosophizing as merely a distraction from piano playing or a defense against anxiety. Since early adolescence he had manifested an unusually contemplative mind and spoken, even pontificated, in ways that suggested a need to probe deeply into fundamentals. His writings, too, veer into philosophical depths from time to time. However, it would be stretching the point to call Glenn a philosopher; he did not take himself that seriously, nor did he write in a philosophical style. Yet he knew two of the leading Canadian philosophers, Jean Le Moyne and Marshall McLuhan, personally, and was aware of their ideas.

Le Moyne was a Montreal-born theologian and writer who had participated in Glenn's 1968 radio program dealing with technological issues, including the achievement by Walter Carlos of *Switched-on-Bach,* an example of electronically synthesized music. Le Moyne's ultra-positive statements about technological innovation pleased Glenn because he spoke of "a kind of Christianization going on in the machine world, in technology."[8] Le Moyne also expressed great reverence for Bach and wrote disapprovingly of Mozart's "frivolity" and the "enormous quantity of prattle" that his music contained.[9] Le Moyne and Gould were jointly awarded the Canada Council's award for outstanding achievements in the arts, humanities, or social sciences: the Molson Prize, which included $15,000, in 1968.

Marshall McLuhan had also appeared in radio debate with Glenn, who called him "communication theory's man of the hour"[10] while harboring mixed feelings about him. "I have now interviewed McLuhan twice," Glenn wrote to a friend in 1966, "and have between times got to know him rather well. He remains for me a subject both fascinating and frustrating in his writings—an extraordinary mixture of wackiness with brilliant perception. I had the feeling, however, that he has in many rather significant ways put his finger on some of the central issues of our time, and notwithstanding all the cafe society cult that is now growing up around him in the U.S., he remains, I think, an intriguing and important figure."[11] In a conversation with John Roberts in 1972, Glenn characterized McLuhan as someone who "did not communicate by answering questions but was more like a medium," while Glenn saw himself as "perhaps somehow closer to the 'the message.' "[12] This dichotomy had become readily apparent in Glenn's radio program about the prospects of recorded music:

> *McLuhan:* The most hopeful thing about this process—about the inevitable lapse of the identity factor in the creative situation, is that it will encourage a climate in which the biographical character of the personage involved will no longer be the cornerstone for subsequent assumptions about his work, and consequently an infinitely more altruistic and extra-historical participation will become inevitable and . . . the way in which the creative act results from and absorbs and re-forms individual opinion and action will be subjected to a most radical consideration.

Gould: We are too close to the invention of electronic material to be able properly to judge its effect upon our world.[13]

If anything resembling a philosophy is to be drawn from Glenn Gould's immense corpus of written and tape-recorded commentary on music, life, and the world, it would have to be a three-dimensional structure comprising his horror of competition, his preference for solitude, and his belief in the equivalency of speech and music. Glenn was convinced that competitiveness is unnatural and corrupting and should be eliminated from human behavior. With no siblings, Glenn never experienced any sort of competitiveness. He was an only child, extraordinarily brilliant, adulated by aging parents, and quite unprepared for the rivalry at large. As a child, he had chafed under classroom conditions, where performance is graded and compared. As a teenager, while entering and winning a number of them, he abhorred the musical competitions where gifted youngsters were pitted against one another. As a concert pianist, he came to detest what he perceived (wrongly, I believe) as a struggle to the death between the performer and the audience. And as a media artist, he expected (wrongly again) that advances in technology would reduce human competitiveness. "Gould claimed to be an avowed socialist [although he was a practical exponent of the stock market] and would spend many hours of conversation berating the capitalist system," wrote Andrew Kazdin, after working closely with him for fifteen years.[14] The attorney of his estate, Stephen Posen, relates that Glenn's stockbroker once told him in jest that even when the market was doing poorly, Gould was his only client who made money. Geoffrey Payzant, a professor of philosophy at the University of Toronto, observed:

> Glenn Gould's writings and recordings are evidences of his intention to separate music from cruelty, to show that competitiveness is not a law of civilized life. Nature may be red in tooth and claw, and competition in the struggle for survival may be a law of nature, but technology (Gould says) intervenes in human culture between man and nature, between man and the beastliness that is in men (at least in the hearts of men such as sit in audiences at concerts and bullfights).[15]

Nowhere in Glenn's philosophy was competitiveness felt to be more rampant than in the concerto, which he believed was basically a musical opposition between soloist and orchestra. One of his greatest ambitions was to produce a series of television programs that would "look at the birth, development, decline and death of the piano concerto. This would be a project which . . . because it would watch the keyboard player rise from the pit, so to speak, flex his muscles vis-à-vis the large ensemble and then . . . disappear, would effectively deal with more than its nominal subject." Glenn was well aware of the immensity of this task. "It would, in essence, cover approximately 300 years of history and by inference, since the formal problems of the concerto are simply an elaboration of other forms, detail, in large measure the processes of sonata and symphony as well."[16] The gigantic project never came about, in part because of his own limitations as a television producer: "I am not really sure that I am visual essayist enough to attempt it."[17]

He did attempt a radio debate on the subject with none other than Dr. Joseph Stephens. Glenn asked Stephens whether he had ever encountered a patient who requested, " 'Doctor, I have this incredible fixation, I want desperately to be up on a stage, at a piano, in front of an orchestra, subduing that orchestra with my playing . . . and in the end to be applauded for my effort while my colleagues get up and meekly walk off the stage. . . .' If you had a patient like that, what would you say to him?" Stephens replied that, though it would be a rare phenomenon, such a patient "would not be suffering from anything unknown to the virtuoso." Glenn disagreed strongly: "I don't think it's at all a rare phenomenon to have that particular kind of exhibitionism turned loose against, as opposed to on behalf of, an audience. I think it is, in a sense, a sort of assault on the audience. . . . there has to be a kind of underlying neurosis when one feels that compulsion to aggressivity." Stephens countered that "it seems greatly oversimplified to see all concertos as simply an assault." But Glenn persisted: "The great evil of the concerto . . . is that attention is being directed away from the person who is listening."[18]

What Glenn never seemed able consciously to perceive or acknowledge was his own extreme competitiveness in having to play faster and more brilliantly than any other pianist, in his need to make every recording sound "different" from what anyone else had ever produced, in his acerbic criticism of Vladimir Horowitz, in his highly successful gambling on the stock market, and in his sheer joy at coming out the winner in conversations and games of wit. In fact, one might consider his having won, posthumously, the biggest competition of all, that of survival in public memory. Among the great pianists who have died within the last two decades—Rubinstein, Kempf, Arrau, Horowitz, Bolet, Serkin—Glenn Gould continues to be the one who is most talked and argued about, seen in films and on numerous laser discs, listened to on records, cassettes, and compact discs, and, even in Canada, venerated as a quasi-saint.

The second facet of his philosophy, if one can call it that, is his championing of solitude. In a 1974 television program, he said that "Solitude is the prerequisite for ecstatic experience, especially the experience most valued by the post-Wagnerian artist—the condition of heroism. One can't feel oneself heroic without having first been cast off by the world, or perhaps by having done the casting-off oneself."[19]

In *The Solitude Trilogy,* Gould paid tribute to conditions of aloneness and having been "cast-off" among minority groups in Canada. He wanted to repeat this effort and also "take a look at the Thoreauvian [sic] way of life as evidenced in present-day America . . . a south-of-the-border adaptation of *my* theme, [i.e.] the relationship of isolation and solitude to one's productive capacity; in effect, to one's life in the world."[20] This project, like the one on competitiveness, never came to fruition. Again, one senses Glenn's ambivalence. Looking at the realities of his life, with its frenetic schedules, the incessant work with technicians and studio crews, the all-night telephone calls to distant friends, and the many trips to the Columbia studio in New York, one wonders just how much solitude he actually allowed himself to experience.

Finally, there are all the written and recorded remarks that Gould made about electronically recorded music. Geoffrey Payzant has divided these into an "Old Philosophy" and a "New Philosophy."

The "Old Philosophy" of recordings is "the conservative view held currently by the majority of people who listen to classical records. It is the view that a good record played on good equipment should bring concert-hall realism into our homes. . . . High-fidelity is both aim and criterion: fidelity to the sounds we might expect to hear if we were present at the actual performance. . . . The performer is supreme, and the technicians are there to see that his performance, intact and unaltered, is accurately preserved in the final result, the disc."[21]

Gould practiced this philosophy only briefly in the early days of his career when he would step into a studio to record and broadcast selections from his concert repertoire. No editing was done; his performance wasn't altered in any way. But already he perceived ways to modify his playing according to the possibilities inherent in the electronic media, remarking: "The microphone does encourage you to develop attitudes to performance which are entirely out of place in the concert hall. It permits you to cultivate a degree of textural clarity which simply doesn't pay dividends in the concert hall."[22] And it didn't take long before he condemned the Old Philosophy for perpetuating a worshipful attitude toward the concert hall tradition, which, in his opinion, accorded "an almost religious devotion [to] music" and wanted music to be "fitted with an acoustic halo, cavernously reverberant, if possible to resemble the cathedral-like sound which the architects of that day tried to capture for the concert hall."[23]

According to the New Philosophy, "neither composer nor performer has final control over any stage in the whole recording process, nobody has. Making a recording is a collaborative process which at any stage leaves open further modifications or adjustments at another stage, and there is no final stage because records are listened to repeatedly, and each repetition is subject to the New Listener's judgments and adjustments. The whole process, however, is presided over by a person who comes into prominence for the first time in the New Philosophy—the producer."[24]

Glenn liked to think of himself as the producer of his own recordings because he invariably made the final decisions about where to splice and how to edit the tapes. However, he was no "tape-wizard."[25] He always depended on specialists for assistance, and it took people with immense amounts of tact, patience, and respect for his artistry to fulfill this necessity. Luckily he found such a person in the exceptional producer Andrew Kazdin, two years his junior and a graduate of the New England Conservatory of Music. Kazdin had received a degree in engineering—Glenn called it a "doctorate"[26]—before going to work for Columbia Masterworks in New York. Their collaboration was of a very high order.

Kazdin helped Glenn maintain the "airtight security to keep away outsiders"[27] from recording sessions. He always followed with a score the music Glenn was recording and thus picked up occasional errors that had to be called to the pianist's attention very diplomatically. Glenn would deny having made a mistake, or say that it didn't matter, or attribute it to his having memorized something incorrectly. But as far as the interpretation of a piece of music was concerned, Kazdin quickly discovered that "it was your life's blood to mention anything. . . . You could feel it through the soles of your feet—that you just didn't tell him how to play the piece. . . . That's suicide."[28] Elsewhere Kazdin stressed: "The fundamental quality that Glenn's producer had to possess was the ability to bathe the recording studio in a kind of nonthreatening Gemüthlichkeit in which Glenn could create his piano interpretations. If the vibrations were wrong, the session was doomed, and so was the producer."[29]

It was customary for Glenn to record a number of different takes of a particular work, usually two or three, but sometimes as many as eight or nine. The takes for works by Bach generally went quickly because "Glenn had a more stable notion of exactly how a Bach piece was going to go before he even started to play."[30] Works by composers he was less familiar with would require more time. Once recorded, or in the "can," to use one of Glenn's favorite expressions,[31] copies of the master tapes were given to him for review back in Toronto, or sent to him. There followed a drawn-out period of gestation that might last months or even years, during which Glenn mulled over in his mind exactly what he wanted the final product to sound like.

When the time finally came for a recording to be released to the public, Glenn would go back to the original tapes and listen to them very carefully, planning precisely where any splices, changes, or insertions had to be made. "[T]he splicing with Gould wasn't just to eliminate wrong notes or fix fluffs of any sort," says Kazdin. "It also very often was the way that the profile of the piece was established. I mean, the interpretation of a piece emerged sometimes only in the juxtaposition of various takes."[32] Whole sections of one take might have to be replaced by splices from other takes to achieve Glenn's goal of a satisfactory interpretation. Above all, the result had to sound like something never heard before. That he succeeded in doing so is a tribute to his creativity. He copied every detail of his editing into his score, and once he felt satisfied with it, he called Kazdin over the telephone and gave him exact instructions to put into *his* score, for example: "on the fourth 16th of bar 32, on the E flat, we change from take 3 to insert 4 in take 2." Kazdin then set to work with the electronic equipment available in the Columbia studios, altering the original takes to correspond in every way with Glenn's wishes.

Once the editing was completed, Kazdin would call Glenn and play the entire tape for him over the telephone, having rigged up a special connection that bypassed the mouthpiece for improved fidelity. It wasn't the ideal way for Glenn to judge the quality of his recordings. "Certainly there were niceties about the sound that could not be detected this way," says Kazdin, "but who cared—[Glenn] *knew* what the takes sounded like, so we'd go on making improvements, and then he'd approve it, and that would be that."[33]

Kazdin's "expertise is, in my opinion second to none" wrote Glenn to John Roberts in 1971, after some technical questions had come up about tapes for a European broadcast.[34] Kazdin no doubt held an equally high opinion of himself; he wrote that "Thinking that somehow I had incorrectly cued the engineer, [Glenn] ran over . . . held up his hand with extended first finger, and said to me, a bit condescendingly: 'Here, let the master do it!' . . . He *was* the master of piano playing. He wanted to deny it, but the phrase accidentally popped out in relation to recording technique—about which I was, and still am, unwilling to acknowledge his superiority over me."[35] Their relationship was that of two masters full of admiration as well as opposition to each other, and Kazdin has written a book about it, *Glenn Gould at Work,* in which he states that "I do not believe that the closeness I felt in our relationship was a self-induced delusion. One cannot survive the literally thousands of hours of telephone calls and personal conversations without coming away with the feeling that there was a friendship that transcended the working relationship."[36]

Working with Kazdin inspired Glenn to become an outstanding technical expert himself. In 1970, he decided that it was much too cumbersome to do his commercial recording with Columbia entirely in New York, and began moving his field of operation to Toronto, where the Eaton Auditorium, site of many of Glenn's teenage performances, was made available to him as a recording studio. The Steinway Company agreed to move his favorite CD 318 there; but the following year, after being returned from Cleveland where Glenn was supposed to record the Grieg Concerto, the piano was severely damaged in an unloading accident in Toronto. Despite extensive repairs, it never sounded quite right to Glenn, and a temporary replacement had to be found. In the meantime, he made recordings using a harpsichord and a substitute Steinway.

Columbia Masterworks was willing to let Andrew Kazdin come to Toronto as Glenn's producer, but rather than try borrowing electronic equipment from the CBC, Glenn decided to purchase his own. At considerable expense ($20,000 in 1970 dollars), he acquired two Ampex 440 tape recorders, three Neumann U 87 microphones, four Dolby 360 noise reduction units, two power amplifiers, three KLH-5 loudspeakers, a two-track editing system (later upgraded to eight tracks, at additional expense), plus all the necessary boom stands, audio cables, and assorted devices needed to do his recordings. At first, when not in use in the Eaton Auditorium, Glenn stored all this equipment in his apartment on St. Clair Avenue. Later, he moved everything to the apartment he rented at the Inn on the Park. When Joe Stephens and I visited him in 1977, Glenn proudly showed us the highly professional and totally self-sufficient editing and recording studio he had built for himself. From concert pianist to radio producer, he was now a technician for all seasons.

23

NEW FACES, NEW CHALLENGES

To hold a recording session in Toronto's Eaton Auditorium, boxes of microphones, cables, recording equipment, tapes, and other necessary items had to be lugged there from Glenn's apartment and then returned. It was a very demanding physical chore that eventually proved too much for the faithful Lorne Tulk, who was working with Glenn and Andrew Kazdin. So Lorne asked a friend, Raymond ("Ray") Roberts, to help him. This was in 1970. Ray was a thirty-one-year-old Coca-Cola salesman, married, who welcomed the extra cash brought in by such part-time work. He was, and still is, an unusually warm, level-headed, reliable, and generous man. Glenn, seven years his senior, felt comfortable having Ray on the team and quickly discovered that he could call on him day or night to run errands and "do different jobs" for him. "I was always his 'gofer' and not one of the musicians," Ray Roberts told me when we recently spent a very long day together to review his memories of their twelve-year relationship.[1] Although Ray never lived with Glenn, he came closer than anyone else to being constantly at his beck and call, to observing and assisting his daily and nightly activities, and to forming a trustworthy account of Glenn's private life up to the time of his death in 1982.

Ray Roberts in Gould's studio at the Inn on the Park, Toronto. Photograph by Lorne Tulk.

Ray also drove to New York with Glenn many times. They would drive all night, sometimes in separate cars. Glenn owned two large automobiles, a 1977 Chevrolet Monte Carlo that he called "Lance," and a black Lincoln Town Car, "Longfellow." The big Lincoln not infrequently developed engine problems. Ray always took care of servicing and repairs to Glenn's cars, a recurring necessity due to Glenn's bad driving habits, which led to many collisions or getting stuck in a ditch somewhere. Ray tried explaining several times that flying to New York was actually safer than driving there at night, but Glenn would have none of that. Crossing the border, he was often checked for drugs. One time he was even strip-searched.

Glenn's work habits were very predictable—"He was a workaholic and felt best when everything was under perfect control." Day and night were reversed for Glenn. Having retired in the morning after the sun came up, he usually got out of bed between three and four in the afternoon, and the first thing he did was to call his stockbroker for the latest market information and to place orders if he wanted to buy or sell something. Other urgent calls were made at that time as well. Then he got dressed, always the same way. His clothes, invariably in basic gray, black, and blue, were purchased at a very expensive men's shop in Toronto. There were times when Glenn lost track of what he was wearing. He might appear with unmatched socks and he might also forget to bathe. At least once he welcomed a guest while wearing trousers that were completely split up the back.[2] When traveling, he brought along many changes of underwear because he sweated a lot when he played and always bathed and changed right after a recording session.

"Why did Glenn dress so oddly?" I asked Ray Roberts.

"Isn't that typical of artists?" he replied. "They like to wear distinctive clothing. It calls attention to them and singles them out from the crowd. Glenn's clothes were always on the formal side."

"But he was uncomfortable about being recognized. Didn't he try to avoid having people approach him, ask him questions, request autographs?"

"I've noticed," said Ray, "that many performers as well as politicians seem to have two personalities, one that's their true self, with normal feelings and reactions, and the other, which is the personality the public gets to see. And sometimes these people don't know which role they're in. It can get very confusing."

Here's an example of instructions Glenn would give to Ray, typically tongue-in-cheek:

ROBERTSIANA
Tues. Oct. 13, 1975 (if not sooner)
1. Arise
1A. Meet with, consult and/or direct Clifford Cartage
1B. Meet with, insult, and/or direct Stanley Ford
re:
1C. I. Radiator Valve
II. Radiator Trim
III. Supervisory Maintenance Personnel

2. Collect library books (3) and return, paying such fines as may be levied.
2A. Make note of said books, and order from retailers and/or publishers if possible

3. While executing above assignments, proceed with physiotherapy, taking heed not to

   a) soil books

   b) electrocute Clifford Cartage handlers and, if deemed necessary,

   c) drown Stanley Ford—

Respectfully and fraternally,
G. Herbert Gould
(representing Busch Enterprises, Scheduling Division).[3]

The radio was always turned on in Glenn's apartment and often the television set as well. "He loved *The Mary Tyler Moore Show,*" says Ray. He would also play tapes and recordings, but seldom his own, which he listened to rarely once they were finished, although he did play them for friends, sometimes commenting about himself in the third person, for example, "Wouldn't you agree that the way Gould brought that voice out in the bass makes for a welcome return to the dominant?"[4] Glenn practiced the piano quite regularly, "but not in the usual way," according to Ray Roberts. He didn't play technical exercises but would try out new ideas and work on them. He didn't like having anyone around while he was working at the keyboard. This was Glenn's only form of physical exercise. Although he knew how to swim, he never went swimming, and he rarely took a walk in the fresh air.

When not involved in making a recording or working on a radio or television show, he'd spend the whole night writing and editing. For a while Glenn rented a room at the Hampton Court Hotel just across Jarvis Street, where the CBC studios used to be, so he could be closer to his work there. Around eleven o'clock he'd stop to call his friends, and this often continued until 1:00 or 2:00 A.M. Usually between 4:00 and 7:00 A.M. he had his only meal of the "day," which always consisted of scrambled eggs, salad, toast, and tea, eaten at an all-night diner. He called it "scrambleds," and on trips he invariably woke Ray up around that time so he could get his "scrambleds." His only other source of nourishment and liquids was the constant drinking of tea, water, orange juice, or coffee (only twice a day), and nibbling on arrowroot crackers. "He dumped Coffee-mate into his tea and coffee." There was never any food in his kitchen, and he never prepared any food for himself. Several attempts at domestication were made by Glenn's women friends—more about that shortly—and by Ray Roberts himself, who tried to advise him on proper diet and would clean up the apartment when it got too messy.

"There were many times when I couldn't agree with him, and I told him so," Ray told me. "I'd complain about his terrible eating habits, and he'd say, 'Dr. Roberts, don't advise me on food.' He called me 'Dr. Roberts' because I had to assist him with his self-administered wax baths and ultrasound treatments for back pain. I worried that he might be overdoing it. I had no training in this field. We had a very comfortable relationship so long as I was always available to help him and do practical things for him. For instance, once I brought my children and their dates along to clean up Eaton Auditorium for him. But when I couldn't agree with him, we talked about my replacement, because it was clear that I would have to be let go. Glenn always stopped a relationship at a certain point when he felt it encroached on his freedom to do what he wanted. He really had no close friends, only over the telephone. His first love was music. But somehow we continued, and no replacement was found."

Glenn had a number of superstitions. One had to do with writing checks. He was often incapable of doing so because he was convinced that it was an "unlucky" day or the check had an "unlucky" number. Andrew Kazdin commented about this: "In some convoluted psychological way, Glenn reasoned that when he wrote someone a check, he was somehow giving away a piece of himself. . . ."[5] On the other hand, there are reports of his unexpected generosity to musicians who needed help. According to the cellist Conrad Bloemendal, who participated in several of Glenn's musical projects, he once wrote a check for $2,000 for a pianist who had just arrived from Czechoslovakia.[6] John Roberts speaks of other generous acts on behalf of fellow musicians. Glenn usually signed his name "Glen" Gould because he was afraid that by writing the second "n" he might end up making too many squiggles. He was also superstitious about giving away copies of his recordings, although he very rarely listened to them. "There might be twenty-five of them lying around," says Ray Roberts, "but if I asked for one, Glenn would say, 'Well, no, Dr. Roberts, it's not lucky today.' "

I wanted to know whether he had any religious tendencies. "The Gold family might have been Jewish at one time," Ray told me, "but there were no signs of that. Nor did he go to church. He was basically an agnostic. But in the later years he became attracted to Zen Buddhism." In 1981, Glenn devoted a radio program to reading selections from *The Three-Cornered World,* a popular work by the Japanese novelist Natsume

Soseki. Lorne Tulk had also told me about Glenn's flirtation with non-Western religion: "You know, he was an unbelievable purist and highly moralistic. Once, when somebody asked me about both his sexuality and about his morality and religion, I said, 'I think he would love for you to have believed he was a Sufi, because that's what he would have liked to have been.' "[7]

Although Glenn liked to gossip about sex, he maintained a high level of discretion about his own sexual involvements, so high that many of his closest friends, for example, Dr. Stephens, John Roberts, and Lorne Tulk, came to believe Glenn was basically asexual. Ray Roberts doesn't agree, maintaining, "He was definitely involved with women." Glenn once told Ray about having had "a torrid affair in his twenties, on one of his tours in the States," and there were several complicated affairs in his thirties, one with a soprano who had collaborated with him in making recordings, and others with women he met while working at the CBC. The singer evidently inspired him to compose a song, unfinished, with the title "Das Kind der Rosemarie" (Rosemary's Child), "and instructions that it be performed "mit grossem [G]efühl und seelicher Kanadischer [R]uhe" (with great emotion and soulful Canadian repose)."[8] The pianist and harpsichordist Greta Kraus, who was a friend of Glenn's and a confidante to some of his women friends, told me that his basic problem with women was that "he could not accept love. . . . I had the feeling that any expression of affection would cause him to panic . . . I know of one affair in which he was possessed with absolute jealousy. . . . He couldn't make one phone call without mentioning her . . . he was stirred by her, was passionately wanting to see her . . . whether it was ever fulfilled? I assume that with the person I'm thinking of, he drove her to distraction. And then, whoosh, it was over, from one day to the next, finished! Absolutely finished. Never a word of explanation, not another word. Well, that's a sick mind, isn't it?"[9]

Glenn's most significant relationship with a woman, in the sense that he said he wanted it to last and even considered marrying her, was with the wife of a well-known pianist, composer, and conductor from the United States. Glenn held this musician in high esteem, studied his scores, and asked him to contribute to his radio discussions. Perhaps he also envied him for being able to combine the role of pianist, composer, and conductor so much more successfully than Glenn ever did. His wife apparently adored Glenn, and in the late 1960s, when serious problems developed in her marriage, she moved to Toronto with her two children to be closer to him. He arranged for them to live in an apartment not far from his own and spent a great deal of time there. Friends like John Roberts and his wife would be invited for dinner; it was a trial at domesticity. And even when they were not together, Glenn would spend hours talking to her over the telephone, until both of them fell asleep. He often mentioned her to Dr. Stephens, who says, "He'd tell me she did this, and she said that. He couldn't seem to get her out of his mind." Indirect evidence of the affair was supplied to me by Glenn's accountant, Patrick Sullivan, who said frankly, "He shacked up with a broad for about a year, some conductor's wife. I know, because I saw the expenses."[10] Some of Glenn's pharmacy bills also include the woman's name, another sign of their closeness. He grew quite fond of her children—especially her son, who was having trouble with his mathematics homework. Glenn would coach him.

We don't know how long it lasted, but their relationship seems to have come to grief when she decided to move back to the United States. My hunch is that Glenn's personality and lifestyle had become unendurable and that she realized a long-term relationship was impossible with so highly narcissistic an individual. Glenn continued to pine for her and kept hoping she would marry him. But Ray Roberts noted no deep regret after her departure. "He didn't wear his heart on his sleeve. I never saw him cry."

"He was usually happy," Ray observes, "but he could be angry, and he swore. Four-letter words would be used when things didn't go right in the studio or with his work. There was no envy or jealousy toward other musicians except Horowitz. He had a thing about him and often commented negatively about what Horowitz did." Whether Glenn knew of Horowitz's homosexuality is a moot point. He never mentioned it to anyone. According to Ray Roberts, Glenn was aware of homosexuals in the studio but felt no attraction and didn't respond to them. "I met Lenny [Bernstein] once," Ray told me, "and Glenn was much aware that he went both ways. He had no interest in that. He came to accept the limitations of bachelorhood, and in the later years was much less involved with women."

Glenn was quite able to display a childlike innocence when it came to sex. Joe Stephens recalls one astonishing phone call in which Glenn reported that he was at a diner and the man sitting beside him brought out some pornographic pictures and asked him if he wanted to buy any. Glenn put on the most amazing posed naïveté, telling Stephens, "I've never seen anything like this in my life. I was absolutely shocked that there were such things."[11] He also shared some thoughts about sex with his Columbia producer, Andrew Kazdin. "It was very common for us," reports Kazdin, "to sit in his car in front of [my] hotel and talk for an hour or more . . . it seemed clear to me that Glenn viewed women with a kind of prepubescent naïveté. His fantasies at once exhibited the immaturity of a teenager and the creative sophistication that could come only with his chronological years."[12]

Glenn was the recipient of many loveletters from women who developed a crush on him, but we know of only one such letter that he wrote. It was discovered, in draft form, among his 1980 papers, but is undated and may have been penned at some other time. Nor is it clear whether it was actually sent to the person he was addressing, someone named "Dell." Perhaps the whole thing was a fantasy. It is interesting to note the analogy to the "Letter to the Immortal Beloved," found in Beethoven's drawer after his death. The identity of the "beloved" in question remains a mystery in both cases. Glenn had written:

> You know
>
> I am deeply in love with a certain beaut. girl. I asked her to marry me but she turned me down but I still love her more than anything in the world and every min. I can spend with her is pure heaven; but I don't want to be a bore and if I could only get her to tell me when I could see her, it would help. She has a standing invit. to let me take her anywhere she'd like to go any time but it seems to me she never has time for me. Please if you see her, ask her to let me know when I can see her and when I can. . . .[13]

The letter stops here.

Although Ronald Wilford was now his official manager, most of the requests Glenn received for his artistic services came to him directly by mail or telephone. Occasional solicitations for a piano recital still arrived "from some small place," and Glenn let Ray handle these calls. His standard response, if Glenn asked for an explanation, was, "Oh, one of those where they want you to play Chopin while pushing a pink piano up York Street naked." This fantasy may have originated partly in Glenn's outspoken fascination for the popular cocktail pianist Liberace. Glenn once told Dr. Stephens that the reason he "had the greatest admiration" for Liberace was "because of the suit that he won in England when he was maligned by some critic who claimed that he was homosexual, and he fought the suit and won."[14]

Another pianist Glenn genuinely respected was the Polish-born virtuoso Arthur Rubinstein. "I'm drunk on it [Rubinstein's recording with the Guarneri Quartet of the Brahms F Minor Piano Quintet]," Glenn told Rubinstein during an interview that was published in *Look* magazine in 1971. "It's the greatest chamber-music performance with piano that I've ever heard in my life." The two pianists debated the value of live versus recorded performances, and the use of edited versus unedited tapes in recordings; "you were born into another world than myself," the elderly Rubinstein told Glenn, then half his age. "Therefore all your own talent is being taken in by that, is absorbed by that, by the circumstances of your entourage."[15] Glenn returned the compliment by publishing a hilarious spoof on Rubinstein's well-known habit of directing his piano playing and often his libidinal activity to an attractive woman in the audience.[16]

A new opportunity opened up for Glenn when he was approached in 1971 by the film director George Roy Hill, who wanted him to provide background music for *Slaughterhouse-Five,* a movie based on Kurt Vonnegut's novel about the disastrous firebombing of Dresden at the end of World War II. Hill was "thinking of Bach and possibly improvisations on Bach themes throughout the film" to provide a whiff of Baroque atmosphere linked to the city. Glenn wasn't exactly wild about Kurt Vonnegut, commenting, "I suspect that much of his work will date quickly and reveal the supposed profundities of an opus like *Slaughterhouse-Five* as the inevitable clichés of an overgeneralized, underparticularized view of humanity."[17] But Hill's invitation was difficult to resist. "Certainly a baroque ambiance for the Dresden sequences sounds both appealing and appropriately ironic," he wrote the director. "I'd be particularly pleased to have a look at the rough cut when available."[18]

When Hill visited Glenn in Toronto, they spent "about five hours" talking together in an airport motel room and agreed to include works that Hill had already selected from Glenn's Bach recordings. But it would be necessary to provide musical continuity, so Glenn went to New York and recorded "wildly imaginative" improvisations on the harpsichord as well as the Bach *Brandenburg Concerto* no. 4 with members of the New York Philharmonic. Hill objected to the sound of the harpsichord, which "simply did not connect," and a piano version was used instead. When *Slaughterhouse-Five* was finally released, Glenn disapproved of the film—"it's not a work of art that one can love"—but critics generally said good things about his contribution, which amounted to fifteen minutes of the sound track. "Bach's music is splendiferously used," wrote Penelope Gilliatt in *The New Yorker.* Another critic praised the music for "offer[ing] a marvelous sense of timelessness. . . . [It] gives added meaning to the setting and an ironic counterpoint to the screen actions."[19]

Three years later, Warner Brothers used excerpts from the *Goldberg Variations* in the sound track of their film *The Terminal Man.* But it was not until 1982 that Glenn was asked to provide his own original music for a film called *The Wars,* based on a novel by the Canadian writer Timothy Findley. Here was the break he needed to show that he was the composer he always said he wanted to be. The producer, Richard Nielsen, sent him a preliminary version of *The Wars,* which Glenn liked very much, but he balked at working on it because one of the scenes showed a dead horse. Only after Nielsen assured him that the horse had not been killed expressly for the film but had "expired from natural causes" did Glenn agree to go ahead. Nielsen and a colleague were invited to his studio for an all-night demonstration of what he had recorded over the years and how it could be matched to scenes in the film. They came away flabbergasted by Glenn's virtuosity in using his own electronic equipment, "timing [the music] before your eyes with the picture, playing it and modulating it . . . really one of the most fascinating nights of my life."[20]

Glenn slaved over the sound track for *The Wars* but composed almost no original music for it. Instead, he assembled, tastefully and with great skill, segments of music by others—Brahms, Strauss, and church hymns like "Abide with Me" that he remembered from his childhood and arranged for children's voices. To provide the exact effect he wanted for these hymns, he even went to the trouble of directing the chorus and the three boy soloists, and wrote "two, excerpts for, believe it or not, harmonica . . . as though they're being played by a doughboy a short distance down the trench . . . my first professional exposure to the harmonica. . . . My ignorance was such that I had to ask what the lowest note of the average government-issue harmonica might be—Middle C, it turns out, but it's not covered in your average text on orchestration."[21] According to Nielsen, "It was a bizarre scene because Glenn . . . was crouched down in a pew where . . . [a]ll you could see was a hand reaching out—looked like a totally disembodied hand. Utterly mesmerizing to watch.[22]

The Wars had some success in Canada, and Glenn thought it "a remarkably fine picture—very understated, rather slow-moving, interesting particularly for what it leaves unsaid and unshown. It's a sort of Canadian 'Winterlight'—the only Bergman film I can relate to—though not quite as well sustained structurally."[23] But distributors in the United States showed no interest, which led to bitter disappointment among the

Canadians. Robin Phillips, the film director, suggested that the music was "too good" for the movie and that "a much more popular music score would have helped the film more." Glenn was furious. "He would just launch into this tirade on the phone about their working problems," recalls his cousin Jessie Greig, on whom, as we shall see, Glenn depended greatly for emotional support at this time. "And he would be so angry."[24]

During the last decade of his life, Glenn's activity as a writer, critic, and essayist was strongly stimulated by a relationship that developed in 1972 (almost entirely over the telephone) with Robert Silverman, a composer, pianist, and editor of a widely read magazine, the *Piano Quarterly.* Bob lives in Vermont and New York but had often been to Canada and appreciated its culture. "I'd admired Glenn since first hearing his recordings," he told me during a long interview, "and I simply wrote him a letter asking whether he'd like to contribute articles to my magazine. I was willing to publish anything he wanted to send me. He'd have total carte blanche in regard to content, length, and style. Well, the timing couldn't have been better because he'd been having all kinds of trouble with *High Fidelity* about getting things published. He called me, said he had an article, 'May I read it to you?' and we were on the phone for over an hour. I told him to send it, and I published it."[25]

Glenn liked the *Piano Quarterly* and became interested in certain issues, one especially that carried the diary of a woman piano teacher with whom he later got in touch. She may have captured his attention because his own mother had been a piano teacher. Glenn was of two minds about teaching. He repeatedly insisted he could never teach the piano because if a student ever wanted to know how he played it would make him feel like a "centipede" when asked to describe in what order it moved its legs; that would produce instant paralysis with the poor creature unable to move any legs at all.[26] John Roberts observed that "it worried Glenn that he really didn't know" how he produced such miraculous results at the piano. "He didn't ever want to think analytically about pianistic things. . . . He loathed pianistic talk, that is, how one actually did things with fingers and hands. All he knew was that he could do it."[27] But he also had a conceit about teaching. To a group of educators he once made the outrageous remark that "Given half an hour of your time and your spirit and a quiet room, I could teach any of you how to play the piano—everything there is to know about playing the piano can be taught in half an hour, I'm convinced of it."[28] As far as I know, no student ever accepted this challenge.

Over the years that Glenn wrote for the *Piano Quarterly*—fourteen articles altogether, including his very long "Stokowski in Six Scenes," which required several issues[29]—he also became acquainted (over the phone) with Bob Silverman's wife, son, and daughter. Once he proposed doing *Hamlet* with the family. Daughter Andrea was supposed to play Ophelia, but couldn't bring herself to do it. Gilbert and Sullivan operettas sung with Bob over the telephone were more successful. All these occasions gave Bob insights into aspects of Glenn's character, for example, his self-indulgent clowning. "Glenn was no actor," says Bob. "He was a college-variety ham."[30]

As far as any reciprocal sensitivity was concerned, Bob, who was older than Glenn, told me that "at no time did I feel that he was thinking of me as a friend. I was a convenience, publishing his material." Glenn would complain to Bob that Ray Roberts didn't pay enough attention to him and was causing him problems, for example, by not taking the car to be serviced properly. "It was the only time I picked up Glenn's class-consciousness," says Bob Silverman. "This man felt himself to be a superior being. Though Ray was not his manservant, Glenn sometimes spoke as though he were. One time Glenn called me from New York: 'I've got a problem. Ray has rear-ended two old ladies on the throughway. I'm calling from the police station in Tappan Zee. Can you get a lawyer for me?' Bob helped him get the matter settled."[31] (I suspect it was Glenn who had done the rear-ending and was letting Ray be the fall guy.)

On two occasions, they met in Toronto. In 1981, Bob stayed for three days: "We went from three or four P.M. to dawn listening to all his tapes, including his string quartet. I told him, 'It's a lousy fugue,' but he totally ignored me and went on to other things. It was around this time that Glenn revealed to me that he'd gotten canned at the CBC. After a lengthy, difficult session, the technicians had rebelled. The board of directors met and decided they couldn't risk losing their staff and with great regret would have to let Glenn go. Glenn told me, 'They were justified, I pushed them too far.' "

According to John Roberts, Glenn was never actually fired as he was not an employee of CBC. The board of directors per se had nothing to do with programming. The head of TV music, John Barnes, who had no musical background, felt Glenn did not understand the technical limitations and time constraints of the CBC. Glenn felt that John Barnes could not or did not understand his developing ideas on music television. His association with CBC went sour.[32]

Bob's second visit was in 1982. "Glenn looked awful. His pants were completely split in the back. He needed a shave. He looked gross, like a blob. He apologized for his appearance. I noticed that his bathroom was full of pills, and he gave me descriptions of a lot of them. After two hours Ingrid [Bob's wife] had had enough and we left."[33]

Though Bob asserted that Glenn always asked if he was disturbing him whenever he called, Joe Stephens maintains the opposite in his case. In 1975, Joe received a call from Glenn in the middle of the afternoon. This was quite unusual, as he only called at night. Joe explained that he was in the middle of rehearsing the *Ophelia Songs* by Richard Strauss, with Mildred Allen, an excellent singer. Expecting Glenn to say, "Sorry, it's obviously not a good time to talk," he was astounded to hear, instead, "Oh, the *Ophelia Songs!* Go get the music." Joe returned with the score. Glenn asked him to turn to such-and-such a page and proceeded to recite every note of the piano score as well as the vocal line, and each dynamic marking. Glenn didn't seem to care that he was interrupting other musicians; he was too intent on displaying his total recall. But Joe was well aware of Glenn's incredible memory, and this display seemed superfluous and inconsiderate.[34]

In terms of boosting Glenn's career as a television artist during the last decade of his life, no new face was more influential than that of Bruno Monsaingeon, a young French violinist who while in Moscow in 1965 "just to learn the language" happened to hear a recording of Glenn playing the Bach Inventions. "It was, for me, something of the intensity of a religious experience," he recalled later. "It completely altered my life." Monsaingeon continued giving concerts, but he also began to write and then produce musical programs for French television, and in 1972 he finally decided "to approach that man of legend" about the possibility of a collaborative project "in which *you* would be the subject." The project was to be financed by a German corporation, Clasart Films, and shown in Europe by the French National Broadcasting System.

Glenn couldn't have been more enthusiastic. He responded with "an enormous letter, fifteen or twenty pages," filled with his own ideas about how to proceed, and inviting Bruno to come to Toronto, which he did in August 1972.[35] Glenn was even prepared to speak in French for the four programs they planned, but as was his custom, he wanted all of his remarks, and Bruno's as well, written out well in advance. "I have . . . had so much experience in drafting dialogue of a similar nature for radio documentaries in this country—dialogue which virtually defies the listener to bet against its having been created for the moment—that I am absolutely confident this system would work and that, with a French translation returned to me, for example, several weeks in advance, my own security with the language would benefit enormously."[36] This plan was eventually abandoned and Glenn's translated commentaries were read by a native speaker.

In 1974, Bruno Monsaingeon brought a ten-man French film crew to Toronto, and the work began, starting "at two in the afternoon . . . until six in the morning." This resulted in a film series called *Les Chemins de la Musique* in four parts, each forty minutes long, bringing out different sides of Glenn as musician and technician. The first, called "La Retraite," deals with his retirement from the concert stage and shows him playing works by Bach, Byrd, Gibbons, Schoenberg, and Wagner (a new piano arrangement made by Glenn of his Prelude to Die Meistersinger). The second program, called "L'Alchimiste," is about a recording session in which Glenn plays a Bach *English Suite,* and with Lorne Tulk's help demonstrates the effect of having the recording microphones placed at varying distances from the piano while playing two pieces by the Russian composer Alexander Scriabin, "Désir" and "Caresse dansée," opus 57.

Bruno Monsaingeon, with his French crew, filming Gould, 1974. Courtesy of Glenn Gould Estate.

The third program discusses Glenn's *So You Want to Write a Fugue,* shows a bit of his *The Idea of North* in a film version that had recently been made, and has him playing selections by Schoenberg, Berg, and Webern. The final program is a complete performance of the Bach Partita no. 6, in E Minor.

Bruno Monsaingeon has published three books about Glenn, mostly containing his own translations of the pianist's voluminous writings.[37] He continues to admire Gould and generally speaks very softly about his eccentricities. But when he was interviewed by Otto Friedrich, he did reveal a typical episode of Glenn's hypochondriacal theatrics:

> When we had that first session [Glenn] bumped into the microphone at some point—very, very gently—and he collapsed into a chair and said, "My God, a concussion." And then he said, "Well, look, in two hours there should be this effect; in four hours, that; in twelve hours—Now in thirteen hours, if this has not happened, then I'm all right." And then I—you know, I was terrified. And he said, "Well I know, I know, once I let my imagination go, I'm lost."[38]

Upon completing their work on *Les Chemins de la Musique,* Bruno and Glenn began planning another series that would be devoted exclusively to his playing of Bach. Glenn insisted on being in total control. Bruno would fly to Toronto and spend evenings in Glenn's studio at the Inn on the Park going over details. They spent three years drafting the programs before the shooting could begin, in 1977, of three remarkable films showing Glenn Gould performing and discussing the music of Bach. This was to be Glenn's legacy to the musical world.

24

APPROACHING MIDDLE AGE

On February 25, 1971, Glenn, then thirty-eight years old, consulted for the first time a physician recommended to him by his massage-therapist Cornelius Dees, himself a patient of this doctor. It was convenient to see John A. Percival, M.D., because his office was located at 262 St. Clair Avenue West, just a few blocks from Glenn's apartment. A distinguished-looking older man, now retired and confined to a wheelchair, Dr. Percival saw Glenn off and on for the next eleven years, until Glenn's death in 1982. He was a general practitioner equipped to step into the shoes of Glenn's earlier primary care physician, Dr. Morris Herman, and, like Dr. Herman, he was keenly aware of Glenn's excessive attentiveness to various sensations in his body and his tendency to get alarmed about them as possible signs of serious disease.

"He obviously needed psychological help," Dr. Percival told me. "Many visits to my office were that he wanted someone to hold his hand. He wanted words of encouragement, something to reassure him, to hear that things were all right after all, because many of his complaints were, I thought, not worthy of any treatment."[1]

"But didn't you make a number of specific diagnoses," I asked, including such conditions as "intracostal fibrositis," "gastroenteritis," "spastic colon," and "prostatitis"? (I'd obtained this information from Dr. Percival's bills, which Glenn had never discarded.)[2] "Perhaps it was necessary to come up with a medical diagnosis in order to collect a fee from Canada's national health plan."

"You're quite right," he said. "These diagnoses came to mind as I listened to Glenn's complaints, but after examining him and sending him off for laboratory and X-ray tests, nothing positive ever showed up. I remember, for instance, examining his prostate manually—he was very cooperative about it—but it obviously was entirely normal. So I had the idea that maybe due to some stress or anxiety he'd started to feel something which I really couldn't identify. Many of the things he came to see me about I would tell him, 'Well really, I don't find anything here,' and I seldom recommended any medication for him. He'd be very receptive to a word of reassurance and encouragement. He'd talk for a while, we'd have a very nice visit, and he seemed to get up quite refreshed after."

I wanted to know, "Did he ever accept advice from you about generally healthy things to do, like not overdressing so much, wearing lighter clothes, getting some exercise, and eating a better diet?"

"I never gave him that kind of advice," Dr. Percival replied. "I accepted Glenn as being rather eccentric. I thought, 'Well, he's happy with his eccentricities and I won't try to have him change them.' "[3]

We will return to Dr. Percival when Glenn, in 1974, developed new and serious symptoms. In the meantime, there were the many stresses associated with work and personal relationships. Glenn was ceaselessly struggling to keep two contradictory strivings in balance—one aimed at achieving the privacy, solitude, and freedom he felt he needed to think and write, the other concerned with achieving success in the electronic media.

More and more music had to be recorded over the next few years for Columbia Masterworks with Andrew Kazdin's help: Bach's *French Suites* and *English Suites;* the Sonatas for Viola da Gamba and Keyboard (with cellist Leonard Rose) and Sonatas for Violin and Keyboard (with violinist Jaime Laredo); Hindemith's Sonata no. 2 in G Major for Piano and five Sonatas for Brass Instruments and Piano (with Gilbert Johnson, trumpet; Mason Jones, horn; Abe Torchinsky, tuba; Henry Charles Smith, trombone—all members of the Philadelphia Brass Ensemble); and Glenn's own piano transcriptions of Wagner's *Siegfried Idyll,* "Dawn" and "Siegfried's Rhine Journey" from *Götterdämmerung,* and the *Meistersinger* Prelude.

He had written his manager Ronald Wilford about wanting to com-

Gould with violinist Jaime Laredo, January 1976. Courtesy of Glenn Gould Estate.

plete the entire cycle of Beethoven's thirty-two piano sonatas, as well as recording all sixteen of the Handel Suites, and more than fifty Haydn sonatas, a stupendous project. Glenn was toying with the idea of switching from Columbia to DGG (Deutsche Gramophon Gesellschaft), but decided that he "could not, in all conscience, abandon the relatively close-up, highly analytical sound which has been the hallmark of our recording at CBS and which reflects, not only my own predilection in regard to piano pick-up but, more significantly, a continuing persuasion as to the validity of the recording experience as a manifestation divorced from concert practice."[4]

Events of a less artistic nature also took their toll on Glenn's limited physical and psychological reserves. In August 1972, he found a stray dog wandering on Jarvis Street. Despite his sympathetic feelings he couldn't bring himself to accept the animal into his own apartment and turned it over to his elderly parents instead. But the dog caused problems, first trying to sleep on Mrs. Gould's bed and then attacking a neighbor's child. After it was taken to Brown's Animal Hospital by the relative of a CBC staff announcer, Glenn thanked the veterinarians for their "special kindness." "It's most encouraging to know that there are people like Mrs. Widman [the relative] who, quite literally, devote their lives to the lot of the animal kingdom and, since I understand from her that you took a special interest in the dog and were more than generous with your time in relation to its care, I do want you to know how very grateful I am."[5]

Over the next few years, Glenn's workload grew very heavy. For CBC Radio, in addition to the programs mentioned earlier, Glenn constructed and participated in a weekly *Music of Today/Schoenberg Series.* This ten-part production began in the fall of 1974 and culminated in a meticu-

CBC Radio where Gould presented many of his documentaries. Photograph by Robert Ragsdale. Courtesy of CBC.

lously worked-out "documentary fantasy," *Schoenberg, the First Hundred Years,* with interviews by the composers Ernst Krenek and John Cage, the conductor Erich Leinsdorf, the musicologist Dennis Stevens, and the Mahler historian Henri-Louis de la Grange. Glenn's contrapuntal *Pablo Casals: A Portrait for Radio* was also broadcast in 1974. For CBC Television, again in addition to programs mentioned earlier, he starred in three major productions for a series called *Musicamera: Music in Our Time.* The first, "The Age of Ecstasy," on February 20, 1974, featured music by Berg, Debussy, Schoenberg, and Scriabin. The second, "The Flight from Order," on February 5, 1975, included Glenn's own transcription of Ravel's *La Valse,* opus 45, quite a divergence from his usual repertoire. This was a virtuoso performance of the highest order, on the same scale as any of Horwitz's flamboyant transcriptions, proving beyond a doubt that he was still one of the world's foremost pianists. Other works on that program were Prokofiev's *Visions fugitives* no. 2, opus 22; seven excerpts from Schoenberg's *Pierrot Lunaire,* opus 21; and Strauss's *Three Ophelia Songs,* opus 67 (with Roxolana Roslak, soprano). The third *Musicamera* show, called "New Faces, Old Forms," was telecast on December 26, 1975, with works by Hindemith, François Poulenc, Schoenberg, and William Walton (his *Façade Suite,* in which a costumed Glenn Gould sings the "Rhapsody" with soprano Patricia Rideout).

It was during this period of intense activity that Glenn developed one of his most distressing symptoms, a peculiar feeling of lightheadedness, almost dizziness, coupled with a slight loss of balance. He consulted Dr. Percival seven times between December 5, 1974, and November 24, 1975, for what the doctor diagnosed as "labyrinthitis," a disorder of the semicircular canals of the inner ear, usually caused by an infection or allergic reaction.

Early in 1975, Glenn's parents sold the house at Lake Simcoe where he had enjoyed such blissful solitude in earlier years. His mother, now eighty-three, was in declining health and being treated for hypertension. She missed the place, but packing and driving there on weekends had become too much for her. Glenn, at forty-two, felt ambivalent about buying the property for himself and declined to do so. His cousin Jessie believed that having to give up their second home "played a tremendous part" in causing his mother's death, and that Glenn thought so too.[6] But the real culprit was Flora Gould's chronic cardiovascular disease. In July 1975 she collapsed while unlocking the side door of their Toronto house for her husband coming home from work. It was a massive stroke and she was taken to the East General Hospital and later transferred at

Glenn's request to the Toronto General Hospital. He leaned heavily on Dr. Stephens during this crisis.

"When Glenn's mother had her stroke," recalls Joe Stephens, "he called me nearly every day to ask me if I had any advice, the names of any specialist, what did I know about strokes, and their treatment, and the prognosis. She was in a coma for several days, and he was very upset about that. He was afraid she was going to die. And I had nothing to offer whatever, except to say that nature will take its course and that I'm sure, since she was in a reputable hospital, she would get the best possible care."[7] Despite Glenn's expressed concern for his mother's grave condition, he did not once visit her in the hospital. In a place full of germs, he feared getting infected and coming down with an illness himself. But before she lost consciousness, he talked to her over the telephone for many hours.

The death of his mother was probably the most traumatic event of Glenn's entire life. Having failed to form a significant bond with any other woman, she had remained a tremendously important figure for him—the only woman with whom he could share his joys and disappointments, his dreams, the reviews of his concerts, and other aspects of his career on a regular basis. And her understanding of his personality was unique. She had given him birth, instantly recognized his musical genius, molded him to become a great pianist, and through his incessant phoning and exchanging of ideas, remained the silent partner in every vicissitude of his hectic career. She was absolutely irreplaceable. Yet though Glenn was in profound distress internally, he displayed little emotion. "He didn't speak much about his mother's death," Ray Roberts told me, "but you could sense the pain."[8] Lorne Tulk recalls the death of Glenn's mother as "a very, very, very moving experience for him. That was the only time ever I saw him in a state where he wasn't really thinking. And if you knew Glenn, you must appreciate that. Even in his sleep he was thinking, you know. And it was the only time I ever saw, and it lasted for about a week, when he simply could not seem to bring his thoughts to jell, couldn't seem to get them organized at all."[9]

Jessie Greig remembers that "Glenn missed [his mother] terribly . . . he was really devastated by her death and he became more introspective. He turned even more to me at that time. Then I became the one he shared his reviews with. . . . It's very interesting, because whenever he would come to something very flattering he'd say: 'Now who would like and enjoy this?' And he always wanted the response, 'Mother.' He was still trying to please her, even at that late date. . . . After his mother's death he phoned and he said that he never knew what the loving support of a family could be until that time. He first became aware of it then."[10]

During the process of mourning, Glenn had recurring dreams about his mother, and he would call Jessie to "tell me in great detail about this dream, about where she was living, and how she knew what we were doing." The cousins had attended church together when they were children, and over the years they occasionally spoke about religious topics, for example, the hymns that he incorporated in his soundtrack for *The Wars*. Jessie says that Glenn was "fascinated by the book of Revelations in the Bible [and] had his own interpretations." She remains convinced that Glenn "believed in God [and] in a hereafter."[11]

Less than a year after the death of his mother, Glenn himself was diagnosed with hypertension. The elevation in his blood pressure was not very impressive at first, so little that Dr. Percival, who was the first to discover it during a routine physical examination on March 11, 1976, told him, "It's nothing to worry about, don't give it a second thought." Dr. Percival's office records no longer exist, but he recalls the blood pressure reading to have been "150 over 90 . . . and I'm not one to have Glenn fussing about this, because he was so suggestible. I remember trying to reassure him: 'We'll just keep an eye on it; it's just borderline; it may be something about the day, the way you're feeling.' But he disputed that right off the bat. 'That is quite wrong,' he said, 'my father has been battling high blood pressure for years.' "[12] Nothing was mentioned evidently about his mother's hypertension and her recent death from a stroke.

As was Glenn's habit, he consulted other physicians about the problem. He went to the Toronto General Hospital complaining of "lightheadedness," and the diagnosis of hypertension was confirmed. On April 19, he was examined by Alexander G. Logan, a specialist in nephrology (kidney diseases) at the Mount Sinai Hospital. An X-ray study of his kidneys and urinary tract was done (intravenous pyelogram) that evidently disclosed no structural abnormalities, but Dr. Logan took Glenn's mildly elevated blood pressure seriously enough to prescribe an anti-hypertensive drug called Aldomet. Aldomet (methyldopa) effectively lowers arterial blood pressure by causing an inhibition of alpha-adrenergic (adrenaline) receptors. It is given in tablet form, and was prescribed for Glenn in a fairly low dosage, 250 milligrams twice a day. Later, this was increased to 500 milligrams twice a day. Patients with severe hypertension may need to take as much as 500 milligrams four times a day.

Glenn kept extremely detailed records of the changes in his blood pressure, which he measured every hour, and sometimes as often as every fifteen minutes. Fearing that his American-made blood pressure cuff might be inaccurate or go "kaput," he purchased two others—one made in Germany, the other in Japan—and frequently compared the readings from the different machines. Here is an example of one day's measurements:

April 24th.
12–30 AM—128.5/100
1–30 AM—126/97.5
2–15 AM—118/90
4–15 AM—119.5/92.5
5–30 AM—111 *LO*/81 *LO*
2–30 PM—120/85 H + A
3–30 PM—122/87
4–30 PM—136/104
6–30 PM—130/98 practice 1 1/4 hrs
8–00 PM—136 *HI*/106 *HI*
9–00 PM—114/90[13]

Judging from these and many other readings Glenn recorded, the medication he was receiving apparently helped keep his pressure within fairly normal limits. His systolic readings (the figure to the left of the slash) would not be considered remarkable for a man in his mid-forties. Only the diastolic readings (second figure, after the slash) occasionally were on the high side, for example, 100, 104, or 106. The highest reading I've been able to find among Glenn's notes is 158/110, but according to both John Roberts and Ray Roberts, the two men closest to him at this time, he did have "really high blood pressure" if he stopped taking the Aldomet. John Roberts recalls an incident when the pharmacy made an error and dispensed the wrong medication. "He immediately felt quite unwell, and on checking his blood pressure, found it to be very high."[14]

Unfortunately, Dr. Logan has not been willing to release any of his clinical findings, which makes it difficult to know whether Glenn had more than the "borderline" hypertension Dr. Percival had diagnosed originally. But we do know from Glenn's own records that on April 15, 1976, Dr. Logan prescribed a second drug for him—Inderal (propranolol), a chemical substance that blocks the effects of beta-adrenergic stimulation, thereby slowing the pulse and respiratory rate. Again the dosage prescribed was very low, 20 milligrams twice a day, much lower than would commonly be used by a patient with heart disease, and resembling the level of dosage often recommended for control of performance anxiety in concert artists and public speakers.

Glenn often worried about his pulse rate, and there were days when he would check it every hour, along with events that he suspected might cause it to fluctuate:

Pulse Chart
Jan. 18 [1977?] (4th. Aldomet at bedtime; 7 3/4–8 hrs solid [sleep])
Wakeup 1:45—104
2:00— "
2:15— "
3:15—102 (after an animated conversation)
3:30—94
3:45—96 (animated conversation)
4:00—88
4:15—84
4:45—90 (phone conversation)
5:00—90
5:08—80 (w.c.)
5:10—88
6:00—88
6:15—82
7:15—82 (Aldomet)
7:30—82
8:00—88
(Aldomet)
12mid—78
5:00 AM—86
5:15—88 (Aldomet)[15]

Despite Glenn's dispute with Dr. Percival about the seriousness of his hypertension, he continued to call him and went to his office about once a month for the rest of his life. However, he never told Percival that he was receiving treatment for hypertension from Dr. Logan and I assume he also kept Logan in the dark about Percival. Was Glenn aware of the Wagnerian similarity in names of his two physicians, Loge (God of Fire) and Parsifal (the Holy Knight)? On May 5, 1976, Dr. Percival noted Glenn to be unusually nervous about cramping sensations in his stomach and prescribed capsules of Librax, one after each meal and one at bedtime. Librax capsules contain a combination of two drugs, 5 milligrams of the tranquilizer Librium and 2.5 milligrams of the anti-spasmodic

Quarzan. And as though it wasn't enough to have two doctors prescribing medication for him, Glenn felt it necessary that summer to consult yet a third physician, Dale McCarthy.

Dr. McCarthy is an orthopedist, specializing in bone and joint disorders, and he listened patiently to Glenn's complaints of chronic tension and discomfort in his shoulders. McCarthy remembers how difficult it was "to make anything specific of these symptoms or the physical findings, which were mostly negative. They didn't fit into any particular pattern but I suspected some kind of inflammatory process stemming from his poor posture and overuse of the upper extremities in playing the piano."[16] McCarthy prescribed non-steroidal anti-inflammatory drugs, first Indocin (Indomethacin), 25 milligrams capsules to be taken at bedtime, and later (in 1978) Naprosyn (naproxen), one 25-milligrams tablet twice a day.

Almost every medication can produce undesirable side effects in addition to the desired therapeutic benefits for which it is prescribed. For example, Aldomet often brings about sedation and dryness of the mouth, and sometimes produces changes in liver function. Indocin, in addition to its anti-inflammatory function, may inhibit the formation of the blood platelets which control bleeding. Glenn always read carefully about what he was taking in his "large medical book listing the effects of all drugs," as Ray Roberts describes it.[17] He also made long lists of symptoms that he intended to discuss with Dr. Logan:

Symptoms (re Logan) *December 22, 1977*

1. Blood pressure escalating—evening 140/100 even without activity
1A. Chills as indication of rise; on occasion absolutely uncontrollable shivering; most frequently mitigated by even small amounts of cold liquid but sometimes [word illegible] this assistance—alleviated by activity.
2. Nostrils—plugged after conversation, especially animated variety ([illegible words] with difficulty in breathing. . . .
3. Gastro-intestinal—hiatus hernia style symptoms for *1 month or so* (!) give history—Barium meal test, etc.
4. Sleep 3–4 hours segments for *4–5 months;* currently improved.[18]

Glenn had always looked rather youthful and quite attractive. But now middle age and the effects of illness and medication began taking their toll. John Roberts describes his appearance as "haggard."[19] Photographs

Gould as he appeared in 1974. Photograph by Robert Ragsdale.

show a more wrinkled face, increasing baldness, and a stooped-over posture. In May 1977, during a meeting in Toronto of the American Psychiatric Association, three psychiatrists—Dr. Joe Stephens, Dr. Robert Fiscella, and myself—visited Glenn in his St. Clair apartment. He greeted us cordially, but not having seen him for over ten years, I was shocked by the tragic deterioration. His face and body had become bloated. He looked fat, flabby, and stooped. (A side effect of Aldomet can be the accumulation of fluid, which leads to weight gain.) His movements were slower than before. His skin, which had always been on the pale side, had acquired an unnatural grayness, roughly the color of steel, due probably to the lack of sunlight. His hair was thin, sparse, and greasy. His eyes seemed smaller, as if sunken inward. But his way of talking hadn't changed at all, his vivacity was still intact. In conversation he was the same exuberant, animated, and funny Glenn, a provocative but charming host and delightful raconteur. And, of course, the subject he most wanted to talk about was himself. It was no longer Glenn the pianist however; what we heard most about was Glenn the radio producer and filmmaker.

Around midnight he drove us to the Inn on the Park for a demonstration of his latest accomplishments. The studio-apartment where he kept his electronic equipment and did most of his work was overheated as usual, and it got to be difficult after a while to pay attention to every tape, every recording, every television program, and every comment that Glenn wanted us to savor. What interested me most was his latest album of Bach, the Six Violin and Harpsichord Sonatas recorded with Jaime Laredo. I had played several of them with Glenn myself during the early years of our acquaintance and remembered the wonderful clarity and rhythmic precision of his playing. But now there were all sorts of curlicues and fancy ornaments which I found inappropriate, if not silly. I must have said something uncomplimentary about the recording, for Joe Stephens remembers Glenn "bristling" at my remarks. Glenn in turn said something that annoyed me very much. The year 1977 was the one I started my research for a biography of Robert Schumann (it has since been published).[20] I mentioned this to Glenn, who came out with his usual invective about the composer, that he was a mediocrity who wrote only the most blatantly showy music, "romantic rubbish." No pianist in his right mind would want to play Schumann's music today (wrong), and his wife really was the better pianist of the two (right). "What you should do, Peter, is write a book about a really important musician," Glenn said to me. Was he thinking of himself?

He played for us the entire tape of *The Idea of North,* which he considered a masterpiece and the most important thing he had ever "composed." Again, my enthusiasm couldn't keep up with his, and I drifted off to sleep in the middle of the program. It would have been helpful if Glenn had served us some refreshments, or even a glass of water, but that always was the furthest thing from his mind. At 3:00 A.M. he drove us back to our hotel.

Joe Stephens, too, was disappointed and worried about this visit, which, as it turned out, was the last time either of us had any personal contact with Glenn. "He looked sick," says Stephens, "but he didn't say a word about that, which I thought was very unusual, considering the way he used to complain to us. And I thought it was so tragic to see this magnificent pianist totally immersed in doing things so far removed from musical performance." Glenn undoubtedly sensed our lack of devotion to his new causes, for he never again communicated with either of us except for his annual Christmas card, which always arrived late. Though I suspected that this sort of precipitous dropping of old friends when he felt they were no longer of any use to him was typical, Joe Stephens took it more personally. I recently asked him, "When did you become aware that this was the end of your relationship?"

"After I got back to Baltimore," he said, "because I was back a week and there was no telephone call."

"Up to that point he'd been calling you regularly?"

"Regularly. And when I came back, expecting to get a telephone call sometime that week, there was no telephone call. I thought, 'This is very odd.' I waited for about one week or maybe ten days. And then I called him. And of course you always got an answering service. And I left a message that I had called—'Please call me back.' No call back. And I think I may have done that three times. And there was no call back. And then I realized that for some reason totally beyond my comprehension, my friendship, if you want to call it that, had been severed."[21]

What neither Stephens nor I, nor anyone else close to him, understood at the time was that Glenn was again experiencing a very disturbing breakdown of control over his hands. The problem was similar to what had happened to him eighteen years earlier, when he became "paralyzed" after the Steinway technician allegedly "struck" his shoulder. But this time there seemed to be no external cause. "Lack of coordination was noticed in second week of June [1977]," he noted in a diary kept almost daily until the problem subsided a year later. He'd noted that "first sign of problem was manifest on upright piano," and it became worse while he was taping a work he had never played before, Alfredo Casella's *Ricercare on the name BACH*.

> Opening theme of Casella was unbalanced—notes appeared to stick and scale-like passages were uneven and uncontrolled [reads the diary]. . . . During next 2 weeks . . . problems increased. It was no longer possible to play even Bach chorale securely—Parts were unbalanced, progression from note to note insecure . . . among other symptoms was inability to articulate chords without arpeggio and to control even those chords at any but the most minimal dynamic levels.[22]

Instead of appealing to doctors for help as he had after the Steinway incident, Glenn this time kept the problem a secret from everyone. He told his producer Andrew Kazdin that for a year no new records could be made for Columbia Masterworks because the Eaton Auditorium which was their recording studio was going to be demolished. (Kazdin later described this as a typical example of Glenn's capacity for "creative lying.")[23] Glenn's diary records that "a summer-long series of practice experiments began. These frequently involved sessions of 2, 3, or even more, hours. 'Constants' from repertoire were used: [Bach] Chromatic fantasia, D major Toccata, G major Toccata, E-flat Haydn [Sonatas] (2 of them) and, for special tests, stock passages such as opening solo (after tutti) in 'Emperor' Concerto, 'Elektra' sequences, and, for confirmations, scale-cadenza from Beethoven G major Concerto (last movement)."[24]

Although we have heard about Glenn's customary unwillingness to think about what his hands and fingers were doing, he now spent hours analyzing their movements, while trying to make adjustments which he hoped would improve matters. Describing this process in his diary, he invented his own terminology, evidently not wishing to consult textbooks on anatomy or experts in biomechanics who might have been able to help in such matters.

Formulas used:

(1) Thumb indents: these were tried in consort with finger indents which were present throughout in an unusual degree . . . harp-like note-by-note sensation . . . and the result produced a reasonably effective method for specific, brief passages with minimal register change . . . but, in all other respects was unpleasant in feel and unworkable in method . . . reacting to overly tense area elsewhere.

(2) During mid-summer, much effort was directed to the hand-knuckles and, initially, it appeared that some progress was made when these were subject to indent pressure. This seemed to foster, on occasion, crescent-like sensation which was sometime solution (circa 1966) . . . but did seem to foster inability to secure repetition in trills, etc. . . .

(3) In late summer, and for a very brief period (not more than 3 or 4 days) experiments with elevated wrists were tried. These were inaugurated to alleviate unnatural burden on indented fingers, thumb, and knuckles. The experiment resulted only in a complete loss of control, especially control of thumb-passing etc.

(4) On various occasions during summer, extreme pressure had been exerted on thumb indents for the purpose of regulating posture, facilitating lower center of gravity and formal position of body. An attempt was made to keep body position in such adjustment that thumb indents would be constant and not subject to variable pressure. These proved unusually

> energy-consumptive and were impossible to pre-set prior to sitting at the piano. . . .
>
> (5) In mid-September [1977] an attempt was made to control all functions from neck. This involved prohibiting movement of neck on a left-right axis and making it an appendage to shoulder. Initial results were dramatic: immediate improvement in all levels of co-ordination was noticed . . . it seemed analogous to breakthrough of May '67. . . .[25]

Alas, the improvement proved to be fleeting: "neck-movement prohibition (inability to look at stop-watch, for example) was fatiguing and excessively restrictive and, in this respect, it called to mind earlier occasions when neck-control had inhibited movement." By the end of September, Glenn was reporting "image problems," meaning that he found himself "sitting farther back than was desirable. . . . Wrist rotation or 'swivel' seemed excessive . . . trill control hazardous . . . frequent 'sticking note' syndrome . . . dynamic unevenness much in evidence." Continuing to search for a solution, he suddenly hit on the idea of tightening the muscles of his face, what he called "The frown (or wrinkled brow) syndrome: This appeared to have (as has been noticed during times of crisis before) a salutary effect. It . . . is hence capable of adding control to trills, etc. . . . I can only conjecture that it relates to neck control and/or thumb elevation mechanism. What is certain, however, is that a wrinkle-free (blank face) expression resulted in immediate lessening of control (especially rhythmic-subdivided count control.) . . ." This suggests that one of the reasons Glenn engaged in so much facial movement while playing is that he felt it gave him better control of his hands. He continued doing "thumb control experiments," and found that a "do not commit yourself to keyboard" style, i.e., raising his hands and fingers, made it possible to generate "certain familiar, and comforting, sensations . . . much increased evenness, etc."[26]

The improvement lasted through most of September, and in October "a new 'image' began to develop . . . possessed of extraordinary naturalness, ease, and spontaneity." Evidently Glenn was beginning to think about his body in a different way. "The answer appeared to be to merge, as one overlap-control unit, the shoulder and body—not, as previously assumed, the shoulder and neck. . . . Thus, the forearm is granted sufficient mobility by the body and upper arm to reach out to applicable areas of the keyboard. . . . During this process, shoulder-body-joins [sic] are felt as overlapping—as though upper arms were united with respective sides of the body. . . ." Glenn went on to describe this newly integrated body image in enormous detail, emphasizing that "it is the *opposite* of all the positions involving the separation of the body from the arm for which specific, self-conscious-style finger controls were required."[27]

But soon there was another setback. On October 14, "it's back to the drawing board. The image of arm-body overlap did not wear well . . . neck grew increasingly sore and immobile . . . still the sensation of loss of spontaneous reaction to the keyboard . . . this manifested itself in stilted trills, etc. . . . Note by note, downward sensation was dominant and when piano was approached, this made playing almost impossible."[28]

In the course of all this dismay and experimentation, Glenn did manage to tape a video program, the fourth installment of CBC's *Musicamera: Music in Our Time,* called "The Artist as Artisan 1930–1940," which was aired on December 14, 1977. It included the Casella *Ricercare on the name BACH* that seemed to have triggered Glenn's problem, as well as works by Hindemith, Krenek, Prokofiev, and Webern. Viewing the tape reveals some of the trouble he was having. In the *Ricercare* he looks like a sick bear, hardly moving, plethorically hunched over the keyboard in such a way that one cannot always see his fingers. He may have wanted to be filmed that way. Looking at the tapes himself, Glenn observed that "Neck-body moved as a confusing unit; thumb was indented to the point of elevation (when not in use); important to tell about indents on other fingers from camera work. . . . So where do we go from here?"

Two new experiments were tried. One consisted of a "fall-into-keyboard approach," the other "involved various attempts to achieve elevation through upper-arm foreshortening." Although his trills seemed improved, Glenn now was bothered by what he called "enlarged veins on hands syndrome." In November that year, he noted "a restoration of control" after driving in his newly acquired Chevrolet Monte Carlo: "It had a remarkable seat (a much less remarkable suspension, however, which made me sea-sick)—a seat which gave much middle back support and which also reclined in the familiar two-door fashion." Another way of stabilizing his back, he found, was to do "much playing in a cross-leg position (right leg over left) and this not only brought back memories of concerts circa 1959 when such positions seemed essential for control and image stability, it also helped to emphasize the spontaneous image of the keyboard and reinforced the ability of the back (as unit) to move forward-backward freely. . . ."

When he visited the Steinway Piano Company in New York on November 9, he was gratified to see that "great improvements had taken place . . . although I avoided repertoire with high concentration of trills.

Gould rehearsing with legs crossed over, 1960. Photograph by Lare Wardrop. Courtesy of Glenn Gould Estate.

. . . There was no neck tension and the image was constant during a 45 minutes to one hour period of practicing."[29]

And so the diary goes on and on—there's a second book yet to come, from January to July 1978. But the question we must ask is why Glenn, at forty-five, would choose to devote so much effort to painstakingly criticizing, dissecting, and correcting the physical dimensions of his piano playing. The most obvious reason, already mentioned, is his dissatisfaction with certain taped performances, such as the Casella piece. But Glenn had long given up any pretense at being a concert pianist expected to do his best in front of audiences. For years he had been producing for the electronic media, where faulty playing can be—and was—easily remedied through splicing. I think that there were deeper reasons for his sudden outburst of pianistic perfectionism. One surely was the recent loss of his mother, who in his conscious and unconscious memory was the incessant corrector of mistakes and prodder toward improved performance. Now that she was gone, these critical functions were entirely within himself. Disconnected from the balancing influence of his mother, he was now tackling the problems of his keyboard performance with the same compulsive fury that he applied to everything else he ever touched: his conversations, his writings, his recordings, his radio programs and television shows. (One is reminded that the breakdown and recovery of his piano technique eighteen years earlier, the "Steinway incident," followed the death of his other piano teacher, Alberto Guerrero.)

Another factor undoubtedly was middle age, normally a time when people review their past, contemplate their diminishing future, and observe, often painfully, the physical decline of the body. A mild to moderate hypertension had flung Glenn into the role of medical patient; he was taking prescribed drugs and losing his attractive youthfulness. But his hunger for control hadn't changed. By taking charge, independently, of his keyboard difficulties, he could maintain an illusion of self-mastery. Interestingly, the diary he kept about these problems is penned much more legibly and coherently than most of his other writings. Reading them gives one the definite impression that Glenn wanted these things to be looked at seriously, possibly even published, perhaps as a legacy for future pianists in trouble and therapists trying to help them.

25

THE LAST YEARS

The second book of Glenn's diary begins January 30, 1978, on an optimistic note:

> I feel now that the proper system is back-as-unit . . . (though it does function best with neck as part of back line) . . . definitely no "*collapsed*" spine, but "collapsed" chest does bring you closer to piano and improves vision. . . . For the past 3 days, everything works. . . .[1]

Considering his emphasis on the posture of his back, it is surprising that the diary says nothing whatsoever about his piano chair. Yet, as is obvious from the films and photographs made of him at the piano during these last years, the chair was no longer giving him adequate support, for the simple reason that the pad he had sat on in earlier years had gotten worn out and was never replaced. This meant that Glenn was now sitting directly on the wooden H-frame, which could only have been uncomfortable if not painful, since his support had to come from a centrally placed board running the entire length of his crotch. The board was attached to the front and the back of the frame, leaving two large empty spaces on either side where his buttocks were unsupported. Thus, the weight of

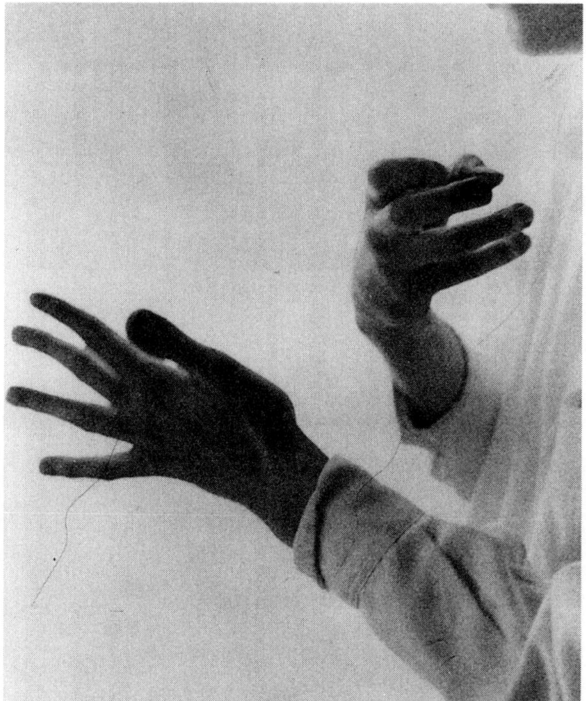

Hands of Gould in conducting gesture. Courtesy of Glenn Gould Estate.

his body had to come down on his perineum and genitals.

I gather that Glenn wasn't consciously aware of this. He treated this chair, built by his father, almost as a sacred object and never complained about it. Nor was the problem picked up by his doctors. Glenn consulted two of them, Dr. Percival and the urologist Philip Klotz, in 1978 about symptoms that he thought were caused by "prostatitis." Both men did a rectal examination and the necessary laboratory studies to rule out an enlargement, infection, or tumor of the prostate gland. "Glenn was very, very worried about his prostate," Dr. Klotz told me. "He was strange. I mean, he was unusual. He didn't volunteer information easily. He was obviously uncomfortable at being here. I think he found the whole thing a terrible pain or drag."[2] Dr. Klotz saw him twice to try to assure him that his prostate was normal. Had he or Percival only watched Glenn playing the piano, the cause of his complaint might have become obvious. (It is a basic requirement of performing arts medicine today that patients be observed while playing their instrument.)

Gould's used-up chair, no padding left on seat. Photograph by Peter Ostwald.

Despite the diary report of sporadic symptoms in February and March 1978—"The wrist had begun to allow an unacceptable rotation . . . shoulder-neck became very sore . . . vision was severely restricted . . . finger-tip nerve tingle . . . brief attack of labyrinthitis"—there seems to have been sufficient improvement for Glenn to contemplate "attempt[ing] a recording in April." For the first time he was considering the "likelihood" that some of his setbacks had "a psychological base." The night before one entry, he had previewed a tape made with a singer he had been involved with, presumably a love affair. "Further, I had not played in three days . . . some 'conducting' had gone on in previous days." When there was significant improvement, Glenn usually attributed it to what he called the "hand-knuckle-bridge," a way of "imaging" his hand as one single, relaxed unit. "It related to the revelation that fingers, ideally, should not be required to move—only, so to speak, to 'be there'—and that all other adjustments should be accommodated by body adjustments."[3]

Anticipating a return to the studio, Glenn's practice schedule became relatively heavy around this time, with up to three to four hours a day devoted to repertoire he was hoping to record for Columbia Masterworks or upcoming CBC programs: Haydn Sonatas, Bach Partitas and the Chromatic Fantasia, Beethoven Sonatas, Strauss's Violin-Piano Sonata. But "the pendulum continue[d] to swing," and in April there was a relapse:

> wrist tightness problems, and, gradually, the separation of one note from the next deteriorates into bumpy grouping and a general lack of fluidity. There was also a general lack of volume control. The fingers permitted only a very restricted, surface contact . . . various experiments with Hand-Knuckle-Bridge were inconclusive. . . .
>
> Suddenly, last night, I determined that in *all* these problems (famous last words) was the lack of *constancy* in shoulder elevation. For one brief moment, and only in right hand, I *had* it; that gleaming, lustrous sound was back and I realized, more than ever, that *that* was the sound of control.[4]

In June, Glenn ventured into the television studio for his contribution to Yehudi Menuhin's *The Music of Man,* which would require demonstrating a new mixing technique for an étude,"Désir," by Scriabin. In addition to the disagreement he was having with Yehudi over spontaneity versus reading of the text, Glenn experienced "extreme tension in the right wrist" and loss of "dynamic contrast control." In July, he "was about to call Andrew Kazdin and set up July [recording] sessions," but being "reluctant to admit an extra-psychic principle at work, I went to apartment at 11:30 P.M. The results were horrendous. G major Toccata fugue, which had become a show-piece was lumpy, inaccurate, uncertain, unrhythmical and ditto everything else that was played."[5]

To judge from his diary, which stops after July 12, 1978, Glenn never again was completely satisfied with the quality of his piano playing. That would have been a plausible explanation for his growing desire to distance himself from the keyboard, embarking on a new career as an orchestral conductor, and devoting more time to reworking his radio pro-

Gould, a solitary figure wandering to Caledon, Ontario, 1980. Photograph by Don Hunstein, CBS Masterworks. Courtesy of Sony Classical.

grams. According to Lorne Tulk, one of Glenn's unfulfilled wishes was to integrate the audio tracks of these programs with films and pictures, a piece of multimedia pioneering.[6] He certainly worked mightily on his Strauss documentary, *The Bourgeois Hero,* in 1978, which involved a cast of eight, including critics, biographers, composers, and conductors. The program is in two "acts," each close to an hour, and consists of six "scenes" about different aspects of Strauss's life, as well as "a rather hard look at his character, including some speculations about the relationship with [his wife] Pauline."[7] There are scenes exploring Strauss's attitudes to his contemporaries, Mahler, Schoenberg, Stravinsky, and so forth, as well as his activities in Germany during the Hitler period.

Another very time-consuming project that made no demands on his ailing piano technique was the film *Glenn Gould's Toronto.* Some years earlier Glenn had met John McGreevy, a young Englishman then working at the CBC who wanted to make films about the world's great cities. McGreevy showed Glenn his recently completed *Peter Ustinov's Leningrad,* and Glenn immediately jumped at the idea of making a film like that.

"It could be his own odyssey to Toronto, his hometown," McGreevy explained to me. "We had a marvelous sympathy for the process, and the design. And he was coming into my world, therefore he was much more willing to accommodate my particular needs. I was after his sensibility, and his wonderful idiosyncrasy, and to do the unusual, as the entire city series was designed to be somewhat idiosyncratic. Glenn would be the only consideration for Toronto. But I don't know that he brought a special language to filmmaking, because he didn't make films himself."[8]

McGreevy asked Glenn to write a script of roughly 4,500 words, to which Glenn responded by producing a manuscript of 45,000 words, telling McGreevy, "You can't touch a thing." McGreevy recalls saying, " 'Well, Glenn, forty-five thousand words, that's a ten-hour film.' So we spent one very long night hacking our way through it, and he took it all in very great spirit because he knew it had to be done." Nevertheless, there remained scenes which McGreevy had to eliminate from the final product. For example, he had "double-shot" a scene where Glenn was driving down Yonge Street when suddenly one of his impersonations, "Ted Slutz," comes out of the crowd, starts to bang on the car, and has a huge argument with him, a good example of Glenn's using an impersonation to project his latent aggression. According to McGreevy, the scene was "god-awful. So to save him from himself, we left it on the cutting-room floor."[9]

Glenn Gould's Toronto turned out to be both entertaining and informative. Gaunt and heavily made up, he wanders about the city divulging historical tidbits and telling quaint stories about himself. Visiting the spacious, bustling Eaton Center with its maze of chrome staircases and open elevators, he expresses astonishment at how much his hometown has changed since he was a boy: "It's absurd! I don't believe it!" Passing the city prison, he comments that a "concert tour is the musical equivalent of a jail sentence." Driving an Eldorado Cadillac (provided by the sponsors), he repeats one of his favorite mottos: "Behind every silver lining is a cloud." And after looking at the Canadian National Exhibition (from the outside—his mother had warned him never to enter such a crowded place), he reports a recurring dream: He is a passenger on an airplane that is about to crash. The stewardess tells him that both pilots are disabled. She begs him to come to the cockpit and take over. Despite his remonstrance that he is completely unqualified to do so, Glenn guides the plane to safety.[10]

There's also a facetious moment when Glenn goes to the Toronto Zoo to conduct a herd of elephants "singing" a Mahler song. He mouths the words in excruciatingly bad German with a nasal tone. The animals look at him quizzically and do some trumpeting. His father had often liked to repeat the story of Glenn's singing to the cows in the country when he was a child, but having to repeat this as an adult and with elephants apparently induced a state of panic in Glenn. As John McGreevy recalls it:

"We'd planned to shoot this scene at six in the morning and at three o'clock in the morning my phone rang. It was Glenn, hoping he wasn't disturbing me, but there he was having just contracted all of the symptoms, bar one, of what he first experienced in 1958 and what was then diagnosed as 'sub-clinical polio.' That's what he said it was, and he'd never had it since '58. There are supposed to be six symptoms. He had the five, but he didn't have the final and definitive symptom, but he just wanted to alert me, in case he didn't show, that I understood the reason why, and I may want to start calling my crew. Well, of course I was shocked. I didn't call the crew. We showed up. He showed up and went on, and we did an absolutely fabulous scene. It was pre-concert nerves, exaggerated in the most baroque way."[11]

The time had come for filming to begin on *Glenn Gould Plays Bach,* the series of television programs that Gould and Bruno Monsaingeon had been working on, writing, perfecting since their last collaboration three years before. It was to be a collaborative effort between Clasart Films in France and the CBC, in whose Studio 7 the first two installments were made. The first, "Question of Instrument," required an entire week (November 19–26, 1979) to complete, and Glenn was obviously not at his best. Peter Mak, the CBC production assistant, told me: "I was in the control room and I felt he was having problems. I thought he didn't have much dexterity in his fingers. He made many mistakes, but wouldn't admit it. I remember him coming to the control room after one recording. What struck me was that he took his shoes off, propped his feet up on the control table—there was a hole in one of his socks—and began talking right away about plans for next day's recordings without saying anything at all about today's session and the problems he was having."[12]

The program begins with Glenn playing the opening fugue from Bach's *Art of the Fugue*. The tempo is slow and stately. It is a fugue that makes no great technical demands, and his performance is spotless, beautiful, very moving. *Art of the Fugue* was the work Glenn cherished above all others by Bach. He had often included selections from it in his concert programs, and in 1962 he had recorded the first nine fugues on the organ of All Saint's Church in Kingsway, Ontario.

> Despite its monumental proportions, an aura of withdrawal pervades the entire work [wrote Glenn]. Bach was, in fact, withdrawing from the pragmatic concerns of music making into an idealized world of uncompromised invention. One facet of this withdrawal is the return to an almost modal concept of modulation. . . .
>
> The harmonic style employed in *The Art of the Fugue,* though rampantly chromatic, is actually less contemporary than that of his early fugal essays and often, in its nomadic meandering about the tonal map, it proclaims a spiritual descent from the ambivalent chromaticism of Cipriano de Rore or Don Carlo Gesualdo.[13]

Since Bach does not indicate a preferred instrument for the *Art of the Fugue,* his last and unfinished composition, it provides an ideal opening for Glenn's impassioned debate with Monsaingeon about whether Bach's music should be played on the piano, an instrument that did not exist in the composer's time. Glenn asserts that Bach was less interested in the texture than the structure of his music. He demonstrates this by playing Bach's own transcription for the keyboard of his Violin Concerto in E Major. And he cites Bach's *Italian Concerto* as an example of a work in which the composer indicates dynamic contrasts that cannot be successfully carried out on the type of keyboard instruments, harpsichords and clavichords, then available. Glenn's final word on the subject is that "the piano can get you a lot closer to Bach's conceptual notions than the harpsichord ever can."[14] In fact, it is possible to achieve dynamic contrasts on both harpsichords and clavichords, the latter showing a greater sensitivity to the actual increase and decrease of sonority.

Next, Glenn (obviously uncomfortable and sweating heavily through his makeup) proposes playing the Bach work he likes least—in fact he says he "hates it"—the Chromatic Fantasia in D Minor. He says it reminds him of the sound track of a Hitchcock movie. As we know from his diary, he had been working on this piece for several years. The performance is very unusual, with great liberties taken in tempo and phrasing.

It sounds choppy in places, with jarring stops and starts, which I assume are the combined product of his dislike for the work plus the technical difficulties he was having at the keyboard. Peter Mak told me, "We ran overtime in filming the Chromatic Fantasia as well as the Partita no. 4 which came afterwards. He had problems with that too."[15]

A vexing predicament for Glenn that year (1979) was his father's romance with Vera Dobson, a widow and longtime friend of the family. Glenn found it utterly unacceptable that his father, despite advanced age and an obvious need for companionship, should remarry and thus besmirch the memory of his beloved mother. The wedding on January 19, 1980—which Glenn did not attend—led to a permanent rift between father and son. John Roberts remembers Glenn agonizing over many drafts of the formal letter that had to be sent excusing himself from being best man at the ceremony. One draft read:

> Dear Father
>
> I've had an opportunity to give quite some thought to the matter of your wedding and specifically to the invitation to serve as your best man. I'm sure that under the circumstances, you (and Mrs. Dobson) would prefer to arrange for a private service—one in which any such conventional ceremonial gesture would be inappropriate; in any case, while I appreciate your kindness in extending the invitation, I regret that I must decline. Needless to say, I wish you much happiness, and I would ask you to pass on my good wishes to Mrs. Dobson.
>
> Most sincerely,[16]

In 1980, Columbia Records issued *The Glenn Gould Silver Jubilee Album,* consisting of works he had taped many years earlier that had never been released, and his newly recorded *A Glenn Gould Fantasy.* Included among the older things were the Strauss *Ophelia Lieder,* opus 67, recorded with Elisabeth Schwarzkopf in 1966; three Scarlatti sonatas; Carl Philipp Emanuel Bach's "Würtemberg" Sonata no. 1 in A Minor; and the Beethoven/Liszt Sixth Symphony transcription (first movement)—all recorded in 1968, plus a reissue of his own *So You Want to Write a Fugue?,* recorded in 1963.

A Glenn Gould Fantasy added to these works was none other than the parody of Horowitz's return to the stage, which Columbia had resisted taping since Glenn had first suggested it to them in 1966. Now, given the green light at last, he proceeded to engage in the fantasy with an incredible outpouring of creative madness. As usual, there were multiple figures speaking about Glenn's prophecy that, in the future, recordings would take the place of live performances. But the voices are predominantly Glenn's impersonations of Karlheinz Klopweisser, Sir Nigel Twitt-Thornwaite, and other alter egos, joined this time by a new character, a Hungarian critic named Márta Hortaványi, author of *Fascistic Implications of the 6/4 Chord in Richard Strauss.* She was played by the attractive young CBC employee Margaret Pacsu, who had recently befriended Glenn and agreed to help him produce his *Fantasy.* It was recorded in three nights at the Inn on the Park, Glenn's studio.

Before the taping began in June, Miss Pacsu observed Glenn washing his hands in water hot enough to leave them scarlet, as though he were preparing for a concert. "I suppose that is mildly neurotic," he admitted. She found the work exhausting: "The pace was really horrendous, and he was very hard to work with [from] the technical point of view, because he knew everything, he could hear everything that he wanted . . . every edit, every single sentence. There weren't four or five versions, there were twenty-five and thirty-five and forty-five. But it was a very satisfactory experience."[17] Highlight of the *Fantasy* was Glenn's impersonation of Horowitz's fictional "return" to the concert stage aboard an oil rig in the

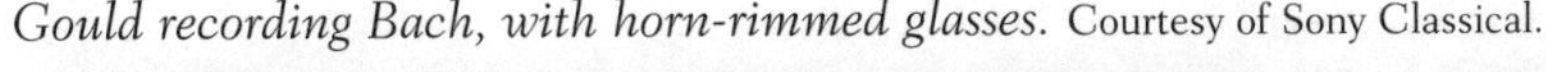

Gould recording Bach, with horn-rimmed glasses. Courtesy of Sony Classical.

Arctic Sea. He begins his program with a bit of von Weber's *Konzertstück,* and as an encore plays his sensational transcription of Ravel's *La Valse.* An announcer tells us that Glenn's piano chair has been washed overboard and he is performing on his knees. The "audience" disappears and Glenn is applauded by the clapping and barking of a single seal.

A much more serious effort, perhaps the most serious film that Glenn ever made, was *An Art of the Fugue,* the second installment of Bruno Monsaingeon's project *Glenn Gould Plays Bach,* produced November 20–25, 1980. As in his previous film about Bach and musical instruments, Glenn wears a blue shirt unbuttoned at the sleeves. He needs a shave and uses heavy horn-rimmed glasses (prescribed as reading glasses by Dr. D'Arcy MacDonald, in March 1976). It is our first glimpse of Glenn wearing glasses in public. Generally speaking, the artist seems more comfortable in this film and speaks with greater animation and vigor. He begins by playing an early fugue of Bach and commenting that not until the composer was in his forties did he reach his peak in being able to integrate contrapuntal material. There follows, with much singing, a prolix discussion of the structure of Bach's Fugue no. 9 from *The Well-Tempered Clavier,* Book II, which Glenn calls "a masterpiece" and goes on to play in its entirety. To judge from this and other performances on the film, he is no longer hampered by any significant hand problems: the articulation is smooth, the tone appealing; there are no sudden stops and starts or weak trills.

At one point, Monsaingeon challenges him but is disarmed by Glenn's unexpected and teasing response:

> *Monsaingeon:* You know, Glenn, in all our discussion you've not once mentioned the word "prelude."
>
> *Gould:* The word "prelude," you say. Well, it's a splendid word. How many times would you like me to mention it?
>
> *Monsaingeon:* Well, if you're talking about *The Well-Tempered Clavier,* how about just as many times as the word "fugue"?
>
> *Gould:* Well, I tell you, I personally think that a lot of fugues in *The Well-Tempered Clavier* are better off without their preludes, and vice versa.[18]

Glenn defends his maverick position by playing a prelude that in his view doesn't fit its fugue, and another that does, for instance, Prelude and Fugue No. 19, from Book 2. After a digression into his distaste for certain Beethoven compositions (specifically the second theme of the "Emperor" Concerto—"such junk" says Glenn), he performs three fugues from the *Art of the Fugue,* including the final one (Contrapunctus XV), which was left unfinished because Bach presumably collapsed while writing it and died shortly afterwards. Glenn's moving performance of this fugue is a fitting closure to the film.

During the year 1980, Glenn made repeated demands on Dr. Percival, who in addition to his usual hearty reassurances responded by writing prescriptions to ease the anxious pianist: Fiorinal (a combination of the barbiturate butalbitol, aspirin, and caffeine) for the treatment of tension headaches; the antibiotic Septra for various infections, colds, and fevers; and the tranquilizers Librax and Valium for Glenn's chronic and acute anxiety.

Early in 1981, a new complication popped up. Glenn's orthopedist Dr. McCarthy discovered him to have an elevated blood uric acid level. This can be a sign of gout, resulting from deposits of uric acid crystals in the joints that produce swelling and pain. Could that have been a cause of Glenn's complaints about his hands and fingers? Dale McCarthy didn't think so when I interviewed him in 1994, nor does the term "gout" appear in Glenn's own copious notes about his health.

Nevertheless, on March 3, 1981, Dr. McCarthy prescribed twenty tablets of Phenylbutazone (100 mgm), an anti-inflammatory drug that may help gout patients by reducing the amount of circulating uric acid in the bloodstream. But this drug is tricky because it can interfere with the formation of blood cells in the bone marrow, resulting in anemia and the loss of white blood cells. We don't know how long Glenn remained on Phenylbutazone, but in November he was put on a less hazardous anti-gout drug, Allopurinal (100 mgm). In December, he received an additional drug for hypertension, Hydrochlorothiazide (50 mgm), which stimulates the excretion of urine.

Glenn expressed considerable dissatisfaction with what his doctors were doing and raised many questions about changes in his medication, as can be seen in the notes he made before one appointment with Dr. Logan.

> Symptoms: *Hand:* now becoming serious. Is Allopurinal a counter (other than for uric acid) and, if so, should it be increased proportionately—otherwise, should another counter be added? Or, if large Aldomet dosage continues, should another Blood Pressure drug be found?
>
> *Foot?*
>
> *Hand asleep*
>
> *Throat—Neck*

Myalgia [muscular pain] etc. as background greatly increased jerks, spasms, stiffness in past week. Does it regulate gland problem. Could it have any relation to Aldomet increase. Does it tie to cough and throat clearing induced by Aldomet?

Labyrinthitis

Blood pressure energy. Does it lead a life of its own? Or does it intersect?

Eye—sty-like sensation developed coincident with Aldomet increase N.S. but annoying, and coupled with glare-like sensation

Antidote to 3 drops (Gantrisin etc.)

Pressure Point describe; does it pose a serious problem, or is it left over of high blood pressure? . . .

(1) If Uric Acid problem continues, is Diazide an acceptable substitute for Hydrochlorothiazide? Aldactone is better and

(2) If 2 Aldomet per [day] can control hypertension and not make hand situation intolerable, ok. Otherwise what can be substituted for Aldomet?[19]

It's truly remarkable that under these circumstances, Glenn was able to proceed with his biggest project in 1981, the filming and re-recording of Bach's *Goldberg Variations,* which had long been planned as the third installment of Bruno Monsaingeon's *Glenn Gould Plays Bach* series. Although Glenn rarely re-recorded anything that he had made earlier, he reconsidered in the case of the *Goldbergs,* which were still selling well in their 1955 version and were widely considered one of his greatest triumphs. He felt compelled to do this for several reasons. The technology of recording had improved enormously over the intervening years. "Somebody had the nerve to invent something called Stereo," he relates to Monsaingeon in the film. "Then a few years later someone else had the audacity to invent a process called Dolby which invalidated the quality of sound in which [the earlier *Goldberg* recording] was done."[20]

Another reason for a remake of the *Goldbergs* was his dissatisfaction with certain interpretive details of the first recording. In an interview with the critic Tim Page, Glenn joked about Variation 15 resembling a nocturne by Chopin or Bizet, and he felt generally that the tempi in the first recording had been too fast. "It was very nice, but it was perhaps a little bit like thirty very interesting but somewhat independent-minded pieces going their own way and all making a comment on the ground bass on which they are all formed." What he was looking for at the mature age of forty-eight was "a way of making some sort of almost mathematical correspondence between the theme and the subsequent variations so that there would be some sort of temporal relationship."[21]

To take advantage of all the latest developments in technology, including the recent introduction of "digital" sound from Japan, it was decided to make the new recording at the Columbia studios in New York, where a Sony digitizer was available on a part-time basis. Glenn also wanted a new instrument to play on, perhaps a Bechstein. Bob Silverman had suggested he try out the Yamaha pianos available at Ostrowsky Piano Company just behind Carnegie Hall. A brand-new Yamaha concert grand stood in the window there, and in order to provide privacy for Glenn while playing on it, Mrs. Ostrowsky hung sheets across the window. He didn't like that particular piano, but just before leaving spotted a dusty, used Yamaha in the back of the store. He liked that one so much that he immediately bought it and ordered it shipped to the Columbia studio for his *Goldberg Variations* recording. Bob Silverman told me that Glenn bought the new one in the window as well, paying for both instruments by check.[22]

The recording was done in six different sessions, from 4:00 P.M. until midnight, in April and May 1981, the entire production being simultaneously filmed by Monsaingeon and his crew. Glenn was very fussy as usual and demanded numerous retakes of each variation, some of which he insisted on bringing back to Toronto for editing on his own equipment. But because of his unfamiliarity with digital editing, the final product was realized—and what a superb realization it is—by the Columbia producer Sam Carter. Andrew Kazdin, Glenn's producer for fifteen years, was no longer involved. The two men had had an unpleasant parting, with Glenn in such turmoil about letting Kazdin go that John Roberts suggested. "I think it's maybe good to go and talk to a psychiatrist. It doesn't mean that one is mentally ill."[23] Kazdin was so deeply hurt—"No regrets, no emotion, no thank you's"—that he attributed the rupture of their relationship to Glenn's "personal dislike" of him.[24] More likely Kazdin had fallen victim to Glenn's habitual way of ridding himself of people he felt were no longer of any use to him. Around this time Glenn even considered letting go of Columbia and any other recording company in order to go into business for himself.

The new *Goldberg* recording, and the film made of the recording, were greatly successful, and the debate still goes on as to which is the "better" performance, that of 1955 or the one of 1981. It's a fruitless debate because both recordings are superb. If you want youthful abandon, spon-

*Gould surrounded by pictures of 1955—*Goldberg Variations *sessions.* Photograph by Don Hunstein, CBS Masterworks. Courtesy of Sony Classical.

taneity, and a miraculous technique, listen to the first. If you prefer stateliness, mathematical precision, the reflective wisdom of middle age, and the clarity of digital sound, listen to the second. In the opening and closing "Aria" of the 1981 recording, Glenn takes much more time, about twice as much as in the 1955 version, and some of the variations are also played at a more leisurely tempo. The fluency and smoothness of his finger action have obviously been restored; the trills are precise and not sluggish. Only by watching closely does one notice that Glenn's hands are often jittery—see, for example, in Variation 17—showing a mild tremor that I assume is a medication side effect. And of course he has visibly aged. The film reveals his puffiness, pallor, and stooped posture.

A look at the "out-takes," those segments that were not included in the final version, reveals the enormous labor of love that went into this recording. Glenn is the true perfectionist, throwing out numerous retakes to eliminate slight defects, imperceptible to the ordinary listener. At one point he is heard to say "shit" because of dissatisfaction with his own performance. But despite the ravages of disease, his playing radiates the enthusiasm and joy of creativity.

26

A FATAL STROKE

One of Glenn's biggest projects in 1982, the last year of his life, was making the musical sound track for a movie, *The Wars,* based on Timothy Findley's novel. He had been invited to write the music himself, as we saw earlier, but decided instead to assemble a collage of works by his favorite composers, as well as hymns that he remembered from his childhood. When Findley met him early that year in a screening room to talk about the film, he was shocked by Glenn's physical appearance:

> He's sick—he's really ill. He looked ill, because the color of his skin was so alarming. And his hair looked dead. It really had that awful look of someone who's been ill in a very major way, so that their hair dies. And it looked like that—it looked like dead hair.[1]

At the last session of working on the sound track with other musicians, the cellist Conrad Bloemendal also noticed Glenn's deterioration, commenting: "It was very scary how unwell and almost ghostlike he looked. He was much more stooped, and he was much thinner. He couldn't see very well. He was a bit wandering with his eyes, and he was stumbling,

Gould in his final struggle. Photograph by Don Hunstein. Courtesy of Sony Classical.

twice, in the studio. It was just like he was going to fall. I was wondering what was going on with him."[2]

But in spite of his obvious handicaps, Glenn persisted in yet another energy-consuming project. He had decided to devote himself seriously to conducting, an old ambition held in abeyance by the crippling back pain and other unpleasant sensations he used to experience after wielding the baton when he was younger and more intent on pursuing the career of a pianist. Now, with his fiftieth birthday approaching in September, Glenn occasionally talked as though he might be ready to give up the piano altogether. Yet he undertook a new project with CBS Masterworks and went to New York in February 1982 to record the Brahms Ballades, opus 10, and again during June and July to record the Brahms Rhapsodies, opus 79.

In preparing for his new career as conductor of a symphony orchestra, Glenn made lists of works that he wanted to perform, including all of

Beethoven's Overtures as well as his *Grosse Fuge* and Second and Eighth symphonies. Other works on his agenda were by Mendelssohn, his Overtures and Third and Fourth symphonies; Brahms, the Third Symphony, Alto Rhapsody, Violin Concerto, and "Tragic Overture;" and Richard Strauss, the *Metamorphosen.* Getting to know the scores of these compositions was no problem because Glenn could easily memorize them. But he lacked the experience of leading an orchestra and would drive secretly to the city of Hamilton, forty miles from Toronto, where he hired members of the Hamilton Philharmonic to practice with. Although he was shy and tense at first, the experience he had gained over the years in conducting his own playing as well as that of small ensembles soon transferred itself into the broader gestures needed for leading an orchestra, and most of the players seemed to enjoy working with him.

The only thing they ever put on tape, in April 1982, was two movements of Beethoven's Piano Concerto no. 2 in B-flat Major, opus 19. Glenn had already recorded this concerto as a soloist, once with Leonard Bernstein in 1957 and again during live performances in Moscow and Stockholm, in 1957 and 1958. But all of these were monaural recordings, and since his other four Beethoven concerto recordings were available in stereophonic sound, he had long hoped to re-record the Second Concerto in stereo as well. In 1978, when Herbert von Karajan was in New York, Glenn had proposed recording the solo part in Toronto and then sending the tapes to Karajan, who was supposed to add the orchestral voices. But Karajan, as we have seen, refused to collaborate on such a scheme. Early in 1982, Glenn phoned the British conductor Neville Marriner, who was guest conducting in the States, to see whether he might be willing to make such recordings with him, but their discussion also came to nothing. Finally he hit on the idea of being both soloist and conductor, but not in the traditional way of leading the orchestra from the keyboard. What he wanted was to conduct from the podium while another pianist, later to be dubbed out, played the solo. Glenn's own interpretation of the piano part would then be added to the tape.

To find the necessary collaborator, Glenn called Martin Canin in New York, and he recommended the young pianist John Klibonoff. Klibonoff agreed, at a price, to come to Hamilton and be Glenn's phantom soloist, but he was not overly impressed with Glenn's ability to lead the orchestra and found it difficult to play the second movement at the excessively slow tempo that Glenn required. Nonetheless, they taped the first two movements of the concerto before this project was dropped.

In July 1982, Glenn recorded Wagner's *Siegfried Idyll* with fifteen handpicked symphony and freelance musicians from Toronto.[3] The clarinetist was Timothy Maloney, now director of the Music Division at the National Library of Canada, who writes:

> We knew we were taking part in something special, and because there was a high level of musicianship, of concentration and commitment and dedication to the task at hand, it was musically very satisfying. . . . Gould was very open and warm with us and we went late into the evening both nights; as we got tired and found it a little more difficult to concentrate . . . he helped lighten things up a lot with his wonderfully dry wit. We joked about a name for the ensemble and Gould came up with two of the best . . . The Academy of St. Lawrence in the Market . . . The Ashes of Toronto.[4]

Glenn worked them relentlessly to produce an elegant, slow-paced performance that emphasized the contrapuntal structure of Wagner's composition, a one-movement serenade incorporating various themes from the opera *Siegfried,* written in honor of his wife Cosima. Because Glenn had chosen to record the chamber music version, employing only a small group of instruments, we cannot tell how he would have managed with a full-size orchestra.

A second recording session had been planned, for Mendelssohn's "Fingal's Cave" Overture, which would have required a much bigger orchestra. The musicians had already been selected and hired when Glenn suffered his fatal stroke. Thus we will never know how far he might have gone in his career as an orchestral conductor. Surely there would have been major obstacles. For one thing, all of his rehearsals had to be held in extreme privacy, behind locked doors. Glenn's intolerance for audiences meant that we would have gotten to know his conducting only by means of the electronic media—radio, recordings, perhaps television. Another negative factor would have been his extreme sensitivity to criticism. Symphony conductors have to put up with a great deal of social stress, grumbling from the players, dissension from boards of directors, hassles about programming, and of course the inevitable griping from the press. To be a successful conductor requires diplomacy, a willingness to face the public—and robust health. I doubt that Glenn Gould with his many psychological and physical handicaps would have gotten nearly as far as some of the other outstanding pianists of our time—André Previn, Daniel Barenboim, Vladimir Ashkenazi, and Christoph Eschenbach—who have become successful conductors.

The last recording Gould made, in New York in September 1982 (the month of his stroke), was as a soloist playing the early Piano Sonata in B Minor, opus 5, by Richard Strauss.

September 25 was Glenn's fiftieth birthday, a significant event because it marked a half century of life and accomplishments. But he was in no mood for celebrating. He knew he was in poor health. His lists of symptoms and complaints had grown longer, with a new and embarrassing one, "urination while asleep," recently added. He visited his doctors frequently, and they kept him well supplied with anti-hypertensive, anti-headache, anti-gout, and anti-anxiety medication. In addition, Glenn would send Ray Roberts out to buy non-prescription drugs: Milk of Magnesia tablets for constipation, Cepacol throat lozenges for soreness and coughing, vitamin C tablets, hydrogen peroxide, and an aspirin-caffeine-codeine preparation called "Frosst 222."[5] Both Glenn's father and his friends at the CBC had wanted to arrange birthday parties for him, but Glenn made it clear that he preferred to be alone. His new stepmother baked cookies and bought a sweater for him, and despite his insistence that he had a cold and wasn't feeling well, she and his father drove over to the Inn on the Park to visit him. Glenn was well enough to go outside to the car with them.

That afternoon, a Saturday, he observed his birthday in his own private way, by phoning a few friends he knew would be able to appreciate a laudatory article about to appear in the *New York Times,* reviewing his newly released *Goldberg Variations* recording. He called Lorne Tulk and read the entire article to him. "It obviously gave him great pleasure," recalls Tulk, "and he also told me, 'I have a surprise for you. I have something for you. But you have to come up and get it, but not right now,' the reason being that he had a cold. He said I should come by next week to pick up the 'surprise.' "[6] Glenn also got in touch with Robert Silverman to tell him to read the *New York Times* piece, and called him back the next day to discuss it. "He sounded extremely cheerful and peppy," says Silverman, "more 'up' than any time that I can remember."[7]

Others remember a more pessimistic tone. Glenn told some of his friends that he did not expect to live much longer after turning fifty. Jessie Greig recalls him as unusually "serious" that entire week before his birthday. "He seemed to think that everything was slipping away from his control." He appeared "obsessed" with ideas about his funeral and told her he was afraid that nobody would attend it. "We'd never talked about anything like that before. He said he wanted to be like Huckleberry Finn and come to his own funeral."[8] John Roberts, then working in Ottawa, remembers Glenn saying that his life's work was finished—"the world has had enough of Glenn Gould."[9] These depressed remarks stand in stark contrast to the optimism Glenn had expressed shortly before his death while talking with Bruno Monsaingeon and John McGreevy about new films he planned to make with them.

Glenn had made a will two years before providing a life interest of $50,000 in a trust fund for his father, and bequeathing his entire estate (approximately $750,000 at the time of his death) to the Salvation Army and the Toronto Humane Society, an organization dedicated to animal welfare. One of his lifelong interests was to have a sort of retirement farm for old cows, horses, dogs, and other animals. Several times he had gone with his father or with John Roberts to look for land to buy on Manitoulin Island, the largest freshwater island in the world, about three hundred miles north of Toronto. Ray Roberts recalls Glenn's yearning to live there himself—a kind of "ideal existence, and he wanted me and my wife to move there too. The 'Puppy Farm' was his vision of a place where all lost, stray, and sick animals would be welcome. But he never thought he had enough money to make it come true."[10]

On the afternoon of Monday, September 27, two days after Glenn's fiftieth birthday, Dr. John Percival received a call from Ray Roberts, who told him, "I'm speaking for Glenn Gould. He thinks he's had a stroke."

"Now why would you say that?" asked the doctor, who for nearly a decade had gotten hundreds of alarming phone calls from Glenn. Ray went on to explain that after awakening that afternoon, Glenn had noticed a loss of sensation in his left leg.

"Well, that doesn't sound like very much," Dr. Percival remembers telling Ray Roberts, ". . . he phoned back about an hour later to say, 'Glenn is not feeling too good, and I don't know what to make of him, but he wants you to come out here and look after him.' " It was in the middle of the afternoon and Dr. Percival had an office full of patients, so he said, 'Well, really, I can't come out at this moment. Why not take him down to the hospital, to the emergency room, and have them examine him to see if it's something serious.' 'Oh,' replied Ray, 'he doesn't want to go to the hospital, he just wants you to come out and look after him.' " Dr. Percival reiterated that he would not be able to come over until later on. An hour or two later, he received another phone call from Ray, between five and six in the afternoon: " 'You know, there is something seriously wrong, he's got a bad headache and his speech is not very clear,' and I said 'Now look, for goodness sakes, you be sensible, you call the ambulance right away and get him to the hospital.' "[11]

Ray says that while Glenn was certain he had had a stroke, he wanted to minimize its consequences by insisting that hospitalization was unnecessary. It may have been his lifelong dread of hospitals as a repository of germs. He was also afraid of the publicity that might ensue. He wanted the doctor just to come over to his studio at the Inn on the Park and treat him there. Ray made other phone calls but soon became convinced there was no alternative to hospitalization. "Then came the question of how to get him there. The last thing in the world Glenn wanted was an ambulance. So we had to get him down to his Lincoln in a [wheel]chair. I put him in the car and drove him to the Toronto General Hospital."[12]

Examined at 8:44 P.M. in the emergency room, Glenn was found to have muscular weakness over the left side of his body, including his face, and some inequality of the deep tendon reflexes. There was no diminution in his responsiveness to sensory stimulation, touch, pain, or change in position. He was drowsy, but had no difficulty speaking. His blood pressure was 124/90 and the pulse rate 104 per minute. A preliminary diagnosis of cerebro-vascular-accident (stroke) with left-sided paralysis was made. It was suspected that the cause might be a blood clot in one of the arteries supplying the right side of his brain, and he was admitted to the neurology department for further observation. There it was noted that Glenn had been seen at the Toronto General Hospital once before, in 1976, complaining of lightheadedness, and found to have an elevated blood pressure, which since then had been managed by Dr. Logan. The neurology staff concurred with the diagnosis of a right frontal brain infarction due to a blood clot causing paralysis of the left side of the body. There was no evidence of a hemorrhage, but a CAT scan of the brain was recommended. It showed enlarged ventricles but no signs of acute bleeding.

The next day, Tuesday, September 28, Glenn was slightly worse. He complained of a frontal headache and kept holding the right side of his head with his hand. The left side of his body continued to be paralyzed, and there was some loss of sensation on that side as well as a defect in vision. But he remained alert, and had a brief visit with Jessie and a longer one with his father, who found him asleep most of the time but occasionally making conductorlike movements with his right arm. Later that evening Glenn was more alert and asked Ray Roberts about the latest stock market results and some income tax matters he wanted cleared up. A television set was brought into Glenn's room, and he talked about wanting to tape a man on one of the channels. There were other signs of incoherence and disorientation. He told a nurse he was in a recording studio. At 10:00 P.M. he asked Ray to call Jessie, and they played Twenty Questions over the phone. Glenn's speech remained articulate but confused.

The following morning, Wednesday, September 29, he was clearly much worse, more lethargic, more incoherent, barely able to move or answer questions, having trouble swallowing, and complaining of fierce headache. The doctors suspected that swelling was developing in the right side of his brain and exerting pressure. Another CAT scan was ordered. It showed that the midline structures of the brain had shifted markedly from right to left, confirming the clinical impression of massive right-sided swelling. A blood-flow study revealed that there was no blood passing through the right internal carotid artery, one of the major blood vessels supplying the brain. Glenn was seen by a consultant in hematology that day who prescribed Persantine (dipyridamole), a drug that inhibits the adhesion of blood platelets, thus reducing the chance of further blood clot formation. Chest X-rays showed that fluid was collecting in the chest cavity. To try to lessen the swelling of his brain, Glenn was started on Dexamethasone, injected by vein; this is a synthetic adrenocortical hormone which has potent anti-inflammatory effects. He also received injections of Mannitol, another way to decrease intracranial pressure, but the effects of these treatments were minimal. That evening he was diagnosed to be comatose and was moved to the intensive care unit.

On Thursday, September 30, a breathing tube was inserted to administer oxygen and help with respiration. Nursing care was stepped up to manage the patient's basic needs. He was by now totally unconscious, and complications were beginning to set in, a rise of temperature and a lessening of urinary output, which were treated by administering liquids by vein, and starting him on Lasix (furosemide), a powerful diuretic. An electroencephalogram to measure brain waves showed that there was still some brain activity present, but it was markedly diminished. Other tests revealed damage to the medulla oblongata (the brain's central controlling mechanism of bodily functions). His father was told that there were signs of incipient brain death and that the prognosis was very grave. This shattering news he shared with the others holding vigil, including John Roberts, who had come to Toronto from Ottawa and was standing by.

A chest X-ray done the following day, Friday, showed that both lungs were infiltrated with fluid at the base. Another electroencephalogram revealed massive loss of brain function on the right side and also some disturbance of function on the left side. All the clinical signs indicated a worsening of Glenn's dire neurological condition; he could no longer breathe spontaneously when disconnected from the respirator. There was no improvement at all on Saturday. One of the doctors concluded that the brain damage was by now irreversible and that his chances for survival were virtually nil. On Sunday, October 3, Glenn's blood pressure had risen to 220/125 and he developed a nosebleed, both probably in reaction to the enormous amount of pressure building up inside his head. There was no longer any hope of recovery, and it was suggested that life-support systems be withdrawn because the patient was in essence "brain-dead." His father agreed, but did not wish this to take place on October 3, as that was his wife Vera's birthday. So on Monday, October 4, a week after Glenn had entered the hospital, he was taken off life support. His heart stopped beating at 11:00 A.M. and he was pronounced dead.

An autopsy was done two hours later. It revealed that there was a blood clot filling the right cavernous sinus, a large vein that runs within the bones of the face above the nose and drains blood from the brain. Lying within this venous sinus is the carotid artery, supplying blood to the brain. The clot in the cavernous sinus was estimated to have been about ten days old, which would have coincided with the time of Glenn's birthday, when he was feeling sick and thought he had a cold. Although no fungi or bacteria could be demonstrated inside the cavernous sinus (Glenn had been given antibiotics while in the hospital), it was suspected that an infectious process most probably had led to the blood clot, since that is the most common cause of cavernous sinus thrombosis. Some clotted blood was observed in the left cavernous sinus as well.

The pathologist found that the internal carotid artery lying within the right cavernous sinus also contained a blood clot, which was the immediate cause of circulatory impairment to the right side of Glenn's brain and the resulting paralysis, coma, and death. The clot in his carotid artery was not as old or well organized as the one in the surrounding cavernous sinus. What could have caused it? A minor degree of arteriosclerosis was discovered in the walls of the carotid artery, but the pathologist felt this was insufficient to account for the kind of blood clot that had developed. He concluded that the clot in the carotid artery most likely was an extension of the older cavernous sinus thrombosis.

The postmortem examination also confirmed the clinical findings of massive brain damage. The right side of the brain was swollen and larger than the left, there were areas of bleeding and destruction of brain tissue, and some of the vital brain structures had herniated downward into the spinal cord canal through the connective tissues that support and confine the brain. The autopsy also showed some enlargement of the left side of the heart consistent with chronic hypertension, and a mildly fatty liver (due, I would assume, to dietary insufficiency). But no physical abnormalities were found in the kidneys, prostate, bones, joints, muscles, or other parts of the body that Glenn so often had complained about.

News of the catastrophe had been suppressed until two days before Glenn died, and the first announcement that he had been admitted to the Toronto General Hospital because of a "severe stroke" included a falsely optimistic note to the effect that it was still too early to determine if there would be any "residual problems."[13] This precipitated a flood of hopeful telephone calls, letters, and telegrams, including ours from San Francisco:

> 10/02/82-14:27
>
> DEAR GLENN. TERRIBLY SORRY TO HEAR ABOUT YOUR ILLNESS. WE THINK OF YOU AND SEND YOU OUR WARMEST WISHES FOR A PROMPT AND COMPLETE RECOVERY, AND ALL OTHER VARIATIONS ON THAT THEME. YOUR GOLDBERGS ARE SUPERB. ALL OUR LOVE.
> LISE AND PETER OSTWALD

Three days later, on Tuesday, October 5, 1982, the world got the whole tragic story: "Glenn Gould, Pianist Is Dead."[14] In my letter of condolence to his father, I wrote that

> your loss is shared by millions who admire and love Glenn's work, and by a few—I consider myself to be one of those so fortunate—whose lives were graced by his friendship. . . . You have given the world one of the greatest musicians of all time, a mind as keen as Mozart's and a pianism as exciting as Liszt's. . . . He will be immortal.[15]

After a short stay in a funeral home where many of Glenn's friends and co-workers paid their respects, his body was laid to rest next to his mother, in the Mount Pleasant Cemetery. His grave is marked by a small two-tone granite stone on which is engraved the outline of a piano. Within this outline we see his name, years of birth and death, and the first three measures of the "Aria" from Bach's *Goldberg Variations.* It was designed, with the help of an artist, by his lawyer Stephen Posen.

A formal memorial service was organized for October 15, at the beau-

"Here I stood, in January 1995, where my friend is buried, nearly four decades after our initial meeting" (Peter Ostwald). Photograph by Peter Ostwald.

"With this final picture of a commemorative plaque, I end my pilgrimage honoring the life and achievements of Glenn Gould" (Peter Ostwald). Photograph by Peter Ostwald.

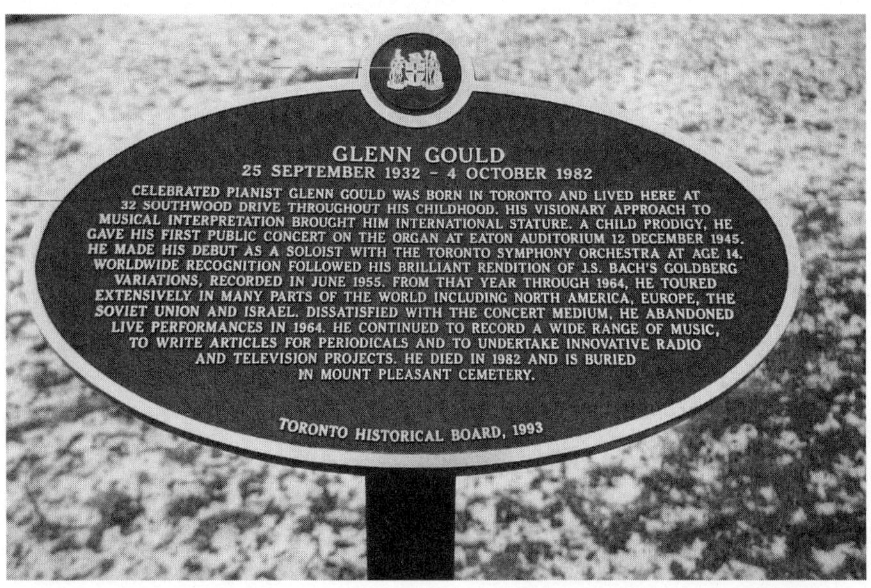

tiful Gothic St. Paul's Anglican Church in Toronto. It overflowed with Glenn's friends, family, co-workers, and admirers. John Roberts gave a superb eulogy, describing Glenn as "having carried the burden of genius all his life. He realized he was a man apart. Everything about him was different . . . a truly modern man and a remarkable innovator. . . . very concerned with the human condition, and, in his own way, the purest and most moral person I have ever encountered."[16]

The high point of the musical program, which included works by Bach, Beethoven, and Brahms, was Maureen Forrester's magnificent rendition of the aria "Erbarme Dich" from Bach's *St. Mathew Passion.* But the most unforgettable moment came at the end of the service, when Glenn's recently recorded "Aria" from the *Goldberg Variations* was discreetly played through loudspeakers installed in the church by Vincent Tovell and his CBC technicians. This not only gave Glenn a chance to have the last word, as he was heard humming with the Aria, but also fulfilled his fantasy of attending his own funeral. Thus, as Bach's ethereal music ended, the frightening specter of death and the terror of inevitable dissolution vanished from Glenn's consciousness.

EPILOGUE AND ACKNOWLEDGMENTS

A few words may be in order about the evolution of this book, which I believe is the first to explore in detail the psychological and psychiatric dimensions of Glenn Gould's life. It comes in the wake of considerable interest in a musical genius who captured so much public attention during his lifetime and has become almost a mythical figure since his death.

Within a year of that death, John McGreevy produced a magnificent commemorative volume, *Glenn Gould: By Himself and His Friends,* pointing out that "Glenn was by nature an ecstatic. His search for ecstasy took on the dimensions of a moral cause, revealing something of the infinite."[1] The book has a foreword by Herbert von Karajan stating that "For the next generation [Gould] will be regarded as an outstanding musician who combined the musical impact of his playing technique with impeccable taste. He created a style which led to the future."[2] Other dimensions of his creativity are commented on by Richard Kostelanetz, Yehudi Menuhin, Robert Fulford, and a roster of friends and colleagues, as well as by Glenn himself. The book is a rich collection of essays, primarily laudatory, as befits a memorial tribute.

More critical is the biography by Otto Friedrich, who was contacted in 1984 by Stephen Posen, the executor of Glenn's estate, and given access to his private papers. Friedrich interviewed many people who had known Glenn personally, myself included. His book, *Glenn Gould: A Life and Variations,* was published in 1989. It gave copious information not only about about Glenn's accomplishments but also about his many eccentricities.[3] I wasn't entirely satisfied with the way Friedrich had handled the medical aspects of Glenn's problems, so I wrote a review of the book for the professional journal *Medical Problems of Performing Artists,* pointing out that "Gould will always remain an important symbol for the treacherous health problems that can beset persons of specialness and charisma, and the challenge of treating them."[4]

That review was spotted by Cornelius Hofmann, editor of the *Bulletin of the International Glenn Gould Society* in Groningen, Holland, who asked whether he could publish it.[5] I agreed and was subsequently invited to attend the Glenn Gould Festival 1992 in Holland (the tenth anniversary of his death), a commemorative festival was also held in Toronto for which I had been interviewed by Ken Winters for a CBC broadcast. At the Holland meeting I presented a lecture on "The Tragedy of Premature Death Among Geniuses, What Does It Mean? Can It Be Prevented?" Many pianists and Gould scholars from around the world were at that meeting, and I had a chance to meet, among others, the violinist and filmmaker Bruno Monsaingeon from Paris; the Canadian musicologist Kevin Bazzana, who was working on a Ph.D. about Gould; Junichi Miyazawa, who wanted to reprint my "Personal Reminiscences" in Japan;[6] Robert Silverman, with whom I had participated once before in an international conference; and John Roberts, founding president of the Glenn Gould Foundation in Toronto.

It was Roberts who urged me most strongly to expand my "Reminiscences" into a book that might deal with some of the more personal issues of Glenn's life which had not found a place in the Glenn Gould literature. Having recently completed a book about the mentally ill dancer Vaslav Nijinsky, I welcomed the idea but was hesitant to pursue it because I had been encouraging a Canadian colleague, Helen Mesaros, in publishing a psychoanalytic study of Glenn Gould. After lengthy discussions with Helen and our mutual friend Bob Silverman, I realized that my approach would be substantially different from hers and decided to go ahead with the work.

To acknowledge the many people who have aided my research, I want to begin with my wife, Lise Deschamps Ostwald, who knew Glenn and has been incredibly supportive, especially during the last year when I became so ill that I really would not have been able to proceed without her assistance. Lise reviewed each chapter before and during the revision stage and made many valuable suggestions. She also assumed major responsibility for organizing the Glenn Gould Film Festival and Symposium presented by San Francisco Performances and the Health Program for Performing Artists, held at the Dolby Facilities in San Francisco on November 18, 1995, an event that brought together members of the medical profession and artistic community. My friend and colleague Frank A. Johnson helped greatly with the symposium in addition to reviewing and commenting on my writing.

It would have been impossible to write this book without the cooperation of Glenn's father, the late Russell Herbert Gould. Furthermore, I could not have proceeded without approval and encouragement from Stephen Posen, attorney of the Gould Estate, who diligently opened many doors for me, facilitating my work and allowing me to do the necessary research. I also extend my gratitude to John Roberts for his constant support. And now I must acknowledge and thank the many other people who also agreed to share their thoughts and memories of Glenn with me. First the doctors: Morris Charendoff, A. A. Epstein, Grant Gould, (Glenn's uncle), Stanley Greben, (and his wife Marylin), Morris Herman, Oscar Kaufman, Philip Klotz, D'Arcy MacDonald, Dale McCarthy, Alan Parkin, John Percival, Joseph Stephens, Marvin Stock, A. H. Thompson, and Herbert Vear.

Next, the musicians: pianist William Aide, cellist Conrad Bloemendal, pianist Carlo Bussotti, pianist Martin Canin, soprano Ellen Faull, pianist Leon Fleisher, violinist Mark Gottlieb, pianist William Corbett Jones, harpsichordist Greta Kraus, pianist Anton Kuerti, violinist Robert Mann, violinist Yehudi Menuhin, composer Oskar Morawetz, conductor Roger Norrington, pianist Michael Oelbaum, musicologist Harvey Olnick, pianist Andras Schiff, cellist Helen Stross, and pianist James Tocco. Next, those who were closely associated with Glenn in his work: his manager Walter Homburger; the filmmaker John McGreevy; his CBC producers Franz Kraemer and Vincent Tovell; his friend and electronic wizard Lorne Tulk; the production assistant Peter Mak; and the publisher Robert Silverman. His childhood friend, Robert Fulford. Patrick J. Sullivan, his accountant. Last but not least, I want to thank Ray Roberts for his patience and generosity in giving me his views about Glenn and assisting me in all sorts of practical ways, and Jessie Greig for allowing me to speak with her over the telephone about her cousin. To Timothy Maloney and his fine staff at the National Library of Canada in Ottawa,

I am deeply grateful for access to the Glenn Gould Archives and help with the copying and transfer of documents, and especially to Cheryl Gillard for her graciousness in responding to so many queries.

I also want to express my appreciation to academic colleagues who generously gave me support and advice during the writing of this book: my wise counselor and friend Leon Epstein; Craig Van Dyke, chairman of the Department of Psychiatry at the University of California; my oncologist for twelve years, Samuel Spivack; to Frank Wilson and Bernard Gordon for their unfailing optimism and support; and a group of fellow doctors, writers (especially John MacGregor), and teachers called the Psychobiography Study Group, which meets once a month to review and discuss the work we are all doing. To the wonderful "F-holes," nickname for my chamber music partners and friends, for years of beautiful music, Paul Hersh, Ted Rex, Stephen Levintow, Bob Bloch, Bob Kadarauch and Jonathan Khuner. I am grateful also to my grammar school friend, Jack Taylor, who provided years of literary enlightenment. Many thanks also to Rosalie Siegel for agreeing to be my marvelously helpful agent, and to Edwin Barber, vice chairman of W. W. Norton & Company, for his superlative work in editing the manuscript.

I really cannot close this book without paying tribute to Glenn Gould, who got all this started by sharing so much with me—his playing, his conversations, his telephone calls, his humor, his charm, his originality, and his problems. Glenn's absolutely unique genius has had an unforgettable influence on the world, and I look forward to other books that will provide insight into the ecstasy and tragedy of his career.

San Francisco, March 12, 1996

NOTES TO SOURCES

Introduction

1. Geoffrey Payzant, *Glenn Gould,: Music and Mind*. Toronto: Van Nostrand Reinhold, 1978, p. xi.

2. Peter Ostwald, *Schumann: The Inner Voices of a Musical Genius*. Boston: Northeastern University Press, 1985.

3. R.T. Sataloff, A.G. Brandfonbrener, and R.N. Lederman, eds., *Textbook of Performing Arts Medicine*. New York: Raven Press, New York, 1991.

4. The UCSF Health Program for Performing Artists consists of the following medical specialists and consultants: Nicholas M. Barbaro, M.D., Neurosurgery; Barry C. Baron, M.D., Otolaryngology; Alexandra Botwin, Ph.D., Clinical Psychology; Nancy N. Byl, MPH, Ph.D., Physical Medicine; Ephraim P. Engleman, M.D., Rheumatology; Paul Fishman, M.D., Psychiatry; Peter Forster, M.D., Psychiatry; Gary S. Gelber, M.D., Psychoanalysis; Bernard I. Gordon, M.D., Dermatology; Leonard Gordon, M.D., Hand Surgery; Edward Green, D.D.S., Dentistry; Madeleine F. Grumbach, M.D., Psychiatry; Daniel F. Hartman, M.D., Otolaryngology; Dorothy Hejna, L.C.S.W., Psychiatric Social Work; Frank A. Johnson, M.D., Psychiatry; Richard Lieberman, M.D., Psychiatry; Robert E. Markison, M.D., Surgery; Leonore Mesches, M.A., Psychotherapy; Peter F. Ostwald, M.D., Psychiatry; Herbert W. Peterson, M.D., Psychiatry; Susan Raeburn, Ph.D., Clinical Psychology; Raphael B. Reider, M.D., Internal Medicine; Michael F. Saviano, M.D., Otolaryngology; Max Scheck, M.D., Orthopedics; Frank R. Wilson, M.D., Neurology—

Research/Education Director; Susan Zegans, M.S.W., Psychotherapy; and Nina Beckwith, Administrator.

Chapter 1, The Concert

1. For a scholarly discussion of this neglected topic of visual aspects in musical communication, see Richard Leppert, *The Sight of Sound: Music, Representation, and the History of the Body.* Berkeley, CA: University of California Press, 1993.

Chapter 2, A Little Night Music

1. Glenn Gould, letter to Thomas McIntosh, January 21, 1957, in *Glenn Gould: Selected Letters,* edited by John P. L. Roberts and Ghyslaine Guertin. Toronto: Oxford University Press; 1992, p. 5.

Chapter 3, Infancy

1. Glenn Gold, birth certificate, Office of the Registrar General, Ontario, Canada.
2. Stephen Posen, executor of the Glenn Gould estate, interview with the author, June 17, 1994, and communication with Lise Deschamps Ostwald, July 1996.
3. Interview with Grant Gould, M.D., October 16, 1994.
4. Obituary of Thomas G. Gould, *Uxbridge Times-Journal,* September 17, 1953.
5. Robert Fulford, interview with the author, June 18, 1994.
6. Letter from H. A. Macdonald Greig, April 29, 1972, in "Keepers" box, Glenn Gould Collection, National Library of Canada. See also "Grieg and his Scottish Ancestry," published by Hinrichsen Edition, London. Glenn Gould's copy of this document, written by J. Russel Greig, who claimed a family connection to Edvard Grieg, was given to him by his cousin Jessie Greig.
7. Notes for an obituary of Florence Greig Gould, written in 1975 by Glenn Gould, in "Keepers" box, Glenn Gould Collection, National Library of Canada.
8. Interview with Mr. and Mrs. (Vera) Gould, June 17, 1994.
9. See Donald J. Shetler, "The Inquiry into Prenatal Musical Experience," in *Music and Child Development,* edited by Frank R. Wilson and Franz J. Roehmann. St. Louis, MO: MMB Music, 1990, pp. 44–62. Another scientist exploring the origins of musical development is Professor Marianne Hassler, at Tübingen University. Her research suggests that certain endocrine events during pregnancy, in particular increased levels of circulating testosterone in mothers, can enhance the proliferation of brain cells of the right cerebral hemisphere in their babies. As a result, they are more likely to become left-handed, to be especially skillful in musical as well as in spatial endeavors, to show signs, both physically and psychologically, of androgyny, and to be unusually susceptible to immune diseases. See Marianne Hassler, "Gonadal Hormones, Brain Development, and Musical Capacities," in *Music, Speech and the Developing Brain,* edited by C. Faienza. Milan: Guerini e Associati, 1994, pp. 138–156.
10. Interview with Mr. and Mrs. (Vera) Gould, June 17, 1994.
11. Interview with Grant Gould, M.D., October 16, 1994.
12. See Martin Greenberg, V. Vuorenkoski, T. Partanen, and J. Lind, "Behavior and

Cry Patterns in the First Two Hours of Life in Early and Later Clamped Newborns," *Annales Paediatriae Fenniae,* vol. 13 (1967), pp. 64–70.

13. Peter Ostwald, "Humming: Sign and Symbol," *Journal of Auditory Research,* vol. 3 (1961), pp. 224–232.

14. Macdonald Critchley and R. A. Henson, *Music and the Brain: Studies in the Neurology of Music.* London: Heinemann, 1977.

15. Russell Herbert Gould, interview in "Glenn Gould: A Portrait" (Part 1), CBC Television, 1985.

16. Peter Ostwald and Philip Pelzman, "The Cry of the Human Infant," *Scientific American,* vol. 230 ( ) pp. 83–90.

17. Christopher Gillberg and Mary Coleman, *The Biology of the Autistic Syndromes* (2nd edition). *Clinics in Developmental Medicine No. 126.* Oxford: Blackwell Scientific Publications; New York: Cambridge University Press, 1992. See p. 50 about Wittgenstein and Bartok.

18. See Oliver Sacks, *An Anthropologist on Mars: Seven Paradoxical Tales.* New York; Knopf, 1995.

Chapter 4, Child Prodigy

1. Jessie Greig, in "Glenn Gould: A Portrait" (Part 1), CBC Television, 1985.

2. Russell Herbert Gould, cited in Otto Friedrich, *Glenn Gould: A Life and Variations.* New York: Random House, 1989, p. 15.

3. See Rosemary Shuter-Dyden and C. Gabriel, *The Psychology of Musical Abilities* (2nd edition). London: Methuen, 1981.

4. Jessie Greig, in "Glenn Gould: A Portrait" (Part 1), CBC Television, 1985.

5. Russell Herbert Gould, in ibid.

6. Grant Gould, M.D., interview with the author, October 16, 1994.

7. Ibid.

8. Russell Herbert Gould, interview with the author, June 17, 1994.

9. Andrew Kazdin, *Glenn Gould at Work: Creative Lying.* New York: E. P. Dutton, 1989, pp. 76–77.

10. Russell Herbert Gould, in "Glenn Gould: A Portrait" (Part 1), CBC Television, 1985.

11. See "Keepers" box, Glenn Gould Archives, National Library of Canada, Ottawa.

12. Russell Herbert Gould, in "Glenn Gould: A Portrait" (Part 1), CBC Television, 1985.

13. Russell Herbert Gould, cited in Friedrich, *Glenn Gould,* p. 16.

14. Glenn Gould, in "Glenn Gould: A Portrait" (Part 1), CBC Television, 1985.

15. John Roberts, interview with the author, June 17, 1994.

16. Russell Herbert Gould, interview with the author, June 17, 1994.

17. Ibid.

18. Grant Gould, M.D., interview with the author, October 16, 1994.

19. Robert Fulford, interview with the author, June 18, 1994.

20. John Roberts, interview with the author, June 17, 1994.

21. Glenn Gould, childhood writing cited in Friedrich, *Glenn Gould,* p. 26.

22. Russell Herbert Gould, interview with the author, June 17, 1994.

23. Ibid.

24. See printed program in "Keepers" box, Glenn Gould Archives, National Library of Canada.

25. Andrew Kazdin, *Glenn Gould at Work,* p. 84.

Chapter 5, A Childhood Friend

1. Robert Fulford, *Best Seat in the House: Memoirs of a Lucky Man.* Toronto: Collins, 1988, p. 36.

2. Robert Fulford, in "Glenn Gould: A Portrait" (Part 1), CBC Television, 1985.

3. Robert Fulford, interview with the author, June 18, 1994.

4. Ibid.

5. Ibid.

6. John Roberts, interview with the author, June 17, 1994.

7. John McGreevy's film *Glenn Gould's Toronto,* released in 1979.

8. Fulford, *Best Seat in the House,* p. 37.

9. Ibid., p. 39.

10. Robert Fulford, interview with the author, June 18, 1994.

11. Grant Gould, M.D., interview with the author, October 16, 1994.

12. Robert Fulford, interview with the author, June 18, 1994.

13. Glenn Gould, notes for an obituary of Florence Greig Gould, in "Keepers" box, Glenn Gould Archives, National Library of Canada.

14. Robert Fulford, interview with the author, June 18, 1994.

15. Ibid.

16. Pierre Berton, interview with Glenn Gould in 1959, cited in Friedrich, *Glenn Gould,* p. 84.

17. Russell Herbert Gould, interview with the author, June 17, 1994.

18. Robert Fulford, interview with the author, June 18, 1994.

19. Robert Fulford, in "Glenn Gould: A Portrait" (Part 1), CBC Television, 1985.

20. Robert Fulford, interview with the author, June 18, 1994.

21. Fulford, *Best Seat in the House,* p. 38.

22. Robert Fulford, interview with the author, June 18, 1994.

23. Glenn Gould, in John McGreevy's film *Glenn Gould's Toronto,* released in 1979.

24. Russell Herbert Gould, interview with the author, June 17, 1994.

Chapter 6, New Teachers and Further Success

1. Glenn Gould, music test, item #59 in "Keepers" box, Glenn Gould Archives, National Library of Canada.

2. Glenn Gould, in "Glenn Gould: A Portrait" (Part 1), CBC Television, 1985.

3. Ibid.

4. John Beckwith, cited in Friedrich, *Glenn Gould,* p. 31,

5. Russell Herbert Gould, interview with the author, June 17, 1994.

6. William Aide, "Fact and Freudian Fable," *The Idler* (Summer 1993), p. 60.

7. William Aide, interview with the author, June 15, 1994.

8. William Aide, "Fact and Freudian Fable," *The Idler* (Summer 1993), p. 59.

9. Ibid., p. 60.

10. Ibid., pp. 59–60.

11. Russell Herbert Gould, interview with the author, June 17, 1994.
12. Robert Fulford, interview with the author, June 18, 1994.
13. Russell Herbert Gould, cited in Friedrich, *Glenn Gould,* p. 49.
14. Greta Kraus, interview with the author, June 18, 1994.
15. Early concert programs, Glenn Gould Archives, National Library of Canada.
16. *Toronto Globe and Mail,* February 17, 1944.
17. Richard Kostelanetz, *Master Minds.* New York: Macmillan, 1967, p. 31.
18. *Toronto Telegram,* December 13, 1945.
19. Glenn Gould, "Advice to a Graduation," in *The Glenn Gould Reader,* edited by Tim Page. New York: Vintage Books, 1990, pp. 6–7.
20. See Ostwald, *Schumann: The Inner Voices of a Musical Genius.* p. 36.
21. Glenn Gould, "Advice," p. 7.
22. Ibid., p. 7.
23. Myrtle Guerrero, cited in Friedrich, *Glenn Gould,* p. 31.
24. Glenn Gould, cited in ibid., p. 31.
25. *High Fidelity Magazine,* vol. 20, no. 6, pp. 29–32, cited by Payzant, *Glenn Gould: Music and Mind,* p. 9.
26. Ibid.
27. *Toronto Globe and Mail,* May 10, 1946.
28. *Toronto Telegram,* May 9, 1946.
29. Cited in Friedrich, *Glenn Gould,* pp. 34–35.
30. Robert Fulford, interview with the author, June 18, 1994.
31. *Toronto Globe and Mail,* January 15, 1947.
32. Friedrich, *Glenn Gould,* p. 35.

Chapter 7, Gaining a Manager

1. Walter Homburger, interview with the author, June 13, 1994.
2. Letter from Russell Herbert Gould to George Smale, October 11, 1947, Glenn Gould Archives, File 1979-20, National Library of Canada.
3. Walter Homburger, interview with the author, June 13, 1994.
4. *Toronto Telegram,* October 21, 1947.
5. *Toronto Globe and Mail,* October 21, 1947.
6. *Toronto Daily Star,* October 21, 1947.
7. Glenn Gould, "Concert Dropout," interview with John McClure, 1968.
8. Glenn Gould, school essay, in File 1979-20, Glenn Gould Archives, National Library of Canada.
9. Jessie Greig, in "Glenn Gould: A Portrait" (Part 1), CBC Television, 1985.
10. Robert Fulford, interview with the author, June 18, 1994.
11. Fulford, *Best Seat in the House,* pp. 41–42.
12. Robert Fulford, interview with the author, June 18, 1994.
13. Glenn Gould, "My Pet Antipathy," in File 1979-20, 23, 132, Glenn Gould Archives, National Library of Canada.
14. Glenn Gould, cited in Friedrich, *Glenn Gould,* p. 39.
15. The book by René Leibowitz, *Schoenberg and His School,* appeared in 1946 in Paris, and in 1949 in translation in the United States.
16. Oskar Morawetz, interview with the author, June 21, 1994.

17. Cited in Friedrich, *Glenn Gould,* p. 159.
18. Jessie Greig, in "Glen Gould: A Portrait" (Part 1), CBC Television, 1985.
19. Glenn Gould, in "Glenn Gould: A Portrait" (Part 1), CBC Television, 1985.

Chapter 8, "My Love Affair with the Microphone"

1. Glenn Gould, "Music and Technology," *Piano Quarterly* (Winter 1974–75), reprinted in *The Glenn Gould Reader,* edited by Tim Page, p. 354.
2. Joseph Stephens, M.D., interview with the author, November 10, 1994.
3. Glenn Gould, see "Music and Technology," in *The Glenn Gould Reader,* pp. 353–354.
4. Ibid., p. 354.
5. Walter Homburger, interview with the author, June 13, 1994.
6. Arthur Rubinstein, *My Early Years,* New York: Knopf, 1973.
7. Glenn Gould, CBC Radio broadcast April 30, 1967, cited in Payzant, *Glenn Gould,* p. 36.
8. Letter from Russell Herbert Gould to Herbert Webber, February 25, 1948, Glenn Gould Archives, National Library of Canada.
9. Russell Herbert Gould, in "Glenn Gould: A Portrait" (Part 1), CBC Television, 1985.
10. Oskar Morawetz, interviews with the author, June 12 and 18, 1994.
11. Bruno Monsaingeon, "Glenn Gould, Composer," Record Booklet, Sony CD SK 47184, 1992.
12. Sony SK 47184.

Chapter 9, Self-Isolation

1. Robert Fulford, cited in Payzant, *Glenn Gould,* p. 5.
2. Fulford, *Best Seat in the House,* p. 46.
3. Ibid.
4. New Music Associates Program on Schoenberg, Berg, Webern, File 1979-20, 44, 16, Glenn Gould Archives, National Library of Canada.
5. Ibid.
6. Fulford, *Best Seat in the House,* p. 46.
7. Ibid., p. 47.
8. Jonathan Cott, *Conversations with Glenn Gould,* Boston and Toronto: Little, Brown, 1984, p. 63.
9. See restricted medical file, Glenn Gould Archives, National Library of Canada.
10. Fulford, *Best Seat in the House,* pp. 44–45.
11. We've already heard Walter Homburger using this expression. Later it was Glenn's friend Robert Silverman.
12. William Aide, interview with the author, June 15, 1994.
13. Glenn Gould, cited in "Profiles: Apollonian" by Joseph Roddy, *The New Yorker,* May 14, 1960, p. 57.
14. Walter Homburger, interview with the author, June 13, 1994.
15. Zara Nelsova, interview with the author, July 12, 1995.

16. Alexander Schneider, cited in Friedrich, *Glenn Gould,* p. 42.
17. This story was told to me by both Zara Nelsova and Oskar Morawetz.
18. File GG 163, Glenn Gould Archives, National Library of Canada.
19. Zara Nelsova, interview with author, July 12, 1995.
20. Harvey Olnick, interview with the author, June 17, 1994.
21. Ezra Schabas and Stuart Nall, *The Musical Courier,* November 15, 1954.
22. Glenn Gould, cited in Friedrich, *Glenn Gould,* p. 42.

Chapter 10, Triumph in the States

1. Zara Nelsova, interview with the author, July 12, 1995.
2. Paul Hume, *The Washington Post,* January 3, 1955.
3. Harvey Olnick, interview with the author, June 17, 1994.
4. Martin Canin, interview with the author, November 7, 1994.
5. Harvey Olnick, interview with the author, June 17, 1994.
6. John Briggs, *The Musical Courier,* February 1, 1955, p. 86.
7. Payzant, *Glenn Gould,* p. 14.
8. Alexander Schneider and David Oppenheim, cited in Friedrich, *Glenn Gould,* p. 44.
9. David Oppenheim, cited in ibid., p. 46.
10. Walter Homburger, interview with the author, June 13, 1994.
11. Ralph Kirkpatrick, Preface to *Bach's Goldberg Variations,* New York: Schirmers, 1938, p. vii.
12. Liner notes to recording of the *Goldberg Variations.* Columbia MS 7096.
13. Friedrich, *Glenn Gould,* p. 52.
14. Glenn Gould, record liner to his first recording of the *Goldberg Variations,* Columbia ML 5060.
15. Glenn Gould, cited by Friedrich, *Glenn Gould,* p. 55.

Chapter 11, First Contact with Psychiatry

1. The study was Geoffey Payzant's *Glenn Gould: Music and Mind.*
2. Glenn Gould, "A Biography of Glenn Gould," *Piano Quarterly* (Fall 1978). reprinted in *The Glenn Gould Reader,* edited by Tim Page, pp. 447–448.
3. Restricted medical files, Glenn Gould Archives, National Library of Canada.
4. Jock Carroll, *Glenn Gould: Some Portraits of the Artist as a Young Man.* Toronto: Stoddard, 1995.
5. Herbert Vear, D.C., interview with the author, June 7, 1995.
6. Gould recorded the date in his personal papers, now in the National Library of Canada.
7. Jock Carroll, *Glenn Gould,* p. 14.
8. Ibid., p. 24.
9. Morris Herman, M.D., interview with the author, June 16, 1994.
10. Stanley Greben, M.D., interview with the author, June 15, 1994.
11. Alan Parkin, *A History of Psychoanalysis in Canada.* Toronto: Toronto Psychoanalytic Institute, 1987.

12. Alan Parkin, M.D., interview with the author, June 14, 1994.

13. Ibid.

14. Stanley Greben, M.D., interview with the author, June 15, 1994.

15. Ibid.

16. Carroll, *Glenn Gould,* p. 25.

17. Glenn Gould, "Gould's String Quartet, Op. 1," liner notes from Columbia MS 6178, 1969, reprinted in *The Glenn Gould Reader,* pp. 227–228.

18. Jock Carroll, *Glenn Gould,* p. 16.

19. Ibid., pp. 9, 10, 17, 25.

20. Ibid., p. 21.

21. Glenn Gould, "Reprinted from *Insight,* Digest of the North Dakota Psychiatric Association," in his liner notes "Beethoven's Fifth Symphony on the Piano: Four Imaginary Interviews," for Columbia MS 7095, 1968. Reprinted in *The Glenn Gould Reader,* pp. 59–60.

22. Jessie Greig, telephone conversations with the author, June 14, 15, and 16, 1994.

Chapter 12, Conflicting Demands

1. "Glenn Gould: Concert Dropout." Conversation with John McClure, bonus record included with Columbia MC 7095, 1968, reissued in 1984 in *The Glenn Gould Legacy,* Vol. 1.

2. Glenn Gould, "Let's Ban Applause!" *Musical America* (February 1962), reprinted in *The Glenn Gould Reader,* edited by Tim Page, p. 247.

3. "Glenn Gould Off the Record; Glenn Gould On the Record," National Film Board of Canada, 1960.

4. Franz Kraemer, interview with the author, June 14, 1994.

5. John Roberts, interview with the author, June 17, 1994.

6. Ibid.

7. Press citations in Friedrich, *Glenn Gould,* pp. 58–60.

8. Glenn Gould, interview with Bernard Asbell, cited in ibid., pp. 59–60.

9. Glenn Gould, "I Don't Think I'm at All Eccentric," *The Telegram Weekend* (Toronto), July 7, 1956. Interview by Jock Carroll.

10. Press citations in Friedrich, *Glenn Gould,* p. 59.

11. Prescription filed in the Restricted Section, Glenn Gould Archives, National Library of Canada.

12. The Glenn Gould Collection, I. "Prologue," Sony Classical SLV 48 401.

13. Ellen Faull, telephone interview with the author, March 11, 1996.

14. See Stratford concert programs in the Glenn Gould Archives, National Library of Canada.

15. Glenn Gould, cited in Friedrich, *Glenn Gould,* p. 274.

16. Glenn Gould, letter to Vladimir Golschmann, March 20, 1958, in Early Correspondence File, Glenn Gould Archives, National Library of Canada.

17. Press reviews cited in Friedrich, *Glenn Gould,* p. 69.

18. Glenn Gould, "Let's Ban Applause!" *Musical America* (February 1962), reprinted in *The Glenn Gould Reader,* p. 246.

19. See Bob Fulford's depiction of Florence Gould in chapter 5 of this book.

20. Glenn Gould, "Beethoven's Last Three Piano Sonatas," liner notes from Columbia ML 5130, 1956, reprinted in *The Glenn Gould Reader,* pp. 54–55.

21. Ibid., p. 57.

Chapter 13, Telephone Calls

1. See Humphrey Burton, *Leonard Bernstein.* New York: Doubleday, 1994.

2. Glenn Gould, letter to Leonard Bernstein, February 7, 1957, in Early Correspondence File, Glenn Gould Archives, National Library of Canada.

3. Leonard Bernstein, cited in Friedrich, *Glenn Gould,* p. 70.

4. This story was first told to me by Anton Kuerti (interview June 17, 1994) but I have heard it from others. It isn't clear whether Lenny's remark was made directly to Glenn or to a group of guests within his hearing. It was not at all unusual for Bernstein to make such blatantly erotic comments in public.

5. Glenn Gould, cited in Friedrich, *Glenn Gould,* p. 234.

6. Leonard Bernstein, cited in ibid., p. 71.

7. Liner notes from Columbia ML 5211, reprinted in *The Glenn Gould Reader,* p. 62.

8. Ibid., pp. 61–62.

9. *Time* reporter, cited in Friedrich, *Glenn Gould,* p. 61.

Chapter 14, Traveling Overseas

1. Glenn Gould, letter to Mrs. Ford, undated, in Early Correspondence File, Glenn Gould Archives, National Library of Canada.

2. Glenn Gould, letter to Herbert C. Moffitt, Jr., M.D., April 16, 1957 in Early Correspondence File, Glenn Gould Archives, National Library of Canada.

3. Glenn Gould, letter to Susan Hamel, April 17, 1957, in Early Correspondence File, Glenn Gould Archives, National Library of Canada.

4. Walter Homburger, interview with the author, June 13, 1994.

5. John Roberts, interview with the author, June 17, 1994.

6. Glenn Gould, telegram to Mr. and Mrs. Gould, May 8, 1957, in Early Correspondence File, Glenn Gould Archives, National Library of Canada.

7. Glenn Gould, letter to Yousuf Karsh, July 8, 1958, in *Glenn Gould: Selected Letters,* p. 13.

8. Note from an admirer, in "Keepers" box, item #92, Glenn Gould Archives, National Library of Canada.

9. Glenn Gould, letter to Yousuf Karsh, July 8, 1958, in *Glenn Gould: Selected Letters,* p. 14.

10. Glenn Gould, postcard to "Banquo Gould," undated, in Early Correspondence File, Glenn Gould Archives, National Library of Canada.

11. Glenn Gould, cited in Friedrich, *Glenn Gould,* p. 65.

12. "Glenn Gould: Concert Dropout." Conversation with John McClure, bonus record included with Columbia MS 7095, 1968.

13. Glenn Gould, "Let's Ban Applause!" in *Musical America* (February 1962), reprinted in *The Glenn Gould Reader,* pp. 245–250.

14. Andras Schiff, interview with the author, May 5, 1994.

15. "Glenn Gould Interviews Glenn Gould About Glenn Gould," *High Fidelity* (Feb-

ruary 1974), reprinted in *The Glenn Gould Reader,* p. 319.

16. Gary Graffman, cited in Friedrich, *Glenn Gould,* p. 66.

17. H. H. Stuckenschmidt, cited in ibid., p. 66.

18. Glenn Gould, letter to his parents from Vienna, June, 3, 1957, in *Glenn Gould: Selected Letters,* p. 7.

19. Ibid.

20. Walter Homburger, cited by Friedrich, *Glenn Gould,* p. 67.

21. Glenn Gould, letter to his parents from Vienna, June 3, 1957, in *Glenn Gould: Selected Letters.* pp. 8–10.

22. Glenn Gould, letter to his parents from Vienna, June 3, 1957, in *Glenn Gould: Selected Letters.* pp. 8–10.

Chapter 15, Strange Illnesses

1. Glenn Gould, "Art of the Fugue," Introduction to Book I of Bach's *The Well-Tempered Clavier,* published by Amsco Music Company, 1972; reprinted in *The Glenn Gould Reader,* p. 21.

2. Now available as part of *The Glenn Gould Edition,* Sony SMK 52684.

3. Stegemann's liner notes, *The Glenn Gould Edition,* Sony SMK 52684.

4. Eric McLean, *Montreal Star,* August 21, 1957.

5. Walter Homburger, interview with the author, June 13, 1994.

6. Letter from Walter Homburger to the Director of the Aluminum Company of Canada in Montreal, August 31, 1956, Glenn Gould Archives, vol. 31, National Library of Canada.

7. Letter from Walter Homburger to Specialty Manufacturing Company, September 19, 1956, Glenn Gould Archives, vol. 31, National Library of Canada.

8. Walter Homburger, interview with the author, June 13, 1994.

9. Critics of the *Buffalo Evening News,* the *New York Herald Tribune,* and a Montreal paper, cited in Friedrich, *Glenn Gould,* pp. 75–76.

10. James Tocco, interview with the author, March 3, 1994.

11. Glenn Gould, interview with Bernard Asbell, 1962, cited in Friedrich, *Glenn Gould,* p. 77.

12. Anton Kuerti, interview with the author, June 17, 1994.

13. Item #67 in "Keepers" box, Glenn Gould Archives, National Library of Canada.

14. Glenn Gould, cited in Friedrich, *Glenn Gould,* p. 77.

15. Glenn Gould, "A Season on the Road," notes in manuscript in the Glenn Gould Archives, National Library of Canada.

16. Item #85, in "Keepers" box, Glenn Gould Archives, National Library of Canada.

17. Author's letter to Glenn Gould, October 1, 1958, personal file.

18. Glenn Gould, letter to Walter Homburger, October 2, 1958, cited in Friedrich, *Glenn Gould,* p. 78.

19. Glenn Gould, letter to Walter Homburger, October 18, 1958, cited in ibid., pp. 78–79.

20. Walter Homburger, interview with the author, June 13, 1994.

21. Glenn Gould, letter to Walter Homburger, October 18, 1958, cited in Friedrich, *Glenn Gould,* p. 79.

22. Glenn Gould, letter to Walter Homburger, October 24, 1958, cited in ibid., p. 79.

23. Item #85 in "Keepers" box, Glenn Gould Archives, National Library of Canada.

24. Walter Homburger, letter to Glenn Gould, October 28, 1958, File 1979-20, 33, 16, 27, Glenn Gould Archives, National Library of Canada.

25. Walter Homburger, letter to Glenn Gould, October 22, 1958, File 1979-20, 33, 16, 18, Glenn Gould Archives, National Library of Canada.

26. Glenn Gould, letter to Bernstein, cited in Friedrich, *Glenn Gould,* p. 80.

27. Letter from "Grandma" to Glenn Gould, October 23, 1958, File 1979-20, 33, 16, 20, Glenn Gould Archives, National Library of Canada.

28. Letter from Sylvia Kind to Glenn Gould, October 23, 1958, File 1979-20, 33, 16, 21, Glenn Gould Archives, National Library of Canada.

29. Glenn Gould letter to the author, October 29, 1958, personal collection.

30. Cited in Friedrich, *Glenn Gould,* p. 80.

31. Walter Homburger, letter to Glenn Gould, October 28, 1958, File 1979-20, 33, 16, 27, Glenn Gould Archives, National Library of Canada.

Chapter 16, In Search of a Home

1. Walter Homburger, letter to Glenn Gould, October 28, 1958, File 1979-20, 33, 16, 27, Glenn Gould Archives, National Library of Canada.

2. Glenn Gould, letter to Richard Kamm, January 30, 1959, File 1979-20, 31, 8, 3, Glenn Gould Archives, National Library of Canada.

3. Glenn Gould, letter to Malka Rabinowitz, February 23, 1959, File 1979-20, 31, 8, 7, Glenn Gould Archives, National Library of Canada.

4. Letter to Glenn Gould, undated, in "Keepers" box, Glenn Gould Archives, National Library of Canada.

5. Walter Homburger, letter to Glenn Gould, October 31, 1958, File 33-16-33 Glenn Gould Archives, National Library of Canada.

6. Glenn Gould, letter to C. W. Fitzgerald, December 27, 1956, Early Correspondence File, Glenn Gould Archives, National Library of Canada.

7. Glenn Gould, letter to the author, January 20, 1959, personal collection.

8. Author's letter to Glenn Gould, February 23, 1959, personal collection.

9. Author's letter to Glenn Gould, January 19, 1959, personal collection.

10. Author's letter to Glenn Gould, February 2, 1959, personal collection.

11. Ibid.

12. Author's letter to Glenn Gould, February 23, 1959, personal collection.

13. Glenn Gould, letter to the author, March 13, 1959, personal collection.

14. Author's letter to Glenn Gould, January 19, 1959, personal collection.

15. John Roberts, interview with the author, June 17, 1994.

16. Winston Fitzgerald, cited in Friedrich, *Glenn Gould,* p. 86.

17. John Roberts, interview with the author, June 17, 1994.

18. Glenn Gould, letter to the author, undated, personal collection.

19. Author's letter to Glenn Gould, December 31, 1959, personal collection.

20. John Roberts, letter to the author, November 21, 1995.

Chapter 17, Dr. Joseph Stephens

1. Joseph Stephens, M.D., interview with the author, May 30, 1993.
2. Ibid.
3. Joseph Stephens, M.D., interview with the author, July 25, 1994.
4. Ibid.
5. Robert Silverman, interview with the author, November 20, 1995.
6. Morris Herman, M.D., interview with the athor, June 14, 1994.
7. Morris D. Charendoff, M.D., letter to the author, May 30, 1995.
8. Hunter J. H. Fry, "Physical Signs in the Hand and Wrist in Overuse (Injury) Syndrome," *Australia, New Zealand Journal of Surgery,* vol. 56 (1986), pp. 47–49.
9. Morris D. Charendoff, M.D., letter to the author, May 30, 1995.
10. Report from a Physiotherapy Clinic at 244 Bloor Street, restricted medical files, Glenn Gould Archives, National Library of Canada.
11. Joseph Stephens, M.D., interview with the author, July 25, 1994.
12. Herbert Vear, M.D., interview with the author, June 7, 1995.
13. Prescription from I. Stein, M.D., undated, restricted medical files, Glenn Gould Archives, National Library of Canada.
14. Joseph Stephens, M.D., interview with the author, July 25, 1994.
15. The Glenn Gould Colllection, II. Sonatas and Dialogues, Sony Classical SLV 48 401.
16. See Peter Ostwald, "Johannes Brahms: Solitary Altruist," in *Brahms and His World,* edited by Walter Frisch. Princeton, NJ: Princeton University Press, 1990, pp. 23–35.
17. Glenn Gould, letter to the author, February 17, 1961, personal file.
18. Glenn Gould, drafts of a letter to Eugene Ormandy, undated, File 1979-20, 23, 20, Glenn Gould Archives, National Library of Canada.
19. Ibid.
20. Eugene Ormandy, letter to Glenn Could, cited in Friedrich, *Glenn Gould,* p. 96.
21. Joseph Stephens, M.D., interview with the author, July 25, 1994.
22. Joseph Stephens, letter to Stanley Greben, M.D., personal file.
23. Stanley Greben, M.D., interview with the author, June 15, 1994.

Chapter 18, The Pitfalls of Composing and Performing

1. Glenn Gould, cited in Payzant, *Glenn Gould,* p. 60.
2. Franz Kraemer, interview with the author, June 14, 1994.
3. Glenn Gould, "Gould's String Quartet, Op. 1," liner notes from Columbia MS 6178, 1960, reprinted in *The Glenn Gould Reader,* p. 234.
4. Harvey Olnick, cited in Friedrich, *Glenn Gould,* p. 163.
5. Glenn Gould, "Gould's String Quartet, Op. 1," liner notes from Columbia MS 6178, 1960, reprinted in *The Glenn Gould Reader,* p. 228.
6. Ibid., p. 229.
7. Maynard Solomon, *Mozart: A Life.* New York: HarperCollins, 1995, p. 115.
8. Payzant, *Glenn Gould,* p. 7.
9. Glenn Gould, "Gould's String Quartet, Op. 1," liner notes from Columbia MS 6178, 1960, reprinted in *The Glenn Gould Reader,* p. 229.

10. Ibid., p. 234.

11. Letter to David Diamond, February 23, 1959, File 1979-20, 31, 8, 5, Glenn Gould Archives, National Library of Canada.

12. Glenn Gould, letter to Otto Joachim (undated), in *Glenn Gould: Selected Letters,* p. 2.

13. Mark Gottlieb, interview with the author, April 14, 1994.

14. Notes for an opera, File 1979-20, 23, 165, item 11, Glenn Gould Archives, National Library of Canada.

15. Glenn Gould, letter to the author, June 29, 1962, in *Glenn Gould: Selected Letters,* pp. 64–65.

16. Glenn Gould, letter to the author, September 14, 1962, personal file.

17. Joseph Stephens, M.D., interview with the author, July 25, 1994.

18. Alfred Frankenstein, *San Francisco Chronicle,* February 8, 1962.

19. Alfred Frankenstein, *San Francisco Chronicle,* February 17, 1962.

20. Glenn Gould, "N'Aimez-Vous Pas Brahms?", written in 1962, reprinted in *The Glenn Gould Reader,* pp. 70–71.

21. Ibid., p. 72.

22. Leonard Bernstein, cited in Friedrich, *Glenn Gould,* p. 103.

23. Burton, *Leonard Bernstein,* p. 328.

24. Leonard Bernstein, comments to the audience before the performance of Brahms's Piano Concerto in D Minor on September 4, 1962.

25. Leonard Bernstein, "The Truth About a Legend," in *Glenn Gould: Variations,* edited by John McGreevy. Toronto, Ontario: Doubleday, 1983, p. 19.

26. Anton Kuerti, interview with the author, June 17, 1994.

27. Newspaper citations from Friedrich, *Glenn Gould,* pp. 105–106.

28. Glenn Gould, in File 1979-20, 23, 165, item 10, Glenn Gould Archives, National Library of Canada.

Chapter 19, Retirement from the Stage

1. Glenn Gould, undated note from the Beverly Hills Hotel, probably draft for a telegram, File 1979-20, vol. 23, 165, item 5, Glenn Gould Archives, National Library of Canada.

2. Glenn Gould, letter to Humphrey Burton, April 17, 1962, in *Glenn Gould: Selected Letters,* p. 55.

3. Lucius Beebe, *Mansions on Rails: The Folklore of the Private Railway Car.* Berkeley: Howell North, 1959.

4. Glenn Gould, letter to the author and his wife, May 24, 1963, personal collection.

5. Glenn Gould, *Arnold Schoenberg: A Perspective.* Cincinnati: University of Cincinnati Press, 1964.

6. Glenn Gould, "So You Want to Write a Fugue," first published in *HiFi/Stereo Review* (April 1964), reprinted in *The Glenn Gould Reader,* p. 234.

7. Letter from Lise Deschamps Ostwald to Stephen Posen, July 25, 1996.

8. Glenn Gould, "So You Want to Write a Fugue," *HiFi/Stereo Review* (April 1964), p. 237.

9. Ibid., p. 239.

10. Glenn Gould, "The Prospects of Recording," first published in *High Fidelity* (April 1966), reprinted in *The Glenn Gould Reader,* p. 331.

11. See the scholarly work of Ronald Kidd on "Concert" and Howard Mayer Brown and James W. McKinnon on "Performing Practice," in *The New Grove Dictionary of Music and Musicians,* edited by Stanley Sadie. London: Macmillan, 1980. Vol. 4, pp. 616–625, and vol. 14, pp. 370–393.

12. Glenn Gould, "The Prospects of Recording," *The Glenn Gould Reader,* pp. 331–353.

13. Ibid., p. 336.

14. Ibid., p. 337.

15. Walter Homburger, interview with the author, June 13, 1994.

16. "Glenn Gould: Concert Dropout." Conversation with John McClure, bonus record included with Columbia MS 7095, 1968.

17. Item #74 in "Keepers" box, Glenn Gould Archives, National Library of Canada.

18. John Roberts, intervieiw with the author, November 17, 1995.

19. Vincent Tovell, interview with the author, June 18, 1994.

20. Ibid.

21. Ibid.

22. Glenn Gould, "Advice to a Graduation," in *The Glenn Gould Reader,* pp. 3–7.

23. Ibid.

24. Joseph Stephens, M.D., interview with the author, November 10, 1994. Recordings released in 1967 and 1968 by Columbia Masterworks.

25. Robert Silverman, interview with the author, November 20, 1995.

26. Glenn Gould, in *Dialogue on the Prospect of Recording,* CBC Radio, January 10, 1965.

27. Paul Myers, in *Dialogue on the Prospect of Recording,* CBC Radio, January 10, 1965.

28. John Hammond, in *Dialogue on the Prospect of Recording,* CBC Radio, January 10, 1965.

29. Leon Fleisher, in *Dialogue on the Prospect of Recording,* CBC Radio, January 10, 1965.

30. Diana Gould Menuhin, in *Dialogue on the Prospect of Recording,* CBC Radio, January 10, 1965.

31. Schuyler Chapin, in *Dialogue on the Prospect of Recording,* CBC Radio, January 10, 1965.

32. Marshall McLuhan, in *Dialogue on the Prospect of Recording,* CBC Radio, January 10, 1965.

33. Eric Till, cited in Friedrich, *Glenn Gould,* p. 208.

34. John Roberts, personal communication to author, December 23, 1995.

35. Yehudi Menuhin, interview with the author, March 15, 1995.

36. *The Glenn Gould Collection,* II. "Sonatas and Dialogues," Sony Classical SLV 48 401.

37. Ibid.

38. John Roberts, interview with the author, November 19, 1995.

39. Yehudi Menuhin, interview with the author, March 15, 1995.

40. Yehudi Menuhin, interview with the author, March 15, 1995.

41. Glenn Gould, letter to Diana Menuhin, April 25, 1966, in *Glenn Gould: Selected Letters,* pp. 87–88.

42. Yehudi Menuhin and Curtis W. Davis, *The Music of Man.* Toronto: Methuen, 1979, pp. 293–294.

43. Yehudi Menuhin, interview with the author, March 15, 1995.

44. Glenn Gould, "Yehudi Menuhin," *Musical America* (December 1966), reprinted in *The Glenn Gould Reader,* pp. 296–300.

Chapter 20, The Solitude Trilogy

1. Glenn Gould, in an interview (1964) cited in Payzant, *Glenn Gould,* p. 56.

2. Glenn Gould, cited in Friedrich, *Glenn Gould,* p. 204.

3. Glenn Gould, "The Idea of North: An Introduction" in *The Glenn Gould Reader,* p. 391.

4. Ibid., p. 392.

5. Charles Rosen, *The Romantic Generation.* Cambridge, MA: Harvard University Press, 1995, p. 5.

6. "Radio as Music: Glenn Gould in Conversation with John Jessup," *The Canadian Broadcasting Book,* 1971, reprinted in *The Glenn Gould Reader,* p. 379.

7. Glenn Gould, "The Idea of North: An Introduction" in *The Glenn Gould Reader,* p. 393.

8. Glenn Gould, "In Search for Petula Clark," *High Fidelity* (November 1967), reprinted in *The Glenn Gould Reader,* p. 300.

9. Ibid., p. 305.

10. Lorne Tulk, interview with the author, June 16, 1994.

11. Citations from the *Ottawa Citizen* and the *Montreal Star,* in Friedrich, *Glenn Gould,* p. 189.

12. Glenn Gould, "The Latecomers: An Introduction," in *The Glenn Gould Reader,* pp. 394–395.

13. Ibid., p. 395.

14. Glenn Gould, "Rubinstein," *Look,* March 9, 1971, reprinted in *The Glenn Gould Reader,* p. 288.

15. Janet Somerville, cited in Friedrich, *Glenn Gould,* p. 187.

16. Lorne Tulk, interview with the author, June 16, 1994.

17. Ibid.

18. *Radio as Music,* first released by the CBC in 1975 as a TV documentary, later as a film.

19. Glenn Gould, cited in Friedrich, *Glenn Gould,* p. 195.

20. Glenn Gould, "Rubinstein," *Look,* March 9, 1971, reprinted in *The Glenn Gould Reader,* p. 288.

21. *Glenn Gould's Solitude Trilogy: Three Sound Documentaries,* CBC Records, PSCD 2003–3.

22. Glenn Gould, letter to Elvin Shantz, January 20, 1973, in *Glenn Gould: Collected Letters,* p. 194.

23. Citations from Friedrich, *Glenn Gould,* pp. 198–199.

24. Janet Somerville, "The Gould Radio Documentaries: Some Birth-Memories," booklet of CBC Records, PSCD 2003–3.

25. Richard Kostelanetz, cited in Friedrich, *Glenn Gould,* p. 114.

26. A. A., Epstein, M.D., interview with the author, June 13, 1994.

27. Glenn Gould, letter to Leon Fleisher, November 14, 1966, in *Glenn Gould: Selected Letters,* pp. 97–98.

28. Joseph Stephens, M.D., interview with the author, November 20, 1995.

29. "Glenn Gould: Concert Dropout." Conversation with John McClure, bonus record included with MS 7095, 1968.

Chapter 21, Changing Views of Composers

1. "Glenn Gould: Concert Dropout," Conversation with John McClure, bonus record included with MS 7095, 1968.

2. Glenn Gould, letter to John Hague, November 5, 1966, Glenn Gould: Selected letters, p. 89.

3. Humphrey Burton, interview with the author, October 23, 1995.

4. Glenn Gould, letter to John McClure, June 11, 1966, in *Glenn Gould: Selected Letters,* pp. 92–94.

5. M2X 35912.

6. Glenn Gould, "Stokowski in Six Scenes," *Piano Quarterly* (Winter 1977 through Summer 1978), reprinted in *The Glenn Gould Reader,* pp. 268, 269.

7. Gould, "Stokowski in Six Scenes," reprinted in *The Glenn Gould Reader,* pp. 270–271.

8. Karel Ancerl, citation in Friedrich, *Glenn Gould,* p. 214.

9. Glenn Gould, "Streisand as Schwarzkopf," *High Fidelity* (May 1976), reprinted in *The Glenn Gould Reader,* p. 308.

10. "Of Mozart and Related Matters: Glenn Gould in Conversation with Bruno Monsaingeon," *Piano Quarterly* (Fall 1976), reprinted in *The Glenn Gould Reader,* p. 33.

11. Glenn Gould, unfinished draft for an essay titled "Why Mozart is a Bad Composer," File 1979-20, 23, 6, Glenn Gould Archives, National Library of Canada.

12. "Of Mozart and Related Matters: Glenn Gould in Conversation with Bruno Monsaingeon," reprinted in *The Glenn Gould Reader,* p. 34.

13. He recorded this concerto twice, first in Stockholm in 1958 with the Swedish Radio Symphony Orchestra conducted by Georg Ludwig Jochum, then in Toronto in 1961 with the CBC Symphony Orchestra conducted by Walter Susskind.

14. Jonathan Cott, *Conversations with Glenn Gould.* Boston: Little, Brown, 1984, p. 56.

15. "Glenn Gould in Conversation with Tim Page," *Piano Quarterly* (Fall 1981), reprinted in *The Glenn Gould Reader,* p. 458.

16. Glenn Gould, "An Argument for Richard Strauss," *High Fidelity* (March 1962), reprinted in *The Glenn Gould Reader,* p. 90.

17. Ibid., pp. 84–85.

18. Glenn Gould, *Arnold Schoenberg—A Perspective,* Cincinnati: University of Cincinnati Press, 1964, reprinted in *The Glenn Gould Reader,* p. 122.

19. Gould, "An Argument for Richard Strauss," reprinted in *The Glenn Gould Reader,* p. 85.

20. Ibid., pp. 85–87.

21. Ibid., p. 88.

22. Ibid., p. 91.

23. "Glenn Gould in Conversation with Tim Page," reprinted in *The Glenn Gould Reader,* p. 453.

24. Glenn Gould in recital, CBC Thursday night, July 23, 1970.

25. Robert Mann, interview with the author, 1994.

26. "The Art of Glenn Gould/Take Thirteen," CBC Radio broadcast August 12, 1969.

27. See for example Gould's "N'aimez-vous pas Brahms?", *The Glenn Gould Reader,* p. 70.

28. Glenn Gould, letter to John Culshaw, June 22, 1968, in *Glenn Gould: Selected Letters,* p. 106.

29. Glenn Gould talking about Wawa, in *"Glenn Gould: A Portrait"* (Part 2), CBC Television, 1985.

30. Glenn Gould, letter to Ronald Wilford, June 8, 1971, in *Glenn Gould: Selected Letters,* pp. 148–149.

31. John Roberts, interview with the author, November 19, 1995.

32. Kazdin, *Glenn Gould at Work: Creative Lying,* p. 128.

33. Glenn Gould, liner notes for Columbia M 32040, 1973, reprinted in *The Glenn Gould Reader,* p. 80.

34. Glenn Gould, letter to Carl Little, June 5, 1971, in *Glenn Gould: Selected Letters,* p. 141.

35. Glenn Gould, letter to Jane Friedman, October 23, 1971, in *Glenn Gould: Selected Letters,* p. 163.

36. Glenn Gould, liner notes for Columbia M 32040, 1973, reprinted in *The Glenn Gould Reader,* pp. 78, 79.

37. Cott, *Conversations with Glenn Gould,* pp. 65–66.

38. Glenn Gould letter to Albert Prefontaine, August 12, 1971, in *Glenn Gould: Selected Letters,* p. 151

Chapter 22, Impersonator, Philosopher, and Technician

1. Cott, *Conversations with Glenn Gould,* pp. 41–42.

2. Ibid., pp. 86–87.

3. Glenn Gould, liner notes to Columbia MS 7095, 1969, reprinted in *The Glenn Gould Reader,* pp. 57–61.

4. Glenn Gould, staging instructions for "Sir Nigel Twitt-Thornwaite," in liner notes for *The Glenn Gould Collection,* XI, "Ecstasy and Wit," Sony Classical SLV 48 416.

5. *Glenn Gould Collection,* III, "End of Concerts," Sony Classical SLV 48 404OO

6. Glenn Gould, "Glenn Gould Interviews Himself About Beethoven," *Piano Quarterly* (Fall 1972), reprinted in *The Glenn Gould Reader,* p. 44.

7. "Glenn Gould Interviews Glenn Gould About Glenn Gould," *High Fidelity* (February 1974), reprinted in *The Glenn Gould Reader,* p. 319.

8. Friedrich, *Glenn Gould,* p. 121.

9. Jean Le Moyne, *Convergences,* trans. Philip Stratford. Toronto: Ryerson Press, 1966, pp. 248–249.

10. Glenn Gould, "The Prospects of Recording," *High Fidelity* (April 1966), reprinted in *The Glenn Gould Reader,* p. 345.

11. Glenn Gould, letter to Goddard Lieberson, May 14, 1966, in *Glenn Gould: Selected Letters,* p. 90.

12. Glenn Gould, letter to Goddard Lieberson, May 14, 1966, in *Glenn Gould: Selected Letters,* p. 90, note 4.

13. CBC Sunday Night/Dialogues on the Prospects of Recordings, January 10, 1965.

14. Kazdin, *Glenn Gould at Work,* p. 99.

15. Payzant, *Glenn Gould,* p. 51.

16. Glenn Gould, letter to Helen Whitney, September 3, 1971, in *Glenn Gould: Selected Letters,* p. 155.

17. Ibid., p. 157.

18. "The Art of Glenn Gould/Take 9," CBC broadcast July 15, 1969.

19. CBC telecast, "The Age of Ecstasy," February 20, 1974, also cited in Payzant, *Glenn Gould,* p. 56.

20. Glenn Gould, letter to Helen Whitney, September 3, 1971, in *Glenn Gould: Selected Letters,* p. 156.

21. Payzant, *Glenn Gould,* p. 40.

22. Glenn Gould, cited in Payzant, *Glenn Gould,* p. 37.

23. Glenn Gould, in "Dialogues on the Prospects of Recordings," CBC broadcast, January 10, 1965, typescript page 3.

24. Payzant, *Glenn Gould,* p. 42.

25. Kazdin, *Glenn Gould,* p. 19.

26. Glenn Gould, letter to John Roberts, September 18, 1971, in *Glenn Gould: Selected Letters,* p. 160.

27. Kazdin, *Glenn Gould at Work,* p. 19.

28. Andrew Kazdin, quoted in Friedrich, *Glenn Gould,* p. 134.

29. Kazdin, *Glenn Gould at Work,* p. 4.

30. Ibid., p. 20.

31. Glenn Gould, letter to Andrew Kazdin, November 21, 1970, in *Glenn Gould: Selected Letters,* p. 127.

32. Andrew Kazdin, quoted in Friedrich, *Glenn Gould,* p. 134.

33. Ibid., p. 136.

34. Glenn Gould, letter to John Roberts, September 18, 1971, in *Glenn Gould: Selected Letters,* p. 161.

35. Kazdin, *Glenn Gould at Work,* p. 96–97.

36. Ibid., p. 42.

Chapter 23, New Faces, New Challenges

1. Ray Roberts, interview with the author, February 26, 1995. All subsequent quotations, unless otherwise noted, are from that conversation.

2. Robert Silverman, interview with the author, November 20, 1995.

3. Glenn Gould, "Robertsiana," File 1979-20, 23, 98, Glenn Gould Archives, National Library of Canada.

4. John Roberts, interview with the author, November 19, 1995.

5. Kazdin, *Glenn Gould at Work,* p. 53.

6. Conrad Bloemendal, interview with the author, June 17, 1994.

7. Lorne Tulk, interview with the author, June 16, 1994.

8. Glenn Gould, "Das Kind der Rosemarie," File 1979-20, 23, 65, Glenn Gould Archives, National Library of Canada.

9. Greta Kraus, interview with the author, June 18, 1994.

10. Patrick J. Sullivan, telephone interview with the author, February 27, 1995.

11. Joseph Stephens, M.D., interview with the author, November 10, 1994.

12. Kazdin, *Glenn Gould at Work,* p. 57.

13. Glenn Gould, draft for a letter to "Dell," undated, in *Glenn Gould: Collected Letters,* pp. 242–243.

14. Joseph Stephens, M.D., interview with the author, November 10, 1994.

15. Glenn Gould, "Rubinstein," *Look,* March 9, 1971, reprinted in *The Glenn Gould Reader,* p. 282.

16. Glenn Gould, "Memories of Maude Harbour, or Variations on a Theme of Arthur Rubinstein," *Piano Quarterly* (Summer 1980), reprinted in *The Glenn Gould Reader,* pp. 290–295.

17. Quotations of statements by George Roy Hill and Glenn Gould, in Friedrich, *Glenn Gould,* pp. 261–262.

18. Glenn Gould, letter to George Roy Hill, September 27, 1971, in *Glenn Gould: Collected Letters,* p. 162.

19. Quotations of statements by Glenn Gould and film critics, in Friedrich, *Glenn Gould,* pp. 263–266.

20. Richard Nielsen, cited in ibid., pp. 266–268.

21. Glenn Gould, letter to Rev. William Glenesk, May 22, 1982, in *Glenn Gould: Collected Letters,* pp. 246–247.

22. Richard Nielsen, cited in Friedrich, *Glenn Gould,* pp. 268–270.

23. Glenn Gould, letter to Rev. William Glenesk, May 22, 1982, in *Glenn Gould: Collected Letters,* p. 247.

24. Quotations from filmmakers and Jessie Greig in Friedrich, *Glenn Gould,* pp. 268–271.

25. Robert Silverman, interview with the author, November 20, 1995.

26. "Glenn Gould: Concert Dropout." Conversation with John McClure, bonus record included with Columbia MS 7173, 1968.

27. John Roberts, in "Glenn Gould: A Portrait" (Part 1), CBC Television, 1985.

28. Cott, *Conversations with Glenn Gould,* p. 31.

29. Gould, "Stokowski in Six Scenes," reprinted in *The Glenn Gould Reader,* pp. 258–282.

30. Robert Silverman, interview with the author, November 20, 1995.

31. Ibid.

32. Letter from John Roberts to Lise Deschamps Ostwald, September 30, 1996.

33. Robert Silverman, interview with the author, November 20, 1995.

34. Letter from Joe Stephens to Lise Deschamps Ostwald, June 20, 1996.

35. Bruno Monsaingeon cited in Friedrich, *Glenn Gould,* pp. 226–227.

36. Glenn Gould, letter to Bruno Monsaingeon, November 12, 1972, in *Glenn Gould: Collected Letters,* p. 181.

37. Bruno Monsaingeon, *Glenn Gould: Le Dernier Puritain; Glenn Gould: Je ne suis pas du tout un Excentrique;* and *Glenn Gould: Contrepoint à la Ligne.* Paris: Fayard, 1983, 1984, and 1985.

38. Bruno Monsaingeon, cited in Friedrich, *Glenn Gould,* pp. 228–229.

Chapter 24, Approaching Middle Age

1. John Percival, M.D., interview with the author, June 16, 1994.
2. Now in the Restricted Archives, National Library of Canada.
3. John Percival, M.D., interview with the author, June 16, 1994.
4. Glenn Gould, letter to Ronald Wilford, December 21, 1971, in *Glenn Gould: Selected Letters,* p. 172.
5. Glenn Gould, letter to Drs. S. Brown and J. G. Hill, August 31, 1972, in *Glenn Gould: Selected Letters,* p. 179.
6. Jessie Greig, cited in Friedrich, *Glenn Gould,* p. 243.
7. Joseph Stephens, M.D., interview with the author, November 10, 1994.
8. Ray Roberts, interview with the author, February 25, 1995.
9. Lorne Tulk, interview with the author, June 16, 1994.
10. Jessie Greig, in "Glenn Gould: A Portrait" (Part 2), CBC Television, 1985.
11. Jessie Greig, cited in Friedrich, *Glenn Gould,* pp. 170–171.
12. John Percival, M.D., interview with the author, June 16, 1994.
13. Glenn Gould, Restricted Archives, File 1979–20, 22, 137, p. 4, National Library of Canada.
14. John Roberts, interview with the author, November 19, 1995.
15. Glenn Gould, Restricted Archives, File 1979–20, 22, 110, p. 6, National Library of Canada.
16. Dale McCarthy, M.D., interview with the author, June 16, 1994.
17. Ray Roberts, interview with the author, February 25, 1995.
18. Glenn Gould, Restricted Archives, File 1979–20, 23, 162, p. 1, National Library of Canada.
19. John Roberts, in "Glenn Gould: a Portrait" (Part 2), CBC Television, 1985.
20. See Ostwald, *Schumann: The Inner Voices of a Musical Genius.*
21. Joseph Stephens, M.D., interview with the author, November 10, 1994.
22. Glenn Gould Diary (Book 1), File 1979–20, 21, 77, pp. 1–3, National Library of Canada.
23. Kazdin, *Glenn Gould at Work,* pp. 151–153.
24. Glenn Gould Diary (Book 1), File 1979–20, 21, 77, p. 4, National Library of Canada.
25. Ibid., pp. 4–10.
26. Ibid., pp. 10–24.
27. Ibid., pp. 33–37.
28. Ibid., pp. 44–48.
29. Ibid., pp. 49–62.

Chapter 25, The Last Years

1. Glenn Gould Diary (Book 2), File 1979–20, 20, 4, pp. 1–2, National Library of Canada.
2. Philip Klotz, M.D., interview with the author, June 16, 1994.
3. Glenn Gould Diary (Book 2), File 1979–20, 20, 4, pp. 11–18, National Library of Canada.
4. Ibid., pp. 27–29.

5. Ibid., pp. 54–63.

6. Lorne Tulk, interview with the author, June 16, 1994.

7. Glenn Gould, letter to Robert Sunter, January 30, 1979, in *Glenn Gould: Selected Letters,* p. 238.

8. John McGreevy, interview with the author, June 13, 1994.

9. John McGreevy, cited in Friedrich, *Glenn Gould,* p. 223.

10. John McGreevy's film *Glenn Gould's Toronto,* released in 1979.

11. John McGreevy, interview with the author, June 13, 1994.

12. Peter Mak, interview with the author, February 25, 1995.

13. Glenn Gould, "Art of the Fugue," Introduction to Book I of Bach's *The Well-Tempered Clavier,* Amsco Music Company, 1972, reprinted in *The Glenn Gould Reader,* pp. 16–17.

14. Glenn Gould, "The Question of Instrument," Vol. XIX of *The Glenn Gould Collection,* Sony Classical SLV 48 425.

15. Peter Mak, interview with the author, February 25, 1995.

16. Glenn Gould, draft for a letter to Russell Herbert Gould, in *Glenn Gould: Selected Letters,* pp. 240–241.

17. Margaret Pacsu, cited in Friedrich, *Glenn Gould,* p. 257.

18. Glenn Gould, "An Art of the Fugue," Vol. XV of *The Glenn Gould Collection,* Sony.

19. Glenn Gould, medical notes, Restricted Archives, File 1979–20, 23, 162, pp. 2–3, National Library of Canada.

20. Glenn Gould, "The Goldberg Variations," Vol. XIII of *The Glenn Gould Collection,* Sony Classical SLV 48 424.

21. Ibid.

22. Robert Silverman, interview with the author, November 20, 1995.

23. John Roberts, interview with the author, November 19, 1995.

24. Kazdin, *Glenn Gould at Work,* pp. 162–163.

Chapter 26, A Fatal Stroke

1. Timothy Findley, cited in Friedrich, *Glenn Gould,* p. 267.

2. Conrad Bloemendal, interview with the author, June 17, 1994.

3. Sony Classical SMK 52 65O.

4. Timothy Maloney, cited in James Strecker, "Glenn Gould: Man, Musician, and Legacy." "Nine Canadians Talk About the Legendary Pianist," *Bulletin of the International Glenn Gould Society,* March–October 1991.

5. List of medications in the Restricted Glenn Gould Archives, National Library of Canada.

6. Lorne Tulk, interview with the author, June 16, 1994.

7. Robert Silverman, interview with the author, November 20, 1995.

8. Jessie Greig, in *Thirty-Two Short Films About Glenn Gould,* a film produced by Rhombus Media.

9. John Roberts, interview with the author, June 17, 1994.

10. Raymond Roberts, interview with the author, February 26, 1995.

11. John Percival, M.D., interview with the author, June 16, 1994.

12. Raymond Roberts, interview with the author, February 26, 1995.

13. *San Francisco Chronicle,* October 2, 1982.

14. *New York Times,* front-page headline, October 5, 1982.

15. Author's letter to Russell Herbert Gould, October 5, 1982, personal file.

16. John Roberts, memorial service tribute to Glenn Gould, October 15, 1982, in the Glenn Gould Archives, File 1979–20, 44, 40, National Library of Canada.

Epilogue and Acknowledgments

1. John McGreevy, ed., *Glenn Gould: By Himself and His Friends,* Toronto and Garden City, NY: Doubleday, 1983, p. 12.

2. Ibid., p. 9.

3. Friedrich, *Glenn Gould: A Life and Variations.*

4. Peter Ostwald, "Glenn Gould: Some Personal Reminiscences," *Medical Problems of Performing Artists* (September 1989), p. 139.

5. Peter Ostwald, "Some Personal Reminiscences," *Bulletin of the International Glenn Gould Society* (Holland; 1991), vol. 8, pp. 23–29.

6. "Ishi toshite tomo toshite," translated by Marie Ogura, in *Wave,* vol. 37, May 1993, pp. 25–33.

INDEX

Abel, David, 30, 31
"Advice to a Graduation" (Gould), 221–22
Aide, William, 71–72, 104
Allan, B. M., 124
Allen, Mildred, 283
Alma Trio, 30
Also Sprach Zarathustra (Nietzsche), 103
American Symphony, 246
Ancerl, Karel, 247, 255
And the Bridge Is Love (Werfel), 178
Applebaum, Louis, 177
"Argument for Richard Strauss, An" (Gould), 251–52
Arnold Schoenberg: The Man Who Changed Music, 206–8
Arrau, Claudio, 71, 104, 266
Arriaga, Juan, 18
Art of Glenn Gould, The, 220, 260
Art of the Fugue, An, 314–15
Ashkenazy, Vladimir, 168, 323
Asperger Disease, 42

Bach, Johann Sebastian, 43, 141
  Anna Magdalena Notebook, 116
  Art of the Fugue, 311, 314–15
  Brandenburg Concertos, 136, 208, 279
  Chromatic Fantasia in D Minor, 311–12
  Concerto in D Minor, 143, 151, 154, 164, 165, 176, 215
  Concerto in F Minor, 18–20, 21, 30, 93–94, 97, 177
  Fantasia and Fugue in C Minor, 75, 76
  Goldberg Variations (Gould's first recording), 17–18, 72, 101, 113, 114–19, 120, 121, 185, 194, 280, 316, 317–18
  Goldberg Variations (Gould's performances), 100, 101, 108, 121, 151, 180
  Goldberg Variations (Gould's second recording), 119, 316–19, 324, 331
  Gould's opinions on, 74, 86, 100, 118–19, 154, 159–60, 217, 244, 245, 269, 316–17
  Inventions, 155, 283
  Italian Concerto, 132, 311
  Musical Offering, 234
  Partita no. 4, 312
  Partita no. 5, 111, 112
  Partita no. 6, 285
  Partitas, 188
  Piano Sonata no. 6 in F Major, 75
  Piano Sonata no. 11 in B-flat Major, 143, 146–47

Bach (*continued*)
Piano Sonata no. 21 in C Major, 80
Piano Sonata No. 29 in B-flat ("Hammerklavier"), 140
Preludes and Fugues, 69
Six Violin and Harpsichord Sonatas, 297
Sonata for Violin and Piano in C Minor, 30, 226
Toccata and Fugue in D Minor, 28
Violin Sonata in E Major, 311
Violin Sonata in G Minor, 28
Well-Tempered Clavier, 159–60, 187, 314
Bachauver, Gina, 188
Bach Medal for Pianists, 174–75
"Back to Bach" movement, 86
Baltimore Symphony Orchestra, 185
Banquo (Gould's dog), 101, 153, 179
Barnes, John, 282
Bartók, Béla, 42
Baudelaire, Charles, 119
Bauermeister, Mary, 262
Beckwith, John, 71
Beethoven, Ludwig van:
deafness of, 77
"Eroica" Variations, 194
Fantasia for Piano, Chorus, and Orchestra, 146–47
"Ghost" Trio, 106–8
Gould's opinions on, 140, 143, 146–47, 210, 244, 245, 252, 262–63, 314
"Grosse Fuge," 140, 176
Liszt's transcriptions for, 254–55, 259–60
Overture to *King Stephen,* 146, 147
Piano Concerto no. 1 in C Major, 84, 132, 177
Piano Concerto no. 2 in B-flat Major, 145, 148, 154, 256, 322
Piano Concerto no. 3 in C Minor, 155, 162, 166, 174
Piano Concerto no. 4 in G Major, 75–76, 78–79, 80, 81, 121, 133, 134, 151, 185, 208
Piano Concerto no. 5 in E-flat Major ("Emperor"), 176, 196, 246–47, 314
Piano Sonata no. 17 in D Minor ("Tempest"), 141, 194, 208
Piano Sonata no. 23 in F Minor ("Appassionata"), 247, 248
Piano Sonata no. 30 in E Major, 109, 111, 138–41, 208–9, 216
Piano Sonata no. 31 in A-flat Major, 138–41
Piano Sonata no. 32 in C Minor, 138–41
Sonata for Piano and Violin in C Minor, 31
Sonata for Piano and Violin in G Major, 31, 226–27
String Quartet no. 13, 176
String Quartet no. 15, 170, 263
Symphony no. 5, 254, 259–60
Symphony no. 6 ("Pastorale"), 254–55
Symphony no. 9 ("Choral"), 138, 147
Variations in F Major, 194
Bennett, Arthur, 64, 121
Bennett, Denton B., 121
Berg, Alban, 61, 87, 152, 178
Gould's opinions on, 201, 256
Piano Sonata, 111, 151
Bergman, Ingmar, 280
Berlin Philharmonic, 155
Bernstein, Felicia, 145
Bernstein, Leonard, 48, 143–45, 169, 205, 210–13, 253, 277, 322
Best Seat in the House: Memoirs of a Lucky Man (Fulford), 57–58, 85
Beverly Hills Hotel, 214
Bizet, Georges, 255
Premier Nocturne, 256
Variations Chromatiques, 256
Blinder, Naoum, 30
Bloemendal, Conrad, 275, 320–21
Boulez, Pierre, 251
Boult, Adrian, 261
Bourgeois Hero, The, 251, 308
Brahms, Johannes:
Ballade in G Major, 75
Ballades, 321
Gould's opinions on, 210–13, 251
Intermezzi, 145, 193–94
Piano Concerto no. 1 in D Minor, 193, 210–13
Quintet for Piano and Strings in F Minor, 160–61, 193, 279
Rhapsodies, 321
Symphony no. 2, 207
Brando, Marlon, 103, 261
Briggs, John, 113–14
Brown, Corrick, 194
Bruckner, Anton, 126, 176, 201, 251
Brunner, Dr., 164
Burton, Humphrey, 193, 214, 245
Busoni, Ferruccio, 156
Butler, Roma, 100
Byrd, William, 256, 257

Callas, Maria, 258, 259
Canadian Broadcasting Corporation (CBC), Gould's collaboration with, 64, 87, 90–91, 94, 106, 125, 132, 137, 161, 178, 179, 200, 204, 208, 219–21, 226, 229, 232, 235, 237, 241, 247, 274, 282, 289, 290, 307, 324
Canadian National Exhibition, 59, 309
Canin, Martin, 18, 21, 112, 166, 167, 169, 322
Cantelli, Guido, 215
Carlos, Walter, 264

Carroll, Jock, 121, 125, 127–28
Carter, Elliott: *Sonata,* 169
Carter, Sam, 317
Caruso, Enrico, 61–62, 66
Casals, Pablo, 178, 206, 240, 290
Casavant Frères, 76
Casella, Alfredo: *Ricercare on the name BACH,* 298, 301, 302
CBC Tuesday Night, 260
Chapin, Schuyler, 225
Charendoff, Morris D., 189–90, 193
Chemins de la Musique, Les, 283–85
Children II or *Richard Strauss Writes an Opera* (Gould), 204–5
Chopin, Frédéric, 43, 48, 74, 87, 166
  Gould's opinions on, 94
  Impromptu in F-sharp Major, 75, 80, 83
  Piano Sonata no. 3 in B Minor, 253
Cincinnati, University of, 216
Claremont Quartet, 204
Clark, Petula, 236
Cleveland Orchestra, 148, 255
Cliburn, Van, 162, 178, 197, 205
Columbia Records, 17, 112, 114–19, 125, 131, 132, 138, 157, 193–94, 223, 242, 246, 249, 253–54, 267, 268, 270, 287, 288, 298–99, 307, 317, 321
Columbia Symphony Orchestra, 177
Committee of the Harriet Cohen International Music Awards, 174–75
Concert for Four Wednesdays, 221
Conservatory Orchestra, 79, 94
"contrapuntal radio," 232–43, 290
Conversations with Casals (Ma Corredor), 178
Conversations with Glenn Gould, 245
Copland, Aaron, 208
Cott, Jonathan, 257, 258
Curran Theater, 179
Curtis Institute of Music, 48

Debussy, Claude, 71
  String Quartet, 176
Dees, Cornelius, 191, 286
Detroit Free Press, 133
Detroit News, 135
Detroit Symphony Orchestra, 133–34
Dialogue on the Prospects of Recording, 223–25
Diamond, David, 203
Dobson, Vera, 312, 328
"Dr. Karlheinz Heinkel," 259–60
Doyle, Arthur M., 124
Dudley, Ray, 72
Dupuis, Albert: Concerto Movement, 75, 76

Eaton Auditorium, 76, 83, 84, 249, 270, 271, 275, 298–99, 309
Elgar, Edward: Violin Concerto, 229
Elsie (housemaid), 39
Emmanuel Presbyterian Church, 48
Epstein, A. A., 242

Fath, Iris, 174
Faull, Ellen, 136–37
Festival: The Anatomy of Fugue, 216
Findley, Timothy, 280, 320
"finger-tapping," 71–72, 104
Fiscella, Robert, 296
Fitzgerald, Winston, 173, 180, 193
Fleisher, Leon, 223, 224, 242–43
Ford, Mrs., 149
Forrester, Maureen, 100–101, 137, 331
Foss, Lukas, 48
Frank, Claude, 111
Frankenstein, Alfred, 208–9
Friedman, Jane, 256
Friedrich, Otto, 180, 238, 285, 332–33
Fuchs, Joe, 112
Fuchs, Lillian, 112
Fulford, Robert, 36, 52–53, 73, 76, 80, 103
  Gould's friendship with, 57–66, 85, 89, 98–99, 100–101

Gibbons, Orlando, 111, 112, 256–57
  Anthems, 257
Gilliatt, Penelope, 279–80
Glenn Gould: A Life and Variations (Friedrich), 332–33
Glenn Gould: By Himself and His Friends (McGreevy), 332
Glenn Gould at Work (Kazdin), 270
Glenn Gould Fantasy, A, 246, 312–14
Glenn Gould Festival (1992), 333
Glenn Gould Off the Record; Glenn Gould on the Record, 131–32
Glenn Gould Plays Bach, 310–12, 314, 316
Glenn Gould Silver Jubilee, The, 312
Glenn Gould's Toronto, 309–10
Gold, Thomas G. (grandfather), 36, 51–52
Goldberg, Johann Gottlieb, 116
Gold Standard Furs, 35, 36, 51–52, 56
Golschmann, Vladimir, 137, 177
Goodman, W., 198
Gottlieb, Mark, 204
Gould, Flora Emma Greig (mother), 35, 36–39
  death of, 290–92, 302–3, 312
  Gould's relationship with, 39–45, 48, 49–50, 52, 55, 56, 59–62, 65–66, 73, 75, 83, 85, 88, 91, 97, 102, 127, 129, 132, 173, 179, 248–49, 258–59, 281, 309
Gould, Glenn Herbert:
  adolescence of, 65–66
  affluent background of, 58
  aggression suppressed by, 49, 55–56, 66, 78, 128, 238–40, 277, 281, 309

Gould, Glenn Herbert (*continued*)
airplane travel feared by, 150, 215–16, 272, 309–10
as animal rights activist, 31–32, 51–55, 56, 280, 289, 325
anxiety of, 110, 114, 121, 130, 132, 149–50, 165, 168–69, 258–59, 263, 287
audience response to, 19, 83, 91, 102, 105–6, 109, 118, 130–31, 132–34, 154, 163, 174, 180, 211, 212, 221, 245, 266
author's first meeting with, 11, 17–34, 132–33
author's friendship with, 142–48, 174–84, 194–96, 206–8, 214–16, 296–98
author's medical letter for, 182–84
autopsy of, 169, 328–29
Avenue Road apartment of, 181, 184
back problems of, 63–64, 189, 275
Bahamas trip of, 121–22, 125, 127–28
in Berlin, 155–56, 157, 165
bicycle of, 92–93
biographies of, 120, 332–33
birth of, 35, 39
body cast worn by, 191, 193
Canadian background of, 17, 25, 64, 95, 97, 110, 114, 150, 194, 195, 203, 231, 267
cancellations by, 164–70, 171, 182–84, 190, 196–97, 214, 217, 247, 256
career of, 58, 65, 81–83, 88, 90, 97, 110–19, 125, 144, 156, 190, 265, 291, 321
as celebrity, 117–18, 119, 132, 180, 188, 198, 273
chair used by, 18, 24, 31, 70–74, 102, 104, 117, 133, 148, 161–62, 209, 304–5, 306, 314
childhood accident of, 63–64, 238, 265
childhood of, 42, 43–66, 265
as child prodigy, 43–56, 58, 62, 67–68, 79–80, 228, 248–49
chiropractors visited by, 23–24, 63–64, 102, 121, 123, 125, 166, 191
Christianity of, 60, 66
competition as viewed by, 50, 210, 213, 222–23, 265, 266, 267
in competitions, 75–76, 80, 162, 265
composers as viewed by, 95, 200
concert schedule of, 130, 131, 134–35, 165, 214–15, 242–43
conducting by, 130, 136, 137–38, 144, 176, 239, 260, 305, 306, 307, 321–23
conservatism of, 202–3
correspondence of, 149, 151–53, 156–57, 166–70, 177, 178, 182, 194–95
counterpoint studied by, 68, 163–64, 193, 200–201, 216–17, 233, 252
criticism avoided by, 187, 188, 296–98, 323
as cultural ambassador, 150
death of, 11, 169, 286, 326–29
debut of, 80
depression of, 163, 290–92, 324–25
diaries of, 298–307
diet of, 274–75, 287
doctors consulted by, 14, 32–33, 42, 102, 121–23, 125, 135, 149–50, 164, 167, 182–84, 188–93, 242, 286–87, 292–95, 298, 315
documentary films on, 116, 131–32, 137, 141, 309–12
dogs owned by, 27, 31, 51, 52–53, 80, 93, 101, 153, 179, 289
Donchery estate leased by, 180, 181, 193
dreams of, 48–49, 127, 129, 258, 292, 309–10
driving by, 101, 128, 157, 186, 209, 272, 282
early performances of, 47–48, 62, 74–76, 78–79, 80, 83–84, 88, 93–97
eating disorder of, 122, 125, 127–28, 133, 150, 158, 164
eccentricity of, 102–3, 109, 112, 121, 122, 128, 133–34, 172, 180, 182, 229, 285, 287
editing by, 207, 212, 239–40, 254, 268–70, 274, 279, 317
education of, 49, 57–58, 62, 67, 69, 76, 84–86, 87, 98, 219, 265
European tours of, 122, 149–58, 161, 162–73
family name of, 35–36, 55, 116
father figures of, 132
fees of, 92
fictional characters impersonated by, 103, 128–29, 239, 258–62, 309, 313
fiftieth birthday of, 324–25, 328
finances of, 106, 109, 119, 165, 170, 265, 266, 272–73, 275, 277, 326
fingers protected by, 46–47, 127, 174
on fishing expedition, 50–51, 61
French spoken by, 283–84
friendships of, 57, 58–59, 66, 84–85, 103, 132, 137, 187, 188, 199, 270, 275, 282, 287, 297–98
fugue studied by, 87, 96, 163–64, 209, 216–17, 234, 253, 282, 285, 314
German accent adopted by, 103, 155, 239, 262, 310
glasses worn by, 313, 314
as "ham," 91, 103, 282
handwriting of, 58, 85
harmony studied by, 68, 216
harpsichords as viewed by, 186–87, 270, 279, 311
hayfever of, 158
high blood pressure of, 169, 292–95, 303

honorary degrees of, 221–22
hospitalizations of, 121, 325–29
hotel rooms of, 127–28, 133, 163, 169, 179, 184, 209, 214
hypochondria of, 21, 22–23, 32–33, 42, 59, 63–64, 92, 102, 109, 113–14, 122–23, 132, 134–35, 164–70, 171, 180, 188, 192, 193, 198, 243, 285, 291, 310, 326
imaginary dialogues of, 262–63
improvisations by, 87–88, 188, 208, 279
independence of, 58–59, 121, 133
infancy of, 39–42
influence of, 119, 154–55, 266–67, 285
influences on, 48, 74, 87, 103–4, 109, 188
"inner model" of, 76–79, 102, 107, 118–19
Inn on the Park studio of, 184, 270, 271, 272, 285, 297, 313, 324, 326
insecurity of, 111, 113–14
insomnia of, 28, 33, 116, 136, 147
intellect of, 22, 59, 65, 291
intensity of, 235–36, 237
interpretation by, 78, 79, 94–95, 97, 106–8, 136, 138–41, 159–60, 161, 163–64, 187–88, 210–13, 246–48, 254, 268, 269, 316–19, 322
interviews conducted by, 232–34, 238, 239–40, 264–65, 290
interviews given by, 104, 120, 133–34, 225, 243
as introvert, 144–45, 174, 198
in Israel, 171–73
Jewish ancestry attributed to, 35–36, 275
kidney problems of, 168–69
Lake Simcoe cottage of, 25–26, 27, 50–51, 58, 60, 63, 68–69, 71, 72, 90, 92–93, 98, 101, 109, 131–32, 172, 187, 215, 217, 229, 290
language as interest of, 66, 126
lawsuit of, 190–91, 192
lecturing by, 151–53, 216, 221–22
liner notes by, 140, 146, 177, 256, 259
love affairs of, 276–78, 306
manipulativeness of, 14, 30, 31, 32, 58–59, 125, 132, 147, 228, 239–40, 272, 285, 303
masking tone used by, 76–78, 102, 109
media coverage of, 117–18, 119, 122, 148, 151, 214
medications taken by, 14, 62, 102, 121, 123, 168, 181, 191, 238–39, 272, 287, 292–96, 315, 318, 324
memorial service for, 324, 329–31
memory of, 30, 45, 64, 66, 68, 94, 106–7, 108, 208, 283, 322
mineral water drunk by, 22, 105, 116–17
modesty of, 174–75, 198
monologues of, 22–23, 25–29, 31, 32, 65, 143, 144, 187, 225, 296–97
as musical genius, 34, 39, 40–50, 67–68, 76, 85, 88, 126, 132, 219, 243, 248–49, 291, 331
musical studies of, 67–80, 104
musicological analysis by, 99–100, 218
narcissism of, 139–40, 142, 144, 277
nervousness of, 21, 31–32, 34, 102–3, 109, 110, 127, 133–35, 150, 294, 310
nervous tics of, 21, 192, 228
neurological problems of, 168, 169–70, 189–93
New York debut of (1955), 111–14
nighttime schedule of, 237, 238, 272–73, 274
as nonconformist, 58, 61, 125–26
"normal" upbringing of, 60
in Northern Territories, 230–36
as only child, 39, 238, 265
as opinionated, 14, 32, 61–62, 65, 87, 94, 123, 297
as organist, 68–69, 76, 83, 206
overdressing by, 21, 24, 102, 106, 116, 122–23, 157, 163, 198, 209, 273, 287
perfect pitch of, 44–45, 68
personality of, 32, 40, 55–56, 102–3, 124, 128, 129, 142, 238–39, 262, 277
personal philosophy of, 263–68
physical appearance of, 19, 24, 59, 145, 282–83, 295–96, 318, 320–21
physical contact avoided by, 189, 191
as pianist, 17–20, 66, 68, 70–79, 88, 101–2, 104, 108–9, 111, 119, 132, 144, 155, 178, 188, 191, 219, 222–23, 242–43, 266–67, 270, 290, 291, 296–97
piano concerto as viewed by, 265–66
pianos elevated by, 18, 24, 133, 147, 148, 174
piano studied by, 43–50, 58, 70–74, 76, 77–80, 92, 98, 103–4
pianos used by, 21, 30, 63, 88, 132, 171, 172, 173–74, 178, 179, 256, 270, 317
playing position of, 18, 24, 31, 43, 70–74, 83, 104, 192, 295, 298–307
practicing by, 72, 106–8, 155, 157–58, 163, 274, 298–307
psychiatrists as viewed by, 121, 128–29
psychosomatic illnesses of, 14, 120, 121–23, 158, 242, 286–87
psychotherapy for, 120–29, 133, 142, 181–84, 187, 192, 197–99
psychotic episode of, 181–84, 185, 262
radio as interest of, 64–65, 66, 90, 101, 131, 139, 219–21
radio programs of, 90–91, 92, 93, 96, 97,

Gould, Glenn Herbert (*continued*)
103, 106, 178, 205, 206–8, 223–25, 230–43, 251, 264–65, 266, 282, 289–90, 307–8
reading by, 87, 177, 178
record collection of, 79, 87, 101, 139, 179, 188, 274
recordings by, 13, 17–18, 72, 74, 91, 94–95, 101, 108, 113–21, 130, 131, 136–41, 144, 154–65, 168, 177, 185, 187, 194, 204, 205, 212, 242, 245–57, 267–70, 274, 275, 279–81, 287–88, 297–99, 306, 307, 316–19, 324, 331
recording techniques studied by, 29, 89, 118, 131, 139, 217–19, 223–25, 229, 264–65, 267–70, 316, 317
record sales of, 119, 219
religious feelings of, 275–76, 292
repertoire of, 83–84, 94, 111, 299, 301
reputation of, 58, 79–80, 97, 105–6, 111, 135, 154, 156, 164, 242, 247
residences of, 179, 180, 181, 183, 184, 193
retirement of, 32, 130, 141, 213, 214–15, 216, 219, 221, 230, 242–43, 244, 284
reviews of, 76, 79, 80, 83, 102, 108, 111, 113–14, 133, 139, 155–56, 161, 162, 208–9, 212, 324
royalties of, 119
St. Clair Avenue apartment of, 183, 184, 198, 270, 286, 296
in Salzburg, 163–65
San Francisco recitals of, 17–24, 33–34, 173, 174, 179–80, 206, 215
Scottish ancestry of, 25, 36–37
sedatives taken by, 28–29, 32–33, 91, 114, 120, 125, 135–36, 149–50, 204, 208
self-confidence of, 85, 104, 133–34
self-image of, 55, 203, 243
sense of humor of, 22, 45, 58, 66, 80, 84, 102, 123, 128–29, 148, 209, 239, 245–46, 259–62
sensitivity of, 238–39
sexuality of, 60–61, 66, 145, 151, 191, 194, 276, 277–78
shoulder injury of, 188–93, 196, 298, 303
sight-reading by, 30, 45, 48, 68, 107, 255
social life of, 49, 57, 66, 85–86, 112–13, 127, 144–45, 147, 150, 180, 193, 201
solitude needed by, 25–27, 66, 68–69, 92–93, 98, 102, 184, 203, 230–31, 232, 235, 243, 267, 287, 308
Southwood Drive home of, 38, 49, 52, 58, 79–80, 179
"splicing plan" of, 139, 268–70
stage fright of, 62–63, 66, 80, 83, 91–92, 154, 174
stage manner of, 18, 19, 20, 79, 80, 102, 104, 105–6, 111, 133–34, 141, 162–63, 180
stroke suffered by, 323, 325–29
style of, 19, 30, 78, 101–2, 144, 155, 159, 160, 162, 248, 288
tape recorders used by, 89, 90, 101, 179
technique of, 70–74, 83, 111, 112, 113–14, 155–56, 186–88, 298–307, 309
technological interests of, 29, 64–65, 66, 89–91, 229, 264–65, 280, 287
telepathy as interest of, 178–79, 181
telephone calls by, 143–48, 149, 177, 180, 181–82, 187, 194, 201, 259, 267, 269, 274, 275, 277, 281, 282, 283, 291, 298, 324, 327
television programs of, 91, 103, 106, 125, 129, 145, 193, 205–6, 212, 216, 219, 220, 221, 225–29, 245, 255, 265–66, 283
tempi used by, 31, 101–2, 112, 138–41, 159, 161, 188, 194, 197, 210–13, 246, 247, 248, 250, 254, 255, 311, 316, 318
Toronto as hometown of, 30, 38, 68–69, 121, 309–10
transcriptions by, 136, 201–2, 254, 287, 290, 314
U.S. tours of, 17–24, 27, 110–14, 133–34
"vacuum cleaner epiphany" of, 76–78, 102
in Vienna, 156–58
vocalizing of, 19, 45, 102, 165, 176, 200, 202, 209
voice of, 66, 68
Washington, D.C. debut of (1955), 111
will of, 325
writings of, 37–38, 84, 85–86, 88, 99–100, 128–29, 140, 166, 201, 217, 229, 249, 251, 255, 259, 262–64, 274, 281–82, 303
Gould, Glenn Herbert, works of:
film scores, 279–81, 320–21
Gould's views on, 32, 132, 144, 176, 202, 203
incidental music, 87
"Kind der Rosemarie, Das," 276
operatic works, 66, 127, 200, 204–5
Piano Pieces, 95–96
piano suite, 87–88
plays, 88
recordings of, 96, 204
Sonata for Bassoon and Piano, 95, 96
Sonata for Clarinet and Piano, 203–4
So You Want to Write a Fugue, 209, 216–17, 253, 285
String Quartet, 32, 125, 126, 176, 200–204, 205, 253, 282
Tod und Verklärung, 66
Gould, Grandma, 169

Gould, Grant A. (uncle), 36, 39, 40, 45, 51–52, 55, 61
Gould, Russell Herbert "Bert" (father), 35–36, 38–41
  Gould's death and, 326, 328, 329
  Gould's relationship with, 45, 46–47, 48, 49, 50, 56, 58, 60, 61, 63, 65, 66, 71, 73–74, 75, 83, 92, 93, 104, 109, 129, 133, 173, 179, 238, 292, 305, 310, 312, 324, 325
Graffman, Gary, 111, 113, 155
Greben, Stanley E., 197–99
Greig, H. A. Macdonald, 36–37
Greig, Jessie (cousin), 84–85, 88, 129, 281, 290, 291–92, 324, 327
Greig, John C. H. (grandfather), 36
Greig, Mary Catherine Flett (grandmother), 36
Grieg, Edvard, 25, 36, 37
  Piano Concerto in A Minor, 255, 270
  Piano Sonata in E Minor, 256
Griller, Sidney, 207
Griller Quartet, 206
Gross, Maurice, 106
Guarneri Quartet, 279
Guerrero, Alberto, 61, 95
  Gould as student of, 70–74, 76, 78–79, 83, 87, 88, 103–4, 105, 116, 179, 249, 303

Hamilton Philharmonic, 322
Hamlet (Shakespeare), 227–28, 282
Hammond, John, 224
Haydn, Franz Josef: Sonata in A-flat Major, 75
Heinze, Bernard, 80
Herbert, Frank, 99
"Herbert von Hochmeister," 259
Herman, Morris, 122–23, 189, 242, 286
High Fidelity, 259, 281
Hill, George Roy, 279
Hindemith, Paul:
  Matthias the Painter, 87
  Piano Sonata no. 3 in B-flat, 91, 94
History of Sexual Customs, A (Lewinsohn), 177
Hofmann, Cornelius, 333
Hofmann, Josef, 48–49
Homburger, Walter, as Gould's manager, 33, 81–83, 88, 91, 92, 97, 103, 104–6, 110–11, 115, 119, 132, 150, 151, 153, 157, 161–62, 163, 167–73, 180, 182, 219, 242
Home Music Club, 83–84
Horowitz, Vladimir, 82, 88, 189, 222–23, 246, 266, 277, 290, 312, 313
Hume, Paul, 111
Hupfer, William, 189, 192
Huxley, Aldous, 140, 263

Idea of North, The, 232–36, 241, 285, 297
Israel Philharmonic Orchestra, 172

James, Mary, 106, 175
Jenkins, Sylvia, 30
Jewish News, 35
Joachim, Otto, 204
Jones, William Corbett, 29–30, 31
Jordá, Enrique, 18, 20, 21, 22, 174
Juilliard String Quartet, 253–54

Kahn, Albert, 240
Kander, Gerhard, 82
Kapell, William, 112, 215
Karajan, Herbert von, 155, 157, 165, 176, 205, 255, 259, 322, 332
"Karlheinz Klopweisser," 103, 262, 313
Karsh, Yousuf, 151
Kazdin, Andrew, 47, 55–56, 247, 265, 268, 269–70, 271, 275, 278, 287, 298–99, 307, 317
Kennedy, Jacqueline, 216
Kind, Sylvia, 169
Kirkpatrick, Ralph, 115, 116
Kiwanis Music Festival, 75, 76
Klemperer, Otto, 145
Klibonoff, John, 322
Klotz, Philip, 305
Kogan, Matilda, 30, 31
Kolisch Quartet, 107
Kollitsch, Wolfgang, 170
Kraemer, Franz, 131–32, 200–201
Kraus, Greta, 74, 276
Krenek, Ernst, 94, 96, 152, 290
Krips, Josef, 176
Kuerti, Anton, 163–64, 212

Landowska, Wanda, 108, 115, 188
Lang, Paul Henry, 212
Laredo, Jaime, 287, 288, 297
Last Puritan, The (Santayana), 177
Latecomers, The, 237–40
Leibowitz, René, 87
Le Moyne, Jean, 264
Lenczner, Michael, 164
Leningrad Philharmonic, 154
"Let's Ban Applause!" (Gould), 154
Leventritt, Rosie, 111–13, 114
Liberace, 117, 278
Lipatti, Dinu, 114–15
Liszt, Franz, 19, 48, 107
  piano transcriptions of, 254–55, 259–60
  Valse Oubliée, 62
Logan, Alexander G., 292, 293, 294, 295, 315, 326
London Symphony Orchestra, 176
Look, 279
Lucerne Festival, 176
Lutrell, Dr., 192
Lympany, Moura, 217

McCarthy, Dale, 295, 315
McClure, John, 131, 244
MacDonald, D'Arcy, 314
McGreevy, John, 66, 309, 310, 325, 332
McLean, Eric, 161
McLuhan, Marshall, 219, 223, 225, 233, 264–65
MacMillan, Ernest, 70, 84, 92, 100–101, 135
Ma Corredor, J., 178
McRae, Colin A., 102
Mahler, Gustav:
  Gould's opinions on, 257
  Symphony no. 2 ("Resurrection"), 137
Mak, Peter, 310, 312
Maloney, Timothy, 323
Malvern Collegiate Institute, 76, 84–86, 87, 98
Malvern Drama Club, 87
Manitoulin Island, 54, 325
Mann, Robert, 253–54
Mann, Thomas, 140
Marceau, Marcel, 106
Marchese, Catherine, 96
Mark, Peter, 23
Marliave, Joseph de, 140
Marriner, Neville, 322
Marshall, Lois, 206
"Márta Hortaványi," 313
Mary Tyler Moore Show, The, 274
Massey Hall, 97
Master Musician series, 206, 229
Master Musician/Yehudi Menuhin, 229
Maybegg, Gerwald, 164
Mazzoleni, Ettore, 79
Mehta, Zubin, 193
Meiningen Orchestra, 107
Mendelssohn, Felix:
  "Fingal's Cave" Overture, 323
  Gould's opinions on, 252–53
  Sonata no. 6, 76
  Songs Without Words, 253
  Trio no. 1 in D Minor, 137
Mennonites, 240–42
Menuhin, Diana Gould, 223, 224–25, 228
Menuhin, Yehudi, 28, 192, 206, 226–29, 307
Metropolitan United Church, 76
Michelangeli, Arturo Benedetti, 247
Miller, Larry, 88
Mitropoulos, Dimitri, 164
Moffitt, Herbert C., Jr., 33, 149–50
Moll, Albert E., 121, 123–25, 129
Molson Prize, 264
Monsaingeon, Bruno, 283–85, 310, 311, 314, 316, 325, 333
Montreal String Quartet, 160, 161, 204
Moore, Howard, 238
Morawetz, Oskar, 87, 94–95, 140, 200
Moscow Philharmonic Orchestra, 151
Moscow State Conservatory, 151
Mozart (Gould's pet bird), 53, 249
Mozart, Wolfgang Amadeus, 45, 62, 67–68, 107, 141
  Gould's opinions on, 22, 66, 76–77, 78, 248–50
  Piano Concerto no. 24 in C Minor, 166
  Piano Sonata no. 3 in B-flat Major, 91
  Piano Sonata no. 6 in D Major, 250
  Piano Sonata no. 7 in C Major, 250
  Piano Sonata no. 16 in C Major ("Sonata facile"), 250
  Piano Sonata no. 17 in B-flat Major, 250
  Piano Sonatas, 249–50
  Sonatas for Four Hands, 74, 143, 249
  Symphony no. 40 in G Minor, 249
Müller, Martin, 166
music:
  atonal, 61, 126, 151, 256
  authenticity in, 139
  Baroque, 86, 87, 115, 116, 224, 249
  contemporary, 61, 71, 86–87, 94, 98, 151–53
  Gould's opinions on, 61–62, 65, 66, 86–87
  pop, 236–37
  on radio, 64
  recorded, 64, 217–19, 223–25, 229, 316, 317
  Renaissance, 86, 257
  Romantic, 86, 201–3, 252–54
Musical America, 229
Musical Courier, 108
Musicamera: Music in Our Time, 290, 301
Music of Man, The, 228–29, 307
Music of Today/Schoenberg Series, 289–90
Myers, Paul, 223–24
"My Plans for the School Year" (Gould), 84
"Myron Chianti," 103, 261–62

Naoumoff, Emile, 95, 96
National Film Board of Canada, 131
National Library of Canada, 121, 184
Neil, Boyd, 165
Nelsova, Zara, 28, 106–8, 110–11
Neveu, Ginette, 215
Newfoundland, 237–40
New Music Associates, 98–101
New Yorker, 104
New York Philharmonic, 143, 144, 210, 211, 279
New York Times, 324
Nick (Gould's dog), 52, 53, 80, 101
Nielsen, Carl, 256
Nielsen, Richard, 280
Nietzsche, Friedrich, 103

Oakland Symphony, 208
Offergeld, Robert, 224

Olnick, Harvey, 108, 109, 111–13, 114, 201
opera, 61, 66, 127, 200, 204–5, 234–35, 251–52
Oppenheim, David, 112, 114–15
Ormandy, Emma, 196
Ormandy, Eugene, 191, 196–97
Ostrowsky Piano Company, 317
Ostwald, Eugene, 97
Ostwald, Kathe, 97
Ostwald, Lise Deschamps, 11–12, 194–96, 208, 209, 214, 215, 216, 333–34

Pablo Casals: A Portrait for Radio, 178, 240, 290
Pacsu, Margaret, 313
Page, Tim, 249–50, 252, 316
Paray, Paul, 133
Parkin, Alan, 124
Payzant, Geoffrey, 13, 120, 265, 267
Pearson, Lester B., 261
Percival, John A., 286–87, 290, 292, 294, 305, 315, 325
performing arts medicine, 14, 190, 305
"Personal Reminiscences" (Ostwald), 333
Peter Ustinov's Leningrad, 309
Petri, Egon, 156, 194
Phillips, Robin, 281
Piano Quarterly, 281, 282
Posen, Stephen, 35, 265, 329, 333
Prokofiev, Sergei: Piano Sonata no. 7 in B-flat Major, 88, 153, 222
"Prospects of Recording, The" (Gould), 217–19

"Question of Instrument," 310
Quiet in the Land, The, 240–42

Rabinowitz, Malka, 172
Rachmaninoff, Sergei, 19, 83
  Piano Concerto no. 3, 48
Radio as Music, 239
Rasky, Frank, 35
Ravel, Maurice, 71
  Valse, La, 290, 314
Recital of Contemporary Music, 96
Reller, Austin, 175
Richardson, J. C., 135, 136
Richard Strauss Festival, 206
Richter, Jean Paul, 77
Roberts, Christina, 132
Roberts, John P. L., 49, 59, 132, 133, 151, 163, 179, 180, 181, 184, 219–20, 255–56, 264, 269, 275, 276, 277, 281, 282, 293, 295, 317, 324–25, 327, 331, 333
Roberts, Raymond ("Ray"), 271–76, 278, 282, 291, 293, 295, 324, 325–26, 326, 327
Romantic Generation, The (Rosen), 234
Rose, Leonard, 21, 136, 137
Rosen, Charles, 234
Rubinstein, Arthur, 19, 92, 238, 240, 266, 278–79

Sacks, Oliver, 42
Salzburg Music Festival, 162, 163
Samuel, Gerhard, 208
San Francisco Symphony, 18, 21–22, 174, 194, 217
Santa Rosa Symphony, 194
Santayana, George, 176
Satie, Eric, 236
Sawallisch, Wolfgang, 166
Schabas, Ezra, 108
Schapiro, Maxim, 110
Schiff, Andreas, 154–55
Schnabel, Artur, 19, 79
Schneider, Alexander, 106–8, 109, 114–15
Schoenberg, Arnold, 61, 87, 152, 178, 223
  documentaries on, 206–8, 290
  Fantasy for Violin and Piano, 227–28
  Gould's opinions on, 99, 140, 201, 216, 245, 251, 289–90
  Ode to Napoleon, 137, 253
Schoenberg, the First Hundred Years, 290
Schoenberg Memorial Concert, 99
Schonberg, Harold, 212
Schubert, Franz: Duo for Violin and Piano, 31
Schumann, Clara, 14, 107, 297
Schumann, Robert, 48, 77, 166
  Gould's opinions on, 14, 297
  Piano Quartet in E-flat Major, 253–54
Schwarzkopf, Elisabeth, 247
Schweitzer, Albert, 229
Scriabin, Alexander:
  "Désir" étude, 307
  Piano Sonata no. 3 in F-sharp Minor, 222
"Season on the Road, A" (Gould), 166
Serkin, Rudolf, 108, 266
Search for Petula Clark, The, 236–37
"S. F. Lemming, M.D.," 128–29, 260
Shakespeare, William, 87, 227–28, 282
Shostakovich, Dmitri, 153
Shumsky, Oscar, 21, 136, 137
Shuter, Rosemary, 45
Sibelius, Jean: Symphony No. 5, 234
Siebenkas (Richter), 77
Silverman, Andrea, 282
Silverman, Ingrid, 283
Silverman, Robert, 281–83, 317, 324, 333
Silvester, Frederick C., 68, 75
Simoneau, Leopold, 137
"Sir Humphrey Price-Davies," 260
"Sir Nigel Twitt-Thornwaite," 261, 313
Slater, David Dick, 38
Slaughterhouse-Five, 279–80
Smith, Leo, 68

Solitude Trilogy, 230–43, 267
Solomon, Maynard, 203
Somerville, Janet, 238, 242
Soseki, Natsume, 275–76
So You Want to Write a Fugue (Gould), 209, 216–17, 253, 285
Stalin, Joseph, 150
Stegemann, Michael, 161
Stein, Irwin, 191, 196, 242, 243
Steinberg, William, 97
Steinway pianos, 132, 173–74, 178, 180, 188–93, 196, 256, 270, 298, 301–2, 303
Stephens, Joseph, 128, 185–88, 191–92, 194–95, 197–98, 199, 208, 214, 222, 243, 266, 270, 276, 277, 278, 283, 291, 296, 297–98
Stockhausen, Karlheinz, 103, 251, 262
Stokes, Aldwyn, 124
Stokowski, Leopold, 28, 156–57, 206, 240, 246–47, 261
"Stokowski in Six Scenes" (Gould), 282
Stout, Alan, 256
Stratford Music Festival, 21, 28, 106–8, 110, 132, 136–37
Strauss, Pauline, 308
Strauss, Richard, 126, 209
  Burleske, 18, 20, 21, 22, 33, 163–64, 208
  Capriccio, 136, 202, 209, 252
  Elektra, 136, 209
  Gould's opinions on, 22, 206, 245, 250–52, 257, 308
  Heldenleben, Ein, 251
  Metamorphosen, 202, 252
  Ophelia Songs, 283
  Piano Sonata in B Minor, 251, 324
  piano transcriptions for, 201–2
  Sonata for Violin and Piano in E-flat, 136
  Stratford program on, 136–37
Stravinsky, Igor:
  Histoire du Soldat, L', 106
  Petrushka Suite, 20
Stross, Fred, 175, 176
Stross, Helen, 175, 176
Stuckenschmidt, H. H., 155–56
Sullivan, Patrick, 106, 277
Switched-on Bach, 264
Symphonia Quartet, 204
Szell, George, 148

Tchaikovsky Competition, 150, 162, 197
"Ted Slutz," 260, 309
Terminal Man, The, 280
Thibaud, Jacques, 215
Three-Cornered World, The (Soseki), 275–76
Time, 148
Tocco, James, 162–63
Toronto, University of, 221
Toronto Conservatory of Music, 49, 67, 221–22
  Gould as student at, 67, 68, 70–74, 76, 78, 80, 87
Toronto Humane Society, 56, 325
Toronto Star, 151
Toronto Symphony Orchestra, 70, 80, 81, 84, 135
Tovell, Vincent, 220–21, 331
"Tragedy of Premature Death Among Geniuses, What Does It Mean? Can It Be Prevented?, The" (Ostwald), 333
Tulk, Lorne, 235–39, 271, 276, 284, 291, 308, 324
Tureck, Rosalyn, 101, 115, 188
Twelfth Night (Shakespeare), 87

Valen, Fartein, 255
  Piano Sonata no. 2, 256
Vancouver Music Festival, 193, 245
Vancouver Symphony, 97
Vear, Herbert, 191
Verdi, Giuseppe: *Falstaff,* 234–35
von Bülow, Hans, 107
von Kaiserling, Count, 116
Vonnegut, Kurt, 279

Wagner, Richard, 126, 205
  Gould's opinions on, 86, 87
  Meistersinger, Die, 157, 217
  Siegfried Idyll, 322–23
  Tristan and Isolde, 61, 203
Wanstead United Church, 62, 75
Wars, The, 280–81, 292, 320–21
Watts, Malcolm, 180, 183
Webern, Anton, 61, 87, 152
  Gould's opinions on, 99–100, 201
  Saxophone Quartet, 99–100
Werfel, Alma Mahler, 178
Whitney, Joyce, 79–80
"Why Mozart is a Bad Composer" (Gould), 249
Widman, Mrs., 289
Wilford, Ronald, 242, 254, 278, 287
Williamson Road Public School, 49, 57–58
Winchester, Miss, 67
Windsor Arms Hotel, 179
Winnipeg Symphony, 64, 132
Wittgenstein, Ludwig, 42

Yamaha pianos, 174

Zen Buddhism, 275
"Zoltán Mostányi," 260